GODS AND MEN

The Origins of
Western Culture

GODS
AND MEN
The Origins of
WESTERN
CULTURE

by HENRY BAMFORD PARKES

New York: Alfred ·A· Knopf

1 9 5 9

L. C. Catalog card number: 59–5425
© *Henry Bamford Parkes, 1959*

THIS IS A BORZOI BOOK,
PUBLISHED BY ALFRED A. KNOPF, INC.

FIRST EDITION

Preface

GODS AND MEN represents an attempt to re-evaluate the Judaeo-Hellenic origins of our cultural heritage. While it is complete in itself, I hope in several later volumes to continue the study of Western cultural development down to modern times.

This is not to be regarded as a general history of Western civilization. I am concerned with the living past, not with the past as a whole. I have concentrated on describing those cultural creations that still have power to shape our thinking and stir our emotions. Nor do I have any particular theory of historical development to propound. All attempts to impose some rigid and comprehensive pattern of historical interpretation—whether those of Spengler and Toynbee or of the economic determinists—seem to me to lead to demonstrably erroneous conclusions. But I have written this book with certain definite convictions. I believe that the main factors in the political and economic development of any society are its general view of life and system of values, that these are reflected in its philosophy, literature, and art, and hence that philosophy, literature, and art are prime materials for the understanding of the past. A sense of the importance of intellectual and aesthetic creation is what I especially hope to convey. It seems to me, for example, that the Greek poets and philosophers provide the fullest explanations for both the rise and the decline of Greek civilization. Similarly, the political decadence of imperial Rome is closely related to its cultural sterility, and the causes are clearly mirrored in its surviving literature and art.

This book has been mostly written during the past five years, but parts of it have been in incubation over a much longer period of time. Some of the ideas that I have expressed about Hellenism first began to take shape more than thirty years ago while I was acquiring an English classical education. Subsequent removal to the United States and immersion in the study of American history confirmed my sense of the essential unity of the Western cultural tradition. I felt that it was impossible to interpret American cultural development, in spite of its distinctive features, unless it was seen as part of a larger whole. The basic American beliefs and institutions, however much modified in the American environment, came from Europe and must be traced back finally to ancient Palestine and Greece. In returning to the origins of the Western heritage, I am trying to understand the present, including the American present.

I am indebted to recent Biblical and classical scholarship for much of my material. The past generation has seen a considerable reappraisal of Hellenic civilization, especially by English classicists, and the undiscriminating idealization prevalent at earlier periods has given place to a more vivid understanding of both its achievements and its deficiencies. It has become easier for us to appreciate the classics since their study has largely ceased to provide support for upper-class rule, just as we can more fully enjoy the Parthenon and the Hagia Sophia now that modern architects no longer try to imitate them. But my main sources have been the works bequeathed to us by the ancient civilizations: the Bible, the writings of classical and early Christian poets and philosophers, and the surviving remains of Greek and Roman art and architecture. In some instances I have vigorously dissented from the traditional estimates, though I have said little with which contemporary classicists would disagree. The blind adulation for Plato and Aristotle is an affair of the past. If I have given expression to some strong sympathies and antipathies, it is because of a sense of the continuing importance of the issues involved. The conflict between democracy and authoritarian rule began in ancient Greece, and the whole of Western political development can be regarded as a long debate between the ideas of the Periclean Funeral Speech and those of Plato's *Republic*. Our religious attitudes and controversies still reflect the conflict between sacerdotal and prophetic conceptions that began in ancient Palestine and the transformation of the teaching of Jesus through the influences of the Helleno-Roman decadence.

One cannot fully understand the Mediterranean civilizations if one knows them through books alone. As I began to realize when I saw Greece, its poets and philosophers lose almost as much of their essential quality when they are divorced from their original environment as did the Parthenon frieze when it was removed to the fogs of Bloomsbury. Thanks to a Fulbright appointment, much of this book was actually written in Greece, partly in Athens, in an apartment overlooking the Acropolis, and partly in the island of Skyros, with its legendary associations with Achilles. I hope that the influence of Aegean sunlight is not wholly absent from its pages.

H. B. P.

Acknowledgments

I should like to thank HANNAH ARENDT for her illuminating discussions of many of the questions dealt with in this book, and for reading and criticizing the chapters on Greece; GEOFFREY BRUUN for reading and criticizing the whole book; HORST JANSON for guidance in finding illustrations; HERBERT WEINSTOCK for editorial assistance; my daughter MRS. NANCY MARR for editorial and secretarial services; and my wife for her constant advice, help, and encouragement.

Contents

Illustrations

INTRODUCTION

THE MYTHS OF
WESTERN
CIVILIZATION

This book is planned as the first of several volumes dealing with the cultural history of the Western world. Western civilization will be treated as a unity, and the main purpose will be to analyze the development of those dominant ideas and beliefs which have given the Western world its creativity and its sense of collective purpose. The present volume is concerned with the origins of the Western cultural heritage in the early civilizations of the eastern Mediterranean, especially with the emergence out of primitive superstition of the Jewish faith in a righteous and omnipotent God and the Hellenic concept of an order of nature, and with the development of the new religion of Christianity in which these beliefs were fused and partially transcended. Ethical monotheism, natural law, and the Christian kingdom of heaven have been the main spiritual principles of Western civilization; and as all of them transcend reason, they must be defined as social myths. This book is written in the conviction that the vitality of any society depends on the continued affirmation of mythical symbolisms created by the collective imagination for the ordering of experience, and that a pure rationalism can result only in social disintegration.

Such a delimitation of subject matter should not be taken as implying any mystical hypothesis about the rise and decline of different civilizations. I do not propose to argue that a civilization is an organism with a life beyond that of the human individuals belonging to it or that all civilizations are destined to pass through the same preordained cycle of growth and decay. The unity of the Western world has been a product of specific historical and geographic factors and should not be attributed to some mysterious biological or cultural necessity. The only reason for dealing with Western civilization as a whole is that it comprises a unified field of study. It is impossible to describe intellectual or aesthetic trends in England or France or the United States without constant reference to movements in other Western countries. Only by including all of western Europe, along with those other sections of the world that have been brought under its influence, can one find a complete and comprehensible line of development. This cultural tradition can be traced back as far as the first millennium B.C., and had its beginnings in the countries of the eastern Mediterranean. On the other hand, it is possible to make a thorough

3

study of the Western mind without making more than brief and occasional references to the civilizations of India and China.

This analysis of the development of Western culture will be mainly concerned with religious, philosophical, and social theory and with artistic expression, particularly with the work of the great imaginative minds. In laying so much emphasis on the higher forms of intellectual and aesthetic activity, I am not supposing that they are determining factors in the rise and decline of cultural attitudes; their historical importance lies not in their being causal, but in their being expressive. A great thinker or artist may have little influence on the culture of his society, but he is always socially significant because he is always receptive to the main currents of thought and emotion among his contemporaries. Thus, his work illuminates the whole spirit and sensibility of his time and may even be a prophecy of social tendencies that have not yet become manifest in action. An analysis of the major intellectual and imaginative achievements of a society is a method of examining its prevalent attitudes, aspirations, conflicts, and anxieties. By taking a series of these soundings one may hope to trace, in broad outline, the general movement of sensibility.

What are the conditions of creativity, and to what factors does Western civilization, in particular, owe its capacity for continuous innovation? History does not present any questions of greater speculative interest and practical importance. For in the entire span of human development creativity has been the exception rather than the rule. Most societies at most periods have remained tradition-bound, and the same sequences of experience have continued to repeat themselves indefinitely. Epochs of progress have occurred only at rare intervals and have always been restricted to particular societies or civilizations, although their more valuable innovations have afterwards become diffused among other peoples. During the past ten or twelve thousand years, in fact, there have been only four major epochs of creativity. All the fundamental elements of man's cultural heritage originated in one or other of these four epochs.

The first such epoch saw the discovery of agriculture and the domestication of animals; these achievements probably occurred in a limited area of the Middle East, whence they gradually spread to other parts of the Old World. This was followed several thousand years later by the building of urban civilizations, which took place initially in Mesopotamia and Egypt, though similar developments occurred at later periods, probably independently, in India and China. The third creative epoch covered most of the first millennium B.C., during which new philosophical, religious, and political ideas were formulated in five separate areas: China, India, Iran, Palestine, and Greece. The fourth, beginning some eight or nine hundred years ago, has been restricted to western Europe and those other parts of the world that have come under European influence. Creativity has not been wholly lacking at other times and places, but has been manifested only at rare intervals and in innovations of relatively minor importance. During the third and second millennia B.C., for example, remarkably few valuable advances took place in the whole Near Eastern area, by contrast with the great technological, aesthetic, and political achievements of the city-building epoch of the fourth millennium and the varied intellectual activities of the first millennium. Throughout the most recent epoch, only the civilization of the Western world has been capable of any consistent progress, and any innovations made by the Asian peoples, in spite of their great preponderance in numbers, have been of negligible significance.[1]

In view of the relative infrequency of creative societies, it should be obvious that no explanation for their appearance can be found in any narrowly materialistic interpretation of history. All societies have lived on the same earth and faced the same biological problems of survival; and while some of them have been handicapped by severe geographic obstacles, the majority have developed in the temperate zone and have had access to adequate natural resources. A society acquires its character not from its physical environment, but from the manner in which it responds to that environment; and while most societies have remained fixed in some rigid pattern of adaptation, a few have made responses that have permitted continuous innovation over periods of centuries. Such responses consist of attitudes and modes of sensibility that become manifest in those collective habit-patterns of thought

---

[1] The more advanced Indian peoples of America passed through creative epochs corresponding to the first and second of the Old World epochs, though at later dates. By the time of the Spanish conquest, Mexico and Peru had reached a stage of development roughly equivalent to that of Mesopotamia and Egypt in the third millennium B.C.

and behavior which we call beliefs and institutions. A creative society is a society whose beliefs and institutions are sufficiently flexible to permit the exploration of new ideas and techniques by its individual members. It may be contrasted with two other types of society: with the tribalism from which it emerges, in which the individual is wholly absorbed into his group and rarely deviates from the traditional mores; and with the state of anomia into which it may degenerate, in which the mass of the population submits to rulers whose authority is based frankly on force, without any claim to ideological justification.[2]

Creativity, in other words, requires freedom. The full implications of this fact, however, are not always recognized. It means that the necessary degree of collective unity and order must be maintained neither by blind adherence to custom nor by force, but by the voluntary loyalty of individuals. How is this loyalty to be assured? By what means is the welfare of the group to be reconciled with the spontaneous vitality of its members? An organic harmony of whole and parts is possible only when there is a common acceptance of a system of values based on a collective affirmation about the meaning of human life. On the institutional level this may be defined as an agreed principle of justice—a principle, in other words, which individuals will support even when it conflicts with their own interests. The rules regulating political and economic relationships must be accepted as legitimate. But a social order acquires legitimacy only through the belief that it is in accord with objective standards and values overruling the private interests of its members. Western man has attributed his standards partly to the will of a righteous God and partly to natural law, and has believed that if he conformed with "the laws of nature and of nature's God," the freedom of the individual and the order of the whole would prove to be ultimately harmonious and always capable of reconciliation. Such a harmony may never be fully realized, and by rationalistic criteria is perhaps incapable of realization. Any rule of justice must always appear

---

[2] There is no adequate English word for this social form, though it has been exemplified among a large part of the world's population for thousands of years, especially in Asia. One may use such metaphorical adjectives as "devitalized," "inorganic," and "mechanistic." Once a society reaches a condition of anomia, any revival of its vitality seems to be impossible except through some external stimulus.

arbitrary and conventional in some of its practical applications, and, as was recognized by the preachers of the Christian gospel, society cannot truly be unified unless legal rights and obligations are transcended by the practice of love and charity. But no specific institutions can be deduced from the Christian ethic, and for most human beings it has been a utopian aspiration rather than a practical reality. The myth of an ideal justice, inherent in the structure of the cosmos, capable of embodiment in human institutions, and providing a standard for settling all conflicts of individual interest, has remained the main support of social organization for Western man.[3]

Both the recognition of individual autonomy and the affirmation of universal standards of justice and morality appeared at a relatively late period in human development. Primitive man, wholly absorbed into his tribal community, had little sense of his own separate identity and recognized no allegiance to any authority higher than the wishes of his tribal gods. These tribalistic attitudes have never been wholly transcended even in the highest forms of civilization; they have always retained much of their strength among the less enlightened masses of the population, and may again become dominant during any period of breakdown and failure of nerve. For culture has developed by a process not of abrupt transformations but of steady accretion, in which new layers are constantly being added and little is ever wholly lost. The mind of the race, like that of the individual, is shaped by its past experiences, and it can never successfully repudiate any phase in its cultural evolution, all of which it must carry with it into the future. In order to appreciate the problems involved in the growth of civilization, one must therefore understand the tribalistic background.

As long as men remained organized into small tribal groups, each individual conformed to the mores of his own community

---

[3] Reinhold Niebuhr remarks: "Evil is always the assertion of some self-interest without regard to the whole, whether the whole be conceived as the immediate community, or the total community of mankind, or the total order of the world. The good is, on the other hand, always the harmony of the whole on various levels" (*The Children of Light and the Children of Darkness,* p. 9). Such a statement expresses the basic faith of Western man. The core of the Western tradition has been the belief that a harmony of the whole exists or is capable of realization.

and devoted himself to its welfare. At the same time he recognized no common bonds with, or obligations toward, the members of other communities. Man was a gregarious animal before he became an individualist, and his loyalty to his own group was combined with feelings of fear, disapproval, and potential antagonism toward all other groups. It is important to recognize that these tribal attitudes must have been constantly strengthened by the struggle for existence and hence that they may be said to have served evolutionary purposes. As men had no power by themselves to control natural forces, they could survive at all only by combining into groups that could act as units. Those tribes which could command the most absolute and unquestioning devotion from their members would be most likely to secure adequate supplies of food, increase their numbers, and be victorious in conflicts with their rivals. Thus, processes of natural selection favored tribal discipline and the total suppression of individuality. The tribe, in fact, became the evolutionary unit, and the tendency of every vigorous community to maintain its distinction from its neighbors, developing and preserving its own special institutions and ways of living, made possible a wide range of different social experiments, the effectiveness of which was afterwards proved through military conflict or economic competition. The whole of history testifies to the vigor and persistence of tribalistic emotions, and even in the most advanced civilizations very few human beings have ever fully transcended them.[4]

The tribal system of organization was accompanied in all parts of the world by similar religious attitudes. The most significant intellectual characteristic of primitive man was his inability to distinguish between objective fact and the subjective processes of his own imagination. Regarding himself as a part of nature, he supposed that he could influence natural phenomena by the performance of appropriate ceremonies, hoping to bring about desired events, such as the return of spring, the increase of the animals

---

[4] In the modern world the nation is the evolutionary unit. In spite of the obvious need for some form of world government, the more advanced nations are right in cherishing their own distinctive values and institutions and resisting absorption into a world community. The task of the twentieth century is not to obliterate the sense of national differences, thereby reducing the whole human race to the same economic and cultural level, but to prevent it from assuming violent forms.

and plants on which he lived, and the removal of famines and pestilences, by means of imitative rituals. At a later period he personified the powers of nature and believed that he could be assured of prosperity by propitiating the gods and securing their protection. Because whatever he felt or visualized with special vividness seemed to him to be objectively real, he also began to project his own aspirations, ideals, institutions, and fears into divine figures. Whenever he affirmed a new political or ethical concept or arrived at a new poetic or technological insight, he believed that in giving expression to it he was merely obeying a divine command.

Thus, each tribe usually developed its own polytheistic pantheon, often including one deity whom it worshipped as its especial patron, the symbol of its traditions, and sometimes its physical ancestor. The members of any vigorous tribe always insisted on the superiority of their own gods and goddesses and hoped that this would be made manifest in material strength and wealth; but they did not usually claim that these were the only celestial beings or ascribe omnipotence to them; nor did they deny the reality of rival objects of worship. The lack of unity on earth was paralleled by a similar anarchy in heaven. This growth of polytheism was presumably due not only to the lack of any clear criteria for differentiating between fact and image, but also to man's fear of assuming the risks and obligations of freedom. He wished to cultivate a sense of dependence on supernatural powers, not only by insisting that as long as he retained their favor he could rely on their protection, but also by making them responsible for all social order and all moral imperatives.

The first major advance in human experience, the change from hunting to agriculture and cattle-breeding, occurred long before mankind emerged into the light of history, and we know nothing about the social conditions that made it possible. The second major advance, the building of urban civilizations, was apparently brought about under the leadership of priestly ruling classes who were believed to be the spokesmen of the gods, and was accompanied by a further elaboration of polytheistic rituals and beliefs. Throughout this epoch of creativity, the belief that divine powers were immanent in human priest-kings seems to have been an effective method of legitimizing the social order, compatible with a remarkable degree of technological and aesthetic innovation. There was, as yet, no full recognition of the autonomy of the individual or of the need for any universal standards of justice and rationality.

Eventually, however, the new environmental conditions began to produce a slow transformation of human attitudes. As more complex social structures and economic systems took shape, ancestral mores and traditions no longer provided adequate guidance, and it became increasingly necessary for individuals to make their own decisions about the conduct of their lives. As different groups came into closer contact with each other through trade or warfare and established permanent commercial or diplomatic relationships, men could no longer think exclusively in tribal terms, but began to look for more comprehensive religious and ethical concepts. With the gradual accumulation of technological observation and experience, moreover, the recognition of objective processes of causation began to develop alongside, and entangled with, the primitive reliance on imitative magic. Thus, human attitudes began to undergo a double transformation: thought began to move from tribalism toward individualism and universalism, and from pluralistic nature-worship toward monistic rationalism.

For several thousands of years after the advent of the first urban civilizations there was no sharp discontinuity in ways of thinking, and men tried to meet their spiritual problems by refining and elaborating the old tribal polytheism. Meanwhile, governments degenerated into military imperialisms maintained by force rather than by effective systems of beliefs. Finally, in the first millennium B.C., came a series of new beginnings in human thought. Almost simultaneously in five different areas, prophets and philosophers began to preach new doctrines, all of which, though in different terms and in varying degrees, recognized the spiritual freedom and independence of the individual, asserted the unity of mankind and of the universe, and adopted a rational rather than a magical view of natural processes. But while the Orientals were concerned mainly with the achievement of inner peace rather than with the reformation of society, both the Jewish prophets and the Hellenic philosophers affirmed beliefs in standards of justice making possible a harmony of order and freedom.

On a superficial view, all subsequent cultural history might be regarded as a prolonged struggle between the old tribalistic attitudes, no longer serving evolutionary purposes but still deeply rooted in the human personality, and the new ideals of individual freedom, the unity of mankind, and rational objective thought. But man advances not by obliterating his primitive heritage, but by transforming it, and any attempted breach of continuity can end only in a reversion to some earlier phase of evolution. The preservation of tribal attitudes in some form remains essential to human survival; but the advance of civilization means that they must be subordinated to higher values.

Unable to live either as isolated individuals or as citizens of the universe, human beings must always remain members of visible circumscribed communities, upon which they are dependent for physical security, ethical guidance, and emotional fulfillment. All social order depends upon the maintenance of the appropriate loyalties, and a new historic epoch begins whenever these are transferred to new forms of organization and become crystallized around new ideals. Identifying himself unquestioningly with the traditions and gods of his own tribe, primitive man never examined the reasons for his own allegiance. But by affirming both the spiritual autonomy of the individual and the reality of universal principles of truth and justice, the philosophers and prophets of the first millennium B.C. called into question all communal loyalties. According to the new view of life, the individual was free to give or withdraw his assent to collective authority. This meant that group loyalties must be legitimized by some universal standard and could not remain effective unless they were believed to have some deeper foundation than the mere need for tribal survival. The community could command allegiance only when it claimed to be the concrete embodiment and manifestation of a cosmic justice.

The affirmation of principles of justice and morality, moreover, lies beyond the scope of rationalistic thinking. By the standards of a pure rationalism, the individual has no motive for concern with anything beyond his own self-interest. His sense of loyalty and moral obligation depends on the intuition that he is a part of some larger whole, and such a conviction transcends reason and is, in fact, the essence of the religious consciousness. It pervaded the attitudes of primitive man, though it led him to the error of believing in the efficacy of magic. When tested by scientific standards of verification, the whole of early religion, with its imitative rituals and the myths designed to explain them and its faith in divine persons who actually intervened in human affairs, appears simply as a mass of error created by fear and maintained by fraud. Yet the primitive conviction of man's organic unity both with his group and with the cosmos is, in some form, essential to human survival. Purely rationalistic thinking, while promising to give man control over physical forces, has the effect of isolating and alienating him from both his social and his natural environment, depriving his ethical and aesthetic values of any claim to objective validity, and emptying his life of all transcendent meaning and significance. Thus, the task of civilized man is not the replacement of religion by reason, but the affirmation of new forms of the religious consciousness which will not conflict with rational and objective thought. The creativity of civilization depends on finding a harmony not only between order and freedom, but also between tribalism and universalism and between religious unity and rationalistic individualism.

Neither of the two peoples who initiated the Western cultural tradition ever achieved such a harmony. For a few generations the Jewish prophetic movement succeeded in infusing the traditional loyalties of the Israelite religion with universalist beliefs, but post-Exilic Judaism, while not forgetting the monotheism of the prophets, largely reverted to tribalistic attitudes. Hellenism, on the other hand, which tried to deduce principles of justice from the concept of natural law, failed to find either a theoretic or a practical reconciliation of freedom and order, and succumbed to the disintegrating effects of an excess of rationalism. Hellenic society finally lost its sense of organic unity and sank into an anomia in which order could be maintained only by the military power, first of the Macedonian dynasties and afterwards of Rome. The basic intuitions of Judaism and Hellenism, however, being combined in Christian theology, and irradiated and revitalized by the new Christian ethic of love, with its promise of a coming kingdom of heaven, were transmitted to the civilization of western Europe, the most recent, and so far the most successful, of man's evolutionary experiments.

Believing always in an ideal justice and in a possible harmony of freedom and order, Western man has sought to realize them in several different forms, and it is possible to distinguish a series of oscillations in Western history between epochs of synthesis and epochs of disintegration. Three successive institutional systems, the feudalism and Catholicism of the Middle Ages, the monarchical state of the Renaissance, and the capitalism and liberalism of the Enlightenment and the nineteenth century have appeared in turn as reflections of the will of God and the cosmic structure.[5] During each period of synthesis the social order has been accepted by most of its members as just, reasonable, and legitimate, and has therefore commanded a voluntary loyalty, without coercion or deliberate indoctrination, and individuals have derived a sense of personal fulfillment and significance from participation in social processes and at the same time have felt free to explore new modes of experience. But each period of confidence and creativity has proved to be transitory, and has been followed by a time of disillusionment during which the established system could be maintained only by intolerance, while loyalties were gradually transferred to new forms of social order and new ideals. Thus cultural evolution in Western society has proceeded by a series of waves. Each forward movement is made possible by a new synthesis of ideas and institutions and continues as long as the order and discipline of society can be harmonized with individual freedom and rational thought. But at a certain point the wave begins to break, the cultural system is shattered into a chaos of conflicting

---

[5] According to traditional European beliefs, the harmony of freedom and order, while inherent in the structure of the cosmos as God had made it, could never be wholly achieved on earth because of human sinfulness; it could be approximated only by a strict discipline of man's corrupted nature. This has remained one of the main ideological supports of European conservatism. Liberalism, on the other hand, has proclaimed man's natural goodness, and has generally affirmed that the harmony of freedom and order could be automatically achieved by the abolition of all restraints. The most extreme expression of liberalism was the laissez-faire economics of Adam Smith. According to Smith, the world had been planned by the "invisible hand" of its divine creator in such a way that there was a preordained harmony between the self-interest of each and the welfare of all; in "the system of natural liberty" each individual would pursue his own advantage, but "the study of his own advantage naturally, or rather necessarily, leads him to prefer the employment which is most advantageous to the society." Perhaps the chief importance of laissez-faire doctrine was that it provided an agreed standard of economic justice; in a laissez-faire economy, thanks to God's "invisible hand," the earnings of each individual would be commensurate with his services to society.

cross-currents, and there is likely to be a retreat from freedom until society can reconstitute its energies for a new advance.

The reason for these oscillations is that as long as society remains creative, human energies cannot permanently be contained within the framework of any particular organizational system. Any such system contains within itself the seeds of its own destruction, for by promoting individual freedom and rational thought it must always bring about the gradual erosion of the institutions and beliefs upon which its stability depends. In the course of time, its institutions, unable to accommodate further innovations, begin to seem oppressive and lose their appearance of legitimacy; its beliefs cease to be consistent with the progress of rational thinking; and individuals develop a sense of alienation from their society and no longer suppose that in fulfilling their social obligations they are conforming with the cosmic design. But these recurrent withdrawals of allegiance have not resulted in any permanent loss of creativity in Western society because they have always been followed by a new crystallization round some new institutional system. When Western man ceased to believe in feudalism, he transferred his loyalties to the monarchical state; and when he began to find monarchy oppressive, he found a new expression of "the laws of nature and of nature's God" in capitalism and democracy. Throughout all institutional changes he has retained a faith in the possibility of harmonizing freedom and order and achieving the brotherhood of the promised kingdom of heaven by conforming with the will of God and with natural law. In different concrete manifestations these have remained the basic social myths of Western civilization. If these myths lose their efficacy, then Western man must either revert to the attitudes of tribalism or acquiesce in the rule of force, either of which means the loss of freedom and creativity.

If all social order, however, depends on the preservation of myths that transcend reason, then must not limits be imposed on rationalistic inquiry? And if the requirements of social order and rational thought are ultimately in conflict with each other, then will not any creative civilization be, at best, a transitory phenomenon? These are perhaps the most fundamental of the enigmas confronting the human species, especially at a time like the present, when conflicting institutional and ideological systems are competing for allegiance.

According to some views of the human predicament, these questions must be answered in the affirmative. If man is inherently an egoist, then he can be induced to subordinate his personal wishes to the welfare of the group only by rigid discipline based on the fear of punishment; and as such fear (except in childhood) usually has little rational basis, it would follow that social order depends on the preservation of beliefs in a righteous God, in rewards and punishments after death, and in other religious dogmas that a rationalistic society is likely to repudiate. If all values, moreover, are merely human constructs or conventions with no claim to any objective validity, so that man finds himself in a universe in which nothing is given for his guidance beyond the brute forces of physics and biochemistry, then conflicts between different value-systems cannot be settled by any appeal to some ultimate standard or by any process of reasoned argument. And as society cannot survive without some basic agreement about values, these must be maintained either by force or by the propagation of illusions. According to these views, that sinners do not go to hell and that the Ten Commandments were not dictated to Moses by Jehovah must be regarded as dangerous truths that society cannot afford to tolerate.

We shall be better able to see all the implications of the problem after this survey of the course of Western thought has been completed. But at this point it can be said that, however man may be constituted by nature, he has appeared throughout all history as a gregarious being, endowed with a sense of moral obligation which causes him to regard himself as a part of some larger organic whole. A perfect society would be impossible without that transformation of the human personality by love which was promised by the Christian gospel, but even the unredeemed and sinful man, though incapable of love for his neighbor, normally acknowledges a sense of duty. The whole to which he owes allegiance has been defined in many different ways; but if this feeling of obligation had been lacking, then no kind of social order could ever have existed from the beginning.[6] The conflict between free-

---

[6] One of the most thoroughgoing exponents of the theory of human egoism (and also of human destructiveness) was Sigmund Freud. According to

dom and order is not only an external conflict between the individual and established social authority. More fundamentally, it is a conflict between different tendencies within the individual personality; and every human being, in proportion as he achieves self-awareness, must, in fact, make his own choices, and look for his own reconciliation between the satisfaction of his personal interests and his sense of social responsibility. Thus, the moral attitude (as distinct from the specific moral rules imposed in any particular society) does not depend upon the propagation of illusions.

Equally inherent in man's nature is the sense of the objectivity of values. Such ideals as justice and beauty have assumed different concrete expressions at different periods of history, but human beings have never been content to regard them as merely conventions; in some form they are felt to have an objective basis, so that man discovers them and does not merely invent them. This is most clearly exemplified in the history of art. Different styles have been developed by different societies, and each individual displays his own preferences; yet through all changes of taste, certain irreducible aesthetic values remain independent of subjective biases. Every true artist feels, indeed, that he is engaged in the revelation of a reality transcending his own subjective impressions, though he may be wholly unable to offer any rationalistic explanation for such a feeling.

The great social myths by which a society is animated are

Freud, "the hostility of each against all and of all against each one" is inherent in the nature of man. Freud's attempts to grapple with the problem of how society ever started are contained in his *Civilization and Its Discontents*. For the sake of security, he supposes, individuals agreed with each other to impose restrictions upon their aggressive and sexual drives, giving up a good deal of their happiness in order to enjoy longer lives. In *Totem and Taboo* he suggests that this may have happened after the young men of a family group had banded together in order to kill (and afterwards to eat) a tyrannical father, and that because their feelings toward him had been ambivalent, containing elements of love as well as hate, they suffered afterwards from a sense of guilt. This revival of the social-contract myth of early liberalism is, of course, wholly unconvincing. If "the hostility of each against all" was the dominant attitude of primitive men, how could they ever have agreed on the mutual acceptance of restrictions? Freud's marked tendency to hypostasize "culture" in the manner of German Romantic philosophy seems to be an attempt to evade this problem; he often speaks of "culture" as though it were an independent spiritual power able to impose its own ideal purposes on human egoism.

imaginative projections of man's sense of membership in a larger whole and of his belief in the objectivity of moral, political, and aesthetic values. If taken literally, they are, by rationalistic standards, always untrue. Yet they convey truths that the human mind cannot apprehend more directly, and as long as they meet human needs and do not lead to the denial or suppression of any important element of human experience, they should not be dismissed simply as illusions. Hitherto, however, the human race has shown a chronic propensity to assert factual certainty in areas where it is unattainable, insisting either that a personal deity exists or that he does not exist, either that man has an immortal soul or that he is wholly a product of matter. In consequence, rationalistic thought comes into conflict with the religious consciousness, and its development eventually seems incompatible with the myths on which social order depends. Any solution of the dilemma of culture can be found only in the development of new modes of thinking which, while admitting that any system of beliefs is, at best, poetic and not literal fact, would at the same time recognize that the truth about the ultimate nature and meaning of human life can be conveyed only through the mythical symbols created by the collective imagination. Twentieth-century physicists have been increasingly compelled to adopt an operational concept of truth, recognizing that their formulae are never exact articulations of the structure of the material universe, which may be ultimately unknowable and even, by human standards, self-contradictory, but accepting them as true for practical purposes as long as they work experimentally. Human beings may perhaps learn to apply a similar concept to the beliefs by which they organize their social and moral life.

Certainty is, in fact, beyond the scope of the human mind; and it is precisely because the human race can never acquire any certain knowledge in the religious and moral realm that it is capable of freedom. If men surely knew either that God existed and would condemn sinners to eternal punishment or that the universe consisted simply of matter in motion and all values were merely human constructs, their range of choice would be narrowly restricted. But their ignorance compels them to make their own affirmations about the nature of reality, choosing a faith to live by and staking their destiny on a wager about its validity. Throughout all history, however, men have been reluctant to recognize that freedom means not merely the power to do as one pleases, but also responsibility for the consequences, and have tried to evade it by attributing their own decisions to the gods, to fate, to chance, or to scientific law. This is the reason for the popularity of all forms of determinism, both religious and scientific.

If the evolution of human society has any meaning, it is to be found in the expansion of human freedom—a process which always involves the possibility of catastrophe as well as that of continued advance. And while freedom in the material realm means the power to control natural forces, in the realm of the spirit it depends on the creation of symbols for the expression of man's sense of moral obligation and his belief in values, in the recognition that these are real objects of knowledge and not merely conventional, but that the contribution of man's own mind and imagination is larger than he has usually been willing to suppose. Ethical monotheism, natural law, and the kingdom of heaven, the central symbolisms of Western society, have often been associated with intellectual dogmatism and moral restrictiveness; but, judged by operational standards, they have, on the whole, been the most successful of man's attempts to organize his spiritual intuitions and experiences and give meaning to his social and moral life.

A Note on Toynbee's Theory of History

The view of history suggested in these pages is, of course, radically different from the interpretation presented with so much eloquence and erudition by Arnold Toynbee. Toynbee's great work is filled with brilliant *aperçus,* and its literary charm and immense learning make it fascinating reading; but its main thesis seems to me to be wholly untenable.

Toynbee splits up world history into a number of different civilizations, twenty-one of which have reached fruition, while eight others have been abortive or arrested, and argues that all of them have passed through the same phases. Brought into existence through a successful response to some kind of challenge, a civilization retains a capacity for further growth and differentiation as long as the members of its elite group retain their creativity. Eventually, however, they lose their capacity for effective responses to new challenges and degenerate into a "dominant minority," while the mass of the population, alienated from their leaders, become an "internal proletariat." Meanwhile the civilization passes through a period of internal warfare, a "time of troubles," which is ended by the establishment of a "universal state," while the internal proletariat usually seek consolation in a higher religion. Finally the universal state is likely to be overthrown by the "external proletariat" of barbarian invaders or to be swallowed up by some younger and more vigorous civilization.

Toynbee never explains what he means by a "civilization" or shows in what sense this hypostasization has any real existence. When we speak of a "civilization," what we really mean, of course, is that the inhabitants of a particular region have acquired certain common and distinctive ways of behaving and of thinking (institutions and beliefs). When the region is largely isolated from the rest of the world (as was the case, for example, with ancient Egypt through most of its history), its civilization can be studied as though it were a separate entity. Most regions, however, have not been isolated, with the result that different cultural patterns merge or overlap, and it is impossible to draw any sharp lines of differentiation. In either case the word "civilization" is an abstraction. When we say that a civilization develops or decays, we are really referring to changes in the habit-patterns of a group of human beings.

It is true that certain kinds of changes have recurred on a number of different occasions. For example: the inhabitants of a particular region often become split into a number of rival states which fight wars with each other (Toynbee's "time of troubles"); the wars result in mutual exhaustion, which leads finally to a transfer of authority to some "universal state" usually originating outside the region. Thus the Sumerian city-states were unified by Akkad, the Greek city-states first by Macedon and then by Rome, and the Italian city-states of the Renaissance by Spain, while the European nation-states of the twentieth century are torn between two competing "universal states," the United States and the Soviet Union. Such a development, however, is due not to any absolute historic laws, but to certain specific factors which may or may not recur, and which have, in fact, recurred much less often than Toynbee supposes; and the change from interstate warfare to unification is a change not in some invisible and intangible phantasm called a "civilization," but in human attitudes, beliefs, and habits of behavior.

Toynbee's thesis makes it necessary for him to argue that each of the entities he identifies as a civilization passes through a time of troubles and ends in a universal state. This is fully true in only about half a dozen cases. Several of Toynbee's civilizations (the Egyptiac, the Arabic, the Orthodox Christian, and the Russian, for example) seem, on the contrary, to begin with universal states. In order to support his argument, Toynbee is compelled to exaggerate a time of troubles (with Orthodox Christian civilization) or invent a hypothetical one (with Andean and Minoan civilizations), to locate the universal state almost at the beginning of a civilization (with the Russian) or after the civilization has ceased to exist (with the Orthodox Christian, which allegedly achieved its universal state in the form of the Ottoman Empire), or to fabricate a universal state that certainly never existed (with the Mayan civilization). His argument seems particularly inapplicable to Egyptian civilization, which—in view of its relative isolation— should have illustrated the process of growth and decay in almost a pure form; Egypt throughout its history alternated between periods of unification and periods of disintegration, and the rule of the pyramid-builders at its beginning was as much a universal state as the New Empire of its old age. Whenever Toynbee finds what looks like a universal state, moreover, he is compelled to postulate a civilization of which it is the climax. The Persian Empire, for example, which unified the whole Near Eastern area, was certainly a universal state; but it could not have belonged to the Sumeric, Babylonic, or Egyptiac civilizations, for their universal states had already been achieved in other forms. Toynbee therefore invokes a distinct Syriac civilization, apparently consisting chiefly of the Jews and the Phoenicians, for the Persians to unify. An even more perplexing universal state is the Arab Caliphate, which cannot be regarded as the climax of an Arabic civilization or as the sequel to any identifiable time of troubles. This is explained by the assumption that the Syriac civilization in some mysterious fashion went underground for a thousand years and then achieved a second unification. Toynbee also fails to account for the fact that a universal state is sometimes brought to an end not by external aggression, but by a renewal of vitality within the civilization. According to his system, for example, the British Raj in India, the Spanish viceroyalties in America, and the Manchu Empire in China were the universal states of the Hindu, Andean, Central American, and Far Eastern civilizations, and hence phenomena of old age. No explanations are offered for the energy currently being displayed by Indians, Latin Americans, and Chinese.

The application of other parts of Toynbee's framework leads to similar procrustean distortions. The thesis that internal proletariats create higher religions, for example, causes Zoroastrianism (actually the religion of part of the Persian aristocracy) to be represented as proletarian, and Tammuz-worship (actually a neolithic survival) to be classified as a higher religion.

PART I

PRIMITIVE
AND NEAR EASTERN
BACKGROUNDS

PART I

PRIMITIVE AND NEAR EASTERN BACKGROUNDS

I

The Culture of the Hunters

In the total span of human development civilization is a relatively recent enterprise, and remains, at best, precarious and incomplete. At what period may have occurred the biological mutations that produced the first human beings is still undetermined. According to the new method of dating by measuring the disintegration of carbon-14 atoms in archaeological specimens, man may have been on the planet for a much shorter time than was formerly supposed. But by any estimate the epochs of savagery cover a vastly greater number of millennia than those of civilization. In the course of his savage experience man acquired habits and attitudes that he never afterwards wholly outgrew, and these have remained a part of his cultural heritage into the twentieth century. Such primitive survivals have been especially important in the development of those mental creations—religion and the arts—which were concerned not with the mastery of man's natural environment, but with the organization and interpretation of his emotions. For this reason a sketch of primitive culture and the rise of the first urban civilizations is an essential preliminary to any study of intellectual history. The patterns of Western thought took shape in the first millennium B.C., but one cannot understand the prophets and philosophers who first formulated the doctrines of ethical monotheism and natural law without some knowledge of the background from which they emerged.

During the first, and probably the longest, phase of their social evolution, men must have lived by gathering fruits and catching small animals. From the beginning, however, they had several advantages over their simian cousins—notably hands released from locomotion and capable of grasping, throats adapted to articulating a wide variety of sounds, and superior brains. Gradually they learned the use and manufacture of stone tools and weapons, and this made it possible for them to kill larger animals and to turn from fruit-gathering to hunting. This first major economic revolution was followed by the discovery of fire and the introduction of clothing, which extended human habitats into colder climates. The paleolithic phase in human history, which was also a hunting phase, lasted, at the lowest estimates, for some thirty thousand years, and has had lasting effects on the human personality. To this day man remains primarily a hunter in his physiological and psychological make-up, and is usually happiest when he can behave as one; he has never found it easy to adjust himself to the necessary repression of his aggressive impulses in the more disciplined and sedentary life of an urban civilization.

Hunting society spread to most parts of the land surface of the globe, with only such minor variations as were necessitated by climatic differences. During this period, for example, the two American continents were first settled by migrants from north-eastern Asia. Tribal organization must have existed in some form since the origin of man, but it acquired its permanent characteristics during the hunting phase. Efficient hunting required close co-operation among individuals who could display some degree of initiative. It was carried on by small tribal units whose members were interrelated by blood or marriage, strangers being admitted only by a process of adoption. When tribes grew too large for effective co-operation, they often became subdivided into smaller kinship groups (known to anthropologists as clans, sibs, or gentes) which continued to regard each other as close allies. Government was normally exercised by individual chieftains assisted by councils of elders, but until the adoption of private property rights no permanent class distinctions or systems of privilege could become established. Although it is dangerous to apply modern political terminology to primitive institutions, one can best describe the spirit of hunting society by calling it republican rather than monarchical, democratic rather than aristocratic.

The oldest and most deeply rooted of all man's ethical principles, and the only principle common to the whole human race, is the taboo against incest. This presumably originated in the need for preventing sexual conflicts and maintaining harmony among members of the same family. More advanced primitive peoples usually went farther than merely prohibiting sexual relationships between siblings and between parents and children, developing much more elaborate systems of marital taboos. Members of the same kinship group were prohibited from marrying each other, but were obligated to find mates in other kinship groups belonging to the same tribal organization. Thus, primitive marriage rules became partly exogamous and partly endogamous. Incest taboos applied to any cohabitation within the clan or sib, all the members of which were considered blood relatives and comprised a closely knit unit bound together by collective interests and obligations. Rules of descent were sometimes patrilineal and sometimes matrilineal. When inheritance was reckoned matrilineally, the continuity of the kinship group was maintained through the female line, and the necessary transferences of group membership were made not by the women, but by the men. Instead of bringing an alien wife into his own kinship group, a young man would be adopted into the group to which his wife belonged.[1]

Most other primitive rules of morality served the same practical purpose of preserving the harmony and economic efficiency of the group, ethical precepts not being distinguished either from tribal laws or from customs and conventions. Once a rule had become established, any violation of it, it was believed, would infallibly lead to some kind of catastrophe and probably to death, and the effects

---

[1] In some early societies the chieftainship was transmitted matrilineally, an individual acquiring the position by marrying either the widow or the eldest daughter of his predecessor. Such a society was not matriarchal, although its women usually had more influence than in patrilineal societies. That a genuine matriarchy has ever existed is highly doubtful. The evidence for it has been exaggerated by some anthropologists, especially by Marxists who have been eager to prove that the subordination of women resulted from the establishment of private property during the neolithic period and did not exist under conditions of "primitive communism." The practice of intermarriage between the heir to the throne and his sister, established in Egypt and some other early monarchies, probably developed as a result of matrilineal inheritance. As the succession to the throne was originally transmitted through the king's eldest daughter, the eldest son could establish a right to it only by marrying her.

Prehistoric Greece was apparently a matrilineal society. Without a knowledge of matrilineal descent and its close association with the clan system, it is impossible to understand early Greek literature, especially the plays of Aeschylus.

of a crime would always be prolonged until the full price had been paid. This meant that good and evil were always in the act, never in the intention, and the man who violated a taboo unknowingly would incur the appropriate penalty as infallibly as the deliberate criminal. Guilt, moreover, was collective as well as individual, being transmitted by the wrongdoer to his children or to the whole kinship group. The group, similarly, had the obligation of avenging injuries suffered by any of its members. Thus, a necessary social objective, the unity of the tribe, was achieved through the development of ir-rational moral fears and guilt anxieties. Such fears were so intense that the violators of taboos might often drop dead in sheer panic at their own temerity.

A similar association of irrational attitudes with socially desir-able results was exhibited by the growth of ritual and magic. These were based on erroneous conceptions of how natural forces oper-ated, but their effect was to assuage anxiety and other disturbing or disruptive emotions and to promote collective harmony. Unable to distinguish clearly between the subjective processes of his own imagination and external realities, and supposing that whatever he felt or visualized with especial vividness must be objectively true, primitive man came to believe that by acting out his wishes in imag-inary forms he could actually influence the course of natural events. This was a misapplication of what is perhaps man's most valuable mental characteristic, responsible for the development of language, of mathematics, and of all his higher intellectual achievements: his ability to think in symbols.

Initially, we may suppose, primitive man, responding to emo-tional pressures like a child or a dreamer, allayed his fears and an-tagonisms by means of symbolic wish-fulfillments. Fearful of an interruption in the sequence of the days and the seasons or an ex-haustion of his food supply, desirous of curing an ailment or aveng-ing himself upon an enemy, he gave expression to his feelings by acting them out in imitative forms. He then came to believe that these enactments produced real results, and that it was only by means of them that he was able to ward off all the dangers by which he was surrounded. This belief may have been partly due to the fact that his wish-fulfillments were, in practice, often fol-lowed by the desired consequences: that, for example, every time he performed a ceremony expressing his anxiety for the return of spring, there was in actuality a rebirth of vegetation, and that whenever he dealt with a physical ailment by enacting his eagerness to be rid of it, he experienced an emotional relief that hastened the physiological process of recovery. Thus confidence in these techniques of imitative control became established, resulting in the elaboration both of group rituals expressive of the normal needs of the tribe and of magical techniques for coping with specific problems.

In this fashion every common tribal interest—the recurrence of the seasons, the increase of the food supply, successful hunting— was likely to become embodied in some regularly repeated ceremony, which usually included group dancing, singing, and feasting. Besides enabling men to express, and thereby to allay, anger and anxiety, such ceremonies also promoted tribal unity and strengthened the loyalty of the individual to tribal traditions, for the emotional excitement they aroused had the effect of breaking down the barriers between individuals and thus fusing all the tribesmen into a collective whole. Meanwhile, whole systems of magical devices were gradually elaborated for curing diseases, punishing enemies, and dealing with other extraordinary crises. The magic-worker usually proceeded by taking something associated either by similarity or by contiguity with the person or object that he was desirous of controlling and then acting out his wishes on it. A human being might be affected, for example, for either good or evil purposes, by the magical manipulation of an image made to represent him, of portions of his hair or fingernails or clothing, or even (in more sophisticated societies) of his name. Certain members of a tribe, marked out either by unusual skills or by some emotional abnormality, usually became particularly adept at these operations, and gradually assumed specialized functions. Released from the duty of hunting, and concentrating on the practice of magic, the shaman, sorcerer, or medicine man was the world's first professional.

In so far as ritual and magic were devices by which man hoped to control his environment, they reflected an erroneous logic that would eventually be dispelled by a more rational understanding of natural processes. But their function was also to enable man to control himself by ordering his emotions and finding socially acceptable outlets for their expression. This function is as necessary in civilized as in savage society, and the methods by which it is accomplished by civilized man are organically linked with those of the paleolithic past. The development both of religion and of the arts can be traced back in a continuous line to the hunting era. The group rituals of the primeval tribesmen were the origin not only of all religious ceremonial, but also of the drama and of poetry and music, while magic gave birth to the visual arts. When paleolithic artists in France and Spain twenty or thirty thousand years ago covered the walls and ceilings of caves with paintings of bears and mammoths, bison and reindeer, their motive was to obtain power over these animals and make them easier to kill. In many of these pictures, in fact, the animals are depicted as either wounded, with darts hanging from their bodies, or close to traps, and there are indications that they were actually used as symbolic targets.

How did primitive man interpret the world in which he found himself, and by what processes did his ritualistic techniques of control acquire religious connotations? Any answers to such questions must, of course, be largely speculative. Ritual has always been one of the most stable elements in culture, and the logic upon which it was originally based is usually not difficult to decipher, whereas religious and philosophical beliefs have been much more variable. The same ritual has often been associated over the course of thousands of years with a series of different theological systems and explained by means of several different myths.

Apparently man's original assumption about the world around him was that all natural phenomena were alive in the same way as he was himself. This did not initially mean that natural objects were regarded as distinct personalities. Primeval man seems to have conceived of nature as filled with an anonymous undifferentiated force, a numinous power, similar to that of the human will. This force was manifested in all forms of movement in the sky or the atmosphere or on the earth, especially in any movement that did not seem to conform to normal expectations, and it might become concentrated in human beings with special talents or even in fetishistic objects. Anybody who touched such an object was likely to be smitten dead, whether the power with which it was charged was, so to speak, positive or negative—as is indicated by the fact that in most early languages the same word was used for "sacred" and "accursed." [2] Such a view of the world might be called religious in so far as it meant that men believed in a cosmic power and tried to maintain a right relationship with it; but the power was not at first personified, and was not approached with a religious spirit of reverence and submission. Through his rituals man hoped to control it and to ensure that its manifestations would be in accord with human purposes.

This feeling of an undifferentiated force at work in nature seems gradually to have developed into the belief that certain objects were not only particularly powerful but also endowed with distinct personalities. Thus the numinous mist that had originally filled the natural world began to disperse, and the figures of the gods slowly became visible. Men attributed will and intelligence to the sun and the stars, to mountains and trees and storms of wind and rain; but there is considerable evidence for the supposition that their earliest deities were animals. During the hunting phase of human evolution they seem to have developed religious attitudes toward the creatures upon whom they depended for their livelihood. The animal that a tribe slaughtered and devoured was regarded as a kind of guardian spirit, sometimes even as a physical relative; he gave his body for the preservation of his human dependents, and in eating it they entered into communion with him and received a share of his power.[3] Fearful of their temerity in doing violence to these divine beings, the primitive hunters developed rituals designed to avert their anger and secure their protection. Thus, the belief in the killing and eating of a god belongs to one of the earliest layers of human thought. It was probably from this notion of animal guardian spirits that kinship groups in var-

---

[2] Among the early Israelites, the Ark of the Covenant, as the residence of the tribal god, was an untouchable object. Once when the Ark was being transported on a wagon drawn by oxen, it was in danger of slipping, and a certain Uzzah put out his hand to steady it. As only the priests could safely handle the Ark, Uzzah was immediately smitten dead, not because he had commited any sin, but because he had made the mistake of touching an object charged with numinous power. See II Samuel, vi, 7.

[3] It is dangerous to engage in psychoanalytic speculations above the meaning of primitive myths and rituals. But it seems a plausible assumption that primitive man transferred to the animals he worshipped emotions and anxieties originally developed during his infantile association with his mother, and that these were subsequently carried over to the worship of the mother goddess during the neolithic phase of cultural development.

ious parts of the world developed the practice of adopting particular animals as their totemistic symbols and embodiments of group unity, though totem animals were considered too sacred to be eaten by their human dependents except on special ritualistic occasions.

Is it possible to make any guesses about the rituals associated with animal worship? Among the cave pictures left by the paleolithic hunters, a few represent human beings wearing heads and skins of animals, only the legs being left uncovered. Possibly animal disguises were assumed merely for the sake of effective hunting. On the other hand, in accord with the primitive confusion between image and reality, human beings may have been identified with the animals they represented, and may have played the central parts in dramatic performances designed to increase the tribal food supply by means of imitative magic. Under such circumstances the performer of the animal role must first have been considered as filled with the divine force that his fellow tribesmen wished to incorporate, and afterwards, carrying his enactment through to its logical and tragic culmination, he must have been slaughtered and ritualistically eaten. There is no direct evidence from the paleolithic period of such a ceremony, but the farther back we can trace the history of any society, the more evidence we are likely to find of human sacrifice and ritual cannibalism. In the ceremonies of which we have direct knowledge the victims were usually criminals, children, or captured enemies, but the accompanying rituals suggest that these were substitutes for a chieftain or medicine man in whom an animal deity had become embodied. We can most plausibly explain man's religious development by supposing that he originally believed not only that he acquired power by killing and eating divinity, but also that this divinity became manifest in human as well as animal forms.

Another tendency in primitive thought made it easy to believe that under appropriate circumstances a man might become filled with divine power. For religion developed as an interpretation not only of man's environment, but also of his own psychic experiences. Awed by the mysteries of his own spirit no less than by those of nature, primitive man was likely to attribute to divine influence any abnormal emotional state, whether above or below the usual level. Medicine men customarily went into states of trance in which they were believed to be in communication with the gods, and many tribes supposed lunatics and sexual deviants to be divinely possessed. In most early societies, moreover, men evolved techniques for deliberately inducing the abnormal forms of consciousness in which they supposed themselves to achieve union with divine power, sometimes by the use of drugs and other physiological stimuli, sometimes by hypnotic dances and music. The wild utterances to which they gave vent on such occasions were regarded as the words of a god and were interpreted as divine commands or predictions of future events. Many peoples attributed any violent or unusual emotion to one of the gods as a matter of course; the individual was then no longer held responsible for his actions, though the gods were sometimes mischievous or even malevolent and the results might be catastrophic.[4]

In particular, any euphoric state of mind in which men felt an enlargement of their normal powers was associated with divine inspiration. The flash of insight that enabled an individual to achieve an original act of creation, whether in art or in technology, was always mysterious, and for early mankind it could be due only to the intervention of a god. Long after the advent of civilization, in fact, poets continued to believe that they wrote from divine dictation; inventors attributed their discoveries to divine aid; and political and ethical reformers insisted that they were proclaiming truths revealed to them by heaven. Certain of

---

[4] Some of the North American Indians have retained a strong belief in divine inspiration. Participants in the sun dances and in the peyote cult try to induce visions and other mystic experiences, in the former case through physical exhaustion accompanied by fasting, in the latter by chewing the leaves of a plant with hypnotic properties. Both the sun dances and the peyote cult have acquired a veneer of Christianity, but the emotional attitudes are primitive.

In the higher religions one kind of experience is still regarded as mystical and attributed to divine influence. By mastering his desires and engaging in contemplative practices in which all thoughts of the external world are excluded, the individual may achieve an inner peace in which he believes himself to be united with a transcendent spiritual power. This is *the* mystical experience, and has assumed much the same form in all the different higher religions. But in primitive religion *any* violent or abnormal emotional state was attributed to the gods and regarded as mystical. Both in the Bible and in Homer there are examples of misleading and catastrophic inspiration. When Jehovah wished King Ahab to be killed in battle, he put "a lying spirit" in the mouths of his prophets in order that they might encourage the king to go to war (I Kings, xxii, 22). Agamemnon explained that when he brought disaster upon the Greeks by insulting Achilles, it was because Zeus had blinded him and deprived him of his reason (*Iliad*, XIX, 270).

the gods, though usually originating in natural phenomena, became especially associated with the advance of human society and with valued emotional attitudes, and were worshipped as patrons of culture.

Another source of religious ritual which can also be traced back as far as the hunting period is the belief in some kind of afterlife. Paleolithic men already buried their dead surrounded by the tools and weapons they would presumably need in their new existence. The notion that man had some kind of spirit distinct from his body seems to have developed among all branches of mankind, and was probably deduced from the fact that he had dreams while his body was asleep; but most primitive peoples regarded the next life as a pale reflection of this one and supposed that the dead were likely to envy the living. Some tribes worshipped the spirits of their departed ancestors; almost all came to believe that if they failed to supply the needs of the dead and make the proper disposition of their bodies, they would be haunted by complaining visitors from the world of ghosts. The tombs of powerful chieftains often became places of fear where by appropriate rituals men might occasionally establish contact with the spirits, but where they were more likely to incur deadly peril. Primitive peoples usually expected the ghosts to be revengeful rather than beneficent, and elaborate ceremonies were often adopted in order to ward off their malevolence.

Animal-worship and the belief in inspiration and in ghosts were probably the most important factors in the growth of polytheism, but there were innumerable other elements in the pedigree of the gods. Almost anything in man's environment might be regarded as a center of numinous power and gradually deified. In different parts of the world, men worshipped the heavenly bodies and atmospheric phenomena, mountains and rivers, rocks and pillars of stone, and almost every familiar variety of tree and animal. Needing reassurance in all the exigencies of daily life, they came to believe that each department of human activity had its own peculiar guardian spirit. Above all, they felt that the unity and welfare of their tribe were embodied in a special tutelary god who might originally have been a totem animal or an ancestral spirit or simply the concretization of communal loyalty. In the course of time, most tribes evolved their own creation myths, inventing grotesque stories about the origin of the world, but the gods to whom this was attributed usually remained rather remote figures. Owing their existence more to intellectual curiosity and poetic inventiveness than to any deep emotional need, they were not worshipped as warmly and assiduously as the lesser, but more cherished, tribal deities.

Initially, there can be no doubt, men deified what they actually saw: it was the visible physical object—the sun, the mountain, the oak tree or bull or snake—to which they attributed will and intelligence. Human thought began to move into a new phase when individuals learned to regard these objects as merely the temporary dwelling-places, or even the symbolic manifestations, of spiritual beings, supposing not that the sun was itself a god, but that a god who transcended nature made use of the sun to reveal himself to man. If the god was not identical with the object, but was merely represented by it, then it followed that he could also be represented by means of human artistry. Men therefore began to make images of their gods; and whereas the early paleo-lithic cave-paintings, being intended to serve magical purposes, had been strictly realistic, later primitive art often sought to heighten and enhance religious emotion by distorting natural forms, making war gods who were embodiments of terror and fertility goddesses with swollen breasts and buttocks who repre-sented solely the functions of sex and reproduction. But the process of abstraction implied in this kind of image-making was beyond the mental capacity of most primitive people, and the average tribesman was incapable of distinguishing the concrete representa-tion from the invisible reality. The idol of the tribal god might be supposed to be merely his symbol, or possibly a vehicle through which his power was particularly concentrated and made mani-fest; but it was often treated as a fetishistic instrument, itself en-dowed with personality, and was sometimes even subjected to magical manipulation if it failed to give prosperity to its devotees.

For a primitive god was never omnipotent, and often seemed to have little more power than human beings. By refusing to worship him men might anger him, but they could also exert pressure on him; and by special magical rituals they could even compel him to act in a desired manner. More advanced societies learned to regard such a procedure as a kind of *lèse-majesté,* and hence as extremely dangerous, but for a long time they did not doubt its efficacy. But tribes normally trusted their own particular gods and wanted them to be powerful, and believed that the gods could be strengthened through human aid. This led to the conception of a sacrifice as a communal meal shared by the tribal deity and his human dependents. By burning certain parts of an animal or by pouring out his blood on the ground before eating the remainder of the carcass themselves, the tribesmen actually provided nourishment for their god at the same time as for themselves. This shared meal was likely to be mingled with rituals handed down from the period when the animal was itself the god and the tribesmen communed with him by literally swallowing his body.

Only very gradually did men attach such transcendent power to the gods that the dependence ceased to be mutual and the sacrifice of treasured objects began to be regarded as a necessary method of placation. Men were very slow to recognize their own weakness and their absolute dependence on cosmic forces they could not control. Not until an even later period did religion become associated with any enlightened ethical principles. The moralization of the gods was, indeed, impossible as long as they retained their connection with natural phenomena, for it was obvious that nature did not behave in accord with any moral rules. What primitive men, both individually and collectively, wanted from the gods was health and strength, riches and long life, and they hoped to attain these things chiefly by ritual and sacrifice rather than by good conduct. The methods of early religion always remained largely magical, and its motivations thoroughly materialistic. Although the tribal gods were regarded as the guardians of tribal morality, and would be angered, it was supposed, if men did not adhere to it, they were not usually considered as its creators, and the behavior attributed to them in myths was often on a lower ethical level than that required of their worshippers. The one moral quality that the gods definitely expected men to display was humility. Almost all primitive peoples supposed that the gods would be provoked to anger if men showed pride or tried to rise above the cosmic status assigned to them, and in a number of creation myths it was suggested that divine jealousy was the original cause of death and the other ills of the human predicament.[5]

Primitive tribal gods were not restricted only in power; existing within the world of space and time, they were endowed with specific physical and temporal locations and could exercise authority only within certain geographic limits, their jurisdictions being normally coterminous with the areas claimed by their worshippers. During the hunting period there was probably little intertribal contact, and each group was likely to elaborate its own system of beliefs without considering the relationship between its own deities and those of other peoples. But when members of different tribes became associated with each other, they did not, in general, doubt the reality of each other's gods. It was assumed that each people would worship its own gods, and would in fact lose its identity if it ceased to do so, and that these gods had power only over their own tribesmen. After the development of agriculture, the gods become attached to particular countries, or even to particular shrines; and foreign visitors were expected to worship them as a matter not only of courtesy but also of prudence, as otherwise the gods might become offended.[6] When several tribal groups came under the same

---

[5] This was why Adam and Eve were expelled from the Garden of Eden. "And the Lord God said, Behold, the man is become as one of us, to know good and evil: and now, lest he put forth his hand, and take also of the tree of life, and eat, and live for ever: therefore the Lord God sent him forth from the Garden of Eden, to till the ground from whence he was taken" (Genesis, iii, 22). Jehovah was angered by the building of the Tower of Babel for similar reasons. "And the Lord came down to see the city and the tower, which the children of men builded. And the Lord said, Behold, the people is one, and they have all one language; and this they begin to do: and now nothing will be restrained from them, which they have imagined to do. Go to, let us go down, and there confound their language, that they may not understand one another's speech" (Genesis, xi, 5–7).

A similar belief in divine jealousy is expressed in the Geek myth of Prometheus.

[6] There are several examples of this attitude in the Bible. When David was driven into exile in Philistia by King Saul, he assumed that he would have to worship the Philistine gods (I Samuel, xxvi, 19). Naaman the Syrian, wishing to worship Jehovah while in his own country, solved the problem by taking with him two mules' burden of Palestinian earth (II Kings, v, 17). Particularly explicit is the story of what happened to the Assyrians who settled in Palestine after the conquest of Samaria. When some of them were eaten by lions, the others decided that this was because they did not know "the manner of the god of the land." So the King of Assyria released an Israelite priest and ordered him to explain how Jehovah should be worshipped. After this, it would appear, the Assyrian immigrants had no more trouble from the lions (II Kings, xvii, 24–8).

government, their mythologies were often fused on the assumption that they had been worshipping the same gods under different names; and when one tribe conquered another, its deity usually became the supreme figure in a new joint pantheon. Theological intolerance scarcely existed before the rise of monotheism. Gods, however, were sometimes capable of migration; and after the full development of polytheism in the early civilizations, individuals often chose which gods they would particularly worship, occasionally importing a new cult from some foreign community.

With the growth of higher conceptions of morality and more scientific views of nature, these primitive beliefs gradually became untenable and were either repudiated or transmuted into vehicles for the expression of new insights and incorporated into more enlightened theologies. This process can be traced in detail in the evolution of the two most spiritually creative of ancient peoples, the Jews and the Greeks. Moses and Homer, Amos and Aeschylus cannot be fully understood without a knowledge of the primitive tribalism and polytheism they were endeavoring to purify and adapt to higher ideals. Even modern man, however, bears the imprint of his early experiences and still confronts similar spiritual problems.

Every organism recapitulates the evolution of the species during its early physiological growth, and a similar process can be traced in the psychic development of the human child. The infant thinks like a primitive, displaying the same tendency to identify with each other images that have become linked by similarity or contiguity, to personify all the objects in his environment, and to act out his impulses in dramatic forms. These magical thought-patterns are only gradually superseded by rational conceptions of causation. Even in adulthood they always remain not far below the surface of consciousness, as is shown by their reappearance in the nocturnal world of dreams. Dream logic, in which everything represents something else and wishes find imaginary fulfillments, is a repetition of the logic that produced primitive magic. More consciously and deliberately, the poet thinks like a primitive, though with an awareness that poetic metaphor, symbolism, personification, and the expression of the basic human experiences in mythical forms are methods of stating subjective attitudes and not articulations of objective realities.

Through the development of irrational rituals and mythologies, primitive thought provided a response to two compelling needs: tribal co-operation and a sense of the unity of man and nature. The human race could not survive at all unless tribal welfare took precedence over the wishes of individuals. Human beings therefore learned to regard with horror any action, such as a violation of the incest taboo, that threatened group harmony; to be fearful of any departure from established mores and attitudes; to project their communal loyalties into the worship of a tribal pantheon; and to regard alien practices and allegiances with acute suspicion. At the same time they sought to relate themselves to the world around them by reading their own subjective thought-processes into external phenomena on the assumption that nature and the human spirit were substantially akin; by creating myths that gave meaning and value to the normal human experiences; and by attributing any new insight or any unusual emotional state to divine inspiration. Both the supremacy of collective over private interests and the sense of man's relatedness to the cosmos are necessary in all societies, and one of the central problems of culture after the growth of civilization is to reconcile them with rational modes of thought.

2

The Culture of the Peasants

Possibly the most far-reaching changes in human history were the discovery of agriculture and the domestication of animals. These apparently occurred eight or ten thousand years ago, marking the beginning of the neolithic era, and can most plausibly be located somewhere in the Middle East, perhaps along the southern shores of the Caspian Sea. The new ways of living were then gradually carried to other regions along different lines of migration. Before the beginning of written records the same kind of agricultural society became established in large parts of Europe and Asia, its archaeological remains being found in such widely scattered areas as the Danubian basin, the western and northern shores of the Black Sea, the fertile crescent bordering the desert of Arabia, and the valleys of the Indus in eastern India and the Hoang-Ho in northern China. In all these regions, neolithic peoples grew cereals, used oxen as beasts of burden, manufactured painted pottery, and made clay images of a fertility goddess. Except in the Americas, where agriculture was probably discovered independently, it seems originally to have been associated everywhere with the same cultural pattern, which must presumably have been diffused from a single center.

Agriculture may at first have been a feminine occupation. It is a plausible theory that the women of a tribe first realized that seeds thrown away near their encampment were producing sprouts and deduced the possibility of deliberately planting them. Early agriculture was associated everywhere with an emphasis on the feminine principle in nature and among the gods and on the analogy between human sexuality and the fertility of the earth. In the beginning the processes of sowing and harvesting may have been left entirely to the women, while the men continued their hunting activities or, if these became unnecessary or impossible, found an outlet for their aggressive energies in forms of inter-tribal warfare which were probably highly ritualized. Such a division of labor was established before the advent of the white men among the less advanced Indian peoples of North America, and was perhaps customary during the early neolithic period in the Old World.

In the end, however, the male members of most agricultural tribes surrendered their primal independence and became tillers of the ground. Thus the hunter was transformed into the peasant. This revolution was followed by a wide variety of social and cultural changes, not all of which were beneficial to the human beings affected by them. Agriculture produced more wealth and economic security than hunting, and stimulated other scientific and technological discoveries; but its invention resulted also in the growth of complex social structures under which the laboring masses supported privileged ruling groups. In spite of the economic advance that it represented, peasant society proved in some respects to be a deviation from the main line of human evolution, and those tribes which retained more of the independence of their hunting ancestors displayed, in the long run, a greater capacity for progress.

Ceasing to be nomadic, a tribe of agriculturalists would become rooted in a particular segment of fertile earth, and their lives would thereafter be largely guided by routines determined by the sequence of the seasons, individual initiative being much more rigidly restricted than among hunters. Land was at first always held collectively by the group, though it might be divided into separate family plots, the extension of the concept of private property to the basic source of production being a very late development in all parts of the world. But in addition to raising food for themselves, peasant communities normally set aside a surplus for the support of their priests or medicine men; and while these professionals might contribute to tribal welfare not only through their control of magic but also by gathering genuinely useful knowledge—most notably, by constructing a calendar for the guidance of farm operations—they were often able to exploit their peasant dependents and become a hereditary theocracy, the mass of the people being gradually reduced to some kind of serfdom. An even more extreme form of oppression was outright chattel slavery, brought about chiefly through the seizure of men and women from more primitive tribes in the vicinity. Agriculture, moreover, made wars of conquest profitable, and wealthy peasant communities, having lost the militancy of their ancestors, were likely sooner or later to be overrun by tribes of nomads, who often succeeded in establishing themselves as feudalistic ruling classes. Thus both internal and external factors tended to produce a concentration of authority in the hands of a few individuals.

These economic and social changes were accompanied by a transformation in the visual arts. Art always expresses the current conception of ultimate reality, swinging between the poles of sensuous representation and pure abstraction in proportion as men accept the finality of the material world or believe in spiritual or intellectual entities underlying or transcending physical appearances.[1] Early paleolithic art had been representational, displaying the belief of the hunters in the final reality of the animals on which they lived and in their power to control them by direct magical manipulation. Throughout the thousands of years of the neolithic period, on the other hand, artists either distorted natural figures, seeking to convey not their physical shapes but the forces and meanings embodied in them, or produced geometrical designs and patterns expressive of unchanging spiritual realities removed from the flux of naturalistic experience. This was the art of a phase in social development during which men were becoming aware of the complexity of the world and were searching for general concepts to explain natural processes. Probably neolithic art can also be linked with the growing irrationality of the social system and the consequent search for a spiritual realm that would both justify

---

[1] While representational art has always been linked with a materialistic concept of reality, abstract art has usually been religious. A few societies (most notably that of classical Greece) have seen the ideal embodied in the actual and have therefore been able to transcend this dichotomy. The abstract art of the twentieth century, however, is a reflection not of religious belief, but of modern man's confidence in his own power to shape and transform the physical world in accord with intellectual concepts of his own invention. Physical objects have lost their reality not, as in religious societies, because of a belief in a higher spiritual realm, but because of trust in the power of human thought.

economic inequalities and provide consolation for exploited classes.

Especially significant in many peasant societies was the development of the institution of kingship. The chieftain of a hunting tribe had usually shared his responsibilities with the tribal elders, but the king was an object of religious adoration, being regarded as divinely appointed and inspired, or even as a god incarnate. He was the successor of the medicine man rather than of the chieftain, and in the beginning his ritualistic functions were probably more important than his exercise of political leadership. The theory of divine right of kings can be traced back in a continuous line from the monarchies of modern Europe, through the Byzantine and Persian empires, to neolithic peasant society. Evidence gathered from primitive peoples in all parts of the world suggests that it began in forms of imitative magic associated with the discovery of agriculture.

In order to ensure good harvests, neolithic tribesmen adopted rituals designed to stimulate fertility, and these were frequently based on the analogy between the reproductive processes of the vegetation and human sexuality. Because many primitive peoples supposed that intercourse at the appropriate seasons, in some instances actually in the fields, would hasten the sprouting of the corn, sexual orgies acquired a religious significance. One individual, however, often became the especial representative of the vegetation spirit and, being identified with the role which he played, was likely to be considered a god. This appears to have been the origin of kingship. While these primal kings may often have exercised the general responsibilities of political leadership, their most important duty was to perform the rituals upon which tribal welfare depended, in particular by successfully cohabiting with the women who represented the earth mother. And while they usually lived in luxury and privilege, released from all obligations of physical labor, they were often destined to tragic ends. Because it was primarily by the exercise of virility that they promoted the fertility of the earth, they were sometimes slaughtered as soon as their sexual powers began to fail. Among some peoples even more savage customs became prevalent. Because the vegetation passed through a series of metamorphoses, being first scattered in the form of seed and then, resurrected as corn, being cut down and devoured, the human being who played the role of the vegetation spirit was sometimes treated in the same fashion; in some instances his body was cut into small pieces which were strewn over the harvest fields, in others it was ritualistically eaten in imitation of the harvest. There are indications that the central figure was often considered not only as a vegetation spirit but also as an animal, usually a horned bull or goat, from which one can plausibly suppose that the ceremony was an adaptation of practices of human sacrifice which predated the agricultural era and had been first established among the paleolithic hunters.

Eventually kings succeeded in freeing themselves from their obligation to serve their subjects by premature death, and the role of sacrificial victim was either enacted symbolically or transferred to somebody else. In some communities a young man would be chosen as the embodiment of the vegetation spirit, and for a given period before being killed would enjoy all the pleasures appropriate to a god. In other instances an animal, a child, or a criminal was sacrificed, and the ritual of killing the vegetation spirit was finally likely to become confused with the practice, also well established among primitive peoples, of removing guilt anxieties by transferring all tribal misdemeanors to a single victim and then slaughtering this "scapegoat" as an atonement for the sins of everybody else. But even after kings had established their right to die naturally, they were still identified with gods and expected to promote prosperity by the performance of customary rituals. The divinity of kingship remained, in fact, the only basis of political authority long after the development of the first urban civilizations.

In the evolution of primitive religion the adoption of rituals based on imitative magic seems normally to have preceded the elaboration of corresponding mythologies. But once a ritual had become established, it was likely to be interpreted by means of a tale about the gods, which then came to be regarded as its *raison d'être,* the original magical purpose being gradually forgotten. In order to explain their agricultural rituals, many primitive peoples devised stories of a marriage between the earth and the vegetation spirit. The earth was seen in feminine terms as a great mother—a conception probably connected with the fact that agriculture was at first carried on primarily by women. The vegetation represented the masculine principle; but because this disappeared during the winter, it was regarded as constantly dying and reviving; and because it was both seed and harvest, it could be considered both husband and son. The earth goddess, it was therefore declared, had been deprived of her lover and had mourned for his disappearance, but had finally regained him either by bringing him back from the underworld or by bearing a son to take his place. The death of the vegetation spirit was, moreover, closely associated with the loss of his sexual power, being attributed in many areas to a fatal wound by which he had been deprived of his masculinity.

The cult of the great mother and her dying and reviving partner became especially vigorous and persistent throughout those Mediterranean and Near Eastern territories where the civilization of the Western world originated. With regional variations, they were worshipped under the names of Ishtar and Tammuz in Mesopotamia, Isis and Osiris in Egypt, Astarte and Adonis in Syria, and Cybele and Attis in Anatolia, while in classical Greece a similar tale was told of the harvest goddess Demeter and her daughter Persephone. Surviving long after the advent of civilization, the myths were gradually embroidered with picturesque details. The people of Mesopotamia, for example, liked to tell how Ishtar had gone in search of Tammuz "to the land from which there is no returning, to the house of darkness, where dust lies on door and bolt," [2] and how in her absence all love ceased among men and animals, and life was in danger of extinction. As she descended into the underworld she was required gradually to remove her garments until finally she stood naked before Eresh-Kigal, the queen of the dead, who reluctantly responded to appeals from the gods of heaven and allowed Tammuz to be sprinkled with the water of life and set free. In the Egyptian version Osiris was first locked in a coffin by his wicked brother Set and floated out to sea, and afterwards torn into fourteen pieces, which were scattered throughout Egypt; but Isis succeeded in gathering together all the fragments except the· genitals, which had been eaten by fishes, after which Osiris revived and was made ruler of the dead. The mourning of Isis for her husband and her long search for his body became representative of all human fidelity and were favorite themes of Egyptian storytellers. In Anatolia, Attis was supposed either to have been killed by a boar or to have bled to death after

---

[2] Sir James G. Frazer: *The Golden Bough,* Chapter 29.

castrating himself in atonement for infidelity to his mistress, and then to have been reincarnated in the form of a pine tree.[3]

The living core of a religion, however, is always its ritual rather than its mythology. It retains its emotional efficacy as long as its adherents continue to fulfill the traditional ceremonial in the belief that through the performance they become linked with a cosmic power and that vital issues of life and death are dependent upon it. The worship of the earth mother and the vegetation spirit endured for many millennia because their separation and reunion were re-enacted every year in symbolic dramas, the completion of which was felt to be a necessary guarantee of communal prosperity. When the people of Mesopotamia chanted their "Lament of the Flute for Tammuz," and when the maidens of Lebanon, watching their river stained with the red earth washed down from the mountains every spring, sang dirges for the killing of Adonis, the god was actually dead; and when they feasted to celebrate his return from the underworld, he had actually come back to life. A projection of constantly repeated cycles of experience, the ritual was timeless, and each recurrence was identified with the original mythical enactment.

In the course of millennia the drama began to acquire new and more spiritual meanings, the killing and resurrection of the male figure becoming symbolic not only of the sequence of winter and spring, but also of the immortality of the human soul. This transformation was facilitated by the fact that the earth was the recipient of the bodies of the dead as well as of the seed. And while the ritual of death and rebirth offered the hope of new life after death, it also conveyed a recognition of the spiritual truth that man can grow to full emotional maturity only by passing through the crisis of a kind of psychic death and rebirth—a truth embodied in the puberty rituals of many primitive tribes and ex-

---

[3] Reminiscences of the vegetation cult were preserved in the medieval Grail legend. The Grail was supposed to be guarded by a king who had suffered a mysterious wound, in consequence of which his land had become waste. Its fertility would be restored through the advent of a young hero belonging to the same dynasty. The Grail seems originally to have been a female sex symbol, its identification with the blood of Jesus being a later amendment of the story. The source of the legend is a controversial question. Jessie L. Weston suggests that the cult of Attis may have been introduced into Britain by the Romans and preserved in Wales during the Dark Ages. See her *From Ritual to Romance*.

pressed in the gospel doctrine that he who wishes to save his life must first lose it. But the elevation of the peasant religion into a vehicle for the expression of more enlightened beliefs was always impeded by the crudity of the original conceptions. Both sexuality and human sacrifice continued to be associated with religion among agricultural peoples in the Near East long after the growth of urban civilizations. Cohabitation with temple prostitutes was still a sacred ritual in Mesopotamia and Syria in the first millennium B.C., by which time the original magical purpose of sexual orgies had probably been forgotten. In Anatolia, especially on the Phrygian plateau, the worship of Cybele was associated with outbreaks of mass frenzy in which men were inspired to imitate Attis by slashing themselves with knives and even emasculating themselves, and the loss of virility was a prerequisite for becoming a priest of the goddess. Human sacrifice was deeply rooted in Palestinian religion before the Israelite conquest, first-born children being dedicated to the gods and presented to them in the form of burnt offerings.[4]

Even more persistent was the tendency to seek a sense of divine possession and union with divine powers by means of collective ecstasies that dissolved all rational limits and conscious restraints. Orgiastic cults flourished throughout the Near East in the first millennium B.C.; and while closely connected with the fertility dramas in which men and women performed the roles of the dead vegetation and the mourning earth mother, they also incorporated elements from even earlier strata of human experience. The celebrants of some of these cults apparently sought union with their god by tearing apart and devouring the flesh, and bathing in or drinking the blood, of a horned animal, usually a bull, in which he had become incarnate. This can only have been a reminiscence handed down for tens of thousands of years from the paleolithic tribesmen who had communed with their animal guardian spirit by eating his body.

Thus agriculture led both to political and economic institutions and to religious practices and beliefs that were obstacles to man's social and moral advance. But while some peoples became pri-

---

[4] As late as the time of the Roman Empire, the tradition of infant sacrifice survived in both Syria and North Africa. The emperors Tiberius and Hadrian found it necessary to legislate against it.

marily tillers of the soil, others lived mainly by breeding animals. In the course of the neolithic era, human geography in the Old World assumed the form it was to retain until relatively recent times. Peasant communities became established in fertile regions, especially along such rivers as the Nile, the Euphrates, the Danube, the Indus, and the Hoang-Ho and along the coasts of the eastern Mediterranean, while nomadic pastoral peoples ranged across the Eurasian plain and the grasslands bordering the Arabian desert. The life of the herdsman was much more primitive than that of the agriculturalist, having undergone much smaller changes since the hunting period, but it was better adapted for political and moral progress. In pastoral society the individual was still required to display initiative, and no elaborate system of class privilege and exploitation could develop. The chieftain of a pastoral tribe was primarily a war leader, not a god incarnate, and decisions were normally reached by processes of democratic consultation. Pastoral religion, moreover, remained relatively free from degrading rituals. Worshipping chiefly divinities of the sky and the weather, and seeing them definitely in masculine forms, pastoral peoples did not usually deify the processes of sexual reproduction or regard human sacrifice as more than an extreme and unusual expedient; and their gods, being nomadic rather than fixed to particular localities, and not normally represented by means of images, could be universalized and spiritualized more easily than the peasant deities. Cultural advance beyond the neolithic phase of human development depended on the assertion of man's power to shape and control biological forces instead of submitting to them; and this was possible only among peoples with a hunting or pastoral rather than an agricultural background.

Although technologically more backward than the peasant communities, herding tribes had more martial vigor and were better able to undertake wars of conquest. The subjugation of a peasant population by pastoral warriors was a recurring phenomenon in the ancient world; and while such an event was always followed by a temporary cultural and technological decline, it often meant a renewal of moral vigor. Two such episodes were of decisive importance in the shaping of the Western tradition: the occupation of Palestine by the shepherd peoples who brought with them the worship of Jehovah and the Mosaic moral code; and the conquest of Greece by Aryan horse-breeders from the Eurasian plains whose chief deity was the sky god Zeus. The spiritual and ethical beliefs of Western civilization took shape during the processes of conflict and amalgamation between the peasant fertility cults and the pastoral cults introduced by the Israelite and Hellenic invaders.

History usually ignores the life of the peasants after the rise of urban societies; yet the agricultural culture established during the neolithic period remained the essential economic basis of all civilization until very recent times, and the cities could not have existed at all if they had not been able to extract an agricultural surplus from the villages. There are good reasons for this historical oversight, however: almost all spiritual and material progress since neolithic times has been the work of nomads or of city-dwellers, while the life of the peasant has remained essentially timeless. Conquering tribes of herdsmen established themselves as ruling aristocracies and then decayed, each of them in turn bringing new languages and new religious beliefs; urban merchants and money-lenders devised methods of exploiting the food-producers and tried to impose their own rationalistic modes of thinking; but village life through most of Europe and Asia retained its neolithic characteristics, and in spite of linguistic and religious changes, the ethnic composition of its people probably remained much more stable than is often supposed.[5]

Prior to the spread of the commercial and industrial revolutions there was no essential change in agricultural techniques; and although the original neolithic fertility rituals, cleansed of their more barbaric elements and adapted to the worship of new gods, gradually faded into popular festivals and folk tales and finally into children's games, the beliefs associated with them retained much of their vitality. Throughout southern Europe, in fact, the traditional conviction that a good harvest depended on the death and resurrection of a god and the worship of a mother goddess was incor-

---

[5] Historians have often exaggerated the importance of language as an indicator of the ethnic composition of a nation. People learn to speak new languages more readily than is often supposed. For example, the Jews during the period of the Persian Empire abandoned Hebrew and began speaking Aramaic (the general language of Syria). That the English speak a Teutonic language by no means implies that the Anglo-Saxon element in their ethnic inheritance is larger than the Celtic or Iberian, just as the Romance language of the French does not prove that they are of Roman descent.

porated into three successive mythologies, the archaic, the classical, and the Christian.[6] Pre-literate, politically impotent, and un-
imaginably conservative, the culture of the peasants rarely affected
the course of history except through its resistance to change, and
its existence can therefore be easily overlooked; but any attempt
to drop soundings into this peasant underworld during any historic
epoch leads to surprising discoveries. Just as there was a prehistoric
element in the mental processes of the civilized human being,
which could come to the surface through a relaxation of conscious
control in sleep or states of trance, so also there was a prehistoric
underworld in the class structure of civilized society. This must
always be remembered in studying the great cultural creations
based primarily on subjective thinking—religion and the arts—
as their value has depended largely on how wide a range of human
experience they could comprehend and synthesize.[7]

---

[6] The celebration of Christ's resurrection is still the chief festival of the
Greek Church. On the evening of
Easter Saturday the whole population
of each village assembles in a dark-
ened church to mourn for his death.
At midnight the priest announces his
return to life, which is greeted with a
sudden blaze of candlelight and ecstatic cries that Christ has indeed
risen. There is a display of fireworks
in the churchyard, and on the next day
every family feasts on roast lamb.
Thus the resurrection is an annually
repeated event, associated with the
revival of the earth's fertility as well
as with the assurance of personal immortality.

[7] Some historians of the French Revolution who have sought explanations
for the failure of the peasants to give
more militant support to Catholicism
have been driven to the conclusion
that, fifteen hundred years after the
official establishment of the Church in
France, the religious beliefs of the rural masses were still essentially pagan
rather than Christian. See A. Aulard:
Christianity and the French Revolution. Visitors to Mexico during the
Church-state conflict of 1926 reached
the same conclusion; but in Mexico

the Church was only four hundred
years old.

Sir James Frazer's The Golden
Bough contains a mass of information
about the survival of neolithic superstitions in rural areas in modern Europe. Frazer does not discuss the possible persistence of prehistoric fertility
rituals down to the sixteenth and seventeenth centuries in the form of a
secret witch cult. The case for it was
overstated by Margaret Murray in her
Witch-Cult in Western Europe, but is
presented more plausibly by Pennethorne Hughes in his Witchcraft. According to the evidence repeatedly
brought out in specific detail by confessions at witch trials, the celebrants
of a "sabbat" (the derivation of this
word is obscure, but it has no connection with the Christian Sabbath)
would anoint themselves with drugs
(such as aconite and belladonna) likely
to induce ecstatic states (including
particularly the sensation of flying)
and then engage in ritualistic dancing, feasting, and sexual orgies. The
leader of the group wore the mask of
an animal (usually a bull or a goat),
and was considered an embodiment of
a god, for which reason he was supposed by Christians to be the devil

in person. He engaged in sexual intercourse with the female celebrants, apparently using an artificial penis (women on trial for witchcraft often described the devil's penis as unusually cold and hard). According to these descriptions, a sabbat was essentially a fertility ritual, and resembled ceremonies still current among primitive peoples in Africa and America. If no witch cult existed, it is difficult to account for all these specific details, or indeed for the whole persecution, though the popular fear of witchcraft was undoubtedly stimulated by clerics and judges and many innocent persons must have been convicted (during the early seventeenth century thousands of persons in England, France, and Germany were put to death for witchcraft). It seems more plausible to suppose that neolithic religious practices lingered on in backward rural areas. The black magic attributed to the witches was also a prehistoric survival, and may occasionally have been effective, partly for psychological reasons and partly through the use of drugs, knowledge of which may have been handed down in rural families.

3

The Theocratic Civilizations

The areas where urban civilization was first superimposed upon the peasant base were Mesopotamia and Egypt, and the time was almost certainly the fourth millennium B.C. At subsequent periods, similar, and apparently independent, civilizations emerged in the valleys of the Indus and the Hoang-Ho, while several millennia later the same process occurred in Mexico and Peru, which by the fifteenth century of our era had reached a stage roughly equivalent to that of Mesopotamia and Egypt in the third millennium B.C. But the Euphrates and Nile valleys were the original sources of the civilization of Western man. For the next three thousand years, in fact—more than half the total span of civilization in the Western world—its history remained the history of these two areas and of those surrounding regions, such as Syria, Anatolia, Iran, and the Mediterranean islands, that came under their influence.

The rise of a civilization was a complex process, dependent mainly on social and institutional changes rather than on any new technological discovery. Its most significant features were the unification of a number of peasant communities into some form of state, the government of which then had command of relatively large economic resources and supplies of manpower; the growth of the division of labor and the increase of classes with specialized functions not directly engaged in the production of food, such as priests, officials, craftsmen, and traders; and the building of cities largely inhabited by such classes. These developments were quickly followed by important cultural and economic advances, particularly by the invention of writing and the keeping of written records and by the use of metals, especially bronze. That this happened first in the valleys of the Euphrates and the Nile seems to have resulted from the need for artificial irrigation; human labor had to be organized for the building of canals that would control and conserve the summer floods of the rivers and distribute the water as widely as possible, and land and water rights had to be allotted to different village communities. This could be accomplished only under the direction of governments holding authority over relatively wide areas.

Man's first answer to the social and political problems involved in the rise of civilization was to strip himself of all responsibility for his own destiny and project all authority upon the gods. The priests who organized the building of irrigation canals and the establishment of central governments attributed their capacity for initiative and creativity to divine inspiration and demanded unquestioning obedience from their dependents on the ground that they were the vehicles of the divine will. Thus, the ancient city was a theocratic institution built around the temple of a tribal deity and ruled by a priest-king who was considered as his nominee and spokesman. In Mesopotamia each city was regarded as the property of its god, and the function of the human ruler was to serve as steward of the god's estates; according to Mesopotamian theology, men had been created in order to relieve the gods of the necessity of labor, and were therefore their slaves. In Egypt the king was actually himself a god, and hence was the owner of all the land and absolute master of all its inhabitants. Thus, the early civilizations were permeated with religion, finding their whole *raison d'être* in the service of heaven rather than of mankind, and maintaining order and unity by absolute obedience to the priest-kings in whom the will of heaven had become concentrated and embodied. In emerging from the protective shell of tribal tradition and confronting the anxieties of a more complex way of life, men sought security by maintaining a feeling of close and comprehensive dependence upon divine powers.

Theocratic civilization was hierarchical and authoritarian, and the beliefs upon which it was based were incompatible with the development of any understanding of scientific law or any concept of historical progress. As the gods were responsible for everything, all phenomena must be attributed to divine intervention rather than to natural causality; and as they had already fully expressed their will in the making of the world and the organization of human society, change was unreal and history meaningless. Man's happiness depended on conformity to the divine order embodied from the beginning in the institutions of the theocratic state. Theocratic principles, nevertheless, provided a workable solution to man's central political problem; by attributing earthly authority to divine appointment, they made it legitimate and gave it a right to unconditional loyalty. As long as faith in theocracy remained vital and unquestioning, the social order was organic and not mechanistic, being based on the willing consent of its members and not on coercion. After six thousand years men have not fully outgrown these theocratic attitudes and are still capable of reverting to them whenever they lose confidence in later and more rational concepts of political order.

For about one thousand years theocracy made possible a remarkable display of human energy and inventiveness. The centuries during which the Mesopotamian and Egyptian civilizations were first established, covering roughly the second half of the fourth millennium B.C. and the first half of the third, were one of the most creative epochs in all history. Having discovered a way of mobilizing and directing human skill and power on a much larger scale than had been possible in peasant society, the peoples of both these civilizations were responsible for astonishing achievements in almost all fields of human activity, most notably perhaps in mathematics, architecture and engineering, and the visual arts. This early efflorescence, however, was followed by a long period of cultural conservatism during which men consolidated and imitated the works of their predecessors and made few significant additions or innovations. Both the Mesopotamian and the Egyptian civilizations passed through epochs of breakdown and disintegration, with a consequent loss of faith in divine guidance; but men failed to affirm any alternative principle of political unity and could restore order only by re-establishing theocratic government, though with an increasing emphasis on military force and coercion. In fact, an interval of nearly two thousand years passed before the advent of another epoch of high creativity, and this developed not in Mesopotamia or Egypt, which were unable to break with their theocratic heritage, but among peoples with no previous tradition of civilization.

Priority in the building of civilization almost certainly belonged to the Sumerians, a people of unknown origin who had apparently first lived in mountainous country, perhaps in Iran, and had then migrated to southern Mesopotamia, where they probably subjugated a peasant population. During the fourth millennium a dozen or more Sumerian cities grew up in the lower Euphrates and Tigris valleys, each of them built around the shrine of a god, while in the fields outside peasants grew corn and date palms and herded cattle. One of the cities usually exercised hegemony over the others; but they remained largely independent in their internal affairs, and changes of supremacy were not infrequent. Sumerian civilization was based on the city-state and proved, in the end, unable to achieve integration on a larger scale. Entrusted by the gods with the management of their property, the priests and officials supervised agriculture on the temple estates and the building and repair of the irrigation canals, promoted trade and craftsmanship, and accumulated wealth; and the temples developed into elaborate financial institutions as well as places of worship and centers of learning. Below this ruling class was a body of free citizens, engaged in industry or cultivating farms, while the base of the social structure consisted of slaves recruited from prisoners of war or from citizens who had lost their freedom through inability to pay debts. Sumerian civilization became predominantly business-minded, and its development was accompanied by a considerable growth of trade both between different cities and with foreign peoples, the metals used by Sumerian craftsmen being imported from Anatolia and Iran and even as far as India.

The Sumerians never forgot that they had created their own means of support by building dry land in what had originally been a watery morass and confining the flood water in canals. This primal struggle with nature and the need for its constant renewal were central in their view of life. According to their mythology, the world had at first consisted of a watery chaos, and order had been established through a cosmic battle in which the gods had vanquished the forces of evil. This battle had to be repeated every spring, not only realistically by repairing the canals and keeping the rising waters under control, but also in symbolic rituals based on imitative magic, which served the purpose of unifying the community under theocratic leadership and concentrating its energies on the labors needed for survival. The priest-king of each city played the role of a god, usually of Enlil, who was the second figure of the Sumerian pantheon, being the son of the sky god Anu, and represented various forms of natural power and energy. In this role the king performed ceremonies depicting the defeat of Tiamat, the demon of the ocean, and the other monsters who followed her leadership. "In these festivals, which were state festivals, the human state contributed to the control of nature, to the upholding of the orderly cosmos. In the rites men secured the revival of nature in the spring, won the cosmic battle against chaos, and created the orderly world each year anew." [1] In other festivals priest-kings also assumed the identity of the vegetation spirit Tammuz, although these fertility rituals, which may have been established among the peasants before the coming of the Sumerians, were not integrated with the worship of Anu and Enlil and did not become part of the official state religion. Enacting these divine roles in religious dramas, the king became closely associated with the gods and was sometimes regarded as of divine descent, though according to the official theology he was always subordinate to his divine master and could not expect immortality. In Babylon, for example, his status was symbolized in an annual ceremonial in which he was stripped of his royal insignia, smitten in the face by a priest, and made to prostrate himself before the image of the city god Marduk and confess his devotion; then, reclothed as a king, he was brought out weeping to show himself to his subjects.

In spite of the irrigation achievements of the Sumerians, they never developed any real sense of security. The movements of the waters were always uncertain; floods were frequent, and the Euphrates periodically changed its course. Mesopotamia, moreover, was surrounded by warlike and nomadic neighbors and was in danger of being conquered if she lost the capacity for self-defense. Fear was therefore always a predominant note in Sumerian religion. The gods could not wholly be trusted, and the unseen world was also peopled by a multitude of demons whose hostility had con-

---

[1] H. Frankfort (ed.): *Intellectual Adventure of Ancient Man*, p. 199.

stantly to be averted by magical rites. Medicine, for example, consisted largely of an elaborate system of devices for exorcising evil spirits. And as the Sumerians had no faith in immortality, their hopes being concentrated on prosperity in this life, they devoted an extraordinary amount of effort and ingenuity to attempts to foretell the future. Retaining the primitive sense of man's unity with nature, and regarding the world as a god-created cosmic order, the order of human society being a reflection and imitation of the macrocosm, they supposed that all kinds of complex interrelationships could be discovered by careful observation. The priests therefore set out to trace correlations between human affairs and natural phenomena in an effort to find foreshadowings of impending catastrophes and thus enable men to guard themselves against coming misfortunes. Their favorite method of divination was to examine the livers of the animals sacrificed to the gods—a practice that spread to other parts of the Near East and was subsequently carried by the Etruscans to Italy and transmitted to the Romans. They also believed that they could foretell events by watching the movements of the stars. The study of astrology originated in the cities of early Mesopotamia, was further developed by the Chaldeans, who took possession of the city of Babylon in the first millennium B.C., and was afterwards transmitted to all parts of the civilized world.[2]

In spite of these irrational elements in their view of life, the Sumerians probably made more important contributions to man's cultural heritage than any other people known to history. They apparently invented writing, although they did not develop a phonetic alphabet and were also handicapped by the necessity of using bulky clay tablets. Writing was used not only for religious and mythological poems and official records, but also for codes of law. The growth of commerce and moneylending led to an emphasis on contractual relationships, and this resulted in the formulation of the world's first legal systems. Sumerian craftsmen worked with soft metals as well as with stone, producing utensils, ornaments, and statues of gods and kings with an extraordinary grace and delicacy, in addition to inventing such objects as the socketed ax and the potter's wheel. In architecture, their most conspicuous creations

---

[2] In 1958 ten astrologers were listed in the Manhattan telephone book.

were the immense brick ziggurats that inspired the story of the
Tower of Babel; these were presumably erected in order that their
gods might have habitations resembling the mountains from which
they had originally come. But they also understood how to build
arches and vaults, although these forms of construction do not
seem to have been widely used, their importance not being recognized until they were adopted by the Romans more than three
thousand years later. The most remarkable achievements of the
Sumerians, however, were in astronomy and, more particularly, in
mathematics. Notwithstanding their lack of an adequate system of
notation, they developed not only arithmetic but also algebra, for-
mulating certain algebraic methods of calculation which they were
unable to transmit to their successors and which were rediscovered
anew in very recent times.[3]

The Sumerian golden age apparently reached its peak before the
end of the fourth millennium. The early centuries of the third
millennium were largely filled with wars among the different
cities, resulting in an increasing use of mercenary instead of citizen
troops and in the militarization of society. Like the Greeks
twenty-five hundred years later and the Italians forty-five hundred
years later, the Sumerians, having achieved political integration on
the basis of the city-state, were unable to make the necessary
transfer of loyalties to any more comprehensive order. Meanwhile, predominance slowly passed to the Akkadians of northern
Mesopotamia, a people who differed from the Sumerians in language and ethnic origin but who had largely been assimilated into
Sumerian civilization. Halfway through the third millennium, Sar-
gon, King of the Akkadian city of Agade, temporarily unified the
whole of Mesopotamia in the world's first military empire. A few
centuries later, supremacy was briefly recaptured by the Sumerian
city of Ur, but through the following millennium Mesopotamia
was ruled either by the Akkadians or by foreign conquerors, and
eventually the Sumerians ceased even to speak their own language.
The culture of Mesopotamia, however, was always based on its
Sumerian foundation, to which other peoples added remarkably
little, and the Sumerian language, although no longer spoken, continued to be studied (like Latin in medieval Europe) as the

[3] See George Sarton: *A History of Science,* pp. 68–74.

1. a. Cave painting from Lascaux, France. The arrows above the back of the horse indicate the magical purpose of this specimen of paleolithic art.

b. Iranian pottery of the fourth millennium B.C. *These exemplify the abstract tendencies of most neolithic design.*

2. *a. A privy councilor and priest of Ma'et,* c. *2500* B.C.

b. Queen Hatshepsut, c. *1485* B.C.

c. The god Amon, c. *1450* B.C.

d. The lioness-headed goddess Uto, c. *900–600* B.C.

Egyptian portrayals of human and divine figures never much varied over a period of more than two thousand years, always conveying an attitude of solemn determination.

vehicle of learning. The economic and cultural traditions established by the Sumerians were, in fact, maintained in some form
in the Mesopotamian cities for more than four thousand years,
and the continuity was not finally broken until the region reverted
to its primeval condition of watery chaos as a result of the destruction of the irrigation canals during the Mongol invasion of the
thirteenth century of our era.

The civilization of Egypt, according to archaeological findings,
first took shape under the stimulus of commercial contacts with the
Sumerians, although after initial borrowings it quickly acquired its
own distinctive quality. Human life was possible only close to the
Nile, which flowed through a narrow valley for five hundred miles
below the first cataract and then broadened into the delta before
reaching the Mediterranean; and the dependence of the whole
region on the annual flooding of the river made political unification essential. In prehistoric times a line of peasant communities
grew up along the Nile valley. These "nomes" were afterwards
combined into the two kingdoms of Upper and Lower Egypt, and
finally, probably near the end of the fourth millennium, the whole
country was united under a single ruler. The Egyptian Old Kingdom, which was the golden age of Egyptian civilization, lasted
through most of the third millennium.[4]

The Egyptian mind was always dominated by an awareness of
man's reliance upon natural regularities—the annual rise and fall
of the river, the daily transit of the sun across the cloudless sky,
and the abrupt division between the desert and the fertile fields of
the Nile valley. Egypt, moreover, being bounded by the sea and
the desert, was through much of its history almost isolated from the
rest of the world and in little danger of foreign conquest; in spite
of her early contacts with the Sumerians, which are known only
through archaeology and were apparently forgotten by the Egyptians themselves, and in spite also of later trade relations with
Phoenicia and some other areas, foreign peoples never had much
reality in the Egyptian view of life. These conditions produced a

[4] The chronology of the early Egyptian dynasties was for a long time a
controversial question; while a majority of Egyptologists dated the Old
Kingdom in the third millennium,
some scholars preferred to place it
about one thousand years earlier. The
question seems to have been finally
settled in favor of the third millennium by the new methods of dating
developed by the physicists.

civilization marked by its extraordinary sense of security and self-assurance and by its attempt to obliterate time and change. Content with their way of life and confident that it would never be disrupted by any accidental or unforeseen catastrophe, the early Egyptians believed that they could perpetuate it through all eternity; and while their primary aim was to transcend mortality by prolonging life beyond the grave, they did in fact succeed in maintaining their institutions for a longer period than any other people in history. Egyptian civilization has always fascinated mankind because of its sheer longevity. In the classical age of Greece the pyramids were already more than two thousand years old—a span almost as long as that separating the Greeks from ourselves —yet Egyptian society throughout this immense period had undergone only minor changes.

Before the unification of Egypt the different nomes worshipped their own tutelary gods, who seem to have originated as totem animals; and under the pharaohs these were combined into a single pantheon. Egyptian theology always remained an extraordinary tangle of deities with indeterminate personalities and overlapping functions, many of whom retained animal shapes and were believed to manifest themselves as bulls or birds. But the unifying religion of the pharaohs and the priests who supported them consisted chiefly of sun-worship. Each successive ruler was supposed to be the child of the sun god Re, who assumed human form for the purpose of begetting an heir to the throne. During the early dynasties he was also a falcon, this being apparently the totem of the nome whose ruler had first united the country. The most popular of Egyptian cults, however, was that of Osiris, the vegetation spirit who had been killed and then acquired immortality as ruler of the dead. In addition to being worshipped as the son of Re, the pharaoh also became identified with Horus, the son of Isis and Osiris, and ultimately with Osiris himself. The deification of the pharaoh was the essential bond of unity of the Egyptian state. The center of all the life of the community and the guardian and symbol of all natural and social order, he was responsible for performing the rituals that ensured that the sun and the river would continue their accustomed movements and for maintaining the irrigation canals and seeing that all classes of Egyptians attended to their prescribed duties.

In the Egypt of the Old Kingdom the pharaoh alone could be a complete individual, though his freedom was narrowly restricted by ritualistic requirements. The chief mark of his individuality was that he, and he alone, had the privilege of assured survival after death. During the early dynasties of the third millennium, a vast proportion of the economic resources of the state was devoted to ensuring that the pharaohs would enjoy their immortality under favorable conditions; human labor on an immense scale was conscripted for building the pyramids where they were buried, while the walls of their tombs were decorated with realistic pictures of Egyptian life, apparently in the magical expectation that they could be surrounded by their accustomed pleasures in the world of the dead. The striving of the early Egyptians for eternity by no means reflected any pessimistic repudiation of the world and the flesh; as their art makes manifest, it was, on the contrary, precisely because of their appreciation of daily life that they were so intent on immortality. The next world was not a recompense for the frustrations of this one, but an eternal prolongation of it. If one can judge from the surviving literary records, the tone of Egyptian society under the Old Kingdom was worldly, materialistic, and optimistic. As all men were officially the slaves of the god-king, society was not yet rigidly stratified along class lines, and ambitious individuals of humble origin could rise to positions of wealth and power in the bureaucracy by displaying skill and prudence, and might even hope that the pharaoh would continue to make use of their services in the next life.

Developing their own system of writing, the Egyptians invented papyrus, which was immeasurably more convenient than the clay tablets used in Mesopotamia. Somewhat inferior to the Sumerians in mathematics and astronomy, and also in metallurgy, they surpassed them in medicine and some other sciences, although their knowledge was always mixed with magical beliefs and never infused with any clear understanding of natural causation. Their literature included not only religious myths and incantations and official records, but also collections of maxims instructing young men how to achieve worldly success and works of fiction displaying a capacity for sophisticated humor. But their finest achievements were in the visual arts, in which they developed styles clearly indicative of the spirit of their civilization.

The main impetus of the arts in Egypt was a determination to affirm the reality of the everlasting world of the gods. Artists created many forceful and vivid portrayals of ordinary human beings and scenes of daily life; but this kind of realism was usually applied only to men and women of the lower classes, with the magical purpose of projecting them into the afterlife for the service of their rulers. The effort toward transcendence was particularly exemplified in bas-reliefs of gods and rulers in which the more important figures were presented frontally and placed side by side without movement or three-dimensional perspective, and in colossal statues of pharaohs whose majestic and impassive features, immune to human suffering and doubt, displayed their immortal nature. The Egyptian sculptor usually presented the human form with arms at the sides, hands clenched, and the left foot forward, and gave it large eyes, broad shoulders, and a slim waist. The shape of the body, the tense positions of the arms and legs, and the solemnity of the features reflected that drive of the human will toward the mastery of the natural world which characterized Egyptian civilization in all its aspects. Though never departing far from realistic representation, these sculptures sought constantly to deny change and movement and to distill out of natural appearances the forms that would be appropriate to eternity.[5] In architecture the Old Kingdom actually came as close to conquering time as is possible for any human enterprise. The Great Pyramid, built of more than two million blocks of limestone each averaging over two tons in weight, which were set in position and bound together with a geometrical accuracy and a thoroughness that modern engineering could hardly surpass, may well outlast the human race.

---

[5] While religious views of life have found their most typical expression in a purely abstract art, they have also been reflected in the treatment of the human figure. A society that affirms a belief in spiritual realities transcending sensuous experience is likely to produce an art in which figures are presented frontally, not in profile, and without movement or three-dimensional perspective. Human forms depicted in this manner give the impression of being removed from the world of space and time and engaged in the contemplation of eternal verities. Throughout art history frontality, immobility, and a restriction to two dimensions have been consistent indicators of a religious view of life. In the history of the Western world this was most clearly exemplified in late Roman and early Byzantine art.

The whole subject is explored by Arnold Hauser in his *Social History of Art*.

During the next two thousand years, Egypt passed through several periods of disintegration in which the monarchy was no longer strong enough to maintain order, and power was assumed by local officials, and several times the country was reunited by new lines of pharaohs. But the mold set so firmly during the early dynasties was never broken; and in spite of a growing emphasis on military force, the development of private ownership of land by priests and nobles, and the gradual democratization of immortality, which finally became the goal of every Egyptian, the priestly castes of the temples always maintained the theocratic tradition. Relatively little was added to the science and culture of the Old Kingdom, styles of art and architecture continued almost unchanged, and the service of the god-king remained the essential unifying principle of Egyptian society.[6]

---

[6] By the sixteenth century of our era, the more advanced American Indian civilizations had reached a stage of development roughly comparable to that of Mesopotamia and Egypt during the theocratic period, and the descriptions written by their European conquerors illuminate the nature of theocratic society in general. By an interesting coincidence, the temple cities of the Mayas in southern Mexico, with their sacred pyramids, their astronomical studies, and their lack of unified government, seem remarkably like those of the early Sumerians, while the authoritarian state socialism of Inca Peru, governed by the children of the sun, strongly resembled that of early Egypt. In the first urban societies of America, as in those of the Old World, order and a sense of security were purchased by the surrender of responsibility to a theocratic ruling class. The weakness inherent in all such systems was vividly exemplified during the Spanish conquest. In Peru a mere handful of adventurers was able to secure mastery over millions of Indians simply by capturing the person of the Inca, thereby paralyzing the nerve center of the whole empire. A similar phenomenon probably occurred several times in the history of the ancient Near East.

4

Near Eastern Imperialisms

During the two thousand years following the theocratic golden age, both Mesopotamia and Egypt passed through several cycles of decline and renewal. Dynasties of rulers would lose their vigor and become incapable of maintaining effective government. Tribes of herdsmen from the Arabian or Libyan grasslands or the mountains of the north would descend upon the rich river civilizations and establish themselves as ruling aristocracies until they, in turn, became effete and were overthrown. These failures of the theocratic principle stimulated questions about divine justice and led to the first attempts to formulate a more enlightened morality giving greater recognition to man's responsibility for his own destiny. But after each disintegration of the central power, order was eventually restored under the leadership of another dynasty of divine kings. Unable to develop any alternative principle of social unity, both Mesopotamia and Egypt could seek only to rebuild the institutions of the past. Such attempts to reconstruct a system that could no longer evoke a vital belief in its legitimacy necessarily resulted in an increasing emphasis on military force and a loss of creativity. Political power, no longer based on the mystique of a religious faith, was gradually rationalized and secularized; the child of the gods gave place to the conquering despot who recognized no checks or limits to his egoism; and the masses of the people, losing their sense of participation in an organic society, could only submit to the caprices of their rulers.

Meanwhile, the institutions of civilization were slowly spreading to neighboring areas. Temple cities similar to those of the Sumerians grew up in Syria and Palestine, in parts of Anatolia, and in western Iran, and the development of the early cities of the Indus valley may have been partly due to Sumerian influence. In the course of the third millennium, migrants from either Syria or the Egyptian delta appear to have settled in Crete, creating a "Minoan" culture which was carried to other Mediterranean islands and to the coasts of Greece and southern Anatolia. Organized into city-states governed by priest-kings, Minoan civilization was clearly an offshoot of the Near Eastern civilizations, but the artistic remains excavated at Knossos and other Cretan sites indicate that it developed along different lines. During its peak period early in the second millennium, it was producing sculpture and painting that displayed a pleasure in the phenomenal world very different from both the Sumerian fear of the gods and the Egyptian craving for eternity. During the same epoch another people, still unidentified, was conducting trading enterprises in the western Mediterranean and along the coasts of northwestern Europe, leaving memorials of its presence in the form of megalithic tombs and stone circles, although it did not establish any enduring civilization among the peasant peoples living in those areas.[1] All these peripheral developments, however, are known only through archaeological discoveries, and prior to the first millennium only Mesopotamia and Egypt had a continuous history.

In both areas the first period of breakdown came in the later years of the third millennium. Mesopotamia was conquered by the Guti, a barbarian tribe from the mountains of the north, while in Egypt the central government disintegrated, presumably because the ruling dynasty lost its vitality, and power was assumed by local officials who developed into a kind of feudal aristocracy. Literary fragments surviving from both regions vividly record men's sense of shock at the failure of the gods and their earthly representatives to maintain the divine order. Mesopotamian temple liturgies tell how: "Order was destroyed. The sacred dynasty was exiled from the temple. The rulership of the land they seized. The divine prince was carried away to a strange land." From Egypt

---

[1] According to the new method of dating, Stonehenge was erected about 1700 B.C. It was reported in 1954 that the double ax, the favorite symbol of the Minoan culture, had been identified on some of the Stonehenge megaliths, but this lacks confirmation.

comes a document known as the *Admonitions of Ipuwer* which describes a state of anarchy. "Behold! that which had never been aforetime has come to pass. The king is taken away by men of naught. Men without faith or understanding have deprived the land of its royalty. They have revolted against the Holy Crown, the defender of Re, which causeth the Two Lands to be at peace. The Serpent is taken from its place, and the secret of the Kings of the Upper and the Lower Land is laid bare. . . . Wherefore when Re first created Man, did he not separate the righteous from the ungodly? It is said that he is the Shepherd of Men. . . . But in this age there is no longer any pilot. Where is he? Does he sleep? His power is not seen." [2] The *Admonitions of Ipuwer* and several other Egyptian writings of this period show the beginnings of a belief in some kind of ideal justice, according to which even the humblest classes in society were entitled to protection and kings might be criticized if they failed to perform their duties.

Early in the second millenium, order was restored in both regions by strong rulers whose regimes showed the trend toward secularization of authority. In Mesopotamia, Hammurabi of Babylon made his city the center of an empire, its god Marduk being henceforth identified with Enlil as the chief deity of the whole civilization, and the laws of the cities were codified into a single system. Surviving monuments depict Hammurabi receiving his code as a gift from the sun god, but it is probably significant that he appointed lay officials to take the places of the priests as judges and administrators. Egypt was reunited by the pharaohs of the twelfth dynasty, founders of the Middle Kingdom, one of whom, Senusret III, set up an inscription that illustrates the increasing reliance upon human rather than divine power. "I have set up my statue on the frontier," declared the Pharaoh after a successful campaign against the Nubians to the south, "not that ye should worship it but that ye should fight for it. I am the King, and what I say I do." [3] But although the proud self-confidence of this assertion reflected the growth of a rationalism markedly different from the religious spirit of the pyramid-builders three quarters of a millenium earlier, it showed also that all security still depended on the person of the pharaoh. For the mass of the people, if not perhaps for himself

---

[2] Christopher Dawson: *The Age of the Gods,* pp. 246–9.   [3] Dawson: op. cit., p. 251.

and his generals, he was still the embodiment of Osiris and the divine child of the sun god.

The restoration of order lasted for only a few centuries and was followed by new waves of barbarian invaders. Egypt was overrun by nomadic herdsmen from Syria or Arabia who founded the Hyksos dynasty. Much more important was the first appearance of the Aryan, or Indo-European, peoples, whose original home was probably in the steppes of southern Russia. The expansion of the Aryans was to continue at intervals over a period of more than two thousand years and to have a profound influence on the whole subsequent development of Western civilization. They were formidable opponents not only because of their nomad militancy and capacity for individual initiative, but also because they had domesticated the horse, hitherto almost unknown in the Near East, and had devised a new implement that had revolutionary effects on warfare, the chariot. Early in the second millennium, tribes of Aryan herdsmen, presumably impelled by economic need, began to press outward from the steppes over a wide semicircle, making themselves masters of peasant societies and imposing their own language and the worship of their own masculine sky deities. They penetrated the Hindu Kush and descended upon the plains of northern India, swept through the Caspian gates into Iran, established the Kassite, Mitannian, and Hittite kingdoms in Mesopotamia and Anatolia, pushed down into the Greek and Italian peninsula and the Mediterranean islands, conquered the Minoan city-states, and overran the neolithic peasant societies in central and western Europe. Eventually they became amalgamated with the peoples they had conquered, and the resultant cultures, combining peasant and nomadic elements, became the foundations upon which new civilizations were afterwards built. But before this took place there was a second resurgence of the ancient river civilizations, led by conquering kings who adopted the new methods of warfare introduced by the Aryans and successfully took the offensive against them.

The next thousand years were an epoch of competing imperialisms. The early theocratic societies had existed for the most part in peaceful isolation from each other, and had relied on militia armies for defense. But the raids of the barbarians, the growth of trade, and the ambitions of military conquerors had now drawn together all the different regions of the Near East, and a series of states aspired to unify the whole region under their own domination. Kings still claimed divine descent, but they owed their authority mainly not to religious sanctions but to their control of mercenary armies, whose delight in plunder and destruction knew no limits. The old theocratic principles were no longer an effective bond of unity, and there were rivalries, especially in Egypt, between the new secular ruling class of generals and bureaucrats and the old priestly hierarchies.

Egypt expelled the Hyksos rulers about 1550 B.C. and became the dominant power for the next three or four centuries. The conquering pharaohs of the eighteenth dynasty maintained an army equipped with horses and chariots and composed largely of foreign mercenaries, extended their empire over Syria as far as the Euphrates, and fought occasional wars with the Hittite and Mitannian kingdoms. Thothmes I boasted that he had "made the frontier of Egypt as far as the circuit of the sun. I made Egypt to become the sovereign and every land her slave." [4] Immense quantities of plunder and tribute were carried back to the Egyptian cities, which were rebuilt with a luxury and magnificence previously unknown, and the temples and statues of the pharoahs grew even more colossal. The society of this epoch, as reflected in its literature and art, was characterized by cosmopolitan sophistication and by individualistic emphasis on wealth and pleasure and on military glory and athletic prowess. Yet in science and learning the Egypt of the Empire made few, if any, advances on the Old and Middle Kingdoms; and its showy architectural monuments, expressive of human vanity rather than of religious belief, were inferior to those of the pyramid-builders in both aesthetic taste and quality of workmanship. Meanwhile, the temple hierarchies, who had acquired ownership of a large part of the wealth and land of the country, were opposed to the secularizing tendencies of the Empire. Eventually Egyptian military power declined, largely because of attacks by Aryan sea raiders from the Mediterranean islands, and the country retreated into its theocratic shell. About 1100 B.C. the leader of the priests himself assumed the throne of the pharaohs. Syria and Palestine had already been abandoned, leaving a vac-

---

[4] Dawson: op. cit., p. 291.

uum partially filled by two new invading peoples: the Philistines, apparently an offshoot of the Minoan civilization from across the sea, and the Israelites from the desert. Henceforth Egypt concentrated all her energies on the task of self-preservation. Except for a brief period in the seventh century, she no longer aspired to govern an empire. For the remainder of her life as an independent state she was notable only for the disillusioned pessimism of her view of life, for her comprehensive and fantastic religiosity, and for her petrified conservatism. In the eighth century her artists were producing painting and sculpture so exactly copied from those of the Old Kingdom nearly two millennia earlier that it is almost impossible for modern critics to distinguish them.

The Hittite, Mitannian, and Kassite kingdoms had already collapsed, presumably because of external warfare and internal rebellions; and supremacy passed next to a new state that had grown up around the temple cities of the upper Tigris: Assyria. The Assyrian kings first emerged as military conquerors in the eleventh century, but this was followed by two centuries of quiescence, during which weaker peoples, notably the Phoenicians of the Syrian seacoast cities and the Israelites in Palestine, were allowed to flourish undisturbed. The period of Assyrian domination over the Near East began in the ninth century. The Assyrian state was one of the most purely militaristic institutions in all history, and the inscriptions set up by its kings fairly drip with blood, recording with complacency the slaughtering of enemy populations by tens of thousands. Enslaved peoples and the images of conquered gods were brought from all directions into the Assyrian capital of Nineveh, which became the richest city in the Near East. The culture of Assyria, as manifested in the immense library of clay tablets gathered by King Sardanapalus, was derived almost wholly from the ancient Sumerians. Much of its art, on the other hand, was vigorously representational. The magnificent hunting scenes that adorned the royal palace conveyed a delight in physical prowess and activity which must have been true to the spirit of Assyrian society.

Assyria was overthrown near the end of the seventh century by an alliance of the Chaldeans, a people from the desert who had become masters of the old city of Babylon, and the Aryan Medes and Persians, who had become the ruling aristocracy in Iran. For

a brief period, Nebuchadnezzar and other Chaldean kings re-
vived the glories of Hammurabi twelve centuries earlier, but the
Persians also had embarked on a career of imperialism, and in 538
B.C. Babylon fell to the Persian conqueror Cyrus. Within a short
period the Persian kings of the Achaemenid dynasty, Cyrus, Cam-
byses, and Darius, created an empire covering the whole of the
Near East and stretching from the Aegean to the valley of the
Indus and from the Caucasus to the Libyan desert.

The Persian Empire lasted for only about two hundred years,
being overthrown by Alexander of Macedon at the Battle of
Gaugamela in 331 B.C.; but it was the most successful experiment
in empire-building that the Near East had known, and some of its
methods, afterwards transmitted to the Hellenistic kingdoms and
to Rome and Byzantium, had an enduring influence on Western
civilization. Previous empires had been held together mainly by
military force, with little attempt to create an effective civil administration, and had meant chiefly the exaction of tribute from
conquered peoples. The attitude of the imperialist power toward
its victims had been symbolized in its treatment of their gods. The
images worshipped by a defeated state had regularly been removed to the capital of the empire in order to demonstrate their
inferiority. The triumph of Assyria or Babylonia meant the supremacy of Ashur or Marduk over the weaker gods of other races. The
Persians, on the other hand, made a real attempt to integrate all
the Near Eastern peoples into a single organism combining the
necessary political unity with cultural and religious heterogeneity.
They created an efficient and reasonably honest administration,
dividing the empire into provinces ruled by satraps whose activities
were carefully supervised by the king. The government maintained order, protected commerce, and built excellent roads
throughout its vast empire, and its collections of tribute were relatively mild. The spirit animating Persian imperialism was indicated by its religious policy. When Cyrus conquered Babylon, he
did not carry away the images of Marduk to Susa or Persepolis;
on the contrary, he became a worshipper of Marduk, and claimed
that he had been chosen by the god as the legitimate successor of
the Babylonian kings. Similarly his son Cambyses, the conquerer
of Egypt, assumed the role of child of the sun god and founder of
a new dynasty of pharaohs.

In spite of their great superiority over previous empire-builders, however, the Persians retained the basic theocratic doctrine. The person of the king remained the only possible focus of loyalty; and while he was not a god (except for his Egyptian subjects), and claimed different divine sponsors in different parts of his empire, he was always divinely appointed and therefore entitled to absolute obedience. It was perhaps because he felt the need for a more effective unifying principle that Cambyses' successor, Darius, became a convert to the new religion of Zoroaster, who preached the worship of a new supreme being not to be identified with any of the established tribal deities and associated with new and invigorating ethical doctrines. But Zoroastrianism was quickly corrupted by the old Iranian polytheism and in its pure form did not remain the official religion of the monarchy for much more than one century.

The Persians gave an interval of peace to the Near East, and their relatively mild rule was welcomed as a liberation by small peoples (like the Jews) who had suffered under the tyranny of the Assyrians and the Chaldeans. But they could not restore the spiritual energy of the ancient societies they had conquered, and, apart from the development of Zoroastrianism, their empire was intellectually not very creative, producing no important new developments in either the arts or the sciences.[5] The principles upon which the Near Eastern civilizations had been founded had long since lost their vitality; and although over the previous two thousand years there had been foreshadowings of new views of life, their full development could be undertaken only by new peoples whose attitudes and institutions were still flexible and had not yet become encrusted with long tradition.

As long as the early civilizations had remained isolated from each other except for occasional commercial contracts, each of them had worshipped its own tribalistic deities without confronting the problem of religious diversity. But during the second mil-

---

[5] The chief monuments of Persian architecture under the Achaemenids were colossal royal palaces with pillared halls. Art was abstract rather than representational, and was based on the principle of repeating the same basic designs, with minor variations, for decorative purposes. The details were often exquisite, but the total effect was usually monotonous. In textiles and to a smaller extent in painting and sculpture, the Persians maintained for many centuries an unbroken tradition, which had some influence on Greek and Roman art early in the Christian era.

lennium, trade and imperialism had brought all the Near Eastern
societies into close and constant relations with each other. Inherent
in economic and political developments was a movement away from
tribalism toward some form of human unity. What was the relationship among the different religious systems, and what bonds of
understanding and co-operation could be established among tribal
groups who believed in different gods? Early peoples did not generally deny the reality of each other's gods, although they liked to
insist that their own were superior—an attitude exemplified in the
subordination of conquered deities to the Assyrian god Ashur and
the Babylonian god Marduk. But this kind of religious imperialism could not provide a spiritual basis for the growing sense of
universalism. The Near Eastern world needed religious no less than
political unification.

The most frequent answer to the problem was religious syncretism. It was assumed that different peoples were really worshipping
the same deities, though with different rituals and under different
names; and as society in the great empires became more cosmopolitan, there was a tendency to merge all the various objects of
worship into a single comprehensive pantheon. Thus, travelers in a
foreign city could participate in the local ceremonies without any
feeling of disloyalty to their own ancestral gods. Universalism, however, required some more positive and dynamic spiritual expression, and this could only take the form of belief in a single supreme
being who was the lord of all mankind and of the whole earth,
thereby symbolizing the unity of the cosmos in the same way that
political unity was focused in the person of the king. Both in Mesopotamia and in Egypt religion began to evolve toward monotheism.
In some Babylonian religious liturgies all the lesser gods became
merged into Marduk, being represented as merely expressions of
different aspects of his personality, while in Egypt the Middle
Kingdom fused the worship of the sun god Re with that of Amon,
an invisible divine force immanent in everything, and made Amon-
Re into a universal god. These deities, however, retained so
many polytheistic and tribalistic associations that they could never
become effective expressions of a new universalist belief. What
was needed was a new beginning in religious thought, but this was
impossible in such long-established civilizations. Such a new beginning seems to have been attempted in Egypt by the Pharaoh

Ikhnaton of the eighteenth dynasty, who set out to destroy the traditional religion and substitute the monotheistic worship of a single creative principle symbolized by the disk of the sun. But this new synthetic religion had no roots in popular sentiment and was bitterly opposed by the priests of Amon-Re; after Ikhnaton's death in 1362 B.C. he was stigmatized as a criminal and his name erased from the official records of Egyptian history, and the country reverted to its traditional polytheism.

Paralleling the trend toward monotheism was the attempt to formulate a higher morality. With the growing complexity of society, men could no longer rely on tribal tradition for comprehensive guidance in all the exigencies of daily life, and were increasingly compelled to make their own decisions. The movement toward individualism as well as toward universalism was inherent in civilization from the beginning. In so far as they were unable to adhere to prescribed patterns of behavior, men needed general ethical principles that could be applied to different situations. Both in Mesopotamia and in Egypt there were numerous expressions of enlightened moral standards, but in both areas these were never disentangled from the traditional magical ways of thinking. In Mesopotamia of the second millennium, for example, the Shurpu series of incantations enumerated a number of moral offenses of which individuals might be guilty, but the purpose of the incantations was the magical cure of disease, on the assumption that this was due to the anger of gods or demons, and purely ritualistic errors and omissions were listed along with transgressions against one's neighbors as equally likely to evoke divine punishment. In Egypt the period of disorder following the collapse of the Old Kingdom produced writings emphasizing the concern of the gods for justice and charity; according to the Instruction for Merika-Re, for example, "more acceptable is the character of one upright in heart than the [sacrificial] ox of the evil-doer." [6] Egyptian moralism became especially associated with the cult of Osiris, the ruler of the underworld. After death, it was believed, every man would stand before him in the Hall of Double Justice and would be required to recite the Negative Confession, swearing that he had not committed a long list of sinful actions. Anybody who had

---

[6] John A. Wilson: *The Burden of Egypt,* p. 120.

lied or stolen or committed violence or lived impurely could not enter paradise. Yet Egyptian notions of immortality remained largely magical; a man could not reach paradise without an accurate knowledge of the road thither as described in the Book of the Dead, a copy of which was placed in every grave for the guidance of the soul; and he might even be assured of salvation simply by carrying with him the symbol of immortality, the scarab beetle.

The traditional thought-patterns inhibited the development not only of moral values but also of science and technology. The Near Eastern civilizations in the second and first millennia made little advance over the age of the theocracies, and remained too much under the influence of magic and religiosity to be capable of arriving at any conception of natural law. The most important new discovery was the use of iron, which began in Anatolia, apparently among the Hittites, and was diffused though other areas in Europe and Asia in a slowly widening circle. It was indicative of the inability of the traditional ideological systems to absorb, and adapt themselves to, new developments that the use of iron was generally prohibited in religious rituals.

A society confronted by new problems but unable to meet them by moving forward to a higher level of development is likely to show a tendency to revert to the past, seeking emotional security in a reaffirmation of tribal tradition. This was illustrated in the revival in Egypt of the art of the Old Kingdom and in the care devoted by the Assyrian and Babylonian kings to preserving the language and learning of the Sumerians. Throughout much of the Near East, however, the most conspicuous spiritual tendency of the first millennium was the attempt to seek spiritual support in the beliefs not of the theocratic civilizations but of the neolithic and paleolithic societies that had preceded it. The old fertility cults had never lost their vitality among the peasants, and these were now interpreted as promising divine aid, salvation from suffering and evil, and personal immortality. Through the traditional orgiastic rituals, by dances, sexual excitement, and collective intoxication, or by tearing apart and devouring the flesh of bulls or goats, men and women continued to seek the experience of ecstasy which they believed to be a proof of divine possession and unity with the god. Isis and Astarte, Ishtar and Cybele had a warmer and more lasting appeal

3. a. *Wall painting representing harvest, from the tomb of Menena,* c.
1400 B.C.

Although conveying a sense of pleasure in the phenomenal world, Egyptian paintings and reliefs never became truly three-dimensional.

b. *Hunting scene from the palace of Ashurbanipal* (*better known as Sardanapalus*), *king of Assyria during the seventh century* B.C.

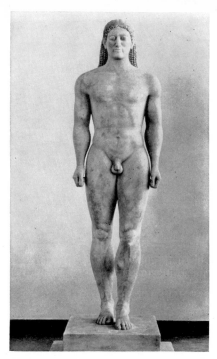

4. *a. Kouros from the late seventh century* B.C.

b. Statue of Kroisos dating from the late sixth century B.C.

The differences between these figures, both of them found in Attica, illustrates the evolution of sensibility and technique in early Greek art.

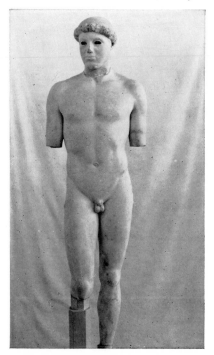

c. Statue of Kritios.

d. Statue found at Anticythera in southern Greece.

The Kritios, found on the Athenian Acropolis and dating from about 480 B.C., shows how the male figure was represented at the beginning of the great age. The Anticythera statue, dating from about 340, displays a technical facility and a lack of vital energy that exemplify the beginning of the decadence.

than the sun gods of the great cities and the war gods of the kings. Nor had the new deities brought by the Aryan invaders struck roots anywhere in the Near East except in Iran, for the Aryan ruling class had been quickly absorbed by the peoples whom they had conquered. In the Hittite kingdom, for example, surviving bas-reliefs show that the Aryan sky god had been symbolically united with the mother goddess; but the sky god was soon forgotten, and the hill country of central Anatolia continued to be the realm of Cybele and the especial center of orgiastic rituals.[7] But the triumph of the mother goddess and her dying and reviving partner was perhaps most complete in Egypt. The Egyptians continued to worship Amon-Re and their innumerable animal deities, but to an increasing extent their religion was centered around the myth of Osiris and Isis, which had now become a promise of universal immortality; and since Isis, queen of heaven and the underworld, earth mother and star of the sea, was generally represented as wearing the horns of a cow, she still preserved a vestige of that animal guardian spirit who had been mankind's first object of adoration in the age of the paleolithic hunters. Within a few centuries all these Near Eastern salvation cults, along with the Near Eastern conception of the divine ruler as the focus of political unity, would be moving westward into Greece and Italy.

---

[7] The orgiastic tradition was so deeply rooted in parts of Anatolia that it survived several changes of religion. In the second century after the advent of Christianity, it manifested itself in the Montanist heresy, the adherents of which believed themselves to be directly inspired by the Holy Ghost and denied the need for any political or ecclesiastical institutions. Though persecuted by the authorities, Montanism was still in existence in the sixth century. After the conquest of Anatolia by the Moslems, a similar emphasis on divine inspiration was represented by the so-called dancing dervishes. At the present moment rationalism is in the ascendant; the dancing dervishes were suppressed by the Turkish government of Kemal Ataturk. But whether police authorities can permanently end a tradition that has probably lasted for at least six thousand years remains to be seen.

5

The Axial Period

The revival of the salvation cults was not, however, the most important spiritual development of the first millennium. This epoch saw also the creation of new values and new views of life that affirmed man's capacity to transcend natural forces and to master and control his own biological drives instead of mystically submitting to them. Making a decisive break with the neolithic and paleolithic past, they represented a new turning-point in human thought. The name "Axial Period" was coined by Karl Jaspers, who applied it to the six hundred years between 800 and 200 B.C.[1] In actuality, most of the creative achievements of the millennium belong to the sixth century, at which time similar developments were taking place in five different areas of the Old World.

Two products of the Axial Period, the ethical monotheism of the Jewish prophets and the rationalism of the Greek philosophers, have largely shaped the attitudes of the Western mind, while a third, the ethical dualism of Zoroaster, contributed indirectly to the Western tradition through its later influence on Judaism and Christianity. This book is concerned only with these three movements of thought, but in order to grasp the full significance of the Axial Period we must extend our field of vision to include India and China, where similar problems evoked comparable responses. Like the Near East, both these Oriental countries had been overrun during the second millennium by barbarian conquerors, India by the Aryans and China by the Chou from the Mongolian steppes, after

---

[1] Karl Jaspers: *The Origin and Goal of History*. The word "axial" has a double significance, meaning that this period was the axis of world history and also that it was concerned with the assertion of values.

76

which there had ensued a period of warfare among a number of small states. As in the Near East, the clash of competing states and peoples, the rise of militarism, the decline of priestly authority, and the growth of individualistic attitudes impelled men to search for new faiths affirming a human rather than a tribalistic view of life. In India the Axial Period saw the mystical teaching of the Upanishads and the foundation of two new religions, Jainism and Buddhism, while in China it produced Taoism and Confucianism. Thus, a panoramic survey shows that the search for new values reached fruition at about the same time in five different regions and in at least eight different forms.

The chronological parallelism seems too remarkable to be dismissed simply as accidental, though history is unable to explain it in rationalistic terms. China, India, Iran, Palestine, and Greece were widely separated from each other, and there is no evidence of any mutual influence.[2] Nevertheless, the sixth century was a period of great spiritual creativity in all five areas. Three religious teachers were almost exact contemporaries. Confucius lived from 555 to 478 and Buddha from 567 to 487, while the most plausible dating for Zoroaster (according, at least, to the most recent authority[3]) is from 569 to about 500. Lao Tzu, the founder of Taoism, and Mahavira, who should probably be regarded as the founder of Jainism, are more shadowy figures, but according to apparently reliable traditions they were living at the same time as Confucius and Buddha. In Palestine the line of monotheistic prophets, which had begun with Amos of Tekoa halfway through the eighth century, reached its culmination near the end of the sixth century with Deutero-Isaiah. Among the Greeks the sixth century saw both the inauguration of philosophical speculation with the work of Thales and his successors and the establishment of democracy at Athens. It would be futile to engage in mystical speculation about the problem presented by the coincidence of dates; but it is impossible to avoid the suggestion that, at rare intervals in history, factors in human affairs make for the emergence of novelties that cannot be satisfactorily explained by any acceptable theory

---

[2] The sixth-century Greek poet Alcaeus appears to have known the prophecies of Isaiah, but there are no other known examples of intellectual communication.

[3] E. Herzfeld: *Zoroaster and His World.*

of causation. The intellectual achievements of the sixth century, considered together, appear to constitute a group of mutations in man's spiritual development comparable to what happens when a new species emerges in biological evolution.

Most of the new doctrines eventually became organized as religious systems into which were incorporated many of mankind's traditional rituals and beliefs; yet with the majority of them the initial impetus was philosophical rather than religious, and the intention was not a reformation or a further development of accepted attitudes, but a new beginning. Most of the thinkers of the Axial Period, for the first time in human experience, began with man as an individual, asked themselves fundamental questions about the meaning and purpose of his existence, and attempted to answer them in rational terms. Repudiating the whole heritage of tribal polytheism and nature-worship, with its amoral concepts of the gods, all of them were opposed to magic in all its forms, to witchcraft, sorcery, and divination, and all of them rejected the fertility cults. They recognized that man could not actually influence natural processes by means of imitative rituals and that the gods could not be coerced or placated by sacrifices or other ceremonial observances. Thus conceptions of both natural and moral law began to be disentangled from the fantasies of the human imagination; man was beginning to think objectively and to recognize the reality of sequences of cause and effect in both the natural and the spiritual realms. And as the Axial thinkers were concerned with the nature of man rather than with tribal welfare, and with the laws of being rather than with the placation of tribal deities, the doctrines they affirmed were of universal scope. Not all of them were explicit monotheists; but implicit in all their doctrines was belief in the unity of mankind and of the cosmos.

Thus individualism, rationalism, and universalism, in varying degrees and proportions, characterized all the thinkers of the Axial Period. Yet as they were men of differing temperaments, emerging from different cultural backgrounds, their specific ethical and philosophical conclusions varied widely. It was, in fact, at this period that the divergencies in spiritual direction between East and West, the one inclining more toward the control of man's inner self, the other more toward the control of his environment, first became clearly apparent.

The Oriental thinkers were primarily concerned with discovering the sources of inner peace by means of psychological self-examination, and were therefore relatively uninterested either in problems of theological definition or in the establishment of political justice. Confucius, the most conservative and least religious of them, preached ethical self-discipline and the performance of social obligations; Lao Tzu believed in submission to natural processes and a mystical identification with nature. In India the eighth and seventh centuries were a period of great philosophical activity, the results of which were recorded in the earlier Upanishads. Hindu thought affirmed that the deities of the Indian pantheon were merely manifestations of a monistic spiritual principle that was also present in the human soul, and that by meditation and ascetic practices man could achieve a mystical unity with the godhead. This ascetic tendency was continued by the religious leaders of the sixth century. Mahavira taught that the soul could eventually become released from the trammels of matter and enter heaven, while Buddha, whose whole system of thought was based on a rationalistic analysis of the human psyche, affirmed that man could find happiness only by becoming released from all desire and thereby achieving nirvana.

In the Near East the approach was ethical and theological rather than psychological, perhaps because the new doctrines developed not in the old centers of civilization, but among more primitive and unsophisticated peoples. The new beginnings of the Axial Period were the work of two relatively new groups, the Persians and the Jews, both of whom had a pastoral rather than an urban background and were offended by the luxury and moral laxity of the great cities. Believing in personal purity and social justice, they affirmed the existence of a single universal deity who required moral perfection rather than rituals and sacrifices. Zoroaster, springing from the class of Aryan warriors who had conquered Iran, preached a militant creed in which all life was represented as a battle between cosmic good and cosmic evil. Ahura-Mazda, the god of truth and light, was opposed to Ahriman, the prince of darkness and of lies, and at the end of time would overcome him, after which the good would be received into paradise and the wicked confined in hell. With the Jewish prophets, on the other hand, there appeared a humanitarian emphasis unique in the ancient world.

Representatives of a weak community that could not defend itself against Assyrian and Babylonian imperialism, they declared that the tribal deity of the Jewish people was also the maker and ruler of the world, that in his own good time he would crush the mighty and exalt the humble, and that man's only duty was obedience to his commandments, the most important of which was justice for the oppressed and exploited.

The Greeks were also a new people, but the main concern of early Greek thought was not with ethics, but with the understanding of nature. Thales and his successors interpreted the world as a unified psycho-physical whole, governed not by the will of supernatural beings, but by natural laws that man could hope to understand. This unitary and naturalistic view of the universe was the origin of the whole modern belief in scientific law. The concept of laws of nature, moreover, was extended by Solon and other Athenians to the sphere of politics, leading to the formulation of new conceptions of political order which provided a democratic alternative to the theocratic and military despotisms of the Orient.

These doctrines seem, among them, to cover almost the whole gamut of possible philosophies of life. Indeed, if one extends the Axial Period forward to include the development of Greek thought during the fifth and fourth centuries B.C. and the preaching of the gospel ethic by the founder of Christianity in the first century of our era, it can be affirmed that no really new ideas have been added since that time. During the past two thousand years mankind, both in the Orient and in Europe, has been living on the spiritual capital accumulated during the first millennium B.C., exploring and developing the assertions of the Axial thinkers and fusing them into new compounds. The only fundamentally new thing has been the development of scientific technology since the seventeenth century, but although this has meant a change in material conditions comparable in importance to the discovery of agriculture or the beginning of urban civilization, it has not brought any growth of new moral or religious ideas.

During the Axial Period man began his spiritual coming-of-age, recognizing his own autonomy as a moral agent and the objective reality of physical and psychological laws of causation. That the process has remained incomplete is scarcely surprising, for if the period is placed within the entire span of man's long evolution it must be regarded as still relatively recent; behind it lay the three thousand years of military and theocratic civilization, preceded by another three or four thousand of the peasant culture and by the countless millennia of the hunting and collecting phases. The doctrines of the Axial thinkers, moreover, meant deprivations as well as gains, for while they offered the individual new faiths and new moral and intellectual goals, they at the same time broke the traditional identification with the natural environment and with the social group which had been reflected in magic and ritual and religious polytheism. When man began to distinguish between objective reality and his own subjective mental processes, he began to lose his sense of unity with nature; and in proportion as he asserted the supremacy of moral or psychological laws derived from his own conscience, he ceased to enjoy the guidance and emotional security he had enjoyed as an unreflecting member of a tribal organism. The problem of human loneliness and alienation had its roots in the thinking of the Axial Period, and came to the surface whenever its positive affirmations ceased to command assent. This, in fact, was the true expulsion from Eden, which in the original Hebrew legend was due not merely to man's disobedience but also to the fact that by eating the fruit of the forbidden tree he had come to know good and evil and had thereby acquired a moral independence that evoked the jealousy of his divine creator.[4]

---

[4] For twenty-five hundred years most poets and philosophers regarded the affirmations of the Axial Period as self-evident truths. During the past three generations, on the other hand, perhaps for the first time, they have ceased to command general assent. Much modern thought can be interpreted as an attempt to return to pre-Axial attitudes and make a new beginning along different lines. Three obvious examples are the philosophies of William James, Nietzsche, and D. H. Lawrence. James denied the assumption of the unity of the universe, which he regarded not as an obvious fact or even as a necessity of thought, but simply as an expression of man's craving for some consoling answer to the mysteries of existence. In place of Axial monism, he preached a thoroughgoing pluralism. Nietzsche (who declared that the Greek world had gone astray when it became intellectualized in the fifth century) refused to accept any general principles of morality and justice, and attacked the doctrine that there was any underlying harmony either in the universe or in society; competition for power was the ultimate reality. Lawrence's whole career was an attempt to recapture man's pre-Axial sense of emotional unity with nature, which he felt had been destroyed by rationalism and moralism; he tried to find it among peasants and other primitive characters, among the North American Indians, and in the artistic remains of the vanished Etruscans.

PART II

JUDAISM

PART II

JUDAISM

The unique achievement of the Jews was to develop religious monotheism without losing the sense of divine personality. Among other peoples monotheism was likely to mean the belief in an abstract spiritual principle, lacking clear-cut outline and distinctive qualities, which could never become a meaningful object of popular worship. Greek philosophy, for example, tended toward some form of monism; but the supreme being of the philosophers had no connection with the Olympian deities of the traditional Greek religion, and remained a mere intellectual hypothesis. The Jews, on the other hand, succeeded in elevating a tribal deity into the omnipotent creator of the universe, and in the course of this transformation their God retained the personal characteristics and the popular devotion that he had acquired as a result of his tribalistic origin. The Jewish God, moreover, became associated with two other unique attitudes: the patron of a weak people who had become organized as a political community at a relatively late period, he became the enemy of oppression and exploitation and the champion of high ethical ideals; and his activity was guided by divine purposes that could be realized only at some future period. Thus, the cyclic processes of nature were no longer regarded as expressions of the divine; God fulfilled himself not in nature but in human history, which acquired a religious meaning and was interpreted as a development toward a preordained consummation. This synthesis of tribalism and universalism resulted in a conception of the supreme being which was in many ways contradictory; God was at one and the same time creator of the natural universe and symbol of moral perfection, omnipotent ruler of the world and loving protector of his chosen disciples. But the emotional power of this Judaeo-Christian theology has been continuously manifested throughout the history of Western civilization.

These special features of the religion of the Jews can be partially understood by means of a historical analysis. Political conditions during their early development made it expedient for them to worship a jealous deity who refused to tolerate or be united with his rivals; and having asserted these monistic claims during his tribalistic phase, he could then, unlike other tribal gods, evolve into the creator of the universe without forfeiting his original traits and associations. Similarly, both the humanitarianism and the eschatological futurism of the Jewish faith can be attributed to material factors—to political and economic conflicts within the Jewish state and to the relations of the Jews with their more powerful neighbors. But while a historical account illuminates the development of Jewish monotheism, it does not wholly explain it; other Near Eastern peoples were confronted by similar problems, but failed to make any comparable response. By rationalistic standards Jehovah must, of course, be regarded as a projection of the Jewish imagination. Yet the religious leaders of the Jewish people experienced him as an immediate presence, continuously participant in all the affairs of the community and invested with a force and vividness of personality unequaled by any other deity in history. The prolonged and intimate relationship between the Jews and their God, as profoundly felt as the marital relationship to which it was often compared, was an unparalleled phenomenon. It resulted in a process of spiritual growth which has had continuing effects on the whole course of Western history, and which found expression in the creation of a literature extraordinary both for its rhapsodic fire and eloquence and for the realism with which it portrayed its human characters.[1]

---

[1] For the authorship and chronology of the books of the Bible, I have generally followed R. H. Pfeiffer: *Introduction to the Old Testament*.

I

The Mosaic Tradition

The earliest event in the Biblical record which is indisputably a part of history was the Hebrew occupation of Palestine. This was a gradual process which may have begun as early as the fifteenth century and was not completed until after the establishment of the monarchy about the year 1000 B.C. Before moving into Palestine, the Hebrews were a pastoral people herding sheep and goats in the grasslands bordering the Arabian desert. This pastoral origin was responsible for many of the special features of their religion, and had a decisive and lasting influence on their political and spiritual development. The prophetic movement of the eighth and seventh centuries was largely an attempt to reassert the simple pastoral virtues that were believed to have been lost after the Hebrews had become agricultural and partially urbanized in their promised land.

The stories of Abraham, Isaac, and Jacob, in spite of their legendary flavor, give a reasonably accurate portrayal of pastoral society. The basic institution was the patriarchal family, which wandered over a wide area in search of grass and water. Families were loosely combined into larger kinship groups, in which authority was exercised by councils of elders, but no elaborate government was possible or necessary. Individual heads of families, enjoying absolute powers over their wives, concubines, children, and servants, developed a capacity for initiative and independent judgment to an extent unknown in settled peasant or urban societies. By contrast with the theocratic empires, these pastoral tribes therefore appeared relatively free and democratic. In spite of their semi-nomadic way of life, they were generally peaceful, and must not be confused with their enemies, the marauding Arab Bedouin from the desert, who appear in the biblical record under the name of Amalekites. But, as with all primitive peoples, the unit was always the family or the kinship group, not the individual. If a crime was committed, the guilt was always collective; and the tribe was obligated to exact vengeance for the killing of any of its members. The Biblical assumption that the sins of the fathers would always be visited upon the children was derived from the mores of pastoral society.

Religious observances were similarly organized around the family. Sacred shrines, attended by hereditary priests, grew up around natural objects that had acquired a numinous quality, such as rock pillars, trees, and springs, and at the tombs of ancestors. But each patriarch exercised priestly functions, and the tribal god was continuously participant in all family activities. Every time an animal was slaughtered for food, its blood was poured out upon the ground as an offering to the god in order that he might share in the communal meal. And although a family often had its own sacred images (the teraphim that Jacob's wife, Rachel, stole from her father Laban), the lack of fixed territorial ties led to conceptions of divinity less material than those prevalent in agricultural communities; the god of a wandering pastoral family could not be permanently attached to any particular place or regarded as resident in any idol or temple made by human hands.

Under what circumstances did the Hebrews become worshippers of Jehovah? [2] There is no good reason to doubt the Biblical story that some of them had settled in northern Egypt and been drafted for forced labor by the pharaohs, and that they then escaped into the desert and adopted a new religious cult under the leadership of Moses. By taking Jehovah as their common god, the Hebrew tribes became united into a political confederation, and it was probably at the same time that they first began to claim common ancestry and call themselves "children of Israel." Associated with the Jehovah cult was the belief that Palestine was their prom-

---

[2] In an effort to approximate the probable Hebrew pronunciation, modern scholars usually refer to this deity as Jahwe, Jahveh, Yahweh, Yahwe, or Yahaweh. This seems unnecessarily pedantic. To be consistent, they should also speak of Moishe instead of Moses.

ised land and that they would have divine assistance in taking possession of it, so that one of its effects was to transform them into a more warlike people. But it is improbable that all the tribes took part in the exodus from Egypt, and there are indications that some of them were moving into northern Palestine several generations before the time of Moses. Which of them introduced the worship of Jehovah, and at what period he was adopted by the other tribes, are still unsettled problems.[3] Even more controversial is the question of whether the Hebrews had already acquired a special religious tradition at a much earlier period. The stories of Abraham, Isaac, and Jacob display so much literary artistry that they must have been composed in their present form at a relatively late period, but the description of their Mesopotamian origin, their religious experiences, and their connections with Palestine may well be a reminiscence of actual events. Popular traditions of this kind usually have some basis in fact.

Buried underneath half a dozen different layers of nationalistic and sacerdotal addition and interpretation, the original doctrines of the prophet who founded the Jewish religion are sunk too deep for excavation. Everything said about Moses in the Biblical record is questionable, and almost all the specific laws and commandments attributed to him were certainly formulated at later periods. The first written record of his life was apparently made by a Jewish patriot in the ninth century B.C., possibly four hundred years after his death. This was afterwards combined with variant versions, rewritten in conformity with the reforming movement of the prophetic epoch, again rewritten and expanded to suit the program of the post-Exilic theocracy, and put in approximately its final form about the year 400. Visible only through this long se-

---

[3] See T. J. Meek: *Hebrew Origins,* Chapter 1. Meek argues that only the tribe of Levi was in Egypt, and that Jehovah-worship was first adopted by the southern tribes and was not imposed upon the north until the establishment of the monarchy. He suggests that the southern tribes may not have settled in Palestine until about two centuries later than their northern brethren. It is undeniable that throughout the history of Israel there were conflicts between the northern and the southern tribes, headed respectively by the tribe of Ephraim and the tribe of Judah, and that Jehovah-worship was always more deeply rooted in the south. On the other hand, popular tradition connected the Ephraimites (descendants of Joseph) with Egypt, and the song of Deborah, which was probably composed in the twelfth century and mentions only the northern tribes, praises Jehovah. Meek supposes that the references to Jehovah may be a later interpolation.

ries of refractions and distortions, the teaching of Moses must remain an enigma. Yet in spite of an almost impenetrable obscurity, it is still apparent that his personality changed the course of history, and that the Israelites who followed his leadership underwent a decisive spiritual experience. Something happened to them while they were still in the wilderness, something that was always cherished in popular tradition and that had a determining effect on their later development. Even from the Biblical record it is obvious that Moses was not a monotheist and that, even by the standards of the ancient civilizations, his ethical concepts were not particularly enlightened. Yet if he did not introduce a new and potentially higher religious belief, the whole of later Jewish history becomes inexplicable.

According to the Biblical story, Moses became a Jehovah-worshipper by flying from Egypt into the desert, seeking hospitality with the priest of a local shrine and marrying his daughter, and undergoing a cataclysmic emotional experience that he regarded as a divine revelation. It has often been suggested that it was from his father-in-law that he first acquired his belief in Jehovah. He then returned to Egypt and introduced the cult to his fellow Hebrews, who were convinced of its efficacy when, during their flight past the Red Sea, they were saved from their pursuers through a sudden movement of wind and tide. This episode is commemorated in the song of Miriam, and is almost certainly historical. Jehovah's origin seems to have been somewhat humble, making a remarkable contrast with his subsequent rise to the position of creator of the universe. He appears to have begun his career as a storm god located on the top of a mountain, possibly a volcano, either in the Sinai peninsula or, more probably, somewhere in Arabia. After his adoption as the patron of the Israelite confederation, he became a peripatetic deity and was transported in the Ark of the Covenant;[4] but for a very long time he retained his early connections with the desert and with storms. In one of the earliest specimens of Hebrew literature, the magnificent war song of the

---

[4] It is possible that the Ark originated in Palestine, not in the desert, and that it was at first a magical divination box rather than the residence of Jehovah. The notion that it contained the Ten Commandments written on stone tablets seems to have been a later addition.

prophetess Deborah, he is described as coming to the aid of his people from the mountains of the south and giving them victory by creating floods of rain that impede the movements of the Canaanite chariots. When Elijah wishes to commune with him, he visits Mount Sinai; and as late as the Book of Ezekiel, which was written early in the sixth century, Jehovah is represented as especially demonstrating his power in thunder, lightning, and rain. The character attributed to him in early Hebrew mythology has a similarly stormy quality. Throughout the Book of Genesis he is as capricious and prone to violence as a mountain wind. When confronted by human pride and disobedience, he is liable to outbursts of such overwhelming and destructive anger that he sometimes commits actions that he himself afterwards regrets.

If the prohibition of images was a part of the original Mosaic religion, it can be attributed, as we have seen, to the attitudes of a nomadic people. But although Jehovah may not have been represented in any concrete form, he was definitely envisaged as occupying a particular point in space. Whenever human beings misbehave in the Book of Genesis, he has to come down and see for himself what they are up to. The Israelites during the conquest of Palestine believed that he was physically present in the Ark, for which reason it was always carried into battle as an assurance of victory (another pastoral people, the Iranians, had a similar conception, going to war accompanied by a wagon bearing an empty throne). After the Jerusalem Temple was built, Jehovah was supposed to occupy a seat in the Holy of Holies between the images of two cherubim.

When Jehovah was adopted by the Hebrew tribes, his primary function became that of a war god, and by leading his people to victory he acquired lordship over the soil of Palestine. Prior to the prophetic movement there was no suggestion that he had any authority over other peoples or other places. The Israelites were obligated not to worship any rival gods, but the constant reiteration of this command and the emphasis on Jehovah's jealousy implied that such gods were equally real. The religion of Moses may have been monolatrous in that it required the Israelites to restrict their worship to a single deity, but it was very far from monotheism. The main reason for Jehovah's jealousy was, no doubt, political; if the Israelite tribes were to become masters of Palestine, it was essential for them to maintain their unity and ethnic identity and prevent assimilation by the previous inhabitants.[5]

Yet although the original Mosaic creed was narrowly tribalistic and had no elements of universality, it already contained the seeds of its astonishing future development. For there were vitally important differences between Jehovah and most other tribal deities. The typical object of tribal worship, usually originating as a totem animal or an ancestral spirit, was a concretization of communal unity handed down from an epoch beyond human memory. The Hebrews, on the other hand, deliberately chose Jehovah as their patron at a particular moment in history. This decision was interpreted as meaning that Jehovah had chosen the Hebrews, from which it followed that he was guided by intentions that could be worked out only through the course of temporal processes. In spite of Jehovah's close association with certain places and natural phenomena, he was a god whose primary self-revelation was through human history rather than through nature. Implicit in the Mosaic tradition was the belief that man's function was not submission to nature, but the achievement of a supernatural purpose, the full meaning of which would become apparent only in the future. Unlike the Mesopotamians, the Israelites never supposed that their destiny was already recorded in the stars; and unlike the Egyptians, they had a religion of time and not of eternity, never becoming obsessed with the cyclic processes of nature and displaying no strong interest or belief in any afterlife.

The relationship between Jehovah and his chosen people, moreover, was essentially contractual. Jehovah had promised to protect them on condition that they obeyed his commandments, honored him with the prescribed rituals, and excluded all rival objects of worship. As described in the Book of Exodus, the contract was sealed in the desert at the foot of the mountain in accordance with the customary legal forms. After Moses had received a long list of commandments from Jehovah, he read them to the Israelites, who "answered with one voice, and said, All the words which the Lord hath said will we do." Moses then ordered oxen to be sacrificed,

---

[5] Some authorities believe that Judaism did not begin to become monolatrous until the time of Elijah. In this case, the jealousy attributed to Jehovah was a later addition to the Mosaic tradition, a reflection not of the political needs of the tribes during the conquest, but of the monopolistic ambitions of the Jerusalem priests.

collected the blood in basins, and sprinkled half of it on an altar representing Jehovah, the other half on the people. Seventy elders of the Israelite tribes then accompanied Moses to the top of the mountain, where "they saw the God of Israel . . . and did eat and drink." [6] The memory of this transaction in the wilderness was treasured by the Israelites throughout all their later history, and shaped their whole religious development. As interpreted by the prophets half a millennium later, it implied that if the Israelite people persistently violated the contract, Jehovah might temporarily transfer his patronage to some other people. The result was that he acquired a mobility and independence not enjoyed by deities inseparably associated with particular tribes. And though initially the Israelites thought exclusively of collective tribal prosperity, to be achieved by retaining Jehovah's favor through the use of the correct rituals, their contract gradually acquired an ethical content, Jehovah being regarded as demanding righteous behavior. It was also significant that in the sealing of the contract the two parties were sharply set apart from each other; the religion of Israel, unlike that of most primitive peoples, never blurred the lines between god and man; it had no deified kings or prophets, no deities descending to earth to beget children with human mistresses.

What laws of behavior were included in the original contract cannot be determined. Later generations attributed to Moses a vast mass of juridical, ethical, and ritualistic regulations, most of which demonstrably originated in Palestine and not in the desert and were certainly adopted by the Israelites at a later period. Probably no part of the surviving Mosaic code, not even the Ten Commandments, was actually promulgated by Moses. It can be assumed, however, that the spirit of the original contract must have been narrowly and intolerantly tribalistic. Throughout their early history the Israelites displayed no compunction about robbing, defrauding, and slaughtering other peoples, and the same attitude was consistently attributed to their divine patron. Jehovah rescued Sarah from Pharaoh's harem after Abraham had passed her off as his sister instead of his wife, at the same time allowing Abraham to keep the gifts he had received through these false pretenses; sancti-

---

[6] Exodus, xxiv, 3, 10–11. Biblical quotations are taken from the King James Version except where this is seriously misleading. In a few instances the new Revised Standard Version is substituted.

fied the blessing fraudulently obtained by Jacob; ordered the Israelites to steal from their Egyptian neighbors by borrowing goods from them on the eve of the exodus; promised to make them masters of Palestine without any consideration for the rights of its existing inhabitants; and ordered that tribesmen who worshipped other gods should be massacred and their women and children enslaved. Even by the standards of the second millennium, Jehovah was a barbaric deity, far less humane than the cosmic spirit worshipped by the Pharaoh Ikhnaton or the Babylonian sun god who had dictated the laws of Hammurabi; and because this tribal deity afterwards became identified with the ruler of the universe, the bloodthirsty actions recorded in the Pentateuch have continued to have an evil influence on Western civilization down to modern times.

Yet while the Israelites were narrowly tribalistic in their attitudes to foreign peoples, they also developed relatively high standards of justice and humanity in their relations with one another. The individualism and equality of their pastoral background were never wholly forgotten, even under the monarchy; and there can be little doubt that this spirit was embodied in the original Mosaic code. Jehovah's contract was made not with a priest or a chieftain, or even with the tribal elders, but with all the people of Israel. The belief that Jehovah was angered by oppression and exploitation was implicit in the Mosaic tradition, though until the time of the prophets this applied only to his Israelite worshippers. And though the elaborate ritualistic rules attributed to Jehovah never had much rational basis, being largely magical in origin, and may have been even more barbaric in their original Mosaic form, they seem to have been free from the more gross sexual practices and grotesque mythological explanations that characterized other religious cults. In this respect also it was of advantage to Jehovah that he became the god of the Hebrews at a particular moment in time. Unlike Enlil and Amon-Re and Zeus, he could evolve toward monotheism without being embarrassed by the amoral rituals and legends that other deities trailed with them from the ages of neolithic and paleolithic savagery.

According to the Biblical story, the Israelites acquired the whole of their religious system through the Mosaic revelation, although their spiritual leaders had subsequently to fight a long battle in order to prevent the pure worship of Jehovah from being contaminated by Canaanite influences. A careful study of the record shows that the real story was much more complex; the occupation of Palestine led to a fusion of religions, as a result of which a mass of Canaanite rituals and beliefs was incorporated into the Jehovah cult, many of them becoming permanent elements of the Jewish faith. Yet there was undeniably a conflict between the two traditions; the Jehovah-worship of the desert, with its nomadic deity, its patriarchal morality, and its association with a pastoral independence and equality, could never wholly amalgamate with the agricultural fertility cults and theocratic institutions of the land of Canaan. It was of decisive importance that some elements in the Israelite population never wholly forgot the Mosaic creed; in spite of the adoption of fertility rituals, Jehovah succeeded finally in retaining his isolation and was never degraded into the partner of a Palestinian mother goddess.

For many centuries before the Israelite occupation, Palestine had contained settled agricultural populations, along with temple cities of the usual theocratic type. To judge from archaeological evidence, in fact, the material level of its civilization was considerably higher before the occupation than it ever was during the period of Israelite rule. With the ebbing of Egyptian imperialism, the country had been left to a number of small separate states, while Philistine immigrants had conquered the southern seacoast. It is apparent from the Book of Judges that the Israelites took possession of the country by a slow process of infiltration, settling first in the infertile hill country of the interior, fighting only occasional wars with Canaanite states, and leaving the cities and the seacoast plains unconquered for centuries. Economically less advanced than their city-dwelling opponents, they relied on militia armies of peasants and herdsmen who fought on foot or rode on asses, any horses or chariots mentioned in the Biblical record being always the property of the enemy. For a long period the Philistines were the masters of most of Palestine, and supremacy did not finally pass to the Israelites until after the establishment of the Davidian monarchy in 1013 B.C. In the end, as is occasionally admitted in the Biblical record, a large part of the Palestinian population, both rural and urban, was absorbed into the Israelite kingdom. In spite of the massacres recorded with such complacency in that highly unhistorical expression of sacerdotal fanaticism, the Book of Joshua, Jehovah's instructions for the extermination of the enemy were never carried out. There was a union of races, leading inevitably to a union of religions.

Palestinian nature-worship seems to have exceeded even that of other Near Eastern peasant cultures in its propensity for gross and revolting rituals. The country was dotted with shrines at which male and female fertility deities, represented by phallic stone pillars and wooden poles, were served by hereditary priests who gained their livelihood from the offerings of the peasants. Sacrifice was not, as with the pastoral peoples, a communal meal shared by the god and the human family, but an offering of first fruits to the deities and their priests in the expectation that the reward would be a good harvest. Orgiastic festivals were celebrated in spring and autumn, accompanied by the usual phenomena of mass drunkenness and the collective conviction of divine possession. As with all fertility cults, there was a pronounced emphasis on human sexuality; both male and female prostitutes were attached to the temples, their earnings being contributed to the sacred treasuries. The chief Palestinian abomination, however, was child-sacrifice; the first-born of every family was the property of the local god and must be given to him as a burnt offering.[7]

Israelite rule over Palestine meant that Jehovah-worship was im-

---

[7] "Goddesses of fertility play a much greater role among the Canaanites than they do among any other ancient people. . . . These Canaanite goddesses were nearly always represented in iconography as naked. . . . Another dominant characteristic of the Canaanite goddesses in question was their savagery. . . . A favorite type of representation shows the naked goddess astride a galloping horse and brandishing a weapon in her right hand. In a fragment of the Baal epic which has just been published (1938), Anath appears as incredibly sanguinary. For a reason not yet known she massacres mankind, young and old, from the sea-coast to the rising of the sun, causing heads and hands to fly in all directions. Then she ties heads to her back, hands to her girdle, and wades up to her knees—yes, up to her throat—in human gore. The favorite animals of the Canaanite goddess were the lion, because of its ferocity, and the serpent and dove, because of their reputed fecundity. . . . A cult-stand of about the twelfth century B.C. from Beth-shan shows a remarkable tableau in relief; a nude goddess holds two doves in her arms as she sits with legs apart to show her sex; below her are two male deities with arms interlocked in a struggle (?), with a dog at the feet of one of them; toward them from below creeps a serpent and from one side advances a lion. This may be considered as a terse epitome of the mythological symbolism of Canaanite religion at the end of the pre-Israelite age in Palestine." W. F. Albright: *From the Stone Age to Christianity* (The Johns Hopkins Press), pp. 177–8.

posed on the whole country, but the traditional rituals continued with little change. Originally a desert storm god and then the traveling war god of the Israelite tribes, Jehovah was now identified with the various Canaanite fertility gods, known collectively as Baalim, and was in consequence split up into a number of different embodiments attached to different shrines, each of which was regarded by the peasants as a separate deity. The fact that he was now represented by a series of stone pillars meant that his worshippers no longer adhered to any Mosaic prohibition of the worship of images. Various indications in the Biblical narrative make it doubtful, indeed, how far the Israelites had ever conformed to any such commandment; King David, for example, had his own household images, the teraphim, which are mentioned in the Book of Samuel without any suggestion that they were a violation of the Decalogue. Along with the Baalim, Jehovah-worship took over the orgiastic festivals and the ritualistic prostitution, which remained a part of the official religion of Israel until the prophetic movement. And although the sacrifice of first-born children was at some period commuted into animal sacrifice, it was revived as late as the seventh century and was believed by some people, including the prophet Ezekiel, to have been one of Jehovah's original commandments.[8]

Meanwhile, the original pastoral republicanism of the Israelites was suffering a similar corruption. Throughout the long period described in the Book of Judges the tribes retained their loose individualistic mode of organization. "In those days there was no king in Israel; every man did that which was right in his own eyes." [9] Leadership was exercised by a series of priests and warriors who owed their position to personal charisma rather than to any hereditary right;[1] and the final political authority, along with the function of judging legal disputes, still belonged to the tribal elders. Jehovah's will was ascertained by the priests through the casting of lots and other mechanical means of divination, or was

---

[8] The prophet explained it as an expression of Jehovah's anger because of Israelite disobedience. "I gave them also statutes that were not good, and judgments whereby they should not live; and I polluted them in their own gifts, in that they caused to pass through the fire all that openeth the womb, that I might make them desolate, to the end that they might know that I am the Lord." Ezekiel, xx, 25–6.

[9] Judges, xxi, 25.

[1] The concept of charismatic leadership was defined by Max Weber, who applied it to Jewish history in his *Ancient Judaism*.

communicated to prophets who cultivated ecstatic states in which they believed themselves to be divinely inspired. But this mode of government, appropriate to wandering tribes of herdsmen, was unsuited to an agricultural and partially urbanized society. According to the Bible, the change to monarchy was motivated mainly by the need for unity in the war against the Philistines, but it must also have been caused by economic factors. The transition from a pastoral to an agricultural society, with the establishment of property rights in land and the growing differentiation between land-owning and servile classes, and the absorption of the Palestinian cities with their commercial and industrial activities made a more complex political and legal system essential. After the somewhat ineffectual rule of Saul, a peasant chieftain whose support came chiefly from the northern tribes, David, of the southern tribe of Judah, succeeded in organizing a military despotism of the normal Oriental type. He ended the domination of the Philistines and conquered the old city of Jerusalem, which became his capital.

Toward the Davidian monarchy the attitude of the Biblical chroniclers remained significantly ambivalent. David's early adventures as an outlaw chieftain when "every one that was in distress, and every one that was in debt, and every one that was discontented, gathered themselves unto him" [2] and his subsequent rise to supreme power, his prowess as a warrior and exploits as a general, his warm personal friendships and numerous love affairs, his talents as poet and musician, his gestures of chivalry and generosity, his occasional acts of treachery and cruelty, the splendor of his kingship—all this made him a saga hero and the most picturesque figure in the whole of Jewish history. The Israelites never forgot that under his rule and that of his son Solomon they had achieved the greatest material power and prosperity they ever enjoyed; and after the final loss of their political independence four centuries later, their hopes became centered on a restoration of David's monarchy under a king of David's lineage. But later chroniclers also recognized that in adopting the institutions of their neighbors the Israelites had lost the republican freedom and simplicity of the age of the judges. The Bible represents the priest

---

[2] I Samuel, xxii, 2.

Samuel as pointing out to the monarchical party that a king would "take your fields, and your vineyards, and your oliveyards, even the best of them, and give them to his servants. . . . And he will take your manservants, and your maidservants, and your goodliest young men, and your asses, and put them to his work. He will take the tenth of your sheep: and ye shall be his servants. And ye shall cry out in that day because of your king which ye shall have chosen you." [3]

All the implications of monarchy became fully apparent during the reign of Solomon, who set out to make Israel a bureaucratic state on the Egyptian model. He maintained a mercenary army recruited from foreigners and equipped with horses and chariots, collected taxes from his subjects and drafted them for forced labor on a royal palace and temple and other public works, appointed officials to control justice and local administration in place of the traditional tribal elders, organized elaborate commercial enterprises, and enjoyed a large harem along with the other appurtenances of kingship. Like his father, he was a priest-king, himself presiding over sacrifices to Jehovah; and the Jehovah cult was now used as an instrument of royal power and remodeled to conform with the usages of other Near Eastern kingdoms. Solomon's main reason for building a temple at Jerusalem was no doubt to make Jehovah a permanent resident of the capital city, and thereby to centralize religion in accord with the centralization of political power. This was contrary to the original nomadic tradition, though the only expression of this fact, in the protest of the prophet Nathan when David had planned a temple, was apparently a very late addition to the Biblical record. "Shalt thou build me an house for me to dwell in?" Jehovah is represented as saying. "Whereas I have not dwelt in any house since the time that I brought up the children of Israel out of Egypt, even to this day, but have walked in a tent and in a tabernacle." [4] Solomon's Temple was filled with elaborately carved images, though none of them seems to have represented Jehovah himself or to have become an object of worship. More significant was the fact that the Temple was surrounded by shrines honoring the deities of foreign countries. The

---

[3] I Samuel, viii, 14–18.   [4] II Samuel, vii, 5–6.

religion of the monarchy was moving toward polytheism, and
Jehovah was in serious danger of becoming, like Marduk or
Amon-Re, merely the presiding officer of a pantheon.

Several rebellions against both David and Solomon had shown
that the primitive republican spirit was still alive, and after
Solomon's death in 933 the northern tribes seceded and formed a
separate kingdom of Israel with its capital at Samaria, leaving
only the tribe of Judah to the Davidian dynasty. Our chief authority for the next three and one half centuries, the Book of
Kings, reflected the viewpoint of the Jerusalem priests after the
seventh-century reforms, and was written on the assumption that
rulers who observed the correct rituals must, ipso facto, have been
rewarded with prosperity while those who corrupted the Jehovah
cult certainly came to bad ends. This thesis could be supported
only by distorting most of the facts, and the true story can be
discovered only by reading between the lines. Judaea, which outside the city of Jerusalem consisted chiefly of pastoral hill country,
seems to have remained more faithful to the Mosaic tradition. In
the richer and more agricultural north, the fertility cults were more
strongly entrenched, and other gods were worshipped alongside
Jehovah. Jeroboam, the first king of Samaria, being determined to
end any dependence upon the Jerusalem Temple, set up shrines for
the worship of a bull (contemptuously described in the Biblical
narrative as a golden calf), though it is probable that this animal
was considered not as a new supreme deity but as a new embodiment of Jehovah or possibly as merely a pedestal on which he
stood while himself remaining invisible. But despite the heresies
of the northern kingdom, it remained stronger than its southern
rival down to the Assyrian conquest of 722, and enjoyed two periods of high prosperity under Omri and his son Ahab (887–853)
and under Jeroboam II (785–744). Much more important than
the ritualistic problems obsessing the author of the Book of Kings
were the increasing economic inequalities. The powers of the
royal bureaucracies and the growth of a money economy produced
their usual effects, and the peasants and herdsmen of the countryside began to fall into debt to urban merchants and aristocrats, and
often ended by losing their land and their freedom and being sold
into slavery. The grievances of the mass of the people were to find
expression in the prophetic movement.

Yet, in spite of religious and economic conflicts, the period of the two kingdoms was the golden age of Hebrew literature. Invigorated by the successful completion of the conquest, writers began to collect the stories of Israel's history since the time of Abraham and of the achievements of Jehovah. Incorporated into the present Biblical narrative, and mingled with the tedious moralizing comments, ritualistic regulations, and long genealogies that were added during less imaginative and more sin-conscious epochs, are a biography of David, probably written by a personal acquaintance during the reign of Solomon, a ninth-century collection of Judaean stories known as the J document, and an eighth-century compilation covering the same ground from a northern viewpoint, the E document. The narrative vigor and vivid character-portrayals of these stories, their primitive enjoyment of human nature and the natural world, their morning freshness and epic scope and energy have never been surpassed in the literature of the world. Other Near Eastern peoples had achieved nothing comparable to them, and what made them possible among the Israelites was the Jehovah cult. The Egyptians and the Mesopotamians, dominated by nature cults that fused past and future into a perpetual present and drew no clear line of distinction between men and gods, had never disentangled history from mythology. It was the memory of the contract with Jehovah in the wilderness that made history a meaningful process and thus enabled these Israelite writers to be the world's first historians. And since they trusted in Jehovah's divine purposes, they expressed a spirit of optimism, a belief in the cosmic significance of human life, which was notably lacking in two other masterpieces probably composed at about the same period, the poems of Homer. Jehovah-worship also made possible the extraordinary realism of Hebrew biography. David was a priest-king and the Lord's anointed, but, unlike the Egyptian embodiments of Osiris and Amon-Re and the Babylonian sons of Marduk, he was a man and not a god. His biographer could portray him with unapologetic awareness of both his greatness and his littleness. The story of his passion for Bath-sheba, his murder of Uriah, and the rebuke of the prophet Nathan was infused with a sense of moral values rarely applied to a country's ruler in any epoch of the world's history.

2

The Prophetic Movement

An analysis of the historical background shows why the religion of Israel, and of Israel alone, was able to evolve into monotheism. Yet prior to the prophetic movement there had been little indication of such a development. Down to the eighth century, Jehovah remained simply a tribal deity, physically located in certain places even if not visibly embodied in any graven image, and exercising authority only over the people of Israel and the land of Palestine. The main object of Israelite religious observances was to retain his favor and thus ensure tribal prosperity. He was considered the patron of the established laws and mores, and was assumed to be particularly prone to anger if his worshippers failed to show him proper respect or omitted any of the prescribed rituals and sacrifices. The Israelites represented him, in fact, as being acutely sensitive about his personal honor; and since the prestige of a god depended upon the welfare of his human dependents, they assumed that he would always come to their aid in times of crisis and could not possibly allow them to be deprived of their national independence. In their numerous arguments with Jehovah, ever since the time of Moses, they had always pointed out how much his reputation would suffer if he deserted or destroyed them during one of his fits of anger instead of giving them victory over their enemies.[1]

---

[1] For example, when the Israelites made a golden calf in the wilderness, Jehovah said to Moses: "I have seen this people, and, behold, it is a stiff-necked people: now therefore let me alone, that my wrath may wax hot against them, and that I may consume them." Moses replied by asking: "Wherefore should the Egyptians speak, and say, For mischief did he bring them out, to slay them in the mountains, and to consume them

The immediate causes of the prophetic movement seem to have been economic and political. The rise of an urban moneyed class, the growing concentration of landownership, and the enslavement of many of the peasants provoked bitter class resentments and aroused memories of the primitive equality and republicanism of the Mosaic period, when the god of Israel had been the god of all the people. One group of reformers, the Rechabites, actually repudiated agriculture and returned to the simple pastoral way of life of their nomadic ancestors. Thus, the pure Jehovah-worship of the desert tradition became identified with social justice, while the Baal fertility rituals were associated with the growth of economic exploitation. In calling for a return to the religion of Moses, the prophets were, at the same time, denouncing both religious syncretism and social corruption.

More important was the deterioration in the international situation. After several centuries of relative peace, the great powers resumed their conflicts. Late in the eighth century, the Assyrians, greediest and most bloodthirsty of all the Near Eastern peoples, began to build an empire in competition with the decadent but still formidable power of Egypt. By any realistic view the two small Israelite kingdoms could not hope to keep their independence, and could survive at all only by paying tribute to Assyria. The logical implication was that Jehovah, in spite of his success in leading his people out of Egypt and making them masters of Palestine, was inferior to Shamash, the sun god of Nineveh. The prophets, however, while recognizing that foreign conquest was inevitable, refused to accept this implication. During this period of national humiliation they began to proclaim the revolutionary doctrine that Jehovah, the tribal god of the Israelites, was, in reality, the sole creator and ruler of the universe, that all the innumerable deities worshipped by other peoples were merely human inventions, that the Assyrians and the Egyptians were, without knowing it, the instruments of Jehovah's purposes, and that the conquest of the people of Israel, instead of being a proof of Jehovah's weakness, had been deliberately planned by him as a punishment for their sins. Such a claim must have been regarded

---

from the face of the earth?" Moses also reminded Jehovah of his promises to Abraham, Isaac, and Jacob. Then "the Lord repented of the evil which he thought to do unto his people." See Exodus, xxxii, 1–14.

by non-Israelites as an astonishing example of tribal effrontery. One can understand it only by recognizing that the central intuition on which the prophetic movement was based was in essence, in spite of its links with the religion of Moses, as novel as the other new beginnings of the Axial Period in China, India, Iran, and Greece.

The prophets were moving from tribalism to universalism, and were thereby enabled to disentangle ethics from tribal mores and allegiances. They saw the world as a unity, and regarded goodness as a spiritual quality, an attitude of mind and heart, and not as a matter of placating an angry god by ritualistic observances. This revolutionary view of the universe and of human life was presented, however, not as a break with the traditional Israelite religion, but as a return to its original Mosaic form. In preaching monotheism, the prophets did not find it necessary to repudiate Jehovah. Thus the new doctrines resulted in a paradoxical compromise with tribalism. The creator of the universe, it was alleged, had, for reasons known only to himself, chosen to reveal himself only to a single people; and although the prophets declared most emphatically that Israel could not count on Jehovah's protection, and that by failing to achieve high ethical ideals she had, in fact, brought destruction upon herself, they did not abandon the assumption that the practice of true religion would result in tribal prosperity. As Israel was obviously destined to be enslaved, it followed as a logical consequence that she must have sinned more grievously than other nations. She alone had known the god of righteousness, and had not remained loyal to him. Denunciations of the wickedness of Israel and predictions of her coming day of doom became the main themes of prophetic preaching. Eventually questions were raised as to whether Jehovah's punishment of Israel had actually been a fair penalty for her misconduct, but these doubts about divine justice were removed by an appeal to the future. In some indeterminate epoch Israel would be purged of her sins, and would finally, under Messianic leadership, become a great nation and be recognized as the spiritual leader and savior of all mankind. In spite of its inner contradictions, this synthesis of opposites proved to have an extraordinary survival power; it enabled Judaism, in defiance of all rational probabilities, to retain its spiritual vitality, and resulted many centuries later in a new religious system that conquered the whole Western world.

The prophets themselves had, of course, no doubts whatever about Jehovah's identity. On the contrary, they were dominated by a most intense conviction of his immediate presence. In spite of the rationality of much of their preaching, they were ecstatic men who heard voices, saw visions, went into states of trance, and believed themselves personally commissioned to proclaim the divine will. Such experiences, it was assumed, could come from no other source than the tribal deity. This attitude can best be understood in the light of Israel's earlier religious development.

Like most primitive peoples, the Israelites had always believed in inspiration, interpreting any disturbance of normal consciousness and self-control as due to spiritual agencies. During their early history, as can be seen from stories in the books of Judges and Samuel, not only the rhapsodic utterances of priests and poets but also the babblings of maniacs were attributed to a divine spirit. Prophecy gradually became professionalized, and schools of prophets, who had developed techniques for the deliberate inducement of states of derangement by means of music and dances and of alcohol and possibly other drugs, earned money by helping peasants to find lost articles, performing miraculous cures, and advising kings about the will of Jehovah. This tradition seems to have been stronger in the northern kingdom, where the orgiastic fertility cults were more deeply rooted; its rulers apparently maintained large bodies of hired ecstatics to encourage their subjects with suitably propitious oracles on the eve of a war or some other major crisis.

Among more sophisticated persons it was recognized that many of these prophets were merely lunatics and that their utterances were misleading; but the popular assumption of divine guidance was not readily abandoned. Jehovah, it was alleged, might deliberately impel his prophets to lie, perhaps because he wished disobedient kings to be led astray. Rationalist criteria were gradually established by the priests, and according to the seventh-century Book of Deuteronomy only those prophets should be obeyed whose predictions had been corroborated by events.[2] But anybody

---

[2] I Kings, xii, 22; Deuteronomy, xviii, 22.

who claimed to be proclaiming the will of God was still likely to be treated with respect. This was why the monotheistic prophets, in spite of their decidedly unpopular doctrines, were able to secure a hearing. Several of them were in serious danger of being lynched or executed, but their auditors were always restrained by an uneasy suspicion that their claims to be Jehovah's mouthpieces might actually be true.

In the tenor of their utterances the monotheistic prophets were sharply different from their professional predecessors. In fact, the first of them, Amos of Tekoa, insisted most emphatically that he was not connected with any prophetic school and had no professional status. They did not claim miraculous powers, and their whole approach to political and social problems was remarkably realistic; in defiance of the traditional Jehovah cult they declared that sequences of cause and effect would follow their inevitable course and that the loss of Israelite independence could not be prevented by magical rituals or appeals for supernatural intervention. Yet their rational insights into the nature of reality and their moral indignation seemed to them to come from an external source and to be impressed upon their minds with a compulsive urgency that they interpreted as a divine command. Their modes of thought and expression were essentially poetic; and although their doctrines marked a great advance toward the capacity for objective thought, they retained the primitive conviction that subjective mental processes were reflections of external forces. In so far as they interpreted certain of their own emotional states as evidences of a spiritual reality, they can be classified as mystics, but they never enjoyed the mystical sense of union with the godhead. Their Jehovah was always an external person, combining the overwhelming power and anger of the old storm god of Sinai with the new demand for moral perfection. By the standards of modern civilization this belief in inspiration tends, of course, to discredit the content of their preaching. It should be remembered that the processes by which men achieve new insights always appear mysterious, even if they are attributed not to supernatural influence but to subconscious forces within the human psyche, and that the only fair test of their validity is operational.

Prior to the eighth century there had been a few individuals for whom the will of Jehovah had been expressed in moral indignation rather than in derangements of consciousness. The prophet Nathan had denounced King David's dealings with Bath-sheba. In the ninth century the mysterious and awe-inspiring figure of Elijah had appeared in the northern kingdom, championing the pure Mosaic tradition and attacking the Baal-worship of King Ahab and his judicial murder of Naboth. Elijah's visit to Sinai, where he recognized Jehovah not in a whirlwind or an earthquake or a fire but in "a still small voice," indicated a spiritual conception of the divine nature, though there is no evidence that he was a monotheist. But Elijah's leadership was transmitted to the miracle-worker Elisha, who headed a professional prophetic school and meddled in politics to no good purpose, encouraging Jehu to seize power from the dynasty of Omri and massacre all its members and supporters. Improbable as it may appear, the surviving records do not indicate that the monotheistic prophets had any real precursors.

The first expression of the new spirit can be located with considerable precision. The time was about 750, and the place was the shrine of Bethel, one of the chief centers of bull-worship in the northern kingdom. Assyria was still only a distant stormcloud rising on the eastern horizon; and Israel had enjoyed a long period of prosperity, at least for the upper classes. Apparently Amos of Tekoa interrupted one of the traditional fertility festivals with denunciatory preachings which seemed to the priest of the shrine to be so dangerously subversive that he sent a warning to the King. According to his own account, Amos was a herdsman and a dresser of fruit trees from the hill country of southern Judaea. In spite of these humble occupations, he was well informed about international politics, and could state his convictions in language that was not only filled with poetic imagery drawn from the life of the wilderness, but was also remarkably terse, forceful, and well organized. If one were challenged to trace the spirit of Western civilization back to its earliest source, perhaps the best answer would be the advent of Amos of Tekoa.

The prophecies attributed to Amos make one of the shortest books in the Old Testament, and some of them, including the consoling Messianic conclusion, were probably added at a much later epoch. But those sections which are plainly authentic make a decisive break with previous religious tradition. In the first place,

Jehovah is presented as the ruler of other peoples besides the Israelites. The book begins with threats of doom for several neighboring kingdoms, each of which, like Israel, will be punished by
God for its misdeeds. And although Amos is not fully or explicitly monotheistic, his basic conception is that divine government
of the world is exercised not through miraculous interventions but
through sequences of cause and effect, so that every event is the
work of God. In a remarkable paragraph he drives home the reality of causation by a series of examples ("Will a lion roar in the
forest, when he hath no prey? . . . Can a bird fall in a snare
upon the earth, where no gin is set for him? . . . Shall a trum-
pet be blown in the city, and the people not be afraid?") and
concludes by asking: "Shall there be evil in a city, and the Lord
hath not done it?" [3] And, in the second place, Amos declares that
God is not placated by rituals and sacrifices, but instead requires
ethical behavior. Jehovah is represented as declaring: "I hate, I
despise your feast days, and I will not smell in your solemn assem-
blies. Though ye offer me burnt offerings and your meat offerings,
I will not accept them: neither will I regard the peace offerings of
your fat beasts. Take thou away from me the noise of thy songs;
for I will not hear the melody of thy viols. But let judgment run
down as waters, and righteousness as a mighty stream." [4] For
Amos righteousness means chiefly economic justice, and the
main reason for the coming conquest of Israel by the Assyrians
is the greed of the upper classes and their enslavement of the
peasants. Israel has "sold the righteous for silver, and the poor for
a pair of shoes." "Those that lie upon beds of ivory, and stretch
themselves upon their couches, and eat the lambs out of the flock,
and the calves out of the midst of the stall; that chant to the sound
of the viol, and invent to themselves instruments of music, like
David; that drink wine in bowls, and anoint themselves with
the chief ointments: but they are not grieved for the affliction of
Joseph: therefore now shall they go captive." [5] Thus for perhaps
the first time in history religion is presented not as a bulwark of
social order, but as a dynamic demand for radical reform. [6]

---

[3] Amos, iii, 4–6.
[4] Amos, v, 21–4.
[5] Amos, ii, 6; vi, 4–7.
[6] Amos's denunciations of the rich

were echoed by another prophet of a
slightly later period, Micah. The last
four chapters of the Book of Micah
were added after the Exile.

The next of the prophets, Hosea, was not concerned with social injustice and lacked Amos's genius for expression (unless he was badly served by his editors), but his basic doctrine was equally novel. Repeating Amos's denunciations of ritualistic observances, he declares that true religion is an attitude of the mind and heart. Jehovah desires "steadfast love and not sacrifice, the knowledge of God, rather than burnt offerings." [7] This conception is conveyed through sexual metaphors, and is reached through an attack on the fertility cults. Israel had originally been married to Jehovah, but had then prostituted herself with the gods of Palestine in the false belief that the Baal rituals produced good harvests. "She said, I will go after my lovers, that give me my bread and my water, my wool and my flax, mine oil and my drink. . . . For she did not know that I gave her corn and wine and oil, and multiplied her silver and gold, which they used for Baal. Therefore will I return, and . . . I will also cause all her mirth to cease, her feast days, her new moons, and her sabbaths, and all her solemn feasts. And I will destroy her vines and her fig trees, whereof she hath said, These be my rewards that my lovers hath given me; and I will make them a forest, and the beasts of the field shall eat them." [8] Hosea's obsession with sex, expressed in vehement denunciations of the ritualistic prostitution associated with the Baal cults, was apparently connected with personal experiences to which he attributed symbolic meanings. [9]

Thus, Hosea was the first prophet to preach a religion of the

[7] Hosea, vi, 6, Revised Standard Version. The Authorized Version incorrectly uses "mercy" for the Hebrew word meaning the love of a wife for a husband.

[8] Hosea, ii, 5–12.

[9] In Chapter i, after some general remarks about the whoredom of Israel, Hosea relates that he married a woman called Gomer and had three children to whom he gave symbolic names. In Chapter iii he describes how he loved a prostitute, bought her out of slavery, and kept her in his house, this being symbolic of Jehovah's love for Israel. A majority of the commentators have supposed that the wife of Chapter i was identical with the prostitute of Chapter iii and have made a romantic story of Hosea's supposed fidelty to his unfaithful spouse; a minority have gallantly taken up the cudgels in defense of Gomer's chastity and insisted that two different women are involved, at the same time defending the honor of the prophet by maintaining that the whole episode related in Chapter iii must have been purely symbolic. Isaiah's private life has evoked similar controversies. Isaiah relates, rather casually, that he had a son by a prophetess, his main concern being with the symbolic name that he gave him. Commentators defend his character by arguing that the wife of a prophet must have been called a prophetess and hence that the child was conceived in lawful wedlock.

spirit. But although this shift of emphasis from the outer to the inner life was a significant advance toward higher conceptions of God, it also led to new and more complex spiritual problems. To interpret religion as love rather than ritual meant a repudiation of the whole primitive heritage, but by identifying the divine husband of his visions with the Jehovah who had ratified the covenant with Israel in the wilderness, Hosea made love into an obligation. How could human beings ever feel assured that they loved God with the total and unquestioning devotion he demanded? Much of the Christian experience was implicit in the religion of Hosea: the anxiety and soul-searching that were reinforced by the belief in original sin, the struggles of the saints to achieve a proper contempt for worldly life and to center all their desires upon God, the mystical transference of sexual drives to the heavenly bridegroom.

The paradoxes involved in the fusion of new spiritual conceptions with the traditional Jehovah cult were even more obvious in the political prophets. If God directed world affairs in order to manifest his power and punish the wicked, then it was not only futile, but also wrong, to resist the inevitable. For Israel to fight in defense of her independence was not merely imprudent; according to the religion of the prophets, it would be disobedience to the divine will. Instead of seeking foreign alliances and becoming involved in international power politics, she should seek only to purge herself of sin and achieve ethical perfection, meanwhile trusting that God by his own methods and in his own good time would bring about the reign of universal justice. The opposition of the prophets to foreign alliances was largely caused by their fear of religious contamination, and their whole attitude to the threat of conquest implied an ethic of non-resistance, but this was predicated not on any rational understanding of the self-defeating effects of power, but on the assumption that a just God was guiding the course of history.

The first individual to wrestle with these dilemmas was Isaiah, a native of Jerusalem and apparently a member of the aristocracy, who was a younger contemporary of Amos and Hosea. If one is tempted to accuse him of a somewhat ignoble fatalism, one should remember that he was struggling to express a more enlightened concept of God. His life was spent doing battle with the profes-

sional ecstatics who uttered consoling oracles in states of derangement or intoxication, with priests who insisted that if Jehovah was
placated with generous sacrifices he would always protect his people, and with the whole primeval heritage of magic and superstition.

Unfortunately, the writings generally attributed to Isaiah (comprising the first thirty-nine chapters of the book bearing his name)
consist of an utterly chaotic mass of personal reminiscences and
disconnected fragments of prophetic exhortation interspersed with
numerous later interpolations and editorial comments. But it is
obvious that he was a poet and a religious thinker of the first rank
and an extremely complex personality. The passage in which he
describes how he saw God in all his holiness and glory and believed himself personally commissioned to be God's spokesman is
one of the classics of religious mysticism. The main theme of his
preaching, as of Amos's, is that God requires justice and not ritual. "To what purpose is the multitude of your sacrifices unto me?"
God is represented as saying; "I am full of the burnt offerings of
rams, and the fat of fed beasts; and I delight not in the blood of
bullocks, or of lambs, or of he-goats. . . . Bring me no more
vain oblations. . . . Your new moons and your appointed feasts
my soul hateth. . . . When ye make many prayers, I will not hear;
your hands are full of blood. Wash you, make you clean; put away
the evil of your doings from before mine eyes; cease to do evil;
learn to do well; seek judgment, relieve the oppressed, judge the
fatherless, plead for the widow." Isaiah was also somewhat of a
puritan, as appears from his detailed and caustic enumeration of
all the articles of clothing worn by the rich women of Jerusalem.[1]

Throughout Isaiah's life Israelite history was dominated by the
menace of Assyria. In the year 722 the northern kingdom was
conquered, nearly thirty thousand of its leading citizens being carried away into slavery; and as Amos and Hosea had predicted,
Jehovah did nothing to save his people. The rulers of the southern
kingdom had now to decide whether to save themselves by paying
tribute to Assyria or to join forces with Egypt and other neighboring states in an attempt at resistance. Throughout most of his career Isaiah was the enemy of foreign alliances and the advocate

---

[1] Isaiah, i, 11–17; iii, 18–23.

of appeasement; and though this was owing partly to a realistic
appraisal of the strength of the Assyrians, it seems also to have
reflected a religious conviction that they were Jehovah's instruments. Assyria was "the rod of mine anger, the staff of my fury.
Against a godless nation I send him, and against the people of my
wrath I command him, to take spoil and seize plunder, and to
tread them down like the mire of the streets." [2] The political
prophecies of Isaiah mingle murky and terrifying forebodings of
Jehovah's coming day of doom with apocalyptic hopes for an age
of universal peace and brotherhood after men have learned to obey
the divine will. Israel will pay the penalty for the worldliness of
her upper classes and their oppression of the poor; but a saving
remnant will preserve the faith, and in some future age other nations will know the true God. "In that day shall Israel be the third
with Egypt and with Assyria, even a blessing in the midst of the
land: whom the Lord of hosts shall bless, saying, Blessed be Egypt
my people, and Assyria the work of my hands, and Israel mine
inheritance." [3] This spirit of religious universalism had no precedents.

King Hezekiah refused to follow Isaiah's advice, and in the year
701 the Assyrian army swept across Judaea, devastated the countryside, laid siege to Jerusalem, and extorted an immense tribute,
but departed without actually capturing the city. Exultant over
the Assyrian withdrawal, the people of Jerusalem attributed
their good fortune to the intervention of Jehovah, and were soon
believing that he had smitten dead one hundred and eighty-five
thousand enemy soldiers in a single night—a story for which there
is no corroboration in Assyrian records, and which is rendered improbable by the admitted fact that Judah had become an Assyrian
puppet state. [4] According to the Biblical record, Isaiah had en-

---

[2] Isaiah, x, 5–6, Revised Standard
Version.
[3] Isaiah, xix, 24–5.
[4] An Assyrian inscription records
that vast quantities of plunder were
carried back from Palestine and that
Hezekiah was shut up in his capital
city "like a caged bird." In addition
to claiming that Jehovah slaughtered
most of the Assyrian army, the
Book of Kings also declares that the
Assyrian king was murdered after

returning to his own country—an
event that actually occurred twenty
years later. In an effort to defend the
authenticity of Holy Writ, Biblical
commentators have frequently claimed
that the slaughter of the Assyrians is
corroborated by Herodotus. But all
that Herodotus says (History, II, 141)
is that when the Assyrians invaded
Egypt (not Palestine), they were defeated because field mice ate their
quivers and bowstrings. The mention

couraged resistance by promising, in the name of Jehovah, that Jerusalem would never be captured. Such a reversion to more primitive conceptions of religion was, of course, in complete contradiction to his whole view of life. Some scholars suppose that under the pressure of the crisis he must have succumbed to tribalistic emotion; others argue that the priestly chroniclers who invented the story of Jehovah's intervention would have been also capable of forging some prophecies to corroborate it.

The next seventy-five years were a period of moral degeneration. Isaiah apparently left no influential disciples; and as Judah had to continue paying tribute to Assyria, there was a general loss of faith in Jehovah. Under the long rule of Hezekiah's son Manasseh, the national god had to make room for the Assyrian sun god, worshipped in the form of a horse-drawn chariot at the entrance of the Jerusalem Temple, and for the Babylonian star cult. Not content with propitiating these foreign deities, the King encouraged the traditional fertility cults, revived infant sacrifice, and was an enthusiastic addict of witchcraft, divination, and necromancy. Nationalistic sentiment seems to have been kept alive, however, by the priests of Jehovah's Temple, who were known as Zadokites from their presumed descent from the priest appointed by Solomon. In 625, successful rebellions by the Medes and the Chaldeans started the disintegration of the Assyrian empire. Judah, then ruled by King Josiah, quickly asserted her independence, and this was followed by a religious reformation designed to re-establish the pure Mosaic tradition. The program of the reformers was the Book of Deuteronomy, which was supposed to have been written by Moses and was allegedly discovered in the Jerusalem Temple in 621.

We do not know the author or authors of Deuteronomy, but the book was obviously a product of the Zadokite hierarchy. Both its conceptions of Jehovah and its proposals for social reform were influenced by the rationalism and the radicalism of the prophets, but it continued to insist on the importance of ritual, and its main emphasis was still narrowly tribalistic. And although its program was in some ways remarkably humanitarian, it clearly reflected sacerdotal ambition; under the pretext of ending idolatry and re-

---

of mice has even caused some commentators to think of rats and there- fore of bubonic plague.

storing the religion of Moses, the priests of the Jerusalem Temple
proposed to establish a monopoly of religious worship and to subject the monarchy to theocratic supervision. They hoped to accomplish these purposes by putting into the mouth of Moses a detailed
legislative program under the assumption that he must have been
able to foresee whatever problems would be faced by the Israelites
six hundred years after his death. The result might be described
as the world's first utopia.

The central doctrine of Deuteronomy is that loyalty to Jehovah
will be rewarded with tribal prosperity. By a curious compromise
with monotheism, he is depicted as being a universal as well as a
tribal god, but it is explained that he has assigned other deities to
other peoples and is himself the god only of Israel. The Jehovah
cult must, however, be purged of all extraneous elements and centralized in a single place; in other words, he can be worshipped
only in the Jerusalem Temple, and all other shrines must be destroyed. This injunction could be justified on the ground of the
traditional association of the village shrines with the fertility festivals, but it also suited the interest of the Zadokites. Most of Deuteronomy consists of a long series of divine commandments in
which elaborate ritualistic regulations and taboos are mingled with
civil and criminal legislation. If, and only if, Israel obeys all these
commandments, she will become a great nation. Thus, the Assyrian domination is attributed by implication to the corruption of
the Mosaic Jehovah cult by Palestinian practices.

Which elements in the Jewish ritual code were formulated at
this period, and which were added after the Exile, cannot be determined with any certainty. But there can be no doubt that Deuteronomy fixed the general pattern for post-Exilic Judaism. Most
of its prescriptions and taboos originally had some magical meaning, and were partly of Canaanite and partly of desert origin; a
few were deliberately added in order to differentiate Jehovah-worship from the fertility cults. But they now lost their initial significance and became simply expressions of loyalty to Jehovah. Animal sacrifice, for example, which had first meant eating the god,
then feeding him, and then placating him, now became a sign of
gratitude. Similarly, the three main agricultural festivals, based
originally on imitative magic, were retained as occasions for
thanksgiving, and in accord with the Jewish emphasis on history

rather than on nature, the most important of them, the passover celebration in the spring, became a commemoration of the exodus from Egypt. Thus ritual retained its central position in the Jewish religion; but it was now purged and sterilized and attributed solely to the arbitrary will of Jehovah. Post-Exilic Judaism, worshipping a god who had ordered his chosen people to circumcise their male children, keep holy the Sabbath day, and adhere to an elaborate code of dietary and clothing restrictions, was in considerable danger of degenerating into a system of mechanistic rules for the maintenance of ritual purity. The final result was very remote from prophetic spirituality and universalism, but as a device for conserving the ethnic identity of a weak people in a hostile world, Jewish ritualism was a work of genius.

In its social legislation Deuteronomy put forward a remarkably bold program of economic radicalism, though it seems to have been too utopian for effective enforcement. Endeavoring to prevent the enslavement of the peasants and re-establish the original equality of Mosaic pastoralism, the reformers prohibited usury and decreed that every seventh year all the slaves should be set free and all debts remitted. It would perhaps be captious to complain that these humanitarian regulations applied only to members of the Israelite community: non-Israelites should be treated charitably, but could be required to pay usury and could be permanently enslaved. But Deuteronomy showed its tribalistic double standard in commanding the Israelites to exterminate the previous inhabitants of Palestine (an injunction that had fortunately become inapplicable by the time the book was written) and forbidding them to intermarry with foreigners on the ground that they might then be tempted to worship foreign gods. Thus purity of worship was to be protected by means of purity of race. Through its influence on Protestant Christianity, the Book of Deuteronomy has been, in fact, the *fons et origo* of racist doctrine in the whole Western world.[5] Judicial powers were to be entrusted to the priests of the Jerusalem Temple, the death penalty being prescribed for

---

[5] Racism developed chiefly in Protestant nations who based their religion on the scriptures rather than on the traditions of the Church, and originated with colonizing groups in contact with non-European races, such as the Dutch and the English. Catholic nations like the Spanish, Portuguese, and French have been refreshingly free from such manifestations of the "chosen people" mentality.

anybody who refused to accept their decisions; and if Israel ever decided to set up a monarchy, the king was not to accumulate wealth or maintain a harem and was to make a copy of the Book of Deuteronomy and "read therein all the days of his life." [6]

For a brief period the Deuteronomist program, at least in its religious aspects, was enforced by the royal government. With puritan zeal King Josiah set out to extirpate all foreign cults and every aspect of the Israelite religion that had been derived from the fertility rituals. He destroyed the horses of the Assyrian sun god and the altars for the worship of the stars; broke in pieces the pillars and poles of the Baalim, desecrated all the local shrines, and ended worship anywhere but in the Jerusalem Temple (thereby creating a large body of unemployed priests); [7] abolished child-sacrifice and ritualistic homosexuality and prostitution; and prohibited witchcraft and divination and all other magical practices and all worship of family idols. According to the enthusiastic commendation of the Book of Kings, "like unto him was there no king before him, that turned to the Lord with all his heart, and with all his soul, and with all his might, according to all the law of Moses; neither after him arose there any like him." [8]

The Deuteronomic reformation, through its influence on Christianity, was an important factor in the shaping of the Western tradition, and some of its moral aspects have had lasting results. [9] In spite of its limitations, there can be no doubt that it represented an advance toward the rationalization of human life. In this and other respects it resembled the Protestant movement of sixteenth-century Europe. The Protestant leaders were, in fact, strongly influenced by Deuteronomy; and in so far as one of their main purposes was to remove from Christianity all elements derived from the pagan background, they had a similar objective. Certain modern writers have been tempted to romanticize the fertility cults, chiefly because they sanctified sexuality, and have drawn a contrast between the license of the mother goddess and the patri-

[6] Deuteronomy, xvii, 19.

[7] According to Deuteronomy, they were supposed to be given positions in the Temple; but the Book of Kings makes it plain that the Zadokites refused to make room for them.

[8] II Kings, xxiii, 25.

[9] Deuteronomy, for example, pro-hibited homosexuality primarily because of its association with the fertility cults. Thus this taboo, which has deeply influenced the moral standards and legal codes of all Western countries, originated in the battle between Jehovah-worship and the Baal cults.

archal severity of Jehovah. It is true that the Deuteronomic reformation, like all the movements of the Axial Period, meant the loss of the sense of unity with nature that had been the essence of primitive religion. Divinity, localized in the Temple or removed to heaven, no longer pervaded the natural world. After the reforms of Josiah, the Israelite peasants could no longer enjoy their agricultural festivals at their traditional shrines; and as sacrifice was permitted only in the Jerusalem Temple, family meals were secularized, and when animals were slaughtered for food, the blood was no longer offered to the god in accord with the old desert ritual. But in spite of its sexual orgies, neolithic religion by no means resulted in gaiety and exuberance. One must not forget the human sacrifices, the eunuch priests slashing themselves with knives during mass frenzies, the pervasive fear of any failure of nature's vital forces, of famine and pestilence, and of the spirits of the dead.

In its immediate results, however, the reformation was a tragic disappointment. Deuteronomy had promised that Jehovah would protect his people if they obeyed his commandments; but it quickly became apparent that his ways were still mysterious. Perhaps, as the Book of Kings suggested, he was still angry because of the sins of Manasseh. The fall of Assyria was followed by a revival of Egyptian ambition, and in 609 Pharaoh Necho invaded Palestine. Trusting in Jehovah's assistance, Josiah went out to oppose him and was immediately killed in a skirmish at Megiddo.[1] Meanwhile, the Chaldeans of Babylon, under King Nebuchadnezzar, aspired to replace the Assyrians. After defeating the Egyptians in 605, they became the dominant Near Eastern power, and Judah was again in danger of losing her independence. This crisis ended all enthusiasm for the Deuteronomic movement. Josiah's successors reverted to paganism, and a new prophet, Jeremiah, revived the doctrines of Hosea and Isaiah.[2]

---

[1] Contrary to his usual practice, the contemporary author of the Book of Kings was too stunned by this event to offer any explanation. Four centuries later, when that dreary rehash of Jewish history, the Book of Chronicles, was written, a reason was discovered. Necho was obeying orders from Jehovah; Josiah was informed of this fact, but refused to listen.

[2] Three minor prophets also belong to this period. Zephaniah and Habakkuk were concerned with the sins of Israel and the threat of foreign conquest; Nahum wrote a stirring poem about the fall of Assyria.

In the career of Jeremiah the conflict between magical and spiritual conceptions of religion, the main theme of all the prophetic writings, reached its highest intensity. None of the prophets was more consistently contemptuous of ritualistic observances; none of them was more convinced that religion meant an attitude of mind and heart which would manifest itself in submission to the divine will and in charity toward other human beings. Jeremiah actually denied that God had ever given Moses any commandments about burnt offerings and sacrifices, and affirmed that when men became truly religious they would no longer have any use even for the Ark of the Covenant.[3] Repudiating all considerations of practical power politics and diplomacy, he looked forward to a new world order when all the people of Israel would have a direct knowledge of the divine will. "After those days, saith the Lord, I will put my law in their inward parts, and write it in their hearts; and will be their God, and they shall be my people. And they shall teach no more every man his neighbour, and every man his brother, saying, Know the Lord: for they shall all know me."[4]

This wholly spiritual and mystical theology, with its utopian implications, ran counter to Israel's nationalistic convictions, and Jeremiah lived in isolation except for a few disciples, without wife or family, and was frequently in danger of murder or execution. Resembling Hosea in his sensitive and emotional temperament as well as in his beliefs, he sometimes longed for death and cursed the day that he was born. In an intimate spiritual autobiography often imitated by later mystical writers, he recorded his bitter complaints against the God who had singled him out to be the spokesman of unpopular truths. Even more than his predecessors, Jeremiah felt his prophetic intuitions as an external force taking possession of his personality against his will. When he resolved to deny his mission and remain quiet, "his word was in mine heart as a burning fire shut up in my bones, and I was weary with forbearing, and I could not stay."[5]

The situation in which Jeremiah was called upon to proclaim what he believed to be the divine will was similar to that which had confronted the more militant and self-confident Isaiah. Once again it was obvious to any rational observer that the Jewish king-

[3] Jeremiah, vii, 22; iii, 16.   [5] Jeremiah, xxiii, 9; xx, 9, 14.
[4] Jeremiah, xxxi, 33–4.

dom was about to be conquered by a foreign power, and once again priests and prophets were arousing popular hopes by declaring that the Jews were the chosen people of Jehovah, and that if he were propitiated by rituals and sacrifices, he would always protect the Temple and the sacred city in which he lived. Like his predecessors, Jeremiah insisted that these hopes were false, that the Jews had forfeited any right to divine protection by their idolatrous religious practices and their failure to achieve economic and social justice, and that Babylonian conquest was in accord with the divine will. "Thus saith the Lord of Hosts, the God of Israel . . ." he declared; "I have made the earth, the man and the beast that are upon the ground, by my great power and by my outstretched arm, and have given it unto whom it seemed meet unto me. And now have I given all these lands into the hand of Nebuchadnezzar the king of Babylon, my servant. . . . Therefore hearken not ye to your prophets, nor to your diviners, nor to your dreamers, nor to your enchanters, nor to your sorcerers, which speak unto you, saying, Ye shall not serve the king of Babylon: for they prophesy a lie unto you." [6] By combining his rationalist and universalist intuitions and his moral idealism with his belief in a personal God directing earthly events, Jeremiah arrived at the conclusion that submission to Nebuchadnezzar was a religious duty and that resistance was actually wrong—a doctrine which he continued to assert with the utmost courage at a time when almost all his fellow countrymen were engaged in a heroic struggle to defend their independence.

The first Babylonian conquest occurred in 597. Defeating the Jewish army and seizing the city of Jerusalem, Nebuchadnezzar deported about three thousand families to Babylonia, including the King and most of the aristocracy and also (as a method of imposing military disarmament) the ironworkers and other craftsmen, but left behind a younger son of Josiah as puppet monarch. But Jewish patriots did not give up hope, and some years later, encouraged by support from Egypt, they precipitated a general revolt against Babylonian domination. This seems to have been accompanied by a revival of the Deuteronomic movement; masters freed their slaves, but (according to Jeremiah) immediately re-

---

[6] Jeremiah, xxvii, 4–10.

enslaved them when the arrival of an Egyptian army made them confident of victory. In 586 Nebuchadnezzar reconquered Palestine, captured Jerusalem after a long siege, destroyed the whole city, including the Temple that had been Jehovah's residence since the time of Solomon, carried away to Babylonia another group of exiles, and made Judaea a province of his empire. Throughout the siege of Jerusalem, Jeremiah, faithful to his anti-patriotic convictions, continued to proclaim the religious duty of surrender. The government put him in prison, but was too respectful of his claims to divine inspiration to have him executed. It is understandable that Nebuchadnezzar should have given him money and invited him to settle wherever he chose. Jeremiah elected to stay in Judaea, but was coerced into going to Egypt with a party of refugee patriots who believed that it would be advantageous to be accompanied by a prophet of Jehovah, even though they paid little attention to any of his prophecies. He apparently died in Egypt a few years later.

The prophetic movement continued for two or three more generations after the Babylonian conquest, but with a new emphasis. The earlier prophets had predicted catastrophe as a punishment for Israel's sins; now the catastrophe had happened, and the Exilic prophets were chiefly concerned with maintaining the faith of their compatriots by promises of rapid restoration. God would quickly reveal his power by destroying the heathen empires, re-establishing his chosen people in Palestine, and bringing about universal peace and justice. These men preached more idealized conceptions of God than their predecessors, but they had a much less realistic grasp of world affairs. Exilic brooding over the sufferings of Israel and the promise of divine redemption induced a feverish apocalypticism that could no longer distinguish clearly between fact and symbol. In the end, their faith in divine intervention, now not for the punishment of Israel but for her transfiguration, proved to have no rational basis, and this recognition brought the prophetic movement to an end. When it became evident that no rapid national restoration would occur, Judaism reorganized its beliefs and institutions under the guidance not of the prophets, but of the Book of Deuteronomy.

The Exilic prophets were largely concerned with the problem

of suffering. As long as the gods had been regarded as amoral natural forces, it had been easy to account for human misfortunes. But the prophets had affirmed high moral standards and attributed them to Jehovah, and had at the same time elevated him to the position of ruler of the world. This presumably implied that suffering was a punishment for wickedness. As Israel had suffered more acutely than most other peoples, it followed that she must have offended God more grievously; and a consciousness of sin, very different from the happy naturalism pervading the earlier Old Testament narratives, became a part of the Jewish temperament and was afterwards transmitted to Christianity. Yet it was not easy for the exiled Jews to believe in Jehovah's justice, especially when they contrasted their own unhappy fate with the prosperity of so many gentile races; and theologians continued to search for more adequate explanations. The more nationalistic of them insisted that the balance would shortly be redressed and that Israel, through divine intervention, would not only be restored, but would also wreak vengeance upon her enemies. One outstanding figure, more faithful to the prophetic spirit, abandoned any attempt to equate sin and punishment and attributed to Israel a mystical mission of atonement.

The most influential spokesman of exilic nationalism was the priest Ezekiel, a member of the Zadokite hierarchy who was among the group deported to Babylonia after the conquest of 597. Narrowly sacerdotal in his view of life, he was obsessed with the need for purity, which he interpreted largely in ritualistic rather than ethical terms. It was perhaps because of his Temple background that his religious intuitions came to him mainly in the form of elaborate visual images rather than of political and moral imperatives. The first half of his writings presents the reasons for Jehovah's punishment of his chosen people. Ezekiel's catalogue of Israel's misdeeds conforms to the prophetic pattern, but emphasizes the worship of false gods and the lack of ritual purity more than the oppression of the poor, and displays little of the burning anger against social evils that had inspired Amos and Isaiah. For the Babylonian exiles the sins of Israel had become historical matters which had to be remembered in order to justify God's actions, not because of any present relevance. Ezekiel describes Jehovah's indignation by narrating a series of symbolic actions and visions of supernatural creatures that seem to have been suggested by the statuary in the Babylonian temples.

Ezekiel's main importance was that he gave specific content, in apocalyptic form, to the hope of national restoration. By divine intervention, he declares, the two Israelite kingdoms will one day regain possession of Palestine and be reunited. Enemies will come against them from the north, "all of them riding upon horses, a great company, and a mighty army," but God will smite them with "an overflowing rain and great hailstones, fire and brimstone." "And seven months shall the house of Israel be burying of them, that they may cleanse the land." "Thus will I magnify myself, and sanctify myself; and I will be known in the eyes of many nations, and they shall know that I am the Lord." [7] Ezekiel ends his book with a detailed description, prosaically meticulous, of the new Temple that will one day be built in Palestine. He does not share the prophetic faith in universalism. Jehovah will demonstrate his power to other nations, but he remains primarily the tribal god of the Israelites, who alone are holy enough to worship him. His sanctuary, in fact, would be polluted by the presence of any non-Jew; one of the sins that had provoked the Babylonian conquest was that "aliens, uncircumcised in heart, and uncircumcised in flesh," had been admitted to the Temple. [8] Ezekiel insists, moreover, even more rigidly than his predecessors, on a direct correlation between virtue and prosperity, and applies it not to nations, but to individuals. Denying the traditional doctrine that the sins of the fathers are visited upon the children, he declares that virtuous individuals can always count on divine protection, while the wicked will always be punished. [9]

This individualistic conception of divine justice was presumably a reflection of growing moral enlightenment, since it showed a recognition that guilt was personal and not tribal. But the assumption that God would protect those who obeyed his will was, of course, derived from tribalistic modes of thought, and the attempt to reconcile it with enlightened moral ideals led to a confusion from which the Western world has never wholly extricated itself. On the one hand, the supposition that God would reward the

---

[7] Ezekiel, xxxviii, 15–22; xxxix, 9–12.

[8] Ezekiel, xliv, 7.
[9] Ezekiel, xviii, 1–32.

virtuous with prosperity led to the conclusion that prosperity must be a proof of virtue. Thus, the Ezekielian doctrine, confirming the self-righteousness of the wealthy and adding insult to the injuries of the poor, provided a mythical support for social and economic conservatism throughout all subsequent Jewish and Christian history. On the other hand, the palpable fact that virtue and piety were not really correlated with prosperity led finally, in some forms of post-Exilic Judaism and in Christianity, to the projection of rewards and punishments into an afterlife.

The epoch in which this doctrine was first formulated seems also to have produced the most eloquent and passionate indictment of it in ancient literature. For the Book of Job was probably written early in the sixth century.[1] Its author is unknown, and may have been non-Jewish. He makes no specific references to Israelite history and religion, and his monotheistic deity is wholly unconnected with Jehovah. Displaying a tough-minded rationalism that seems more Greek than Jewish, he ignores the whole prophetic attempt to justify God's ways to man in terms of an enlightened morality. He was unquestionably the greatest poet and the most learned man of all the Old Testament writers, and if his book ends with a vast cosmic question mark, it cannot be said that any subsequent generation has come closer to solving the mystery he propounded.

Making use of a folk tale long current among the pastoral tribes on the edge of the Arabian desert, the author presents a man who has always lived uprightly but who, nevertheless, is abruptly tumbled from the height of prosperity into the most abject misery. Three friends suggest to him, tactfully at first but finally with brutal frankness, that he must have offended God; but Job continues to insist that he has not sinned more than other human beings and does not deserve his misfortunes. In recounting his virtues (in Chapter xxxi) he claims not only that he has refrained from all wrong actions, but also that he has always been generous to his servants and to strangers and the poor, displaying a moral sensitivity that cannot be matched even in the writings of the prophets.

---

[1] For the date of the Book of Job, see Robert H. Pfeiffer: *La Problème du Livre de Job*. Pfeiffer assigns it to this period largely because it seems to have preceded, and had a profound influence upon, Deutero-Isaiah. Most other scholars have preferred a later date.

Meanwhile, wicked men continue to flourish, thus demonstrating that God deals out rewards and punishments with no regard whatever for human merits. At the end of the poem, God appears in a whirlwind and rebukes Job for questioning his ways. Describing how he has imposed order upon chaos in the natural world, setting the stars in their places, controlling the winds and storms, and creating all the wild animals, he shows that his power and wisdom are beyond human comprehension. Man can only recognize his own weakness and accept his fate without either protesting against it or attempting to justify it. Thus, the God of the Book of Job is identified with the natural universe and has none of the ethical qualities that the prophets sought to attribute to him. Yet in presenting God as the sole creator of the universe and depicting the creation as a work of the divine intelligence, this unknown writer is more explicitly monotheistic than any of his predecessors and also comes close to the conception of scientific law; and his descriptions of the natural order display both a sense of wonder and an eye for concrete and specific detail unsurpassed in any ancient literature except that of Greece.

Although the Book of Job was outside the main stream of Jewish thought, its conception of the deity apparently had a profound influence on the next of the major prophets, generally known as Deutero-Isaiah. This unknown writer, who was responsible for Chapters x1–1v of the Book of Isaiah, appeared late in the sixth century, during the period when the Babylonian Empire was succumbing to the growing power of the Persians under King Cyrus. Combining the nationalism of Deuteronomy and Ezekiel, the universalism of the first Isaiah, and the spirituality of Hosea and Jeremiah, and adding a new interpretation of world history which is peculiarly his own, he should probably be regarded as the culminating figure of the whole prophetic line. His writings consist of one long rhapsodic paean of rejoicing over the coming restoration of Israel, expressed with a continuous poetic intensity not equaled by any other Biblical writer. Through his faith in divine intervention he was stimulated to propound a theology that was to have a lasting influence on the course of Western thought. On the mystical level his mind operated with such white-hot fervor that apparently incompatible doctrines became indissolubly welded into a new unified world-view. His God is at one and the same time the cosmic creator of the Book of Job, the moral judge of the prophets, and the national deity of the Israelite people, and the contradictions among these different conceptions are transcended by means of the myth of the suffering servant, which afterwards developed into the central mystery of Christianity.

Although the earlier prophets had regarded Jehovah as the ruler of all peoples, they had not grasped all the implications of this belief; the transformation of a tribal into a universal deity was too revolutionary to be completed immediately. But by identifying the prophetic God with the God of Job, Deutero-Isaiah became perhaps the first religious teacher in world history whose monotheism was fully explicit and consistent. With the evident conviction that he has made a new discovery, he affirms again and again the uniqueness of the God of Israel. "I am the first, and I am the last; and beside me there is no God. . . . Is there a God beside me? Yea, there is no God; I know not any. They that make a graven image are all of them vanity. . . . Before me there was no God formed, neither shall there be after me. I, even I, am the Lord; and beside me there is no Saviour." [2] And as Jehovah is the only God, it follows that all men everywhere must eventually come to worship him and obey his will. Deutero-Isaiah is still a Jewish nationalist in that he believes Israel to be Jehovah's chosen people, bound to him by the mutual love and loyalty of an indissoluble marriage; but Israel has a universal mission to exhibit the divine love to all nations. "Unto me every knee shall bow, every tongue shall swear." "I the Lord have called thee in righteousness, and will hold thine hand, and will keep thee and give thee for a covenant of the people, for a light of the Gentiles; to open the blind eyes, to bring out the prisoners from the prison, and them that sit in darkness out of the prison house." [3]

This mission, however, can be accomplished only through suffering. Denying any correlation between misconduct and punishment, but insisting nevertheless that the course of history is infused with a divine purpose, Deutero-Isaiah affirms that Israel has received "double for all her sins," and that her function is to make atonement for other peoples. This novel conception is conveyed through descriptions of the "righteous servant" whose role in the

---

[2] Isaiah, xliv, 6–9; xliii, 10–11.   [3] Isaiah, xlv, 23; xlii, 6–7.

divine scheme is that of a universal scapegoat, and who may partially have been suggested by the fertility myths of a dying and reviving god. Applied afterwards to the founder of Christianity, it seems originally to have referred to the whole Israelite community. "Surely he hath borne our griefs, and carried our sorrows," men will say about him; "yet we did esteem him stricken, smitten of God, and afflicted. But he was wounded for our transgressions, he was bruised for our iniquities; the chastisement of our peace was upon him; and with his stripes we are healed. All we like sheep have gone astray; and we have turned every one to his own way; and the Lord hath laid on him the iniquity of us all." [4] By rationalistic standards this myth of redemption through vicarious suffering must remain a mystery. But it pointed toward a fundamental transvaluation of values by which the importance of a community would no longer be measured by its material power; and its spiritual efficacy in giving meaning to historic processes and promising to redeem mankind from its burden of guilt has made it one of the fundamental religious doctrines of the Western world.

Of all the Old Testament writers, Deutero-Isaiah has had the most pervasive and lasting influence on the Western mind. His God, at the same time the maker of the universe, the moral judge, and the loving protector of his chosen people, became the God of Christianity, while the rhapsodic phraseology with which he proclaimed God's power and mercy and the mystical meaning of suffering is familiar to all Western peoples. Yet none of the Old Testament writers seems to have more completely misinterpreted contemporary events; on the level of historic fact Deutero-Isaiah was the victim of a tragic delusion.

The rise of Persia seemed to the exiled Jews to be an indication that the expected day of national deliverance was close at hand, and some of them even expected that Cyrus would acknowledge the supremacy of Jehovah. This delusion seems to have been caused by Cyrus's policy of conciliating conquered peoples by professing to be a worshipper of their tribal deities. For Deutero-Isaiah, Cyrus is the agent of God—not, like earlier conquerors, for the punishment of the chosen people, but for their salvation.

---

[4] Isaiah, xl, 2; liii, 4–6.

Having destroyed the power of Babylon, he will re-establish the Jews in Palestine and rebuild the Temple, and all men everywhere will recognize that this is Jehovah's doing. Cyrus is Jehovah's shepherd, his anointed one, entrusted with a mission to inaugurate the reign of universal justice. "I will go before thee, and make the crooked places straight," Jehovah is represented as saying to Cyrus; "I will break in pieces the gates of brass, and cut in sunder the bars of iron; and I will give thee the treasures of darkness, and hidden riches of secret places, that thou mayest know that I, the Lord, which call thee by thy name, am the God of Israel. For Jacob my servant's sake, and Israel mine elect, I have even called thee by thy name; I have surnamed thee, though thou hast not known me." [5] Deutero-Isaiah even pictures the desert being transformed into a garden and a highway built across it for the triumphal march of the exiles from Babylonia back to Jerusalem.

Everything that actually happened after the rise of the Persian Empire proved merely an anticlimactic negation of these prophetic hopes. Cyrus captured the city of Babylon in the year 538, and with the approval of the Persians a few of the exiles then returned to Judaea and assumed leadership over the peasants and herdsmen who had continued to live there under Babylonian rule. A Jewish community was reconstituted under the leadership of Zerubbabel, a prince of Davidian descent, and another Temple was built in Jerusalem. But Palestine continued to be controlled by the Persian authorities, who showed no inclination to regard Jehovah as more than a minor tribal deity; and the new Temple was so inferior to its Solomonic predecessor that it appeared "in comparison of it as nothing." [6] Meanwhile, the inhabitants of the former northern kingdom of Samaria, who had not come under the influence of the prophetic movement, adhered to a more primitive form of the Mosaic religion; they refused to co-operate with the Judaeans and eventually built a separate temple for themselves on Mount Gerizim. Two hopeful prophets, Haggai and Zechariah, encouraged the efforts of the Jews by assuring them of divine assistance; and Haggai, the more nationalistic of them, predicted that Jehovah would soon manifest his power by overthrowing the horses and chariots of the heathen kingdoms and making Zerub-

---

[5] Isaiah, xlv, 2–4.　　　　　　[6] Haggai, ii, 3.

babel the promised Messiah.[7] During a period of disorder following the accession of Darius to the Persian throne in 522, Zerubbabel was secretly crowned king. But Darius quickly asserted his
authority, and Zerubbabel was removed by the Persians, by either
death or imprisonment, after which the Davidian dynasty disappeared from history.

This disillusioning fiasco virtually ended the prophetic movement. The struggling and impoverished Judaean community, led
by Zadokite priests but largely composed of ignorant peasants and
herdsmen, bore little resemblance to the sacred nation, chosen by
Jehovah to reveal his power to all peoples, that had been envisaged
by both Ezekiel and Deutero-Isaiah; and most of the exiles preferred to stay in Mesopotamia or Egypt, where their opportunities
for achieving wealth and comfort were much more substantial.
Three later figures were afterwards added to the prophetic canon,
but none of them displayed the spirituality and universalism of
their great predecessors. Malachi, directly reversing the doctrines
of Amos and the first Isaiah, insisted that the Jews could count on
Jehovah's assistance if they worshipped him with the correct rituals; Obadiah delivered a nationalistic diatribe against the neighboring people of Edom; and Joel was inspired to make apocalyptic
predictions of a coming day of doom because of a plague of lo-
custs.

---

[7] Haggai, ii, 21–3.

3

Post-Exilic Judaism

A fter the Babylonian captivity, Judaism produced no creative thinkers comparable to the major prophets, and showed a strong tendency to revert to its tribalistic origins.[1] Recognizing that Israel had no immediate prospect of regaining her political independence, and relegating the Messianic hope to some indefinite future, the priestly leaders of the Jewish people concentrated on the task of preserving their ethnic and religious identity and preventing assimilation. The Jews must remain sharply distinguished from all gentile races; and as Judaism could no longer be based on a territorial state, it could survive only through a strict adherence to the laws of its national religion. Thus Israel built around herself a hard, bitter shell of ritualism and intolerance. Forgetting the prophetic insistence that God was responsible for evil as well as for good, and ignoring Deutero-Isaiah's intuition that the mission of the righteous servant could be fulfilled only through suffering, theologians continued to affirm the tribalistic doctrine that virtue would always be rewarded and wickedness punished. Israel as a nation would eventually triumph over her enemies, and (as Ezekiel had declared) Israelite individuals who obeyed the law could count on divine protection. The constantly reiterated predictions in post-Exilic literature of divine rewards for the chosen people, coupled with vengeance upon sinners, often displayed an attitude of sanctimonious self-righteousness in which hate was a conspicuous element.

---

[1] Most Jewish historians have a much higher opinion of the post-Exilic period. See especially Louis Finkelstein: *The Pharisees.*

Yet though the intolerance of post-Exilic thought marked a degeneration from the rational insights and the moral grandeur of Amos and the first Isaiah, it must always be remembered that Israel could not otherwise have preserved for posterity the monotheism and ethical idealism that were her great contributions to Western thought. In spite of its tribalistic rigidity, Judaism continued to believe in a Messianic mission to the gentiles, and thus still held the seeds of universalism encapsulated within it. The form of the belief varied widely. Sometimes the Messiah was envisaged as an earthly conqueror, a king of the Davidian line who would make Jerusalem a world capital, though—with a significant reminiscence of the original democracy of the Mosaic tribes—he would appear not on horseback or in a chariot, but riding humbly on an ass.[2] For other writers the Messiah would be a supernatural being, an agent of Jehovah who would establish universal peace and justice, not by material power, but through spiritual influence. But in all its manifestations the Messianic myth meant that historic processes were moving toward a new and higher order, and that the Jewish people had been chosen by God to bring redemption to all mankind. Representing a paradoxical fusion of high ethical ideals with faith in supernatural intervention, and of universalism with tribalism, the myth had become, in fact, the keystone of the whole structure of Judaism, for it provided a reason for continued fidelity to Jehovah in spite of so many disappointments. It was thus a striking illustration of the fact that, while a people cannot survive without strong tribal loyalties, such loyalties cannot remain vital and persistent unless they are justified by some universal faith.

A large part of the Jewish people remained residents of foreign countries. The exiles deported by Nebuchadnezzar had not been enslaved, and in the business civilization of Mesopotamia some of them quickly rose to affluence, while Egypt became another important center of Jewish life. The Persian Empire maintained peace and order over a vast area of the Near East for two hundred years, and Jews were soon engaging in commercial and industrial activities in many different cities and even rising to high positions in the royal bureaucracy. Thus Israel was already displaying her remarkable capacity for flourishing in an alien environment. That

---

[2] Zechariah, ix, 9.

Judaism was able to retain its identity in spite of the loss of its territorial base was due to the monotheism introduced by the prophets; prior to the prophetic movement Jehovah had been solely the god of Palestine, and it would have been impossible for the Jews to continue worshipping him on alien soil. But as a result of the prophetic movement, by a paradox that has continued for twenty-five hundred years to bewilder the gentile world, Judaism had become a potentially universal religion in spite of the fact that it still remained the faith of a tribal community. Although the Jerusalem Temple continued to be the center of the faith and the only place where sacrifices could be celebrated, Jews in other cities began to meet in synagogues for prayer, singing, and the study of the scriptures. And although the Deuteronomic emphasis on racial purity was never forgotten, gentiles could be adopted into the Jewish community if they were willing to repudiate all their previous connections and accept the whole Mosaic code. Throughout the next five hundred years, until the process was checked by the Christian schism, Judaism added appreciably to its numbers through the conversion of proselytes.[3]

The task of reorganizing the Jewish ritual code in order to make it more comprehensive and more rigid seems to have been first undertaken by exiled priests in Mesopotamia soon after the Babylonian conquest, and was continued after the rebuilding of the Temple. The laws attributed to Moses were considerably expanded, and the traditional folk legends about the creation of the universe, the Garden of Eden, and the early patriarchs were rewritten in order to give added emphasis to the importance of ritual. Sabbath-day observance, for example, was traced back to the beginning of time when God made the world in six days and then rested on the seventh. Even more explicitly than the prophets, these priestly legislators insisted that the Jews were the elect people of the one true God, all other gods being merely human inventions; but the chief mark of their election was that they had been entrusted with the ritual code that God had ordained for the maintenance of holiness and purity, and their mission to re-

---

[3] S. W. Baron (*Social and Religious History of the Jews,* I, 171) estimates that by the beginning of the Christian era nearly one fifth of the population of the eastern half of the Roman Empire was Jewish. Most gentile historians prefer a lower figure.

deem the gentiles was postponed to the Messianic age. The enlightened moral doctrines of Deuteronomy and the prophets were
never forgotten, and Judaism continued to be distinguished by its
high ethical and economic standards; but this renewal of ritualism
led inevitably to a superstitious and mechanistic emphasis on outward observances and on the letter as well as the spirit of the law.
Its chief significance, however, was that it prevented assimilation.
The Jews were set apart by such practices as circumcision and
Sabbath-day observance; they were strictly prohibited from marrying gentiles; and their elaborate dietary rules made it almost impossible for them even to eat with their non-Jewish neighbors.
While some of the taboos were of value in promoting cleanliness
and preventing infection, a large number had originated either in
magic or in the battle with the fertility cults. There was no rational basis, for example, for the prohibitions against mixing wool
and linen in the same garment and against seething a kid in its
mother's milk.

Little detailed information has survived about Jewish history
during the Persian period, the darkness being only partially lightened by the books of Ezra and Nehemiah. The Book of Ezra begins with a highly unreliable account of the rebuilding of the Temple and the conflict with the Samaritans—the interest displayed by
the Persian government and the number of returning exiles being
vastly exaggerated—and then describes how the scribe Ezra came
from Mesopotamia to Palestine early in the fifth century and persuaded the Jewish community to adhere more strictly to the Mosaic
law. A generation later, Nehemiah, a Jew who had risen to a high
position at the Persian court, secured a commission as governor of
Judaea, in which capacity he was able to impose a number of
ritualistic and economic reforms. Ezra remains a shadowy figure,
of doubtful historicity; but Nehemiah is self-revealed in his own
memoirs as a high-minded, honest, and efficient public official
with a marked tendency to be complacent about his own virtues
and quick-tempered with his opponents. The main concern of both
Ezra and Nehemiah was to prohibit intermarriage, Jews who had
taken gentile wives being required to divorce them. Two charming
works of fiction show that this severity was not universal. The Book
of Ruth gives an idealized portrait of a Moabite woman who is
represented as an ancestor of King David (Deuteronomy had

strictly prohibited any relationship with Moabites, who could not even be admitted as proselytes), while the Book of Jonah depicts God as concerned about the salvation of the great gentile city of Nineveh.

Ezra and Nehemiah seem to have had considerable success in reshaping the Judaean community to accord with the Exilic ideal of a priestly nation. The Mosaic code apparently prevailed even among the rural population, to judge from the absence of any reference to fertility cults in post-Exilic literature. But Nehemiah's attempts to enforce the radical economic program of Deuteronomy were soon abandoned, and the third century saw a growth of sharp class divisions similar to those which had helped to evoke the prophetic movement. The form of government was theocratic,[4] and the Zadokite priestly families, who (under Persian supervision) combined religious and political authority and were supported by taxes and Temple offerings, became the nucleus of a landowning aristocracy that grew increasingly secular-minded and responsive to alien currents of thought. Its worldly philosophy of life was exemplified in much of the Book of Proverbs. Meanwhile, many of the middle class, especially in the cities, retained a stricter fidelity to the national religion, for which reason they became known as Hasidim ("the pious"). The Zadokite families, in spite of their growing skepticism, continued to control the Temple services, but Hasidic doctrines were propagated in the synagogues by professional students and exponents of the scriptures, generally referred to as scribes. In the second century Hasidicism led to the formation of a pietistic organization, the Pharisees, while the rival sect of the Sadducees represented the point of view of the priestly aristocracy.

In so far as they denounced the sins of the upper class and preached a God of justice and purity, the Hasidim were the heirs of the prophetic movement, but they never recaptured either its burning anger against economic exploitation or its contempt for merely ritualistic observances. Because the ultimate authority now belonged to the officials of a foreign empire, conscientious Jews, able to do little to improve conditions, could merely put their trust in a god of vengeance. Reflecting an impotent middle-class resentment against aristocratic license, Hasidic doctrine was perme-

---

[4] The word "theocracy" was first coined by the Jewish historian Jose- phus in the first century of our era to describe post-Exilic Palestine.

ated with a fatalistic sense of dependence upon a deity who could be trusted, sooner or later, to punish sin. It preached an ethic of pacifism and non-resistance, but this was predicated not on any mystical faith in the virtues of turning the other cheek, but on the assurance of supernatural intervention. The chief Hasidic documents were the Book of Chronicles, a reinterpretation of Jewish history which surpassed even the Book of Kings in its insistence that God had always come to the aid of pious rulers, and the Book of Psalms. More than most other sections of the Bible, this collection of religious poetry has had a continuing appeal to all Western peoples; and when its authors glorify divine omnipotence or celebrate the great events of Jewish legend, they often reach the same note of cosmic wonder as the Book of Job and the major prophets. But it must be added that the main theme of the entire book, repeated in all but a dozen of its hundred and fifty chapters, is the certainty that God will reward the righteous who obey the law, and the rewards expected by the psalmist usually include the promise of destruction for his enemies. Some of the psalms express a tribalistic hatred of foreign powers; even the beautiful lament of the exiles "by the waters of Babylon," for example, concludes with the assurance that the daughter of Babylon will be destroyed. "Happy shall he be, that taketh and dasheth thy little ones against the stones." [5] But in nearly a third of the collection the "enemies" whose death the psalmist so confidently prays for and anticipates are not gentile nations, but individual Jews who do not share the religious convictions of the Hasidim. In the words of Psalm 58, "the righteous shall rejoice when he seeth the vengeance: he shall wash his feet in the blood of the wicked. So that a man shall say, Verily there is a reward for the righteous: verily he is a God that judgeth in the earth." [6]

The chief importance of the Hasidim in the history of religious thought is their adoption of several new doctrines that were afterwards incorporated into Christianity. Their insistence that God would always protect righteous individuals could be made plausible only if rewards and punishments were projected into an afterlife.

---

[5] Psalm 137, 9.
[6] The most extreme expression of pious hate is Psalm 109. See also 3, 5, 6, 7, 9, 13, 17, 18, 21, 23, 25, 27, 30, 31, 35, 38, 40, 41, 42, 43, 44, 54, 55, 56, 57, 59, 61, 64, 68, 69, 70, 71, 86, 92, 102, 119, 138, 140, 141, 142, 143.

The Sadducees, being endowed with privileges in this world and uninhibited about enjoying them, had no interest in immortality, and continued to deny it. But the Hasidim and their successors, the Pharisees, began to preach belief in a bodily resurrection and in heaven and hell. They also departed from strict monotheism by peopling the unseen world with a multitude of angels and by postulating the existence of evil spirits in revolt against God. The chief source of these new doctrines was the Zoroastrian religion, which had been adopted by the Persian monarchy in the reign of Darius.[7]

Zoroaster is the most obscure of the great innovators of the Axial Period. All the original written records of his teaching were apparently destroyed when Alexander's army burned the palace of the Persian kings at Persepolis in 330. The sacred book of the Zoroastrian religion, the Zend-Avesta, is a chaotic mass of fragments which seems to have been compiled from oral tradition early in the Christian era. Yet Zoroastrianism, though in a corrupt and partially paganized form, remained the official religion of Iran until it was conquered by the Mohammedans in the sixth century of our era, and has been preserved down to the present day by the Parsees, a small community of exiles who took refuge in the Indian city of Bombay. According to the most plausible interpretations, Zoroaster was born into an aristocratic family in the eastern part of Iran about 569. The Zend-Avesta records that at the age of thirty he rejected the traditional Iranian polytheism and began to seek religious illumination, and that at the age of forty, after numerous mystical experiences, he began to preach a new religion, his first convert being a chieftain named Vishtaspa. Vishtaspa can probably be identified with the Hystaspes who, according to Herodotus, was the father of King Darius.

Unlike any other Axial philosopher, Zoroaster explained suf-

---

[7] The Egyptian religion also had taught belief in immortality and in rewards and punishments in the next life. But both the pre-Exilic prophets and the Hasidim (unlike the Jewish aristocracy) were always vehemently opposed to Egyptian influences. Presumably this was partly because of memories of the Mosaic period and partly because of a conviction that the Egyptian emphasis on eternity was incompatible with the historical ori- entation of Jehovah-worship. When Isaiah accused the Jewish aristocracy of making a "covenant with death" and an "agreement with hell," he was probably referring to the alliance they had made with Egypt. The prophetic and Hasidic movements, however, were less hostile to Mesopotamian influences, and Hasidic belief in evil spirits was partially derived from Mesopotamian mythology.

fering and evil by affirming a dualistic view of the universe. The forces of the supreme god, Ahura-Mazda (or Ormuzd), stood for truth, justice, and light, and were arrayed in cosmic battle against the powers of darkness and the lie, headed by Ahriman (or Angra Mainyu). At the end of time, Ahura-Mazda and his angels and archangels would win a final victory over Ahriman and his daevas (demons), after which the righteous would be received into paradise and the wicked confined in hell. Man was free to choose between good and evil, and could most effectively aid in the victory of Ahura-Mazda by practicing the virtues of truth, justice, courage, and industry, and by the constructive activities of an agricultural and pastoral life ("Whoever cultivates the corn cultivates righteousness," said Zoroaster; "he follows the Mazda-worshipping religion with a thousand beasts, and strengthens it with ten thousand sacrifices").[8] Thus, the Zoroastrians preached a pure, virile morality, with the promise of rewards in an afterlife. Repudiating all forms of magic and idolatry, they adopted light as the chief symbol of the good, and worshipped Ahura-Mazda by tending perpetual fires in shrines open to the sky.

As can be seen from the later chapters of the Book of Daniel and from a number of subsequent documents, including especially the Christian Book of Revelation, the Zoroastrian world-view was incorporated into the Jewish religious tradition with relatively little change in spite of its discrepancies from Mosaic and prophetic doctrine. Originating as the creed of the conquering aristocracy who created the Persian Empire, Zoroastrian dualism was transformed into a consoling promise of divine vengeance for oppressed classes. In the writings of the prophets, Jehovah's day of doom had meant foreign conquest or some other natural catastrophe; and though the nation, Israel, would survive and eventually rise to world-leadership, there was no promise of immortality for individuals. But later Hasidic thought shifted the whole historic process to another plane and gave it a new dimension; the day of doom, now postponed to the end of time, would be followed by the immortality of the pious and the damnation of the wicked. And whereas the prophets had always insisted that every event, evil as well as good, was the work of Jehovah, in later Hasidic literature evil

---

[8] Ralph Turner: *The Great Cultural Traditions,* I, 368.

was attributed to demons, so that God's benevolence toward the righteous was saved by means of an apparent sacrifice of his omnipotence.[9] Satan had first appeared in the Bible (in the books of Job and Zechariah) as a kind of roving investigator or prosecuting attorney in Jehovah's world, being apparently modeled after the police officials known as the King's Eyes and Ears, who were sent out by the Persian monarchy to test the loyalty of its satraps. Through the influence of Zoroastrian dualism he acquired the characteristics of Ahriman, the prince of lies, was gradually elevated into the chieftain of a body of rebel angels, and was then identified with the snake who had tempted Eve in the Garden of Eden.[1] This meant that the human race had been corrupted at its origin—a conception which an ex-Pharisee, Paul of Tarsus, developed into the Christian doctrine of original sin.

The growing tension in Judaean society led finally to an explosion early in the second century. By this time the Persian Empire had been overthrown by Alexander and replaced by a group of Hellenistic monarchies, Palestine being a part of the kingdom of Syria under the Seleucid dynasty. Hellenistic culture then began to percolate into the Jewish community, and was enthusiastically adopted by members of the Jerusalem aristocracy, even including some of the priests. A gymnasium was erected for the celebration of Greek games, and a number of young men even underwent an excruciatingly painful operation in an effort to conceal the fact that they had been circumcised. In the year 168, however, King Antiochus Epiphanes made the mistake of trying to Hellenize Judaea by force; the Jerusalem Temple was rededicated to the worship of Zeus, and the observance of all Jewish rites was prohibited under penalty of death. This precipitated a popular rebellion, headed by a provincial priestly family, the Hasmonaeans,

---

[9] According to II Samuel, xxiv, 1, "The anger of the Lord was kindled against Israel, and he moved David against them to say, Go, number Israel and Judah." (Presumably taking a census was considered as sinful because it was a step toward the creation of a bureaucratic state on the Egyptian model; its purpose was to facilitate taxation and forced labor.) I Chronicles, xxi, 1, which was prob-ably written in the third century, declares, on the other hand: "Satan stood up against Israel, and provoked David to number Israel."

[1] After the triumph of Christianity, Satan was also identified with the gods of paganism, and thus assumed the appearance of the horned god who had been mankind's first and most lasting object of worship.

the ablest of whom was Judas Maccabaeus, and supported by the more moderate of the Hasidim. The more extreme members of this group, on the other hand, continued to trust in God rather than in human effort, and mostly preferred martyrdom to effective resistance; even when they took up arms, they allowed themselves to be massacred in preference to violating the ritual code by engaging in military activity on the Sabbath day. But the Hasmonaeans aroused the nationalistic feelings of the peasants and, after a quarter of a century of almost constant fighting, succeeded in winning the independence of Judaea. Simon Maccabaeus, the only survivor of the Hasmonaean brothers, then ousted the Zadokite high priest and assumed the office himself. His son and successor, John Hyrcanus, added the title of king and considerably enlarged the Jewish state by military conquest. He subjugated the Samaritans, destroying their temple on Mount Gerizim, and took possession of Galilee to the north and Idumaea to the south, not only compelling alien groups to conform to the Jewish law, but also forcibly circumcising them. But after they had achieved power, the Hasmonaeans quickly forgot their religious convictions and allied themselves with the worldly and rationalistic Sadducees, and their policies led to murderous civil wars in which thousands of Pharisees were massacred. Hasmonaean kings continued to rule Palestine until it was absorbed into the Roman Empire in 63 B.C.; but their ambitions, cruelties, and debaucheries had long since forfeited the support of all pious Jews.[2]

Two Biblical documents, the books of Daniel and Esther, reflect popular sentiments during the Maccabean period, and are significant chiefly for their feverish and virulent nationalism. Daniel is a Hasidic manifesto, expressing the conviction that God will always come to the aid of pious Jews who obey the law. A series of stories, placed during the period of the Babylonian captivity, tells how Daniel and other exiled Jews are several times in danger of death because they refuse to violate the dietary code or worship idols, but are always miraculously preserved, whereas enemies of the Jewish people are destroyed. The story of the lions' den, for

[2] Alexander Jannaeus, king and high priest from 104 to 78, was probably the most depraved of these descendants of the Maccabean brothers. Josephus describes how on one occasion he caused eight hundred of his Pharisee opponents to be crucified and then had their wives and children butchered while he enjoyed himself with his concubines before their eyes.

example, ends with an account of the lions killing Daniel's opponents, along with their wives and children. The later chapters of the book, written in that apocalyptic form which had now become one of the most popular methods of Jewish religious expression, describe the Hellenistic monarchies and the career of Antiochus Epiphanes, and conclude with predictions of the resurrection, the last judgment, and the Messianic age. Esther, on the other hand, is the product of a wholly secular tribalism, unredeemed by any note of religious idealism. The book does not even mention God or the ritual code, and Esther is represented as entering the harem of a gentile king, concealing her nationality, and ignoring the dietary rules without any suggestion that this may mean the loss of divine protection. Thanks to Mordecai's able leadership and Esther's physical charms, the Jews not only save themselves from destruction; with the approval of the Persian authorities, according to the book's complacent conclusion, they are also allowed to slaughter no less than 75,800 of their opponents.[3]

Even after the establishment of Roman rule, nationalistic sentiment remained a vital force in Palestine, especially among the Galilean peasants, despite the fact they had not been assimilated into the Jewish community until the reign of John Hyrcanus. But the disappointing outcome of the Maccabean wars tended to corroborate those interpretations of the Messianic hope which, like the Book of Daniel, expected its realization by supernatural means. While the wealthy Sadducees adapted themselves to Roman civilization, as formerly to Hellenism, the Pharisees continued to adhere strictly to the law and to await divine intervention. About two centuries after the advent of the Maccabees, the Messianic hope was restated in a more spiritual form by Jesus Christ. The Christian Church was strongly influenced by Pharisaism, but condemned its self-righteousness and its excessive legalism, reaffirmed the prophetic doctrine that God required love and charity rather than ritualistic observances, and adopted Deutero-Isaiah's conception of

---

[3] The Book of Judith, included in the so-called Apocrypha, was probably written by a pious Jew as a response to Esther. Like Esther, Judith uses her physical beauty to save the Jews, assassinating their enemy, the Assyrian general Holofernes. But, un- like Esther, Judith is able to do so without entering a gentile bed or violating the dietary laws. On the contrary, it is because of her strict adherence to the laws that she is able to escape from the Assyrian camp with the head of Holofernes.

the suffering servant. In this form the Messianic myth took possession of the whole Western world, which thus came to believe, as
all the prophets had predicted, that it owed its salvation to the
people chosen by Jehovah. But, by a tragic paradox, Israel was excluded from this consummation of her national hope.

Through the triumph of Christianity the whole Jewish religious
system, which had gradually evolved during the thousand years of
national life that had elapsed since the time of Moses, was incorporated into Western culture with only minor changes and omissions. The deity worshipped throughout the Western world was the
God of Moses, of the prophets, and of the Hasidim, being at one
and the same time the creator of the natural universe, the author of
the moral law, and the protector of his chosen people. But because
the Jews were supposed to have broken the covenant originally
made in the desert at the foot of Mount Sinai, the promises made
to the Hebrew tribes, it was declared, had been transferred to the
Christian Church. Like the prophets, Christians believed in the
unity of the cosmos and of mankind and in a God of holiness and
and righteousness; but, like the authors of Deuteronomy and the
Psalms, they believed also that God rewarded the righteous and
punished the wicked. Christianity retained a sense of both collective
and personal dependence upon divine guidance and protection in
this world, believing that events were directed by a just deity who
might chasten his chosen disciples for their own good but would
never wholly abandon them. Any discrepancies in the allotment of
prosperity and suffering in this life would be wiped out on the
day of judgment, when (as Zoroaster had affirmed) the righteous
would be rewarded in heaven and the wicked condemned to
eternal punishment.

Similarly, the ethical standards of the Western world were largely
of Jewish origin. Though it rejected the ritual code (with the exception of Sabbath-day observance), Christianity retained the Jewish moral code, including especially the Ten Commandments. The
official sexual rules of Western society, for example, were derived
mainly from the laws attributed to Moses, reflecting the relatively
strict standards of patriarchal pastoralism and its battle with the
fertility cults. The numerous conflicts and contradictions within
the Western ethical system were all present in Judaism, and were
caused by the adoption into Christianity of the entire Jewish na-

tional heritage and the assumption that every part of it was a product of divine inspiration. Thus, Christianity became a religion of both war and peace, both conservatism and radicalism. Christians could imitate the bellicose and bloodthirsty nationalism of the Mosaic tribes, the Davidian monarchy, and the Book of Esther, or they could advocate the pacifism of Jeremiah and the non-resistance of the Hasidim. Like Ezekiel and the authors of the Psalms, they could trust in God to remedy injustice; or, like Amos and the first Isaiah, they could denounce the wickedness and covetousness of the upper classes and make revolutionary demands for a new social order.

The most significant feature of the Jewish heritage, however, was its view of history. Other ancient peoples had believed in a golden age, but had always located it in the past at the beginning of time. Israel alone looked forward to a golden age in the future and interpreted history as a meaningful and progressive movement toward this Messianic consummation. Originating in tribalistic loyalty, and reflecting the determination of a weak people to retain its identity in spite of conquest and enslavement, the Messianic hope was given universal scope by the prophets and became the end toward which all earthly events were moving. In various manifestations, religious and secular, spiritual and materialistic, it became one of those dynamic social myths which give meaning and direction to human life and which have more influence on human action than any rational philosophy. Unless its importance is understood, the development not merely of the Jewish people but also of the whole Western world becomes unintelligible.

The essence of the Messianic myth is the belief that in some future epoch, after some kind of revolutionary transformation, the conflict between freedom and order will be transcended. Ethical and political conflicts will cease, and external discipline and authority will no longer be necessary, because all men will act freely and spontaneously in harmony with the divine will and with each other. Jeremiah gave the myth its first clear expression when he looked forward to an age when all men would know God directly. "After those days, saith the Lord, I will put my law in their inward parts, and write it in their hearts; and will be their God, and they shall be my people. And they shall teach no more every man his neighbour, and every man his brother, saying, Know the Lord:

for they shall all know me." [4] Thus mankind would regain the primal innocence of the Garden of Eden, and the end of history, like its beginning, would be the realization of perfect freedom.

In its cruder, more literal forms, the Messianic hope has always had a special appeal to oppressed and rebellious classes. Throughout the history of Christianity a series of radical movements have expected its speedy realization by supernatural means. It was the Second Coming of the early Christians, the Age of the Holy Ghost of the medieval mystics, the Millennium of the Saints which inspired the Calvinists and the revolutionary sects of the Reformation and which the Puritans hoped to achieve in New England. In a secularized form, divorced from religion and read into the structure of the material universe, the same hope haunted the imagination of the eighteenth-century *philosophes* with their confidence in the spontaneous virtue of the natural man, exploded into history in the Jacobin dictatorship of the French Revolution, and developed into an even more potent social force, associated with atheism but still recognizably derived from the prophecy of Jeremiah, in the Marxist doctrine of a coming kingdom of freedom when the state would wither away and all men everywhere would live in concord and equality.

By rationalistic standards, of course, the realization of any such dream is forever impossible; and as a long series of utopian experiments have demonstrated, any attempt to achieve it can lead only to some form of totalitarian tyranny. Some degree of conflict between spontaneous impulse and social discipline is inherent in all civilized living. But myths transcend rational analysis, and their true function is not to provide a program for action, but to express the ethical affirmations by which a civilization is animated. Implicit in the Messianic myth is the belief in an ideal harmony of freedom and order, an ideal standard of justice reconciling all divergent interests. According to the religious beliefs of Western man, conflicts between individuals and the group, or between groups and the totality of mankind, are caused solely by human imperfection, not by any inherent necessity. The harmony of the whole may be incapable of perfect realization in this world, but it nevertheless serves as a standard for the judgment of all social or-

---

[4] Jeremiah, xxxi, 33–4.

ganization, thus making individual freedom possible and subordinating power to higher values. This faith in an ideal harmony, mythically embodied in the will of a righteous God, was the most important Jewish contribution to the Western heritage. Incorporated into Christianity, it was afterwards broadened and liberalized by fusion with the Hellenic concept of natural law and given a new ethical meaning by the teaching of the gospel.

PART III

HELLENISM

PART III

HELLENISM

A t about the time when the Hebrew tribes were moving into Palestine, another group of migratory peoples, whose original home had been somewhere in the plains beyond the Danube, was taking possession of cities and farmlands in Greece and the Aegean islands and reducing the previous inhabitants to serfdom. Hellenic culture, like that of Judaism, originated in a series of invasions followed by a fusion of races and religions. The two cultures developed along sharply divergent lines partly because of differences in the initial process of amalgamation.

Unable for several centuries to achieve mastery over the Canaanites and the Philistines, and afterwards in constant danger of attack from Egypt or Mesopotamia, the Israelite herdsmen and peasants clung to their ethnic identity and to the Jehovah cult on which it depended, hoping that their God would protect them as long as they obeyed his commandments. The Aryan conquerors of Greece, on the other hand, were a warrior people equipped with horses and chariots who quickly established themselves as a ruling aristocracy throughout the mainland and then turned to piracy and further expansion overseas. Serenely confident of their own powers and right to dominance, uninhibited in the expression of their emotions and unafraid of anything in nature, they displayed none of the Jewish conviction of human dependence upon divine omnipotence. Controlling subject races throughout Greece and the Aegean islands, they were not bound by rigid tribalistic loyalties, but developed an ethos founded on personal ties and the individualistic pursuit of glory. Trusting in their own strength, and convinced that the gods did not help the weak, they worshipped beings akin to themselves who differed from men only in their superior powers and in their freedom from death. Their religion was essentially a deification of man's natural vitality, and expressed a realistic acceptance of the limits of human life rather than any hope of magical or supernatural protection. The ultimate authority over the universe belonged, in fact, to impersonal fates whose decisions were binding upon men and gods alike.

Thus, the ruling aristocracy during the period of the conquest developed an initial inclination toward a humanistic ethos. Virtue meant the cultivation of typically human qualities rather than submission to biological forces or to the will of deities that transcended nature. This attitude was afterwards diffused, largely through the

147

poems of Homer, among the main body of the Greek people and
was the main source of the unique qualities of Hellenic civilization.
Making possible both the enjoyment of natural existence and a
realistic recognition of human limitations, and promoting confidence in man's capacity to guide his own life by rational thought,
it gave Hellenism its astonishing psychic health, its freedom from
either moralistic or intellectual repressions.

Almost equally important in the evolution of Hellenism was the
influence of the environment. In the Orient, geographic factors had
led to the growth of bureaucratic despotisms by which the state was
embodied in a god-king and remained a remote and mysterious
force for the mass of the people. In Egypt and Mesopotamia only a
centralized power could control irrigation, while the Hebrew tribes
were compelled to surrender their freedom to the Davidian monarchy by the need for military security. In the Greek peninsula, on
the other hand, with its mountainous interior and long, indented
coastline, difficulties of communication impeded political unification; nor was this necessitated either by economic need or by any
threat of foreign invasion. Thus, Greece remained divided into a
multitude of small communities, most of which quickly turned to
the sea and lived largely by foreign commerce. The city-state became the main Greek institution and focus of loyalty, making
possible a wide range of political experimentation, and leading
finally to the growth of democracy. Unlike other conquering tribes,
the Greeks did not abandon the primitive republican spirit of their
pastoral background after they had become a settled civilized people; they moved toward wider diffusion of political power rather
than its concentration in a single god-king.[1]

---

[1] The environment must have contributed to the unfolding of the Hellenic spirit in other and more subtle
ways. With its dry and rocky soil,
Greece offered men little ease or comfort, and only a rugged and combative
people could cope with such unfriendly
conditions. But it was a land of incomparable beauty, and its mountains and seas were bathed in a light
that gave all objects an exceptional
sharpness and distinctness of outline
and produced colors of an extraordinary range and intensity. In such a
country it was easy to believe that

divine powers were immanent in nature and that they were to be apprehended primarily in aesthetic rather
than in moral terms. And where all
visual impressions were so vividly defined, men were impelled to develop
a corresponding mental clarity. The
atmosphere of Greece was conducive
to conceptual thinking.

The influence of geography on national character is a little-explored
field of historical investigation, though
a beginning has been made by Ellsworth Huntingdon in *Civilization and
Climate* and other books. Despite ex-

Thus, an analysis of the early development and the geography of Greece can partially explain the special quality of her civilization; yet no combination of historical and environmental interpretations can wholly account for the Greek achievement. After every possible material cause has been taken into account, there remains something elusive and apparently almost miraculous which is recognizable in every typical creation of the Hellenic genius and which no later people has been able wholly to recapture. Perhaps the most pervasive characteristic of the Greek mind was its unfailing eye for the whole, manifested both in the capacity for philosophical generalization and in the unity and harmony of its works of art. To what genetic factors can one attribute this innate compulsion to find in all phenomena an underlying order; or the exuberant imagination that poeticized every object in the natural world with mythical inventions; or the intuitive good taste that purged the polytheistic heritage of all its elements of grossness and savagery and make it a vehicle for expression of humanistic values?

Worshipping gods who were essentially projections of human skill and beauty, the Greeks believed that man was closest to divinity when he was most completely himself.[2] Confidence in man and cultivation of man's natural capacities were always the hallmarks of the Greek spirit. This sharply distinguished Greek culture from that of the peoples of the Near East, where transcendental religiosity led both to superhuman aspirations and to conduct that was often subhuman. For this reason Greek literature and art were always focused on human beings and displayed, in fact, no interest in their physical environment except as the scene of human

tensive ethnic and cultural changes, the inhabitants of different countries often display similar characteristics for thousands of years. The modern Greeks have most of the qualities of their classical predecessors, except—alas!—their genius. The ancient inhabitants of France and Spain, as described by Roman historians, strongly resembled the modern French and Spaniards. The practical and empirical inclination of British thought showed itself as early as the fourth century in the heresies of Pelagius. It is difficult to account for such continuities unless one attributes them to the influences of geography and climate.

[2] Skeptics have always liked to ridicule the anthropomorphism of popular religion. "God made man in his own 'image," it has been said, "and man made haste to repeat the compliment." But when the gods are not seen in human terms, they become subhuman. Perhaps the greatest achievement of the Greeks was to humanize their gods. Herodotus noticed that the Greeks differed from Orientals in "believing the gods to have the same nature with men" (I, 131).

activities. Yet though the early Greeks were not concerned with
nature apart from man, they regarded man as a wholly natural being and supposed that his ideals of beauty and morality and justice
were inherent in his natural development and therefore in accord
with the processes of the natural world, instead of being derived
from some transcendental source. The ideal was implicit in the
actual, and nature was infused with divinity. This was an eternal
reality underlying and giving meaning to sensuous phenomena, and
man could apprehend it in moments of vision. Whereas Judaism
had found its standards in the gradual unfolding through history
of the will of God, Hellenism affirmed a timeless perfection immanent, though not fully realized, in the natural world.

This confidence in nature sustained Hellenic civilization during
its golden age of the sixth and fifth centuries, and led to the concept of natural law, the supreme Greek contribution to the heritage of human thought. By virtue of this faith in nature as both
normative and intelligible, the Greeks laid the foundations of
Western political and philosophical theory and of Western science.
The faith was manifested in the production of works of art representing the ideal forms immanent in human bodies rather than
static and transcendental abstractions; in the composition of a
literature whose outstanding quality was its simple and direct recognition of the realities of human experience; in the development of
naturalistic systems of thought based on the assumption of the
unity and uniformity of the cosmos; and in the search for ethical
and political principles by which order, instead of being maintained
by force or by the authority of a god-king, could be harmonized
with the free expression of man's natural vitality. As the aristocratic governments set up during the conquest gave place to the
democracy of the city-state, everything in nature and society was
laid open to rationalistic investigation, and trust in human instinct
and intelligence was carried to its ultimate limits.

But while the Greek achievement remains an astonishing proof
of the potentialities of individual freedom and rational thought,
the quick descent of Greek society into decadence after the fifth
century illustrates the dangers of any attempt to maintain social
order by reason alone, without the support of a system of myths.
For while the Greeks continued to follow the guidance of nature,
they gradually lost the belief that it was infused with ideal forms

and principles of justice. The concept of natural law ceased to be normative and became purely descriptive. As thought became less religious and more consistently rationalistic, natural morality became identified with the pursuit of self-interest, while art no longer attempted to reveal the divine powers immanent in nature, but degenerated into realism. With the erosion of the mythical basis of society, the turbulent individualism that had always characterized the Greek people was no longer held in check by any communal loyalties. The city-state system was destroyed by internal and external conflicts, and was not replaced by any broader form of integration based on a faith in universalism. Eventually order could be maintained only by submission to force, without democratic participation, and sensitive persons began to turn away from social life and seek salvation in private philosophies. This state of political disintegration lasted through the long period of the Hellenistic and Roman empires.

Hellenism might have retained its vitality if it had preserved its original happy confidence in nature and had succeeded in combining it with a religious universalism. Instead, there developed a spiritual counter-movement, beginning with Orphic mysticism and culminating in the philosophy of Plato, which turned away from nature as a realm of illusion and imperfection and affirmed that the ideal forms that gave it beauty and significance existed, independently of matter, in a transcendental realm of abstract ideas. Greek thought had always been non-historical, lacking the concept of progress in time toward some future goal. With Plato and his successors, ideals were removed not only from history but also from nature, and were transferred to an unseen eternal world of which this world was merely an imperfect copy. Man could achieve goodness, justice, and beauty not through the natural unfolding of his personality, but by imitating a transcendental and unchanging pattern of perfection. With this repudiation of its original naturalism, the Greek mind lost its aesthetic and intellectual creativity. Hellenism degenerated into a petrified culture devoted to copying the achievements of the past.

This Greek experience suggests that social order and cohesion cannot be preserved without a belief in values and ideals that cannot actually be deduced from nature by reason alone, even though they may be regarded as immanent in the natural world and identified with natural law. Without such a belief, the movement toward individualism and rationalism, when carried to its logical conclusions, leads inevitably to the breakdown of society. This dilemma first became apparent toward the end of the fifth century B.C. At that time the fundamental problems confronting any rationalistic civilization were, for the first time, fully explored, and the answers given to them by different Greek thinkers have had an enduring influence on all subsequent Western thought and culture.

I

The Foundation of
Greek Civilization

Our earliest written source of Greek history, the Homeric epos, although probably not composed in its present form until the ninth or eighth century, describes conditions of about the year 1200, and its essential accuracy has been remarkably confirmed by archaeological discoveries. Homer depicts most of the Greek mainland as controlled by a warrior aristocracy, variously known as Achaeans, Argives, and Danaans, who appear to have come down from the north not many generations earlier and ended the domination previously exercised by the Minoan rulers of Crete. Thus, Homeric society was in some ways similar to that of Western Europe immediately after the dissolution of the Roman Empire; like the Goths and the Franks, the Achaeans were a barbarian people who took possession of a long-established civilization. Except in Crete, however, their arrival does not seem to have been followed by the destruction of the Minoan cities; and although there was a marked cultural decline, there was no sharp break in cultural continuity. It is therefore probable that they achieved control of Greece not by outright conquest, but by a process of gradual infiltration, perhaps coming first as mercenaries and then seizing power and legalizing it by marrying Minoan heiresses.[1]

---

[1] The Cretan city of Knossos, which had apparently been the capital of a Minoan empire, was burned about the year 1450; but there is no archaeological evidence of destruction elsewhere. Two kinds of script, known as

153

In the Homeric period a supreme king was ruling at Mycenae in the Peloponnese while subordinate chieftains held authority elsewhere.[2] But the Achaeans had not forgotten their original pastoral individualism; and the kings, whose primary function was to provide leadership in war, were not despots on the Oriental model, but were expected to seek advice from their leading vassals. As has often happened during periods of disorder, the loyalties that maintained social cohesion were personal rather than tribal or religious; and Achaean adventurers would often leave their homelands and enlist in the service of powerful princes elsewhere in return for protection and economic support. The peasants and slaves, on the other hand, had no rights whatsoever, and were rarely mentioned in the Homeric poems except as examples of human misfortune. During times of peace, not even the chieftains were above working with their hands on their estates (Odysseus, for example, built his own house), but their favorite activity was war, and its chief purpose was plunder.[3] Piracy was a respectable occupation, and groups of Achaean adventurers delighted in raiding wealthy communities in Egypt and the islands (Egyptian records of a slightly earlier period complained of attacks by "people of the sea") and carrying

---

Linear A and Linear B, have been found in the Minoan cities. In 1953 an English amateur archaeologist, Michael Ventris, succeeded in decoding Linear B, which turned out to be an early form of Greek, written not in the alphabet that the Greeks borrowed from the Phoenicians several centuries later, but in characters adapted from the Minoans. This must have been the language of the Achaeans. Linear A, which has so far remained untranslatable, presumably represented the original Minoan language. Apparently the Achaeans took over the Minoan cities as going concerns and employed Minoan scribes to keep their records.

[2] Surrounded by mountains on three sides and overlooking the whole plain of the Argolid, the hilltop of Mycenae was well situated for defense. It was, moreover, in almost the mathematical center of Agamemnon's empire. But its continuing power to stir the imagination is due to Aeschylus.

The modern visitor can easily visualize Agamemnon riding home across the Argolid and Clytemnestra awaiting him at the entrance to the palace. Similarly, the acropolis of Thebes, the red earth of the Theban plain with which Antigone buried her brother, and the lonely crossroads on the way to Delphi where Oedipus killed his father have been infused with a lasting human significance by Sophocles.

[3] There is no standard practice for the transliteration of Greek names into English. Originally the Latin forms were regularly used. During the past century there has been a gradual shift to the Greek forms. It is now customary to speak of *Odysseus* instead of *Ulysses*. On the other hand, *Ajax* still has the preference over *Aias*, and *Achilles* never becomes *Achilleus*. I have adopted the most usual forms without trying to be consistent.

home golden and brazen goblets and tripods, tapestries and weapons of war, slaves and concubines. Social conditions were barbaric and anarchical, and life for all but the ruling aristocracy must have been miserable and uncertain. The Achaeans, however, respected certain simple rules of morality in their relations with each other; individuals were expected to show each other hospitality (which always included an exchange of costly gifts), to keep sworn promises, and to act generously toward suppliants instead of taking advantage of their weakness.

The expedition against Troy almost certainly occurred early in the twelfth century, although we may conjecture that its chief purpose was to win control of the sea route into the Black Sea rather than to recapture an abducted queen. The Trojans seem to have belonged to another group of Aryan invaders closely related to the Achaeans, and worshipping similar gods. Minstrels at the courts of Achaean kings must have soon begun to celebrate this ambitious enterprise; and though they undoubtedly embroidered the story with picturesque details, they are not likely to have fabricated the main personalities. What professional ballad-singer, called upon to glorify the achievements of the ruling families, would have invented so unkinglike a character as the foolish and irresolute Agamemnon, or would have described a sordid quarrel between the king and one of his leading vassals about the ownership of a concubine if this had not been supported by historic fact? But although the protagonists of the Homeric poems may well have been actual people, they and their children are the last individuals who can be named and identified for a period of about five hundred years. Not long after the siege of Troy, a new wave of invading Aryan barbarians, the Dorians, descended upon Greece, conquering the Peloponnese and ending the hegemony of Mycenae. A number of refugees, including both Achaeans and descendants of the earlier inhabitants, fled across the Aegean and took possession of the section of the coastline of Asia Minor that became known as Ionia. The whole Greek world then sank into a dark age, the history of which is almost completely unknown.

When Greece next emerged into the light of history, in the seventh and sixth centuries, it presented a very different picture. Kingship almost everywhere had faded into a mere ceremonial office, and the Greek world no longer recognized any single leader.

Although the sentiment of Panhellenic unity was maintained by means of the quadrennial athletic festival at Olympia, there was no effective political co-operation; and the Greek world was divided into a large number of independent city-states, the polis having replaced the individual chieftain of the Homeric period as the focus of loyalty. The pressure of an expanding population had led to a large-scale movement of overseas expansion, and Greek cities had been founded not only throughout the Aegean and the coast of Asia Minor, but also in the western Mediterranean, especially in Sicily and southern Italy. The states were mostly governed by aristocratic families who emphasized their purity of blood and claimed descent from the Achaean and Dorian conquerors, and ultimately from the gods; but many of them had begun to live by industry and foreign trade rather than by agriculture, and economic institutions were becoming more commercial and less feudal. Although some of the Dorian states, especially Sparta, maintained a rigid separation between the conquering race and their peasant subjects, elsewhere the two ethnic groups were becoming fused into a single Greek people, and a common culture was emerging from their diverse religious and social traditions. It was of considerable importance that the Aryan element in the cultural heritage remained dominant, so that the beliefs and mores introduced by the Achaean and Dorian conquerors were the foundations of the civilization of the polis, while the peasant and Minoan tradition, though never eliminated, became recessive. This was comparable to what had happened in Palestine, but it was brought about by a slow process of amalgamation, without the intolerance displayed by the priests and prophets of the Jehovah cult.

The Greek religion of the classical period was obviously a fusion of two elements which may be described as chthonian and Olympian, and which apparently corresponded to the original class-race division between the mass of the people and the Aryan aristocracy.[4] Chthonian religion was essentially a religion of the

---

[4] This interpretation of Greek religion was developed chiefly by Cambridge scholars, such as Jane Harrison. It has been restated for general readers by W. K. C. Guthrie in his *The Greeks and Their Gods*. Some classicists disagree with much of it, arguing that the contrast between Aryan and pre-Aryan beliefs has been exaggerated and that some features of the classical religion which have usually been regarded as Olympian, such as the worship of Pallas Athene, were actually of Minoan origin. The Minoans cer-

peasants, being directed, so to speak, earthward rather than sky-ward; it was certainly the older of the two elements, and its tra-ditional beliefs and cult practices, though not much in evidence during the classical period, proved in the end to have more vitality and more survival power. The Aryans, on the other hand, were a hunting and pastoral people who had turned to warfare as their main occupation, and they brought with them deities located in the sky rather than beneath the earth. In the course of their mi-gration they had stayed long enough beside Mount Olympus, in northern Greece, to regard its cloud-capped peak as the seat of heaven, but their deities were, in general, nomadic and therefore universal in scope, and were not restricted to particular shrines and localities. Chthonian religion was infused with a nocturnal spirit of fear and magic and mystery, while the daytime clarity and realism of Hellenism were associated with the worship of the Olympians. And while the chthonian religion emphasized the feminine principle, the Olympians were strongly patriarchal.

Thus, Greek religion was a palimpsest on which different char-acters were inscribed by different races, and through an analysis of ritual and legend it is possible partially to decipher the earlier layers and recapture the beliefs of the peasant society that flourished in Greece before the coming of the Achaeans. Like all the agricultural peoples of the neolithic age, the peasants worshipped a mother goddess, and their culture was pervaded with a religious reverence for femininity as the source of life. Archaeological remains make it evident that women enjoyed much more independence than their successors of the classical period. In the wall-paintings of the Minoan palace at Knossos, women are more prominent than men, and are shown engaging in bullfighting and other athletic exercises, usually with bare breasts, artificially narrowed waists, long flowing skirts, and an air of high sophistication.[5]

---

tainly worshipped female deities, but the supposition (maintained by Sir Arthur Evans, the excavator of Knos-sos) that these were all forms of the mother goddess may be untenable. This does not mean, however, that the religion of the peasants had not re-mained essentially neolithic up to the time of the Aryan invasions. The Minoans of the Cretan cities were a small sophisticated ruling class, and it is unlikely that they held the same beliefs as the mass of the population.

[5] Probably Minoan society cannot fairly be described as matriarchal, but its rules of descent were almost cer-tainly matrilineal. Authority seems to have been transmitted through the fe-male line, a chieftain acquiring his position by marrying the widow or

In honor of their mother goddess, the peasants engaged in fertility rituals, including mass intoxication, sexual orgies, and human sacrifice. They also revered the spirits of the dead and performed elaborate ceremonies at the tombs of departed heroes in order to avert their hostility and win their protection. The spirits were often believed to be re-embodied in the form of snakes, apparently because these animals came out of the ground and, owing to their capacity for shedding their skins, seemed to be immortal. This worship was largely a product of fear, since it was supposed that the spirits would be angered if their corpses were not given appropriate care. On the other hand, if they were pleased, they might show their beneficence by rewarding their worshippers with lasting prosperity. These two chthonian cult systems were closely connected, the earth being both the recipient of seed and the resting-place of the bodies of the dead; and besides being responses to man's economic anxieties, both of them implied some possibility of human deification. Through participation in the orgiastic fertility rituals, individuals could achieve a sense of possession by a divine spirit. The heroes whom they worshipped were, moreover, men who had in some sense become gods after death.

The beliefs of the Aryan invaders were relatively free from these irrational hopes and fears. There was an impassable barrier between earth and heaven; a man could not become a god, and when he died, his shade went down to the underworld of Hades instead of staying in his tomb to trouble or reward his posterity. The gods were not mysterious powers of nature with shifting con-

---

daughter of his predecessor. A careful study of the Homeric stories makes it evident that this was still partially true in the Achaean period, although the system was no longer understood when the poems were put in their final shape half a millennium later. The plot of the *Odyssey* depends on the fact that whoever marries Penelope will acquire the lordship of Ithaca, Telemachus being merely the heir of his father's personal possessions, while the marital misfortunes of the sons of Atreus may have reflected a conflict of institutions; the Achaean brothers, Agamemnon and Menelaus, have the patriarchal attitudes of the invaders, but their wives, the sisters Clytem-

nestra and Helen, behave with the independence of Minoan princesses. Phaeacia, as described in the *Odyssey*, is apparently an idealized Minoan community; Nausicaa, heiress to the throne, is interested in finding an attractive stranger for a husband; and when Odysseus comes to the palace, it is significant that he seeks protection from the queen rather than the king. A similar situation is implied in the story of how Oedipus, on becoming king of Thebes, marries Jocasta, who is the widow of the previous ruler. It is a plausible theory that the Achaean chieftains had actually first acquired power over Greece by marrying into Minoan ruling families.

tours, capable of embodiment in a tree or an animal, who must be worshipped with bestial rituals. On the contrary, they were sharply defined figures, conceived in the likeness of men and women; and the chief ritual they required was an offering of food in order that they might share in the feasting of their worshippers. There was little spirituality in the Olympian religion, and its moral doctrines were those to be expected of a race of conquering warriors; but at least it never sank below the human level. Pindar summarized its essential quality when he declared that "there is one race of men, one race of gods; both have breath of life from a single mother. But sundered power holds us divided." [6] This sense of kinship between gods and men, combined with a keen awareness of the barrier between them, was one of the foundations of Hellenic civilization.

After the Aryans took possession of Greece, they imposed their masculine sky deities on the subject population in somewhat the same fashion that the Israelites had imposed Jehovah-worship in Palestine. There was, however, one obvious and extremely important difference in the manner in which the two systems developed. The Israelites had found it necessary to preserve their ethnic identity, and Jehovah therefore remained solitary and inviolable. The Achaeans, on the other hand, had intermarried with the previous inhabitants of Greece, and they therefore attributed the same form of behavior to their gods. Instead of extirpating the peasant cults, they incorporated them into the Olympian religion and gave the peasant deities an Olympian clarity and humanity. When the Greek pantheon reached its full quota of inhabitants at some period after the invasions, it was a combination of Aryan gods and pre-Aryan goddesses. The three brothers, Zeus, Poseidon, and Hades, along with such other male figures as Hermes and Apollo, had been introduced by the invaders, but these were now living, not very harmoniously, with several forms of the mother goddess, whose characteristics had been portioned out among such diverse figures as Hera, Demeter, Pallas Athene, Artemis, and Aphrodite. Behaving like an Achaean king, Zeus had taken the goddess Hera as his official wife, but he had also been united with several other manifestations of the mother goddess who were wor-

---

[6] *Nemeans*, VI, 1, translated by R. Lattimore.

shipped at local shrines, and was therefore represented as indulging his fancy with a variety of concubines. His polygamous proclivities and stormy marital relationship with Hera were, no doubt, reflections of actual conditions in many Achaean households, while his rule over the gods, who acknowledged his supremacy but frequently tried to thwart his decisions, was an exact copy of Achaean kingship.

Meanwhile, the peasants still performed the traditional rituals at the innumerable local shrines; and—just as after the adoption of Christianity during the Dark Ages, and again among the Indians of Mexico and Peru a millennium later, pagan deities were transmuted into Christian saints—so the chthonian deities and dead heroes of the indigenous inhabitants were identified with the gods of the Achaeans. Zeus, in particular, was worshipped in many different forms at different places, appropriating the characteristics and ceremonies originally associated with local vegetation gods and dead chieftains and (in Jane Harrison's words) "trying to look as though he had been there all the time." In other instances, tomb rituals were not transferred to the new deities, but the original recipients were forgotten and were finally replaced by well-known figures of the heroic period, with the result that such men as Agamemnon, Achilles, and Hector were honored with religious rituals in various different parts of Greece. Much the same thing had happened in Palestine, but among the Jews the Jehovah cult was eventually purged of these extraneous additions; the Greeks, on the other hand, delighted in all this mythological confusion and felt no compulsion to reduce it to order and consistency. The bewildering complexity of Greek religion was indicated by Plato's summary of it as including "the institution of temples and sacrifices, and the entire service of gods, demigods, and heroes; also the ordering of the repositories of the dead, and the rites which have to be observed by him who would propitiate the inhabitants of the world below." [7] But though the Greeks failed to rationalize their religious ceremonies, they showed the essential quality of their genius by humanizing them. As their civilization developed and the Olympian beliefs spread to the peasant population, sexual orgies, human sacrifice, and the other savage elements of the neo-

---

[7] *Republic,* translated by Benjamin Jowett, p. 427.

lithic heritage gradually disappeared, and the traditional deities lost their original animal qualities and became projections of human beauty and intelligence. Only the persistence of certain epithets and associations revealed that Hera had originally been a cow and Pallas Athene an owl, and that the Zeus who was worshipped at certain shrines had at first been the spirit of a dead chieftain who was believed to be reincarnated as a snake.

The religion of the Greeks was never wholly humanized. Savage rituals lingered on in rural areas, such as the landlocked Peloponnesian province of Arcadia, and even reappeared in the most advanced states during times of crisis. It is startling to find that as late as the time of the Persian invasion, the Athenians were still paying divine honors to a sacred snake on the Acropolis and were still capable of reverting to human sacrifice. Despite the growth of rational thought during the fifth century, generals were still liable to be deterred from military operations by an eclipse of the moon or some other unfavorable omen. The chthonian cult of heroes who had achieved divine status through their extraordinary powers and their services to mankind always remained a most important part of the Greek religion, being exemplified particularly in the cult of Heracles. The Olympians, moreover, retained some of their original associations with aristocratic rule; and, standing for intelligence and sanity and the acceptance of limits, they could not satisfy the demand of frustrated and oppressed groups for redemption from suffering. It is significant that the class conflicts following the rise of the polis were accompanied by a resurgence of the chthonian fertility cults and chthonian mysticism in the worship of a different deity, the enigmatic Dionysus, god of all forms of intoxication.[8] The realism and sobriety of Hellenism were hard-won acquisitions always in danger of being swept away by outbreaks of religious emotionalism. One cannot appreciate the Greek achievement unless one recognizes the continuing strength of superstitious fears and mystical aspirations among the mass of the Greek people. In a country of such awe-inspiring grandeur, fear of the gods was indeed an understandable emotion. It was symbolic of the

---

[8] It was formerly supposed that the cult of Dionysus was introduced into Greece for the first time in the eighth century. The recent decoding of the Minoan script has revealed that he was already being worshipped in the pre-Homeric period.

whole Greek genius for humanizing nature that the cloud-capped
heights of Helicon and Parnassus were regarded as the homes not
of maleficent storm spirits but of Apollo and the Muses.

The Homeric epos played a decisive role in stabilizing and popu-
larizing the Olympian theology and the mores and view of life associated with it. For the classical Greeks, Homer was not only the
supreme poet, but also a religious and moral teacher who established the characters and functions of the gods; and his works
were studied almost as reverently as was the Bible among the Jews.
Composed at a time when the barbaric feudalism of the Achaean
age was being transformed into the commercial and democratic
society of the polis, the Homeric epos looked wholly to the past
rather than to the future, commemorating the values and social attitudes of the old warrior ruling class. Although a careful reading
of the poems shows that they by no means express full approval of
these values, they tended to confirm the aristocratic families in the
conviction that they alone were entitled to leadership. But their
main social importance was in diffusing relatively rational and enlightened conceptions of the nature of the gods and of their ways
of manifesting their power in the lives of human beings. The
civilization of the Greek golden age owed an incalculable debt to
the Homeric epos, which remains the one indispensable source for
the understanding of the Greek spirit.

The poems were composed somewhere in the region of Asia
Minor which had been settled by Achaean refugees at the time of
the Dorian conquest. Here professional minstrels must have continued, generation after generation, to recount the traditional stories
of the heroic age. Finally some new development, perhaps the institution in the island of Delos of a religious festival calling for
several days of continuous recitation, caused some of the stories to
be organized into two long epic poems. Most historians of literature
regard the poems as the end-products of many generations of
gradual accretion rather than as the compositions of a single man
of genius. Most poets and literary critics, on the other hand, prefer to believe in the existence of Homer, and on such a question
they probably speak with more authority. Certainly the *Odyssey*,
which is as carefully constructed as any modern novel, reads like
the work of a single mind; and although the narrative sequence of
the *Iliad* contains numerous inconsistencies, as though passages

originally composed for other purposes had been clumsily patched together, the poem has unity of a more important kind: of tone and mood. But while we may suppose that one great creator was responsible for the poetic genius of the poems, it is obvious that their philosophy and view of life were social products. The sophisticated *Weltanschauung* of the epos must have been the result of a long spiritual evolution.[9]

Anybody habituated to Judaeo-Christian conceptions of the deity is likely to have difficulty in understanding how Homer could have been regarded as a religious teacher. Religion in the Western world has become associated with feelings of awe and humiliation before a holy and omnipotent god who cannot, without blasphemy, be supposed to have any human weakness or imperfection. But the gods of Homer scarcely differ from his human characters except in being endowed with superior powers and free from death. They fight on opposite sides of the Trojan War, deceive and quarrel with each other, disobey the commands of their supreme ruler, and feel sexual desire and other human emotions. What is one to make, for example, of the episode recorded in Book XIV of the *Iliad*? After Achilles has quarreled with Agamemnon and retired from the war, his mother, the sea goddess Thetis, persuades Zeus to give some victories to the Trojans in order that the Greeks may realize that they are helpless without their leading warrior. This angers Zeus's wife, Hera, who hates the Trojans, and she resolves to distract her husband's attention from human affairs by arousing his sexual desires. Confronted by his wife in her best clothes and perfumes, Zeus assures her that she is more attractive than any of his mistresses (seven

---

[9] Such episodes as the building of the Greek wall and Helen's naming of the leading Greek warriors to Priam are out of place in a poem dealing with the tenth year of the war. But this does not prove that they were not written by Homer; other authors have been known to change their plans in the middle of composition. Acceptance of Homeric authorship does not mean, of course, that we have the poems precisely as Homer composed them. The text of the poems was not officially fixed until the sixth century, when Pisistratus, tyrant of Athens, ordered copies to be made. During the two or three centuries between Homer and Pisistratus there was plenty of time for interpolation. One obvious addition is the catalogue of the ships in Book II of the *Iliad*, which was apparently inserted largely to please the Boeotians and the Athenians, who are not mentioned elsewhere in the poem. Another is the description, in Book XI of the *Odyssey*, of celebrated sinners being punished in Hades; this does not correspond with the normal Homeric conception of the afterlife, and must have been derived from the doctrines of Orphic mysticism.

of whom he names to her), insists on going to bed with her immediately, and then falls asleep, thereby enabling the pro-Greek
faction among the gods to reverse the tide of battle. How could
deities who behaved in this fashion ever have been objects of
worship, and in what sense was the poet who told such a story a
religious teacher? A discussion of these questions will do much to
illuminate the whole genius of Greek civilization. Without a sympathetic appreciation of the meaning of the Homeric gods, in fact,
one cannot understand Hellenism.

The outstanding quality of the religion of Homer is its humanism. It contains nothing that degrades man to a subhuman level;
nor, on the other hand, does it encourage him to hope for deification. The whole chthonian element in the Greek religious heritage
is conspicuously absent. Although several embodiments of the
mother goddess are included in the Homeric pantheon, they have
lost all their original fertility associations and are portrayed in a
thoroughly Olympian spirit. Hera has become domesticated as
the wife of Zeus, Pallas Athene is the sexless and almost masculine
goddess of intelligence, and Artemis is the chaste patroness of wild
animals, with no traces of their common derivation from the great
peasant deity who had symbolized all the mysteries of reproduction. The Homeric heroes do not believe in imitative magic or in
animal gods, and they indulge in no bestial ceremonies. The chief
ritual is an offering of food to the Olympians, and the only instance
of human sacrifice—the slaughtering of Trojan prisoners at the funeral of Patroclus—is mentioned briefly and apologetically, with
no reference to its religious significance, and attributed to the
frenetic rage of Achilles. The author of the poems, in fact, can be
seen constantly softening the more savage elements in the legendary
material with which he is working; it is from other Greek authors
that we learn of such episodes as Agamemnon's sacrifice of his
daughter Iphigeneia when the Greek fleet was becalmed at Aulis
and Orestes' killing of his mother Clytemnestra at the command
of Apollo.

Nor does Homer describe any mystical or orgiastic experiences
in which men believe themselves to be possessed by the gods, or
recognize the chthonian cult of the spirits of the dead. His heroes
are not buried, but cremated; and though their shades survive in
some fashion in the underworld of Hades, to which they cannot be

admitted without the appropriate funeral ceremonies, they have no power over the living, and there is no reason to be afraid of them. In the Homeric world the death of the body means the end of all power of action; and the shades, as Odysseus discovers when he visits the underworld, spend their time regretting that they are no longer alive. As Achilles tells him, it is better to be the living slave of a poor man than a king in the world of the dead.[1]

Thus, one of the most significant consequences of the Homeric religion is a recognition of the limits of human life. It promises no magical control of natural phenomena and offers no supernatural compensation for misery and frustration. Its cosmology is, in fact, a magnified reflection of actual social conditions, the Olympians being larger versions of Achaean kings; and there is a sharp line of demarcation which cannot be crossed. A man cannot become a god,[2] and may expect to evoke divine anger if he tries to step beyond his status, just as a peasant cannot become a king. The notion that human beings must accept the limitations of mortality, and that any display of *hybris,* or indeed any excess of any kind, will evoke the *nemesis* of a corresponding retaliation, was deeply rooted in the Greek mind, and was one of the sources of the later Greek doctrine of natural law. But the gods are reasonable beings who act from intelligible motives, and they live in a daylight world in which all contours are clear and definite, without mystery and without any evocation of irrational hopes or fears. The Homeric heroes face this world without illusions, knowing that they must rely primarily on their own strength and capacity for endurance, and that the gods do not help the weak. Such a view of life could have originated only among a ruling aristocracy the members of which were free to express their feelings and use their power to the limits of their capacity and were not tempted to expect divine redress for their frustrations. We may conjecture that the Achaean warriors actually held the beliefs that Homer attributed to them, although

---

[1] Cremation had replaced burial sometime during the period of the Aryan conquests, presumably because migratory peoples could not continue to care for the tombs of their dead. Its effect, of course, was to put an end to the traditional fear of the spirits; after a corpse had been reduced to a handful of ashes, it could no longer be regarded as a threat to the living.

[2] In rare instances, however, men may become immortal. Menelaus, for example, wins this promotion because, as the husband of Helen, he is Zeus's son-in-law.

with more savagery and more superstition, and that their religion was afterwards refined and rationalized by their descendants in the Ionian cities.

How do the gods manifest their power in earthly affairs and in the minds of human beings? What events and what emotional states are attributed to divine influence? Such questions take us to the heart of any system of religious beliefs, which always derives its vitality from the conviction that certain human experiences are caused by the intervention of an external spiritual force. For the Jews, at least after the prophetic movement, the voice of God was identified with moral imperatives; his power was exercised in the punishment of sin and the protection of his chosen people. God was above the natural world, which had been partially corrupted by human disobedience, and manifested himself in events running counter to normal expectation, such as the destruction of the strong and the glorification of the humble and oppressed. But in the Homeric religion there is no separation between divinity and nature. On the contrary, the natural world is itself infused with divine powers, and the gods express themselves through natural processes. In the world of Homer, as Walter Otto has declared, "the divine is not superimposed as a sovereign power over natural events; it is revealed in the forms of the natural, as their very essence and being. For other peoples miracles take place; but a greater miracle takes place in the spirit of the Greek, for he is capable of so regarding the objects of daily experience that they can display the awesome lineaments of the divine without losing a whit of their natural reality." "There has never been a religion in which the miraculous, in the literal sense of transcending the natural order, has played so slight a role." [3]

At first sight this may seem a paradoxical assertion, since throughout the Homeric poems such gods as Zeus and Hera and especially Pallas Athene are constantly interfering in human affairs. Many modern readers are likely, in fact, to dismiss these continual celestial machinations as tedious and unnecessary and to complain that they merely delay the course of the story. It must be admitted that Homeric religion is not consistently naturalistic, and still contains relics of primitive superstition. A storm or a pestilence is usually attributed to the anger of one of the Olympians, with the

---

[3] Walter F. Otto: *The Homeric Gods,* translated by Moses Hadas, pp. 6–7.

implication that it might have been avoided if mortals had been more careful to pay him the requisite honors and sacrifices. Several times during the fighting on the Trojan plains a god saves some warrior from death by snatching him off the battlefield and transporting him to safety. But there is no suggestion of anything miraculous in the vast majority of these divine interventions. The action of the gods takes the form not of reversing the natural course of events, but of accentuating tendencies already inherent in a situation, usually by enhancing the power of those human beings whose strength or intelligence or beauty has already made them divine favorites. Throughout both the *Iliad* and the *Odyssey* (in marked contrast to many of the Biblical narratives), the main lines of the story in no way depend on supernatural intervention; Achilles could have killed Hector, and Odysseus could have made his way home to Penelope, without any aid from heaven. For Homer the gods are continuously participant, nonetheless, even though they may be invisible except to the eye of the poet. Whenever a Homeric hero feels new reserves of strength in battle or is flooded with some intense emotion or inspired with sudden insight or endowed with unexpected good fortune, one of the gods is present. For the Greeks this sense of enlargement was in itself divinity. The core of the Olympian religion was the conviction that at these critical moments human life touched a new dimension and was infused with influences from a higher order of being. "The shadow of a dream is man, no more," declared Pindar. "But when the brightness comes, and God gives it, there is a shining of light on men, and their life is sweet." [4]

Examples of divinity manifesting itself in this fashion can be found in every book of the Homeric poems. When Achilles wishes to kill Agamemnon and then thinks better of it, his impulse of self-control is attributed to Pallas Athene. Hector, stunned by Ajax but quickly regaining his strength, owes his recovery to Apollo. Priam, spending the night in the tent of Achilles, decides to leave before his host is awake because of a warning from Hermes. As a more detailed illustration, let us consider what happens when Odysseus encounters the princess Nausicaa after being thrown ashore in Phaeacia. According to Homer, it is Pallas Athene who

---

[4] *Pythians*, viii, 95.

impels Nausicaa to go to the seashore with her attendants to do the family laundry, at the same time suggesting to her thoughts about her need for a husband, and Pallas Athene who, when the girls are playing ball after lunch, arranges that the noise should awaken Odysseus. When the hero, naked and dirty, emerges from the thicket in which he has been lying asleep, it is similarly the goddess who gives Nausicaa courage not to run away, and who, after Odysseus has washed and clothed himself, "made him greater and more mighty to behold" and "shed grace upon his head and shoulders." [5] Plainly, all these events could have been narrated without any reference to Pallas Athene; but without the goddess, Homer could not have conveyed the full emotional quality they held for the participants. It is normal for human beings to feel that such a chain of happy accidents is somehow providential and, at the moment of love, to have the sensation of suddenly perceiving a beauty not present before. For Homer such feelings were an indication that one of the Olympians had been at work.

For the early Greeks, man experienced divinity through the exercise of his natural vitality. This meant that there were many gods, whose wishes might sometimes conflict with each other; and it was wise to honor all of them rather than incur antagonism by too exclusive a devotion. The favorite Greek virtue of temperance (*sophrosyne*) meant the recognition, in due proportion, of all aspects of human nature and of the appropriate deities. One of the most meaningful of Greek legends was the story of Hippolytus, who dedicated himself to chastity in the service of Artemis and was, in consequence, destroyed by the jealousy of Aphrodite. And although the sense of insight and enlargement given by the gods irradiated human life with a new beauty and significance, it might also lead man to sorrow and destruction, for the Olympians were not moral, at least by human standards, and rarely displayed pity. The passion inspired by Helen's beauty was the work of the gods, and her abduction by Paris was contrived by Aphrodite, but the result was the slaughter of the noblest of the Greeks and Trojans and the final ruin of Troy, which was what the gods had planned. There were, in fact, heavenly powers who deliberately induced madness and moral blindness; when Agamemnon brought the Greeks

---

[5] *Odyssey*, translated by S. H. Butcher and A. Lang, vi, 227–38.

to catastrophe by insulting Achilles, it was because the gods had temporarily taken away his reason in order to do him mischief.

On a few occasions, more often in the *Odyssey* than in the *Iliad,* Homer suggests that the gods are the guardians of morality and that men bring sufferings upon themselves by sin. "How vainly mortal men do blame the gods," exclaims Zeus at the beginning of the *Odyssey*. "For of us they say comes evil, whereas they even of themselves, through the blindness of their own hearts, have sorrows beyond that which is ordained." [6] But such attempts to read a moral meaning into earthly affairs are not characteristic of Homer's cosmology, which is normally much less consoling and more realistic and very remote from the ethical monotheism of Jehovah-worship.

Apart from the shadowy Hades (whom Homer rarely mentions), the Olympians are powers only of light and vitality and affirmation; and the ultimate authority over the universe belongs not to any beneficent intelligence, but to the dark and mysterious fates. The fates determine the broad outlines of human life, bringing sorrow and death to all men; and free will, human and divine, is effective only within these limits. A man, for example, may incur suffering beyond his fate if he acts foolishly or criminally. The gods can protect a warrior as long as his death is not yet decreed; but when his appointed day comes, they have to abandon him to the fates and to the darkness of the underworld, where they have no jurisdiction. Although Homer sometimes seems to identify the decrees of the fates with the will of Zeus, he feels that they are binding upon the gods and that even Zeus cannot reverse them. In Book VIII of the *Iliad,* for example, Zeus is described as measuring the fates of the two sides in golden scales in order to find out which is ordained to be victorious. Even more significantly, in Book XVI he wishes to rescue his son Sarpedon, whose death has been decreed; but when rebuked by Hera, he recognizes that if he attempts to thwart the decisions of the fates, his own authority over gods and men will be undermined. In the Homeric world there is an area of contingency within which divine and human intelligence can control events, but man's ultimate destiny is fixed not by the Olympians, but by impersonal powers who cannot be

[6] *Odyssey,* i, 32–4.

placated either by sacrifices or by moral virtue. In later Greek thought, the Homeric fates developed into the concept of natural law.

Such a view of life can be regarded as an appropriate reflection of the barbaric individualism of the heroic age; it offers little satisfaction to man's moral questionings or his search for justice. But it is true to human experience not only in its bleak recognition of misery and death, but also in its conviction that life at its moments of highest intensity is somehow touched with influences from another order of being. This sense of a sudden brightness and irradiation, of a significance beyond rationalistic explanation, is a normal human emotion, though in a materialistic age it is no longer regarded as evidence of any religious reality. It is, in fact, the genesis of aesthetic appreciation, and all artistic creation is an attempt to capture it and make it permanent.[7] The intuitions upon which the Olympian religion were founded were primarily aesthetic rather than moral. Out of these moments of vision and euphoria the Greek imagination created a world of divine beings who embodied at all times the beauty and vitality that men could experience only at rare intervals.

By Judaeo-Christian standards it is, of course, difficult to understand how Homer's Olympians could have been objects of religious reverence. They are heartless and even cruel; they feel sexual desire, and are by no means monogamous; and they are not omnipotent. Except when being deceived by Hera, Zeus is generally represented as keeping world affairs well under control; and when threatened with a revolt by the other gods, he can convincingly remind them of his superior power. But even Zeus has to conform to the decisions of the fates. As for the lesser gods, they take part in the battles on the Trojan plains, and are sometimes even wounded by mortal warriors. Even more alien to Judaeo-Christian attitudes is

---

[7] "What is meant by 'reality'?" wrote Virginia Woolf in *A Room of One's Own*. "It would seem to be something very erratic, very undependable —now to be found in a dusty road, now in a scrap of newspaper in the street, now a daffodil in the sun. It lights up a group in a room and stamps some casual saying. It overwhelms one walking home beneath the stars and makes the silent world more real than the world of speech—and then there it is again in an omnibus in the uproar of Piccadilly. Sometimes, too, it seems to dwell in shapes too far away from us to discern what their nature is. But whatever it touches, it fixes and makes permanent." Mrs. Woolf's "reality" is what the Greeks meant by the presence of divinity.

the element of humor in Homeric religion; Aphrodite, captured in bed with Ares by her husband Hephaestos, is an object of laughter to gods and men alike. But humor no less than beauty was for the Greeks a gift from the gods. The Olympians represent not the ethically good, but everything that elevates human beings, whether for good or evil, above the necessities of their fate-bound existence.

When economic and social developments compelled the Greeks to grapple with the problem of justice, they could no longer find sustenance in the Olympian religion. These amoral figures could not be transformed into vehicles for ethical idealism. But the Homeric world was not yet consciously aware of such problems. Homer assumes as unquestionable postulates the type of society which the Achaeans have created and the mores and values associated with it. The chieftains rule by right of birth even when they fail to display the heroic virtues expected of them; Agamemnon is neither wise in counsel nor resolute in battle, but he is still the bearer of the royal scepter and the descendant of Zeus, and his decisions must be obeyed. The rank and file must submit in silence to the will of their Achaean masters. Achilles can denounce Agamemnon and propose to put an end to the war; but when the low-born Thersites expresses the same sentiments, he is beaten by Odysseus and treated as an object of general contempt. These class lines are reflected in the structure of the universe, Zeus being the king of the gods in the same way that Agamemnon is the king of men.

Achaean morality was rooted in the intuitive feeling, akin to the aesthetic sense, and only remotely derived from any considerations of social utility, that certain actions were honorable and others shameful. Such chivalric virtues as courage, courtesy, generosity, and the pursuit of glory were marks of nobility, and it was shameful to violate an oath, to take advantage of the weakness of a suppliant, or to deny a corpse the correct funeral rites. Neither marital infidelity nor piratical raids against alien cities and the enslavement of their inhabitants had as yet been subjected to moral judgments. This aristocratic sense of honor and dishonor was expressed in the untranslatable word *aidos*. The hero was the man who displayed the chivalric virtues in the highest degree and who, in particular, was dominated by the passion for glory, the only quality by which an individual could achieve a kind of immortality and thus become like the gods. It was not only because of his prowess in battle, but also because of his lust for undying fame and his sensitivity to insults that Achilles was the noblest of the Greeks, the most nearly perfect example of moral excellence (*arete*).

The Homeric poems were based on the ethos that had developed in the barbaric past and which, at the time when the poems were composed, was beginning to be challenged by the rising forces of commercialism and democracy. Like other great writers, Dante and Shakespeare being notable examples, Homer upholds the traditional system of values during a period of rapid transition, expounding the aristocratic conception of *arete,* with its emphasis on military and athletic prowess, hereditary arrogance and class privilege, and the lust for glory, in the same way that Dante accepted the values of medieval Catholicism and Shakespeare those of feudal honor and the divine right of kings. But a great writer is always too complex to be given a political label: his view is always so comprehensive that he transcends whatever system of values he adopts, and thus points toward the future even when his vision seems most concentrated on the past. While Homer accepts the ethos of the barbaric age, he at the same time passes an implicit judgment on it, thereby arriving at an essentially tragic view of human life. This is perhaps the main reason for attributing the poems to a single creative mind; it is difficult to suppose that works presenting the world in these profound and sophisticated terms could have been the collective product of generations of anonymous ballad-singers. The sense of tragedy is intermittent in the *Odyssey,* which is concerned with its hero's adventures in the fairyland of the western Mediterranean and his final triumphant homecoming; but the *Iliad,* which deals exclusively with war, is pervaded by it. It is this quality especially that makes it one of the supreme achievements of the human mind.

While Homer glorifies the manifestations of heroic *arete,* he constantly emphasizes its consequences in the misery and death of human beings. The world is of such a nature that the immortal glory that great men necessarily desire can be attained only through slaughter and destruction. Thus, the warriors of the *Iliad* are trapped by a tragic destiny, and in moments of self-awareness see themselves almost as somnambulists, carried by fate and the compulsions of their own pursuit of *arete* to catastrophic ends. For the hero there is no escape, since he cannot cease to be heroic, but the possibility of a happier alternative is never forgotten. This is one of the functions of the frequent similes with which the battle scenes are interspersed; drawn from the daily activities of a hunting and pastoral people, they serve as a constant reminder that war is not man's only occupation. The climax of the whole poem, moreover, is the meeting between Priam and Achilles, when for a brief period the two men put aside the hatreds that destiny has imposed upon them and join each other in a common grief. It is, in fact, impossible to read the *Iliad* without feeling that it is the work of a man who especially admires humanity and courtesy and gentleness, in which respect also Homer resembles Shakespeare.

The tension between the savagery of the action and the humane standards of the narrator reaches its highest expression in the character of Achilles. In his outward behavior, Achilles is the barbarian chieftain of the Achaean age, constantly impelled by frenetic and uncontrollable emotions, whether of resentment against Agamemnon's seizure of his concubine, of grief for the death of Patroclus, or of rage with Hector. This was no doubt the Achilles of history. But Homer also gives him the consciousness of a civilized man, so that he is capable of moods of reflection in which he can wonder at, and deplore, the events in which he is involved and the necessities of his own heroic character. Offered a choice between long life and eternal glory, he can only choose glory; and because of this choice he is destined (as he tells Priam) to spend his days away from his home and father, bringing misery and destruction upon the Trojans, and in the near future to be killed himself. The recognition makes Achilles the saddest of all the Greeks, but he cannot abandon the pursuit of *arete* by withdrawing permanently from the war; in his meeting with Priam he can only blame Zeus for giving evil fortune to Greeks and Trojans alike. Heroic values lead to destruction, but no other values are possible, and the hero can only face realistically the tragedy of his own predicament.

2

The Rise of the Polis

How could the aristocratic values and view of life recorded in Homeric poems be adapted to the conditions of an increasingly commercial and democratic society? This was the problem confronting Greek thought after the rise of the polis. In the search for a solution, political and philosophical theorists arrived finally at doctrines which, though partially developed out of Homeric conceptions, were as revolutionary as the other new beginnings of the Axial Period in the Near East, and of even greater importance in their ultimate consequences for the Western world. Social and economic conflicts led in Palestine to a religion of ethical monotheism. In Greece they produced the belief in natural law.

The early history of the polis is wrapped in mystery, but it is plain that during the early centuries of the first millennium, Greek society was undergoing a gradual transformation, the details of which can be partially deduced from the evidence of myth and legend. Like all primitive peoples, the early Greeks had been divided into kinship groups holding their lands by communal ownership, without private property, and obligated to exact vengeance for injuries suffered by any of their members. This social system must have been established among the original peasant inhabitants, but it continued long after the coming of the Aryans, as can be seen from numerous indications in the Homeric poems. By what processes it gave place to the institutions of the polis we can only speculate, but it is obvious that the main motivating force was that, owing to the scarcity of fertile land and the pressure of an expanding population, the Greek world was turning to commerce and industry and developing the practices of a money economy. At some period before the seventh century, the communal landholdings were generally broken up into private properties; individuals, freed from the traditional kinship ties and obligations, began to move from farming into the new urban occupations; and kinship groups were combined into city-states which took over the responsibilities of government and the administration of justice. These changes were not always advantageous for the mass of the people, since the establishment of private property in land led to the expropriation and enslavement of many of the peasants by the moneyed classes. But, like the analogous changes occurring in Europe in the later Middle Ages, they unquestionably promoted social and cultural progress. The ambitious individual could enjoy much wider opportunities as the independent citizen of a polis than as a member of a kinship group. The new ways of living developed most quickly among the Greek colonists in Asia Minor and Italy, where traditional institutions had no deep roots, and down to the fifth century these areas were economically and intellectually more productive than mainland Greece.

This growth of individualism appears to have had some connection with the adoption of patrilineal laws of inheritance. As we have noticed, pre-Aryan Greece almost certainly reckoned descent through the mother, in accord with the general reverence for femininity so conspicuous in the artistic remains of the Minoan civilization. It is probable that Greek kinship groups were originally based on matrilineal descent and that the shift to a patrilineal system after the Aryan invasions tended to make them less cohesive and weaken their authority. These suggestions have little concrete evidence to support them, but in Greek thought the change in the rules of descent was undoubtedly in some way associated with the rise of the civilization of the polis. The climax of the *Oresteia* of Aeschylus, which celebrated the supercession of the duty of private vengeance by the rational justice of a court of law, was the assertion of patrilineal inheritance by the goddess Pallas Athene.

Athenian legend and history give some indication of the kind of changes which must have occurred in all parts of the Greek world. Historians declared that sexual relations were at first entirely promiscuous, and children did not know who their fathers were, which suggests a matrilineal society as it would look from a patriarchal viewpoint. One early king, Cecrops, was given credit for establishing marriage laws and patrilineal rules of descent. A later king, Theseus, was believed to have founded the Athenian city-state by uniting a number of clans under a single government, setting up a central council and a town hall at Athens, and (as described by Thucydides) compelling all the inhabitants of Attica to resort to the new metropolis and have their names inscribed on a single citizen roll. Citizenship of the polis was thus given precedence over membership of a kinship group. Clan loyalties long continued, however, to be an obstacle to effective city-state government, and it was not until the reforms of Cleisthenes at the end of the sixth century that these traditional groupings were finally swept away and replaced by political subdivisions based solely on geography and not on ancestry.

When the polis first took shape, it was, of course, governed by a king, or, more frequently, by wealthy families claiming descent from the Achaean and Dorian conquerors. Though there are some evidences of conflict between landowning and moneyed interests, the shift to a commercial economy seems generally to have been made by aristocratic groups, not by some newly emergent bourgeois class. It was mostly members of the old ruling families who acquired large estates and used them for the production of oil and wine and other commercial products, moved into the cities, developed a variety of different industries, built fleets of merchant vessels, and lent money to the peasants and sold them into slavery when they were unable to repay it. This same class had at first a monopoly of political office and controlled the council, which was usually the main organ of government. In the course of time, however, the disintegration of the traditional kinship ties and the massing of individuals in new urban communities led to the rationalization of political attitudes and to demands for more democratic institutions. Living in the intimacy of the polis, men could see for themselves how governmental decisions were made and quickly learned to protest against injustice. Middle-class citizens claimed that political rights should no longer be limited to families of aristocratic descent, while the exploited peasants, still remembering the tradition of communal ownership, began to demand a cancellation of debts and a redistribution of the land. Before the end of the seventh century, most of the more advanced states were torn apart by class conflicts that often developed into bloody civil wars.

One of the main obstacles to the creation of a new order was the Homeric ethos. The Homeric conception of *arete,* characteristic of an individualistic warrior aristocracy and manifesting itself in war, athletics, and class arrogance, could not easily be harmonized with the justice of an ordered political community. To some extent the Homeric sense of glory was successfully transformed into a sanction for civic loyalty; throughout Greek history warriors who died in battle for their polis were promised immortal fame as their appropriate reward. But Greek political life was always turbulently individualistic, and the blame belonged partly to the models for imitation presented in the Homeric poems. Throughout the golden age, the Greek cities were afflicted with a series of ambitious adventurers who copied the *arete* of Achilles in much the same way that the Western world in the nineteenth century was cursed with would-be Napoleons, and when their demands for glory were not satisfied, they would sulk in their tents or go over to the enemy. In spite of the constant idealization of patriotism in Greek literature and art, political ties and obligations were, in actual practice, extremely loose. There is much truth in Maurice Hutton's suggestion that the Greek citizen, in weighing his duty to his city, never forgot to ask how far loyalty would profit himself.[1]

In one state, Sparta, the ruling class both retained its privileges and kept individual ambition under rigid control by the drastic method of freezing all institutions at a pre-commercial stage of development. Descended from Dorian conquerors, the Spartans were masters of a large mass of peasant "helots" who outnumbered them at least twenty to one. Frightened by a helot rebellion halfway through the seventh century, they adopted a code of laws, the purpose of which was to prohibit all those economic, social, and intellectual developments which were leading to race fusion and class conflict in other states. According to legend, this code was the

---

[1] Two notorious examples from Athenian history may be cited. When Themistocles, the chief author of the Greek victory at Salamis, lost his political leadership, he took refuge with the Persians and died an official of the Persian king. When Alcibiades was deprived of his generalship in the expedition against Syracuse, he promptly gave his services to the Spartans.

work of a legislator named Lycurgus. The Spartans were to remain purely a warrior ruling caste, and were to be educated for
war in the service of the state and for nothing else. Agriculture was
left to the helots, who were required to turn over to their Spartan
masters a fixed proportion of what they produced, and trade to
foreigners. The Spartans refused, in fact, even to build a walled
city, but continued to live in scattered open villages. As a further
obstacle to the growth of any mercantile class, a system of iron
coinage was adopted, making money too bulky to be hoarded or
transported easily. The system of government among the master
race was a mixture of monarchy, aristocracy, and democracy, but
political conflicts were thereafter rare, partly because the Spartans
were always afraid lest any disunity should provoke another helot
rebellion, partly because they were too thoroughly indoctrinated
into obedience to authority to be capable of novel ideas.

The laws of Lycurgus proved their effectiveness in that the
Spartans not only retained their control of the helots, but also remained for centuries the masters of most of the other Peloponnesian states and the leading military power of all Greece. Yet, as
with all attempts to impose an uncompromising logical pattern
upon social processes, the final result was in some respects the opposite of what must have been the original purpose. The intent
had probably been to perpetuate a Homeric type of society, but the
Spartans had to surrender all the individualism so characteristic of
the Homeric heroes, and could retain their dominant status and
their warrior code of values only by living in conditions of rugged
discomfort and making a total surrender to the needs of the state
of all private interests and wishes. Obviously, privilege acquired at
such a cost was emptied of all its value. Sparta, nevertheless, had
an extraordinary and lasting fascination for all those Greeks, especially in the aristocratic classes, who were alarmed by the tur-
bulence accompanying commercial and intellectual progress. Undisturbed by the total lack of mental activity and by the savage repression of the helots, who were quietly murdered when they
showed any symptoms of independence, anti-democratic philosophers regarded Sparta as almost a model community. Here was a
society that had successfully resisted change and had maintained
an effective caste system in which different groups were assigned
to different functions in accord with their hereditary capacities.

Every member of the master race was a loyal and self-effacing instrument of the community, and the welfare of the state was always held to be more important than the happiness of individuals.
Sparta represented the totalitarian solution to the political problem,
and because of the admiration felt for it by the Athenian aristocrat
Plato, it has had a lasting influence on Western thought.

During the seventh and sixth centuries the only viable alternative to the Spartan system seemed to be dictatorship. Most of the
rich commercial cities passed through revolutionary upheavals,
often accompanied by wholesale massacres of defeated groups;
but the overthrow of aristocratic rule usually meant the transfer of
power not to the people, but to ambitious adventurers claiming to
represent their interests. These "tyrants" enforced order and often
promoted commercial expansion and patronized the arts. The age
of the dictators was marked by a rapid growth of architecture and
sculpture and by the beginnings of lyric poetry and philosophy.
Most of the Ionian and Italian cities continued to be governed by
tyrants as long as they remained independent units. But in spite of
the considerable services of these men to Greek civilization, Greek
thought was almost unanimous in condemning them. The tyrant
ruled by force and fraud, and of all possible types of government
this was the worst. Power had to be legitimized, and with the
breakdown of tradition this meant that it must be based on some
rationally acceptable principle. Never having accepted the theocratic doctrines on which the Oriental monarchies were founded,
the Greeks were faced with the task of finding or creating standards for a new political order. *Dike,* which in the Homeric poems
had meant an established custom or practice, gradually acquired
the connotation of a norm by which existing practices might be
judged, and was then abstracted into *dikaiosyne,* the ideal righteousness and justice. The attempt to define *dikaiosyne* remained
the central preoccupation of the Greek mind throughout the golden
age of the sixth and fifth centuries.

In Palestine a similar situation had led to the prophetic movement, but among the Greeks it was less easy to identify the official
religion with the demand for justice. The gods of Homer had become the gods of the polis, each city usually adopting one member
of the Olympian pantheon as its special patron; but they remained
closely associated with the aristocratic families, who, indeed,

usually claimed to be descended from liaisons between gods and mortal women, and nothing in the Homeric poems suggested that Zeus had any concern for the rights of the lower classes. After the rise of the polis, Apollo, who had been pro-Trojan and relatively unimportant in Homer, had developed into the favorite Greek deity, giver of laws and sponsor of culture, spokesman of moderation and self-control, and symbol of all expressions of form and order and the recognition of limits. His shrine at Delphi, built on a rocky incline at the foot of one of the spurs of Mount Parnassus and overlooking the gorge through which the Pleistos ran down to the Gulf of Corinth, became the most important Greek religious center. The priests of the shrine, claiming to interpret oracles that were mouthed by an illiterate peasant priestess during states of hypnosis, gave advice to the whole Greek world on a wide variety of political and spiritual problems. But although they often used their influence with remarkable wisdom, there could be no doubt that Apollo was not friendly to democracy.[2]

The earliest known attempt to transform the Olympians into defenders of popular rights is in the works of Hesiod. This Boeotian peasant poet, who probably lived in the ninth century, recorded aspects of Greek life not otherwise represented in literature. Convinced that the world was steadily deteriorating, and that this was primarily because of human wickedness, he celebrated hard work, honesty, and sobriety, and seems deliberately to have sought to counteract the Homeric emphasis on war and military glory. His mythological compositions show that the early Greeks could picture the origins of the world in images as savage and grotesque as those of any other primitive people. The *Theogony* describes how Earth first bore Heaven and then, in union with him, gave birth to a series of gods and also of Titans and other monsters; how one of the sons of Earth and Heaven, Cronos, castrated his father and became ruler of the world and then swallowed his own children to prevent them from overthrowing him; and how his youngest son, Zeus, was saved by his mother, who gave her husband a stone to swallow instead, and eventually, after a series of battles with his

[2] "Know thyself," "Nothing in excess," and several similar maxims were carved on the vestibule of Apollo's temple. It was characteristic of the Greeks that the religious awe induced by surroundings of such breath-taking sublimity was used to support these humanistic moral doctrines.

father and with the Titans, became the king of gods and men. Such
lurid fancies suggest how deeply the Greeks were indebted to
Homer for humanizing and rationalizing their religious beliefs. But
the peasant society for which Hesiod spoke also liked to believe
that Zeus had somehow become the guardian of justice, and in
Hesiod's *Works and Days* this doctrine was asserted with an almost
Hebraic concern for the rights of the humble and oppressed.
"For those who practise violence and cruel deeds far-seeing Zeus,
the son of Cronos, ordains a punishment." "There is virgin Justice,
the daughter of Zeus, who is known and reverenced among the
gods who dwell on Olympus, and whenever anyone hurts her with
lying slander, she sits beside her father, Zeus the son of Cronos,
and tells him of men's wicked heart, until the people pay for the
mad folly of their princes who, evilly minded, pervert judgment
and give sentence crookedly." [3]

The Hesiodic conception was reaffirmed by a number of later
poets and philosophers, but Zeus never acquired the ethical qualities of Jehovah in popular belief. The social tensions accompanying the rise of the polis manifested themselves instead in the
growth of mystical salvation cults that ran counter to the beliefs
and attitudes associated with the official worship of the Olympians.
These cults strongly resembled the worship of the mother goddess
under the names of Isis, Astarte, and Cybele in different parts of
the Near East, but it seems unnecessary to postulate any Oriental
influence on Greek society. Pre-Aryan Greece had been pervaded
with similar beliefs, which had retained much of their vitality among
the peasants; and it is understandable that the revolt against aristocracy should have caused a resurgence of this spiritual underworld
of primitive mysticism and hysteria. Like the rise of tyranny, it reflected the breakdown of the traditional order under the impact of
economic change and class conflict. It is significant that most of the
tyrants patronized the new cults and gave them official status.
Only against this background of popular emotionalism and irrationality can the creative effort responsible for the Greek golden
age be appreciated in its full significance.

The first manifestation of this resurgent primitivism was the
Bacchic frenzy, which seems to have originated in Thrace and to

---

[3] Hesiod: *Poems,* translated by H. G. Evelyn-White, pp. 21, 23.

have swept across Greece in the eighth century. In honor of Dionysus, god of fertility and intoxication, of the sap rising in the trees, of the reproductive seed, and of wine (of the whole wet principle in nature, according to Plutarch), hordes of worshippers, among whom women seem to have been especially prominent, assembled at night in forests and on the tops of mountains and worked themselves into a frenzied exaltation by dancing to the sound of flutes, fondling snakes, and devouring the raw flesh of the animals in whom their god had become incarnate. At these times they believed themselves possessed by a divine spirit, endowed with supernatural powers, and assured of immortality.

According to a later story, Dionysus was the son of Zeus and a mortal woman named Semele, a princess of the Boeotian city of Thebes; Semele had been blasted by lightning before her son was born, but the infant god had been rescued from her womb by Zeus and afterwards born out of Zeus's thigh. But the original Dionysus plainly had no place in the Olympian pantheon, and was the product of complex atavistic emotions that were incapable of explanation by any kind of rationalized myth and could be understood only by relating them to more primeval stages in man's long spiritual evolution. Unlike the official deities of the polis, Dionysus was a popular god, offering to oppressed classes a temporary escape from reality and a promise of salvation which they could not obtain from the sober, unpitying Olympians. But Dionysus was perpetually dying and being reborn, disappearing and returning, and hence was a revival of the old vegetation deity whose worship underlay that of the new gods of the ruling class and must still have survived among the peasants. And as he was also embodied in an animal whose raw flesh was ritualistically devoured by worshippers who themselves wore horns and were possessed by his spirit, his origins went back even beyond the agricultural era to the paleolithic hunters.

How the cult was brought under control and domesticated we do not know. Memories of the Dionysiac madness, including the tearing of its opponents limb from limb, survived into the historical period, and were preserved for all time in the *Bacchae* of Euripides. But by the sixth century Dionysus had become one of the Olympians, with regular festivals, purified of their original hysteria, in the leading cities, and had even become reconciled with the god who stood most conspicuously both for reason and self-control and for upper-class rule. In his temple at Delphi, Apollo took Dionysus under his protection, allotting him a share of the festivals and allowing his image to be carved on the back pediment. In the course of centuries, in fact, the two gods seemed to merge into each other, sharing the same functions and epithets. This union of Apollo and Dionysus, of order and enthusiasm, aristocratic restraint and popular emotionalism, can fairly be regarded as symbolic of the whole development of Greek culture.

The popular craving for redemption, which seems to have found its extreme expression in the worship of Dionysus, led also to more intellectual mystery cults equally alien to the official religion. In the Homeric world there was an impassable barrier between earth and heaven, and man could not become a god. But a happy immortality was the promised reward for initiation into the mysteries. This desire for immortality was associated with a sense of sin and with a search for purification from fleshly taints which conflicted with the dominant attitudes of Greek civilization but must be regarded as also an expression of the Greek spirit. In reaction against the total naturalism of the official religion, with its consistent acceptance of all carnal emotion in both gods and men, a counter tendency was developing toward a total repudiation of the material world.

The most famous of the mystery cults was located at Eleusis, in Attica, at the shrine of the harvest goddess Demeter, an Olympianized form of the mother goddess. This was sponsored by the Athenian government, and did not involve any repudiation of the traditional gods and the ethos associated with them. The Eleusinian mysteries have remained perhaps the best-kept secret in all history: though they were celebrated annually for over one thousand years, almost all that is known about them is that the initiates witnessed some kind of dramatic spectacle, apparently associated with the growing of the corn, and believed that this entitled them to happiness in the next life. But the consolations provided by this official cult were too mild to cure any acute sense of sin. Some individuals suffered from a spiritual restlessness and malaise that demanded a new revelation, and they found it in the doctrines of Orphism. This was allegedly the creation of the legendary musician Orpheus, known in mythology for his unsuccessful attempt to rescue Eurydice from the underworld, and was apparently a sterilized and intellectualized variant of Dionysus worship.

The theological poems attributed to Orpheus were collected and written down in the sixth century, although they were probably composed at some earlier period. They presented a view of life more akin to Hindu mysticism than to the naturalism of the Olympians. Dionysus, the last of a series of supreme beings, had been begotten by Zeus, but had been torn to pieces and devoured by the wicked Titans. Pallas Athene had rescued his heart, as a result of which he had been born a second time, returning to life as the divine principle of unity and purity, while Zeus had blasted the Titans with lightning. The race of men, born from their ashes, was a mixture of the wicked Titanic element and the good derived from the dismembered fragments of the body of Dionysus. Thus, man was tainted with original sin, but his soul was divine and immortal, and he could find salvation by ascetic practices. The Orphic writings described in detail the experiences of the soul after death, emphasizing the punishment of sinners and the rewards of the pure, and promising that after a series of reincarnations the disciples of Orpheus could achieve final redemption and reunion with God.

Orphism never won many adherents. It seems to have been strongest in the cities of southern Italy, where golden plates engraved with the Orphic motto "I too am of divine descent" have been found in a number of graves. But it had a conspicuous influence on some of the philosophers, especially on Pythagoras and Plato, and through Platonism on Christianity; and in the ages of decadence following the collapse of the polis, the pessimism that it represented steadily increased. The more ascetic aspect of Christianity, its tendency to regard the body as intrinsically evil and to interpret salvation as the purification of man's immortal soul from all fleshly taints, was of Hellenic and not of Jewish origin.

It is obvious that the seventh century was a critical period in Greek development, both the spread of tyranny and the rise of the salvation cults being suggestive of the social disintegration that finally overwhelmed the Greek world three or four hundred years later. To see a similar tendency reflected in the lyric poetry written in the Ionian and Aegean cities, the chief literary achievement of the period, is perhaps not wholly fanciful. The surviving fragments suggest that most of it was the expression of a sophisticated individualism devoid of any sense of communal obligation. This was exemplified in the satires with which Archilochus ridiculed the chivalric ideal, in the hedonism of Mimnermus and some of the work of Alcaeus, and in the highly personal love poems of Sappho.

The threat of disintegration evoked the creative effort of the Greek Axial Period, and this first showed itself, as far as we know, in the thought of two men active in the early decades of the sixth century: Thales of Miletus and Solon of Athens. These are shadowy figures whose views of life can be only tentatively reconstructed from the few fragmentary remains embedded like fossils in the writings of their successors. But later generations, presumably with reason, looked back to them as great innovators, and an analysis of what survives of their doctrines corroborates this verdict. Their significance becomes even greater when it is remembered that they were probably almost exact contemporaries.

All the thinking of the Axial Period saw the world as a unity and endeavored to arrive at rational conceptions of cause and effect. But whereas the Jewish prophets had found their principle of unity in the will of a single divine creator and the Hindus had been primarily concerned with the psychological processes by which man could achieve a state of blessedness, the Greeks approached nature directly and attempted to postulate generalized laws that would account for all phenomena. They were not concerned only, however, with explaining the natural universe; they were also looking for standards and values that could be applied to man's ethical and political problems. Natural law thus had a dual role, being both descriptive of natural processes and normative for the ordering of human society. This is why Thales and Solon must be linked together, although one is remembered as the founder of Greek science, the other as a political theorist and reformer.[4]

Such a conception of natural law was the product of a religious faith in the divinity of nature; and the work of Thales and his im-

---

[4] Among the more useful books on the development of Greek thought are John Burnet: *Early Greek Philosophy;* F. M. Cornford: *From Religion to Philosophy;* Werner Jaeger: *Paideia* and *Theology of Early Greek* *Philosophers;* Leon Robin: *Greek Thought;* and George Sarton: *History of Science.* For applied science, see Charles Singer and others: *History of Technology,* vol. II.

mediate successors was, in fact, as much theology as science. They proclaimed their doctrines in a tone of prophetic conviction rather than of scientific caution, and made little attempt to support them with experimental evidence. But Greek thinkers, unlike the Jewish prophets, did not find it possible to make much use of traditional beliefs. Most of them retained Zeus as a convenient word for the totality of the universe and the religious reverence it inspired, but this wholly depersonalized symbol had no real organic relationship with the all too human king of the Olympians. Yet, although Greek philosophy, while not repudiating the official religion, seemed able simply to bypass it, leaving it encapsulated in some wholly separate mental compartment, it owed an immense debt to its Homeric heritage. It was the naturalism of the Homeric religion, its identification of the gods not with magic and miracle but with normal processes, that caused the Greeks to turn directly to nature for guidance; and it was because of the Homeric conception of an impersonal fate whose decrees were binding upon gods and men alike that they were able to evolve the doctrine of natural law. Their first attempts to construct a working model of the universe can be regarded, moreover, as reflecting the Homeric belief that any excess evoked retaliation, *hybris* being always followed by the appropriate *nemesis*.

The rich Ionian city of Miletus, located near the mouth of the Maeander River at a point where it could control much of the traffic between the Greek world and the kingdoms of the Asiatic hinterland, was an appropriate birthplace for the scientific spirit. Of the life of Thales virtually nothing is known with certainty, but tradition represented him as a universal genius who discovered mathematical methods for measuring heights and distances, worked out new techniques of navigation by the stars, predicted an eclipse, diverted the course of the River Halys, planned a confederation of the Ionian cities, and, on being twitted for impracticality, made a fortune by foreseeing from weather conditions that there would be a big olive harvest and then cornering the market for olive-presses. Such stories are a welcome proof that Greek philosophy did not initially display the bias toward pure speculation and the contempt for practical utility for which all Greek thought has been reproached. The one certain fact about Thales is his assertion that there was a single underlying substance from which everything had emerged and to which everything must return. Aristotle's statement that Thales believed everything to be full of gods shows that he regarded this substance as psychophysical. The fact that he identified it with water is relatively unimportant. For the first time in history (as far as we know) human thought had embarked on the enterprise of explaining all phenomena in terms not of the activities of divine or demonic persons, but of uniform naturalistic laws of causation.

The theories of Thales' two immediate successors and fellow Milesians, Anaximander and Anaximenes, have survived in more detail. Anaximander (who propounded some kind of evolutionary hypothesis suggesting that men and other land animals were generated from fishes) described the first substance simply as indeterminate, while Anaximenes identified it with air and supposed that all phenomena were produced through its condensation or rarefaction. In the thought of Anaximander it is possible to discern the beginnings of a cosmology that was more fully developed by an Ionian of the following century, Heraclitus of Ephesus. Out of the first substance, which was eternal and perpetually in motion, emerged the specific elements; and because these were variously hot or cold, moist or dry, they were in opposition to each other. All phenomena could be explained in terms of the endless conflict of opposites, and movement in one direction must always be counteracted by a corresponding movement in the opposite direction. Thus, nature was a self-regulating balance of contrary forces. There was an obvious similarity between these physical theories and the emphasis of Greek ethics on the achievement of *sophrosyne* and the avoidance of *hybris,* and Greek political theory was to make use of the same conception in defining justice. A summary of Anaximander's teaching, preserved by a later philosopher, underlined the analogy. "From what source things arise, to that they return of necessity when they are destroyed; for he says that they suffer punishment and give satisfaction to one another for injustice according to the order of time." [5]

Heraclitus, a thinker of remarkable power and profoundity who is said to have died about the year 470, displayed the same assumption that the sanctions of justice were to be found in nature.

---

[5] Arthur Fairbanks: *The First Philosophers of Greece,* p. 12.

Interpreting the world as an order governed by law, he insisted on the universality of change and conflict, and identified with the transforming power of fire the basic force that kept everything in motion. "All things come into being by conflict of opposites, and the sum of things flows like a stream." "This order, the same for all things, no one of gods or men has made, but it always was, and is, and ever shall be, an ever-living fire, kindling according to fixed measure, and extinguished according to fixed measure." Justice meant a balance of opposites, and hence could be defined as strife. Heraclitus cited as an example the tension between the string and the frame in a bow or a musical instrument. "Harmony lies in the bending back, as for instance of the bow or of the lyre. . . . Opposition unites. From what draws apart results the most beautiful harmony. All things take place by strife." Thus, tension was the regulating principle of both nature and society. "The sun will not overstep his bounds; if he does, the Erinnyes, allies of justice, will find him out." "Men should know that war is general, and that justice is strife. . . . They would not have known the name of justice, were it not for these things." [6]

This was a comprehensive intellectual system which could be applied both to physical phenomena and to the movements of human society, but which still displayed a strong tendency to think mythically rather than empirically, in terms of general forces rather than of specific causal sequences. Both the virtues and the weaknesses of the Heraclitean philosophy were exhibited by Herodotus, whose description of the conflict between Greece and the Orient was written during the middle decades of the fifth century. Most of his readers have been so charmed by his vivid anecdotes and his fascinating anthropological information that they have regarded him as primarily a delightful storyteller, but one should not overlook his philosophical intentions. Regarding Greece and the Orient as opposites, he showed how, from the time of the Trojan War down to his own day, each of them in alternation had been encroaching on the other and paying the appropriate penalty for its injustice. The defeat of the Persians in their invasion of Greece early in the fifth century was merely the last of a series of such acts of reparation. Most of Herodotus' stories of individuals exemplified the same sequence of *hybris* and *nemesis*. Thus, Herodo-

---

[6] Fairbanks: op. cit., pp. 29, 33, 37, 39.

tus saw all history and biography as illustrations of a general law. He failed to show, however, that this general law was actually inherent in the movement of events, and to this extent his work fell short of a truly scientific attitude. Injustice was always punished not because it started a counteracting chain reaction that could be empirically verified, but because of a mysterious necessity in the nature of things, the final *nemesis* often having no real connection with the original act of *hybris*.

Yet in spite of the mythical tendencies in the thinking of the Milesians and their disciples, and in spite also of their lack of understanding of the experimental method, they have justly been regarded as the founders of Western science. The Near Eastern civilizations had accumulated a mass of empirical observations, especially in medicine, mathematics, and astronomy, and the Greek philosophers borrowed from them extensively and may have added relatively little. But neither in Egypt nor in Mesopotamia had there been any impulse to unify scientific knowledge by searching for generalized hypotheses freed from religious preconceptions. The notion of natural law had been lacking. The essential contribution of the Milesians was to see the world as a unity, and this made them the authors of the scientific world-view as distinct from the gathering of scientific information.[7] Thus, what gave birth to the scientific spirit was not observation or practical utility, but a new intuition, the content of which belonged as much to the field of religion as to that of science. This fact deserves emphasis, as does the fact that, in seeking for principles of unity in nature, the Milesians made use of conceptions derived from the current climate of opinion. Throughout the whole subsequent history of science, general theories (as distinct from the observations they have systematized) have been the products of intuition and

-----

[7] In sharp contrast with the boldly generalizing tendency of the philosophers was the empiricism of Greek medicine. Hippocrates and his disciples, who maintained a medical school on the island of Cos, insisted on the careful observation of what actually happened in states of disease, and regarded all general hypotheses as useless and misleading. They probably surpassed all other Greek scholars in concrete contributions to human knowledge. Their conception of health as the norm that natural physiological processes always sought to achieve, so that the function of the physician was to assist nature, had a considerable influence on the ethical thinking of the later philosophers, especially Socrates and Aristotle. Yet, in spite of its contributions to medical science, the Hippocratic school was far less important than the Milesians in the general development of human thought.

have shown a high degree of correlation with social conditions.[8]

The concept of a balance of opposites, which Anaximander and Heraclitus used for the interpretation of nature, was applied by Solon to society. Athens was torn apart by class conflicts that seemed likely to end either in dictatorship or in civil war, and in the first decade of the sixth century Solon was entrusted with authority to enact a program of reform. Himself an aristocrat who had been engaged in commerce but had been content with only a moderate fortune, he set out to find an acceptable compromise among class interests. While he canceled the debts of the peasantry and prohibited the enslavement of Athenian citizens, he refused to support any redistribution of property; and while he revised the Athenian constitution to give greater representation to the mass of the people, he left the government, on the whole, still under aristocratic control. He also drafted a written code of laws and reformed the judicial system in order to give fuller legal protection to the rights of poorer citizens. He described the purpose of his program as follows: "To the common people I have given such a measure of privilege as sufficeth them, neither robbing them of the rights they had, nor holding out the hope of greater ones; and I have taken equal thought for those who were possessed of power and who were looked up to on account of their wealth, careful that they too should suffer no indignity. I have taken a stand which enables me to hold a stout shield over both groups, and I have allowed neither to triumph unjustly over the other." [9]

----

[8] The abandonment of the finite and static Ptolemaic cosmology at the end of the Middle Ages was a reflection of the breakdown of the feudal order and the growth of individualism. This is shown by the fact that the doctrines of the infinity of the universe and the motion of the earth were stated, on purely philosophical grounds, by Nicholas of Cusa early in the fifteenth century, long before Copernicus, Kepler, and Galileo gave them scientific justification. The Newtonian cosmology, in which the universe was a product of natural laws promulgated by a divine creator, reflected the monarchical state of the seventeenth century. Darwin's theory of evolution, with its emphasis on the struggle for existence as the mechanism of progress, was derived from laissez-faire capitalism (and was afterwards used by Herbert Spencer as a new justification for capitalism). The modern world was losing the belief in absolute truths and values and coming to regard each individual as the center of his own universe long before Einstein formulated the theory of relativity. Such examples raise the problem of the nature of scientific truth. One can only conclude that the subjective element in all general hypotheses is larger than is usually supposed; man builds scientific data into comprehensive structures by his own creative activity.

[9] Ivan M. Linforth: *Solon the Athenian*, p. 135.

The reforms did not end class struggle at Athens, and a generation later the popular leader Pisistratus established a tyranny that was continued by his sons after his death in 527 and was not overthrown until near the end of the century. But although Solon's specific reforms were short-lived, the ideas upon which they were based were remembered by the Athenians and were revived after the fall of the dictatorship. Athens eventually adopted a thoroughly democratic form of government, but its political greatness was due to something much more important: its belief in the rule of law. It was Solon, as far as we know, who first explicitly affirmed this principle, putting it into effect (according to his own declaration) by giving Athens a written code that provided for the fair administration of justice. This recognition that justice depended on the supremacy of law, which has been one of the basic principles of Western civilization, was originally derived from the assumption that there were laws of nature which should serve as norms and standards for man-made laws. The legitimacy of political order depended on its conformity to the order of the natural universe, which had acquired for the Greeks the kind of religious authority the Jews gave to the will of Jehovah.

Depending on a religious faith, this dual role of natural law could easily be undermined by critical analysis. Why should human beings be obligated to follow the guidance of nature, particularly after it was demonstrated that the laws they read into the natural universe were largely products of their own intuitions? Yet the belief that justice meant conformity to "the laws of nature and of nature's God" has persisted throughout the whole history of Western civilization. This tradition can be traced back in a continuous line as far as Solon. In some of the surviving fragments of his poems, he depicted Zeus, in conventional fashion, as punishing the wicked, but in a remarkable elegy quoted in one of the speeches of Demosthenes he presented a more naturalistic conception of the workings of justice, suggesting that excess led of itself to an equally violent reaction. The ruin of Athens, he declared, would come not from the gods, but directly from the actions of its own citizens. The greed of the rich meant degrading bondage for the people, and would provoke war, civil strife, and secret conspiracies. The remedy could be found in a universal obedience to a system of law which would preserve moderation and balance divergent interests. "A law-abiding spirit createth order and harmony, and at the same time putteth chains upon evil-doers; it maketh rough things smooth, it checketh inordinate desires, it dimmeth the glare of wanton pride and withereth the budding bloom of wild delusions; it maketh crooked judgments straight and softeneth arrogant behavior; it stoppeth acts of sedition and stoppeth the urge of bitter strife. Under the reign of law, sanity and wisdom prevail ever among men." [1]

[1] Linforth: op. cit., p. 143. The last sentence is a somewhat free translation. What the Greek says is "Under it [i.e., a law-abiding spirit] sanity and wisdom prevail ever among men."

3

The Athenian Golden Age

The later decades of the sixth century were a period of bold philosophical speculation provoked by the new impetus given to thinking by the Milesians. In political development, on the other hand, most of the Greek world continued to show symptoms of decadence. While the more backward mainland states were still controlled by the old aristocratic families, many of the advanced commercial cities remained under the rule of tyrants, and interludes of democratic government were usually both brief and bloody. Meanwhile, the Ionian cities, which had been the main centers of intellectual activity, were deprived of their independence by the expanding empire of the Persians, and showed themselves incapable of forgetting their internal conflicts even in order to resist foreign conquest. Athens alone succeeded in moving forward to a new political system by which democracy was established and legitimized and the rule of the people reconciled with the rule of law. In consequence, she became not only the richest and most powerful of the Greek states, but also the chief center of intellectual and aesthetic activity. The Greek golden age of the fifth century was the age of Athenian predominance.

Athens was conveniently located for maritime expansion; but her rise was caused not only by material factors, but also by the legal security enjoyed by her citizens and by a liberal immigration policy which encouraged the entry of merchants and craftsmen from other cities. The tyranny of Pisistratus proved, on the whole, to be a beneficial interlude, for he promoted economic and cultural progress, undermined the power of the aristocratic families, and did not unduly interfere with the legal rights of private citizens; and after the overthrow of his son and successor Hippias at the end of the sixth century, conditions were ripe for a new experiment. Some of the old families hoped to re-establish aristocratic government; but one upper-class group, under the leadership of Cleisthenes, turned to the people and secured the adoption of a thoroughly democratic constitution. Thereafter the final authority in Athens belonged to the assembly of all citizens, executive responsibilities being entrusted to elected officials, while the old aristocratic council of the Areopagus survived only as a court of appeals in cases of homicide. The law courts were similarly democratized, decisions being rendered by large popular juries. For the next three quarters of a century the proceedings of the assembly continued to be dominated by members of upper-class families who had the prestige, leisure, and oratorical powers needed for political leadership, but the city had definitely adopted the principle of *isonomia:* equality of all citizens before the law.

Thus, the Athenians had established a new foundation for political authority. Justice no longer meant adherence to traditional customs or obedience to a hereditary ruling class or a divinely appointed king; it meant conformity to laws in the making of which all citizens participated. The feeling of exhilaration which they derived from this achievement lasted through most of the fifth century, until the failure of democracy in the Peloponnesian War, its most memorable expression being the Funeral Speech that Thucydides put into the mouth of Pericles. Claiming that "our form of government does not enter into rivalry with the institutions of others, we do not copy our neighbours, but are an example to them," Pericles eulogized the individual freedom enjoyed by all Athenians in their public and private lives, the legal principle of equal justice for all, and the scrupulousness with which every citizen obeyed the magistrates and the laws.[1]

The effectiveness of these democratic institutions was proved, soon after their adoption, in the wars of Persia. When some of the Ionian cities attempted to regain their independence, they received help from Athens. The Persians crushed the rebellion, destroying the city of Miletus and slaughtering all its inhabitants, and then

---

[1] Thucydides: *History of the Peloponnesian War,* translated by Benjamin Jowett, ii, 36.

turned their attention to the presumptuous Athenians. In 490, Darius sent an expedition against Athens, but the heavy-armed Athenian hoplites won a decisive victory at Marathon. Ten years later, Darius' son and successor Xerxes personally led a large army across the Dardanelles and through Thrace for the conquest of Greece. In this crisis, the Greeks were by no means united; Persian rule, though despotic, was relatively enlightened; and as the Ionians had discovered, submission did not mean much more than paying tribute, whereas unsuccessful resistance meant total destruction. The oracle of Apollo at Delphi predicted Persian victory—an error by which it forfeited the spiritual influence it had exercised for the previous two or three centuries—and the Persians won some support from tyrants and aristocracies. It was the Athenians who were most determined on resistance, and their leaders interpreted the war as a conflict of principles and of civilizations: Hellenic liberty and the rule of law against Oriental despotism and the rule of a king. Fortunately, the Spartans, though with some hesitation, were also willing to fight for Greek independence, and the Persians were defeated in a series of three decisive battles. Athenian sea power was mainly responsible for naval victories at Salamis and Cape Mycale, while the Spartan army played a leading role in crushing the invading land forces at Plataea.

Once the security of mainland Greece had been secured, the Spartans withdrew from the war, but the Athenians organized a confederation of maritime city-states, the Delian League, in order to maintain Greek control of the Aegean and liberate Ionia, and fighting continued for another thirty years before the Persians were finally willing to accept their defeat and make peace. Supplying most of the armed forces of the League, while all but three of the other member states made their contribution in money, Athens was able to use it in order to establish her own predominance and make herself the mistress of the eastern Mediterranean. For the half-century following the battles of Marathon and Salamis, she was riding the crest of a wave, invigorated by the conviction that she had discovered the principles of civilization and was capable of teaching them to the rest of the Hellenic world and of defending them against the barbaric despotisms of the Orient.

Compared with almost any other community in human history,

the Athens of this period seems almost miraculous, whether one judges by the high levels of political capacity or by the number of men of creative genius she produced. Why was one relatively small city, during a period of only two or three generations, able to make so many contributions of such lasting importance to human thought? Obviously no adequate explanation can be found in materialistic factors, either of biology or of economics. In their ethnic inheritance the Athenians did not differ significantly from other Greek peoples: and although their self-confidence was supported by rising economic prosperity, they never became a really wealthy community. The material basis of all Greek society was meager and uncertain, and even the aristocratic families—to judge from the surviving inventories of their possessions—must have lived plainly and enjoyed little physical comfort. There was less accumulated surplus wealth in classical Greece than in the cities of the oriental empires or of the Hellenistic kingdoms of a later period. The Athenian achievement is a permanent refutation of the notion of any close or necessary relationship between economic and cultural productivity. It was the result not of surplus wealth, but of favoring institutions and beliefs.

As a forcing-ground for human creativity, no social organization in history has ever surpassed the Greek polis. Perhaps the chief reason was that it was sufficiently small to give every individual a sense of responsible participation in public affairs. Even Athens at the height of her power probably had less than fifty thousand adult male citizens, and most of the other cities were considerably smaller. There was little specialization, for in addition to his normal occupation every citizen was occasionally a soldier and, in democratic Athens, a voter in the assembly, a juryman, and a critic of the drama. The Funeral Speech insisted particularly on the versatility displayed by the Athenians—unlike the Spartans, who let their rulers make decisions for them and were trained exclusively for warfare. Such conditions constantly sharpened and stimulated every human aptitude.

It was the whole human personality, not merely man in his function as voter or soldier, which belonged to the polis. When Aristotle defined man as a political being, a being who lived in a polis, he was presenting a comprehensive definition. To remain aloof from communal activities was to be guilty of idiocy, a word that originally meant concern with one's private affairs. The Greeks were aware of the problem of conflicting allegiances, as the *Antigone* of Sophocles bears witness, and the growth of Orphism shows that a few of them were capable of seeking individual salvation. But for the men of the golden age the individual was always a part of his community, his gods were the gods of his polis, and his character and values were shaped by social institutions, which meant that virtuous men could exist only in virtuous societies. The identity of ethical and political values was, in fact, almost axiomatic. Not until the failure of all political idealism in the Hellenistic and Roman period did the classical world as a whole finally lose its faith in the possibility of political justice and make that divorce between ethics and politics which has been transmitted to the Western civilization by Christianity.

The society of the polis had, in fact, the intimacy of a fraternal organization and was much more than a mere unit of government. Its bond of unity, as Aristotle declared, was friendship. Almost all life was lived in public, in the streets and in the market place rather than in the privacy of a home. The citizens could form their political judgments of each other by personal acquaintance; and, as the comedies of Aristophanes bear witness, anybody's personal eccentricities and idiosyncrasies were known to everybody. Such a lack of privacy would have been oppressive if it had been combined with puritan values; but the Greeks never cultivated hypocrisy or entertained any illusions about human nature. The sexual and scatological jokes of the comedians were as inherently a part of the Greek way of life as the love of beautiful forms, and this love would, in fact, have been unreal if it had not been based on a total acceptance of everything human.

Inheriting the Homeric morality associated with the worship of the Olympians, the Greeks continued to believe that *arete* was achieved not by the suppression of nature, but by its perfection. To a large extent the barbaric ethos of the old ruling families, with its glorification of physical beauty and athletic prowess, was transmitted to the society of the polis. Handsome features were a gift of the gods; and a victory in one of the athletic festivals meant civic honors and was sometimes a recommendation for political office. Pindar, the Boeotian poet of the early fifth century, devoted all the resources of his incomparable lyric splendor and

eloquence to celebrating the winners of the chariot races and boxing matches and tracing their ancestral connections with the
Olympians. Intellectuals sometimes deplored this emphasis on
athletics. "Our wisdom is better than the strength of men or of
horses," insisted the philosopher Xenophanes. "This is indeed a
wrong custom, nor is it right to prefer strength to excellent wisdom.
For if there should be in the city a man good at boxing, or in the
pentathlon, or in wrestling, or in swiftness of foot, which is honored
more than strength (among the contests men enter into at games),
the city would not on that account be any better governed." [2]
Such complaints usually had political implications, in view of the
close association of athletic prowess with the old ruling-class ethos;
it is significant that Pindar was one of the more anti-democratic
of Greek poets, even to the point, apparently, of showing pro-
Persian leanings during the invasion. Yet in spite of a continuing
tendency to regard the *arete* of the successful athlete as a justification for aristocratic privilege, democratic communities retained the
traditional respect for bodily perfection. The gymnasium was one
of the central institutions of the polis, and most citizens appear to
have visited it regularly. It was with good reason that the Greeks
felt themselves to be superior to most of the Oriental peoples in
masculine strength and vigor. Even Greek intellectual activity
mostly took place out of doors and was associated with physical
exercise. The typical philosopher did not develop his ideas either
in a study or in a classroom, but while walking and conversing
with disciples.

From the diffusion of the aristocratic ethos the Greeks derived
also their conviction that civilized living meant the constructive
use of leisure. The Puritan glorification of work as a valuable moral
discipline was wholly alien to the Greek mind. Although this attitude sometimes supported anti-democratic conclusions, their importance should not be exaggerated. It is true that both Plato
and Aristotle regarded physical labor as degrading to those who
devoted themselves to it, and advocated a social system in which
a ruling class of leisured gentlemen would be supported by slaves;
and this has led some modern critics to condemn all Greek thought
as vitiated by a contempt for the economic basis of human life.
But the Greek civilization of the golden age must not be judged

---

[2] Fairbanks: op. cit., p. 73.

by Plato and Aristotle, who lived in an age of disillusionment and
reaction. The leaders of the Athenian democracy did not consider
that the average individual was degraded because he had to work
for a living, provided that he had leisure for other activities besides work. The Funeral Speech claimed that "to avow poverty
with us is no disgrace; the true disgrace is in doing nothing about
it" and boasted that "even those of us who are engaged in business
have a very fair idea of politics." [3]

Nor did early Greek thinkers consider it beneath their intellectual dignity to devote their minds to practical problems. The sixth
and fifth centuries were, in fact, an age of considerable advance
in metallurgy, shipbuilding, engineering, and other industrial arts,
although in general the Greeks were technologically less inventive
than their Oriental predecessors. What was typically Greek was
not any contempt for the economic substructure of life, but rather a
conviction that it was only a means and never an end. The Greek
aesthetic achievement would have been impossible if Greek society
had not been permeated with this attitude. The architectural monuments of the Orient had been the work of royal or priestly despotisms. In Athens, on the other hand, it was the people who were
willing to spend the surplus wealth of their community so lavishly
on the adornment of their city. No other society in history has devoted so large a proportion of its resources to the arts and relatively so little to physical comfort.

Two evils in the society of the polis must be admitted: the enslavement of part of the laboring class and the subordination of
women. In common with every other civilized people down to
modern times, the Greeks considered it legitimate to hold members of more backward and supposedly inferior races as chattel
slaves. Nor was enslavement restricted to foreigners, since it was
sometimes imposed upon the citizens of Greek communities when
they were defeated in interstate warfare. In democratic Athens,
however, the line between slaves and free laborers was not sharply
drawn (except in the silver mines of Laureon, where slaves were
employed under conditions that comprised one of the blackest
marks on the Athenian record); they worked side by side at the
same occupations, and conservatives like Plato and the anonymous
author of *The Constitution of the Athenians* complained that it was

---

[3] Thucydides, ii, 40.

impossible to tell them apart and that even the slave population was infected by the spirit of democratic liberty. Before the end of the fifth century, radical philosophers were beginning to doubt the traditional theory that some races of men were inherently suited for enslavement. Unfortunately these liberal tendencies were ended by the fall of the democracy, and in later centuries the dependence on slave labor increased.

The subordination of women was associated with the rise of the civilization of the polis, their social position having markedly deteriorated not only since the Minoan period but also since the composition of the Homeric poems. The society of the polis was definitely masculine; there were no women in the Platonic dialogues, and even the Funeral Speech allotted only two short sentences to the widows and mothers of the dead, declaring that a woman earned her greatest glory by being not "talked about for good or evil among men." [4] But against the fact that even the democratic Athenians felt that the respectable woman belonged in her home, her proper function being to give pleasure to man, must be set the evidence of the drama. A community which could produce the *Antigone* of Sophocles, the *Alcestis* of Euripides, or even the *Lysistrata* of Aristophanes knew that heroism, intelligence, and strength of will were by no means masculine monopolies. Nor should the prevalence of homosexual love be overestimated. This was an aristocratic cult, common in conservative communities like Sparta and Thebes, where it was supposed to be more conducive to virility and training in warrior virtues than the love of women, but practiced in Athens only in wealthy and anti-democratic circles. References in Aristophanes make it evident that the average Athenian regarded it as an aberration.

The way of life of the polis provides, however, only a partial explanation of the Athenian achievement. The greatness of Athens was due not only to the institutions and values she shared with other Greek cities, but also to the dynamic self-assurance derived from the successful establishment of democracy and the triumph over the Persians. For two or three generations, until both the course of events and the trend of thought made such optimism untenable, Athenians could believe that both individual virtue and political justice were in accord with nature and therefore could

----
[4] Thucydides, ii, 45.

be realized through the release of man's spontaneous energies, not through inhibition and restraint. This was one of those rare and happy periods in human history when order and freedom appear to be in harmony and the individual achieves a sense of full self-realization through participation in the activities of his society. Based on a religious faith in the divinity of nature, this confidence in human potentialities was eventually undermined by the growth of rationalism and confuted by the catastrophe of the Peloponnesian War; and after men had lived through the Athenian disillusionment, they could never wholly recapture the sense of exhilaration which had preceded it. But something of the spirit of the golden age can be partially recaptured from the surviving fragments of its aesthetic expression.

The visual arts are often the most reliable gauge of the spirit of a civilization, reflecting it directly without the intellectual disguises and distortions that the use of words makes possible in literature.[5] A distinctive style has arisen whenever favorable economic conditions have enabled artists to produce comprehensive expressions of the view of life of their society; and while its value is partly dependent on mastery of the technical media, it is also determined partly by historical factors that transcend narrowly aesthetic criteria. There are some societies whose views on life are so narrow and impoverished or so conflicted and disharmonious that a great art is impossible. The supreme aesthetic achievements have been the products of ages of confidence when men have believed in an ultimate harmony behind phenomena and have trusted their own capacity to comprehend and organize the whole of experience. At such periods, aesthetic form, reflecting the order believed to be inherent in the universe, appears as natural and organic, not as an artifice imposed upon content and limiting its expression. The conflict between the classic emphasis on order and the romantic emphasis on spontaneous expression appears only in ages of doubt.

The Greek sense of organic order was reflected most directly

---

[5] It is perhaps for this reason that art history is so far ahead of other branches of cultural history. For a long time most art history has been written on the assumption that the spirit of a society is reflected in its art and that this can be understood through the analysis of style and form, not merely of content. These conceptions seem to have remained unknown to most historians of literature, at least in English-speaking countries.

and completely in religious architecture. In contrast with the grandiose and ornate constructions of the Oriental despotisms, the Greek temple was always a simple building, flat-roofed and usually four-sided, with rows of columns surrounding the inner shrine that housed the statue of the deity. But the unity of the total design was combined with extraordinary subtleties of detail, producing the effect of an organic growth rather than of a geometrical construction. The proportions were most carefully planned to convey a sense of harmony and serenity, and the rectangular appearance was, in actuality, an optical illusion, all the lines being slightly curved. The rounded columns with their delicate variations of width seemed in the Greek sunlight to be almost alive, especially when they were built of the glowing marble that the Athenians quarried from Mount Pentelicon. Unlike the Egyptian pyramids and Babylonian ziggurats and the domes and spires of later Western styles, the Greek temple was designed to harmonize with its environment, not to dominate it or negate it. With its horizontal lines it rested on the earth instead of soaring above it, and was built with a view to its external appearance rather than to the shaping of inner space. The Greeks liked to choose sites of the greatest natural beauty, preferably on the tops of hills overlooking the sea, and the vistas of distant mountains and the movements of the sun were integral parts of the whole aesthetic impact.

Like the polis that produced it, the Greek temple was incapable of adaptation to more complex social forces. Later Greek and Roman architects, seeking to meet new purposes and new forms of the religious consciousness, broke completely with the classical tradition and concentrated on the shaping of inner space by developing the potentialities of the vault and the dome, which had been unknown to their fifth-century predecessors. In modern civilization, with its different needs and aspirations, the prestige of the Greek style has been, on the whole, an obstacle to healthy artistic development. But the greatest masterpiece of Greek architecture, its crowning achievement both in size and in subtlety of detail, the Parthenon built on the top of the Acropolis in Athens in honor of the tutelary goddess of the city, remains one of the supreme expressions of man's capacity to create an ideal harmony. Fronting the sunset and overlooking the semicircle of mountains that girdle the Athenian plain and the blue waters of the Aegean, its glowing

marble columns have continued for more than two thousand years
to affirm the power of the human spirit to find order, beauty, and
serenity in earthly life.

Almost all the temples of Greece succumbed eventually to earthquakes, to barbarian vandals or Christian fanatics, or to the slow
ravages of time, the remains being reduced to piles of rubble or
buried under thick layers of silt. It is therefore impossible to write
the history of Greek architecture in any detail. In sculpture, on the
other hand, one can trace a continuous evolution from the archaic
beginnings to the final decadence. We cannot reconstruct Greek
art in its full glory, as nothing survives of the work of any major
figure before the fourth century. Our knowledge is based on the
works of anonymous minor craftsmen and on inaccurate copies of
earlier masterpieces made during the Roman period. But enough
has been preserved to show the movement of style and technique.

Throughout its early history, Greek sculpture was evolving in
response to spiritual impulses that reflected the whole Greek
view of life, the development of sensibility and the growth of
technical mastery being aspects of a single process. Through the
dark age following the Aryan invasions, art seems to have been
wholly geometrical. The creation of human figures apparently began early in the seventh century, the initial impulse being obviously
due to Egyptian influence. The earliest statues were closely copied
from Egyptian models, displaying the same physiological configu-
ration, the same tense positions of body and limbs, and the same
air of solemn determination. But whereas Egyptian art had
been permeated by faith in a static and eternal world transcending
time and mutability, the art of early Greece sought to reveal a
beauty immanent in nature. Its purpose was to render an ideal;
but this ideal was to be found within the phenomenal world, being
manifested in moving bodies in a three-dimensional space. For
two hundred years successive generations of anonymous Greek
craftsmen were steadily moving away from the Egyptian model
and learning how to convey a Hellenic naturalness and spontaneity,
their favorite subject being the figure of a *kouros,* a young man,
possibly representing Apollo. The body ceased to be symmetrical
and rectangular and became curving; the weight was no longer
evenly distributed on both legs; the head was posed at various
angles instead of always front-face; the arms and legs were given

more relaxed positions; and the features acquired the smiling and graceful self-assurance appropriate to an Olympian. Equally indicative of the Greek spirit was the evolution of the relief. Egyptian relief had had only two planes, a front and a background, with no foreshortening, and the figures had been presented only front-face or in complete profile. But Greek carvers set themselves the task of suggesting movement in space, and during centuries of slow technical evolution they discovered how to convey a sense of depth by using foreshortening and by carving figures at different angles.

The great period of Greek art, as of Greek civilization as a whole, lasted only as long as men could retain a vital religious belief in ideal forms immanent in nature. With the growth of rationalism, art was destined to lose its religious quality and degenerate into the realistic rendering of human emotions and the portrayal of a purely sensuous beauty that had lost all spiritual vitality. These tendencies were already visible in the sculpture of the late sixth century, especially in the Ionian cities; but after the Persian wars they were abruptly reversed. The rise of Athens to cultural leadership was accompanied by a revival of religious idealism, which was reflected in almost all the surviving work of the fifth century. Its leading representative was Phidias, whose chief works were colossal statues of the Olympians made for the temples on the Athenian Acropolis and for those on the site of the great athletic festival at Olympia. According to Greek commentators, he gave to his representations of gods and goddesses an austere dignity and solemnity which had been lacking in the work of his immediate predecessors and which disappeared from Greek art after the fifth century. For the Athens of the golden age, the Olympians, though thoroughly natural, were still objects of religious awe, and even Aphrodite had not yet become merely a desirable woman.[6]

---

[6] See Gisela M. A. Richter: *Three Critical Periods in Greek Sculpture* (published by the Clarendon Press, Oxford), pp. 5–7. After noting the beginning of realism in the sculpture of the early fifth century, as manifested in "the new representation of the human figure in a number of new, agitated stances" and the use of "facial expression to indicate emotion—surprise, joy, exaltation, grief, fear, exertion—as well as old age," Miss Richter goes on: "We should have expected that Greek sculptors, once in possession of the necessary knowledge, would have progressed along the path of greater naturalism and have initiated an era of realistic sculpture. This, however, was not the case. The logical continuation of these experiments did not come for more than a century later when Lysippos initiated the Hellenistic period and

Seeking to represent the divine forms that gave beauty and significance to nature, all the art of the great period reflected the belief that man became godlike in moments of heightened vitality. It was devoted exclusively to the portrayal of the human figure in isolation from its environment; and being concerned with the manifestation of unchanging realities, not specific events, it was unaware of time and change. The greatest Greek statues conveyed an extraordinary sense of an organic energy emanating from vital centers within the human body, an energy always effortless and therefore graceful and assured. It was in this fashion that the Olympians revealed themselves to man. The same concentration on ideal forms abstracted from specific times and places was displayed in funeral stelae representing grief with a consummate tenderness and delicacy, large numbers of which have survived, and in the carving of scenes of action on the friezes and pediments of temples. These were frequently depictions of battles between gods and titans or between men and centaurs, thus serving as reminders that civilization was not achieved without a struggle with savagery, but the greatest of Greek reliefs, the portrayal of the Panathenaic procession on the frieze of the Parthenon, was a lyrical celebration of human grace in movement.

In the long history of man's aesthetic self-expression, classic Greek art is merely one of the many possible styles, and its standards are not universal. The modern spectator may sometimes prefer the art of the archaic period, before its original hieratic stiffness had given place to the flowing lines of the fifth century, just as he may find the simplicity of the Italian primitives more expressive than the too easy mastery of the great Venetians. It is difficult to judge the art of the golden age fairly without being biased by its Hellenistic and modern imitators who copied its external appearances but lost its vital energy. Post-Renaissance Europe was inclined to judge all art by Greek standards and—misled by the fact

---

Greek realism, properly speaking, began. What was the reason for the delay? I think we shall find it in the personalities of a few great artists whose genius directed and determined the trend of Greek sculpture during the second half of the century. The greatest of these was Pheidias. He imparted to the art of his time an idealizing trend, a sublimation of natural forms, and thus retarded the realistic rendering of nature." Thus, Miss Richter attributes the revival of idealism to personal factors. Phidias and his associates, however, were products of the Athens of their time, and their work reflected the climate of Athenian opinion after the Persian wars

that the subjects of Greek art were themselves beautiful—to forget that the aesthetic value of art was to be found in the method of representation, not in what it represented. The copying of Greek models by men who lived in a wholly non-Greek society resulted in a sterile academicism against which Western artists rebelled in the late nineteenth century. The Western world had to find its own non-representational styles, appropriate to a society that no longer accepted the guidance of nature but believed instead in man's capacity to shape the natural world in accord with ideas and values of his own invention. Yet only by recognizing the non-universality of Greek art can one appraise the Greek achievement in its true proportions. The Greeks believed that they were revealing a divinity eternally present in nature. In reality they were creating new aesthetic norms and canons expressive of a new view of life.[7]

A similar movement, first from static to dynamic conceptions of reality, and afterwards from religious awe to a disillusioned rationalism, can be traced in the history of the other chief art form of the Athenian polis, the tragic drama. There are a number of conflicting theories about the origins of the drama, but it is agreed that it began as a ritual, in the singing of choral songs at festivals of the god Dionysus. Ritual is always static and collective, its purpose being to summarize certain recurrent elements in human experience and prevent any break in the continuity of natural processes. The transformation of the Athenian Dionysiac rituals into tragic drama, which apparently took place under the tyranny of Pisistratus during the middle decades of the sixth century, was brought about partly by the addition of an individual performer who gave answers to the chorus, and partly when new compositions, dealing with other myths besides those of Dionysus, were substituted for the traditional choric dithyrambs.[8] In this development was mirrored the whole evolution of the Athenian polis from

[7] The Greek ideal of the human figure has, on the whole, been accepted by Western man throughout his later history. Most Western portrayals of the female nude have conformed to the Greek canons, as can be shown by measuring the proportions; in the Greek model, for example, the distance between the breasts is roughly equal to that from the breasts to the navel. Northern Europe during the Middle Ages preferred a different type, represented in much German and Flemish painting. This "Gothic" nude has smaller breasts, a much longer torso, and a larger stomach. Both types are equally "natural."

[8] *Hypocrites,* the Greek word for actor (from the New Testament use of which is derived the English word "hypocrite"), originally meant an answerer.

the rule of tradition to the rule of law. Tribal groups had been brought together in a political community giving legal rights to individuals, and the authority of *dike*, established custom, had been transformed into *dikaiosyne*, the ideal justice that must be interpreted and implemented by human intelligence. By a parallel process, the worship of Dionysus ceased to consist merely of the traditional group songs and dances, developing into dramatic performances portraying specific individuals and presenting new interpretations of the meaning of life. And just as the stability of the Athenian commonwealth lasted only while men retained their belief in the ideal justice after which man-made laws were patterned, so the drama remained a vital art form only as long as its authors continued to believe in religious truths which it was their duty to expound.[9]

The original functions of Athenian tragedy were therefore both religious and political. A dramatic performance was an act of worship, but of worship paid to deities who required the exercise of human reason and not merely the repetition of traditional rituals. More significantly, it was a means for promoting unity among the citizens of the polis, inculcating loyalty to the new institutions of city-state society, and giving religious sanction to the change from agrarian tribalism to urban individualism. These religious and political motivations determined the work of the first great Athenian dramatist, Aeschylus, who lived through the period when democracy was established and the Persians were defeated, and who himself fought at Marathon. His main purpose was to interpret and justify in religious terms, as an expression of a divine design, the Athenian creation of an ordered democratic society under

---

[9] Possibly the highest of all literary forms, poetic drama is also the rarest. It can flourish only at a time when individuals have been released from tribalistic constraints, but when the social order is still permeated with religious values, so that the destinies of individual men and women are felt to have a universal significance. It was possible in ancient Athens because of the belief in the divine origin of the polis. It was possible again in the England of Elizabeth, the Spain of the Hapsburgs, and the France of the early Bourbons because the monarchical state was seen as a reflection of the God-created order of the cosmos (political doctrine pervades the histories and tragedies of Shakespeare no less than those of Aeschylus). When faith in the religious significance of human society begins to fade, it is no longer possible to present the fortunes of individuals in poetic terms, and dramatists and writers of fiction turn to prose. Genuine poetic drama ended in ancient Greece with Euripides and in modern Europe with Racine.

the rule of law. Unlike every other major figure in Greek thought, Aeschylus had a dynamic rather than a static conception of reality, interpreting history as a meaningful progress toward higher levels of civilization and thus overcoming the most significant weakness in the whole Greek way of life. All his surviving plays are inspired by history, and cannot be understood without a knowledge of the social and institutional changes in the evolution of the Athenian commonwealth. In Aeschylean tragedy the rise of the polis is projected against a vast cosmic backdrop comprising all of space and time, with a sublimity matching that of the Jewish prophet Deutero-Isaiah, who, only a few decades earlier, had similarly given a universal meaning to the moral evolution of his own people.

Concerned with the progress of the human race from savagery to civilization, Aeschylus gives little attention to individual characterization. His men and women are victims and instruments of social and cosmic forces and are condemned to work out their destinies with little opportunity for any exercise of free will. Suffering is the result of fate rather than of human error, certain families being condemned to crime and catastrophe in each successive generation. The historical reality reflected in the Aeschylean concept of the ancestral curse was the primitive tribal society in which the individual was absorbed into his kinship group and had the duty, in particular, of exacting vengeance for the killing of any of his kinsmen. As long as the punishment of crime was a private obligation, murders necessarily had to follow each other in endless sequence. But the chain could be broken and the individual could become the master of his own fate when kinship groups were brought together in a political organization based on rational principles of justice. Thus, the emphasis on fate in Aeschylean tragedy is an expression of the tribalistic phase in human development, and Aeschylus' real subject is man's rise to the dignity of individual freedom. His audience undoubtedly understood all these social implications, for it was within Aeschylus' own lifetime that the traditional Attic kinship groups had been finally dissolved by the reforms of Cleisthenes.

For Aeschylus, moreover, as for the Jewish prophets, the struggle for justice had cosmic overtones. Knowing that the Olympians had been brought into Greece at a relatively late period, he read prog-

ress and evolution into the whole structure of the universe by identifying the rise of the polis with the triumph of Apollo and Pallas
Athene over their chthonian predecessors. The typical Aeschylean
tragedy begins with a conflict between different divine figures and
ends with a reconciliation that carries human society to a higher
level. Behind these figures is the inscrutable Zeus, the supreme
being who has decreed that men can learn wisdom only by suffering [1] and who himself also, apparently, can realize his own
nature only through a process of growth. Aeschylus' sonorous
catalogues of outlandish peoples and places are a constant reminder of the infinite extent of space and time, while his rough-
hewn, compressed style, in which words highly charged with meaning are thrown alongside each other with a minimum of con-
nectives, suggest a mind wrestling with truths almost beyond the
power of human language to express. An Aeschylean tragedy gives
the impression of being built out of blocks of granite.

Dealing mainly with man as the puppet of destiny, the plays of
Aeschylus cannot be fitted into the Aristotelian tragic formula.
According to Aristotle, the ideal tragic theme is the passage from
happiness to misery of "a man who is highly renowned and prosperous, but one who is not pre-eminently virtuous and just, whose
misfortune, however, is brought upon him not by vice and depravity but by some *hamartia*." [2] Linguists disagree as to whether
hamartia always refers to a moral flaw or may also mean a mistake
of judgment; but in either case the Aristotelian view implies that
the tragic hero brings catastrophe upon himself by his own actions,
even though the punishment may far outweigh the original mis-
demeanor. The punishment of a wholly virtuous man would, according to Aristotle, be an offensive spectacle. Thus, a moral meaning must be read into the course of events, suffering being presented
as the result of some kind of error. In actuality this critical dictum,
which Aristotle derived supposedly from the works of Sophocles,
leads to a total misunderstanding of the meaning not of Aeschylus
alone, but of all the Greek tragedians, none of whom presented
life in these consolingly moralistic terms. Causing countless generations of commentators to search for the *harmartia* of which

---

[1] *Agamemnon*, 177–8.
[2] Aristotle: *Poetics*, translated by W. Hamilton Fyfe, XIII, 5.

Greek tragic heroes might conceivably have been guilty, often with
the most ludicrously inadequate results, it has probably been the
most misleading statement in the whole history of criticism.[3]

Of the seven surviving tragedies of Aeschylus, the *Persians,*
which deals with the reception of the news of Salamis at the court
of Xerxes, is complete in itself, while the *Agamemnon,* the
Choephori, and the *Eumenides* together make up the *Oresteia.* The
other three plays are tantalizing fragments of lost trilogies, but a
knowledge of the social background makes it possible to guess at
their meaning. The *Suppliants* presents the fifty daughters of
Danaus flying from their cousins, the fifty sons of Aegyptus, who
are determined to marry them. As the opening lines of the play
make sufficiently clear, the Danaids have a horror of marrying such
close relatives; they have the attitudes of a tribal society in which
marriage within the kinship group is strictly prohibited. We know
that in the two last sections of the trilögy the Danaids were forcibly
married; that by order of their father all but one of them murdered
their husbands; and that this one was then put on trial for disobeying her father and was acquitted through the intervention of
Aphrodite. According to the most plausible interpretation of
Aeschylus' theme, the sequence must have ended with the institution of new and more enlightened marriage laws which released
individuals from the endogamous taboos of tribal society and thus
resolved the conflict presented in the opening lines. *The Seven
Against Thebes* is the concluding section of a trilogy dealing with
the curse on the family of Oedipus, and describes how Oedipus'
son Eteocles, by killing his brother and at the same time dying,
ends the curse and thereby saves the city of Thebes from further
misfortune. Thus, Eteocles, who is presented as a noble but
doomed character, sacrifices himself and his family for the sake of
the polis. The meaning of *Prometheus Bound* is more obscure, for
Zeus is presented as a tyrant who has wished to destroy mankind
and has condemned Prometheus to unending torment for taking
pity on the human race and teaching them the arts of civilization.

---

[3] It is because of the Aristotelian
conception that a tragedy is generally
defined as a play that ends unhappily.
But the distinguishing features of Greek
tragedy were the seriousness of the
theme and the elevation of the style,
not the details of the plot. A number
of Greek tragedies end happily. To
avoid confusion, perhaps we should
abandon the word "tragedy" and speak
simply of "poetic drama."

5. *a. Pallas Athene, found on*   *b. Flute-player from the so-called Ludovisi*
the Acropolis of Athens.   *throne, found in southern Italy.*

Both these masterpieces of anonymous Greek craftsmen date from the
first half of the fifth century.

c. The Parthenon, completed in 433 B.C.

6. *a. Roman copy of the Cnidian Aphrodite of Praxiteles.*

b. The Hermes of Praxiteles, found at Olympia and probably dating from about 320 B.C.

c. Horsemen from the Parthenon frieze, representing the Panathenaic procession.

We are told that Prometheus will one day be released by Heracles, who, as a descendant of the Danaid who accepted marriage with her cousin, presumably represents the civilization of the polis. At the end of the trilogy the progressive aspirations that Prometheus embodies must somehow have been reconciled with the brute power represented by Zeus. But how the despotic Zeus of *Prometheus Bound* could have developed into the wise and beneficent supreme being of the other plays is a mystery.

Aeschylus' last and crowning achievement was the *Oresteia* (produced in 458), with the exception of the *Iliad* the greatest masterpiece of Hellenic literature. Through most of the trilogy, representing the savagery and superstition of man's primeval heritage, the psychic atmosphere remains thick and murky and the sense of doom is intense and unremitting. In the background is the bloody feud between the sons of Pelops, Atreus and Thyestes. The first drama of the trilogy presents the murder of Atreus' son Agamemnon by his wife Clytemnestra and her paramour Aegisthus, the son of Thyestes. In the *Choephori* Agamemnon's son Orestes avenges his father by killing Clytemnestra and Aegisthus, and is immediately driven mad by the Furies, ancient chthonian spirits of vengeance whose function is to punish any violation of tribal taboos. In the *Eumenides* Orestes is still pursued by the Furies, but their power has now been challenged by new and younger deities, Apollo and Pallas Athene, who have more regard for human sufferings than for the maintenance of "ancient right." The case of Orestes is submitted for decision to the Athenian law court of the Areopagus; and after Athene has expounded the meaning and sanctity of the rule of law, and Apollo and the leader of the Furies have spoken for the defense and prosecution, the judges decide for acquittal, the deciding vote being cast by Athene herself on the ground that inheritance is patrilineal and that Orestes' duty to his father therefore outweighed that to his mother. The reason for the decision, meaningless to modern readers, would have been understood by the play's original audience, who remembered the connection between matrilineal rules of inheritance and tribal taboos and obligations of vengeance. After the acquittal the Furies continue to complain because younger deities have overridden ancient right, but are finally persuaded by Athene to recognize their defeat, accept a new home in

Attica, and transform themselves into guardian spirits of the polis. Thus, the rational justice of the new civilization not only liberates the individual from the taboos and the family vendettas of tribal society; by taming the Furies it also enables him to overcome his own inner fears and pangs of guilt. No work in world literature has a theme of more far-reaching significance or is more unequivocably on the side of the forces of light.[4]

Phidias and Aeschylus were the spokesmen of an Athens that believed that, under divine guidance, order had been united with freedom, the *dikaiosyne* of the polis with the *arete* of the individual. Interpreting the Athenian constitution as an expression of divine and natural law and attributing its growth to the will of the Olympians, Aeschylus, speaking through the mouth of Pallas Athene in the *Eumenides,* gave religious sanctions to the rule of law and infused civic loyalty with a spirit of religious universalism. But this faith was never clearly expressed in theological terms, and in the course of the fifth century it was gradually undermined by the growth of rationalism. One of the most significant features of the Funeral Speech (allegedly delivered in the year 431) is that it makes no reference whatsoever, even in the most perfunctory terms, to any of the gods. Even the games and sacrifices are mentioned only on the ground that they supply Athenian citizens with healthful recreation. And as social cohesion cannot be maintained by reason alone without the support of the emotions, the gap was filled by the substitute religion of patriotism. Greek civilization could have remained creative only by moving forward from the particularism of the city-state to a broader unity. For a generation after the Persian wars Athens seemed capable of providing leadership in such an advance. But in the end she fell back into a narrow and intolerant tribalism.

As the manifesto of an enlightened faith in human freedom,

[4] The English Marxist George Thomson has shown how a knowledge of the social background illuminates the plays of Aeschylus. In accordance with Leninist practice, Mr. Thomson indulges in periodic outbreaks of vituperation against the dishonesty of "bourgeois" scholarship; but, apart from these displays of Communist bad manners, his *Aeschylus and Athens* is a valuable study. English-speaking scholars have usually approached Aeschylus in purely literary terms, and have therefore failed to understand his real subject matter. Most historians of Greek literature are frankly unable to offer any explanation either for the refusal of the Suppliants to marry their cousins or for the emphasis on patrilineal descent in the *Eumenides*. See, for example, Moses Hadas: *A History of Greek Literature,* pp. 79–82.

the Funeral Speech remains, of course, one of the beacon lights of all Western history. The Athenians, according to the speech, believed both in the legal liberty derived from the equality of all citizens under the law and in the right of the individual to do as he pleased without incurring anger or even "sour looks" from his neighbors; yet at the same time they had a healthy fear of disobeying the laws, "having a special regard for those which are ordained for the protection of the injured as well as to those unwritten laws which bring upon the transgressor of them the reprobation of the general sentiment." As free citizens, moreover, they developed every side of the human personality, achieving all-round adaptability rather than specialized skills. They were "lovers of the beautiful, yet simple in our tastes, cultivating the mind without loss of manliness;" [5] yet this did not prevent them from surpassing other peoples in political wisdom and military courage. Whereas other peoples "from early youth are always undergoing laborious exercises which are to make them brave, we live at ease, and yet are equally ready to face the perils which they face." "To sum up, I say that Athens is the School of Hellas, and that the individual Athenian in his own person seems to have the power of adapting himself to the most varied forms of action with the utmost versatility and grace." [6]

The speech, however, was delivered in time of war, and its main purpose was to stir the patriotic emotions of its auditors and give them motivations for self-discipline and self-sacrifice. The generation that had fought the Persian wars had found its sanctions in religious belief, interpreting Athenian civilization as an expression of divine and natural law. But Pericles offered instead the worship of the state as an end in itself, and offered no higher purpose. "I would have you day by day," he declared, "fix your eyes upon the greatness of Athens, until you become filled with the love of her; and when you are impressed by the spectacle of her glory, reflect that this empire has been acquired by men who knew their duty

---

[5] *Philokaloumen te gar met' euteleias kai philosophoumen aneu malakias.* Literally, "we love beauty with economy, and wisdom without softness." More freely, "we cultivate the arts without extravagance, and philosophy without loss of vigor." In this famous and untranslatable sentence Pericles seems to be contrasting Athenian good taste with the lavish ostentation of Asiatic art styles, though he may also be defending himself against accusations that he had spent too much money on the adornment of the Acropolis.

[6] Thucydides, II, 37–41.

and had the courage to do it, who in the hour of conflict had the fear of dishonor always present to them, and who, if ever they failed in an enterprise, would not allow their virtues to be lost to their country, but freely gave their lives to her as the fairest offering which they could present at her feet. . . . Make them your examples, and, esteeming courage to be freedom and freedom to be happiness, do not weigh too nicely the perils of war." [7]

Probably no community in history has been more worthy of the devotion of her citizens. Athens had become the visible embodiment of all that was noblest in the Hellenic spirit. But her inability to develop the religious universalism that had been implicit in the work of Aeschylus led to the ruin of Hellenic civilization.

---

[7] Thucydides, II, 44.

4

The Debacle

The immediate cause for the decline of Greek civilization was the Peloponnesian War. After the Persians had been defeated, the sense of Panhellenic unity, never effectively embodied in institutions, grew steadily weaker, and a struggle for supremacy between the two leading states finally became inevitable. Armed conflict began in 431 and, after continuing intermittently for nearly thirty years, ended in the victory of Sparta and the destruction of the Athenian Empire. The political consequences of the war proved to be transitory. Athens regained much of her power within a generation, and interstate warfare continued until the establishment of the Macedonian hegemony by the Battle of Chaeronea in the year 338. But on the spiritual level the triumph of the mindless militarism of Sparta over the city that had glorified freedom and intelligence was a traumatic event from which Greek culture never recovered.

What factors brought about this catastrophe? Plato regarded it as an illustration of the inherent weaknesses of a free and democratic society and of the need for an authoritarian order based on the belief in transcendental values; and through the influence of the Platonic philosophy, which has served as the main intellectual foundation of European conservatism, the outcome of the Peloponnesian War may be said to have had lasting effects on the Western cultural tradition. Whatever we may think of Plato's conclusions, the defeat of Athens did, in fact, illuminate certain of the perennial problems of human society, and a study of its causes is still rewarding, especially in view of the parallels between the political condition of fifth-century Greece and those of the Western world in recent generations. Such a study must take account not only of the political condition, but also of the whole intellectual and spiritual development of Greek civilization. For the Athenian debacle was associated with the growth of a rationalistic individualism devoid of any belief in unifying moral values, the manifestations of which can also be traced in philosophy and literature.

The primary need of the Greek world, as of the Western world in the twentieth century, was for unity. But this can never be achieved by political methods alone; state interests and interstate rivalries cannot be transcended without the affirmation of a universal ideal and standard of justice.[1] By combining some two hundred of the smaller Aegean cities into the Delian League during the Persian wars, Athens had begun to assume leadership in a movement for unification. This may be regarded as a practical manifestation of that faith in the spiritual unity of Greek civilization and in the principles of democracy and the rule of law that had inspired the *Oresteia*. Though Athens always dominated the League, the smaller states received substantial benefits in the form of naval protection, the promotion of trade, the use of the Athenian currency, and the right of appeal to the Athenian law courts with their high standards of justice. As long as they maintained democratic governments, they were not disturbed in the management of their internal affairs. This forward policy was supported chiefly by the commercial and democratic elements at Athens, and by

---

[1] The ideal solution of such a problem is, of course, the transfer of sovereignty to some kind of federation; but this is made impossible by that very exacerbation of tribalistic hatreds that makes it necessary. Sovereignty depends on human attitudes, and is essentially psychological; that form of authority to which men give their primary loyalty is sovereign; and loyalties cannot easily be transferred. Once loyalties have become fully crystallized around individual states, the only practicable way of preventing chronic warfare is for one state to assume leadership and make itself the embodiment of the principle of universality. This can most easily be accomplished by a peripheral state not previously involved too deeply in interstate rivalries. Thus, Greece was finally united by Macedon, which was able to represent the Panhellenic ideal in spite of its cultural backwardness. The unification of European civilization has been attempted both by France (under Napoleon) and by Germany, each of which failed because it did not transcend its own national self-interest. Today two peripheral powers, the United States and the Soviet Union, are competing for leadership. It can be predicted that victory will go to the power that most genuinely represents universalist ideals.

similar groups in other cities. The aristocratic landowning families throughout Greece, on the other hand, continued to oppose Athenian predominance; there was, in fact, an oligarchical pro-Spartan group even in Athens itself. Yet if the Athenian democracy had retained the support of all the satellite states, it is unlikely that it could ever have been defeated by the Spartans.

Unfortunately the unifying idea was too weak and the forces of particularism were too strong. After the removal of the Persian threat, some of the Aegean cities wished to leave the league, and Athens responded by using force against them. Thus, the league gradually degenerated into an empire, held together not by common interests and ideals, but by Athenian power. This degeneration began under the leadership of Pericles, who was largely responsible for guiding Athenian foreign policy from 461 to his death in 429. A disciple of the philosophers, and no worshipper of the Aeschylean Zeus, Pericles, as the Funeral Speech indicates, offered the Athenian democracy no loyalty higher than the greatness of its own polis. While he advocated moderation and warned against excessive ambition, he frankly affirmed that Athens could retain her supremacy only by arousing fear. His successors in the leadership of the democracy remembered this dictum and forgot the prudence with which Pericles had applied it. Cynically avowing their exclusive concern with Athenian interests, they exacted heavy tributes from the satellite states, imposed crushing penalties upon any that attempted to secede from the empire, tried to extend Athenian domination throughout the whole Greek world (most notably by the unsuccessful invasion of Sicily in 415), and thereby caused such a general hatred that the Spartans were able to appear to most of the other Greek states as the protectors of their liberties. Thus, the defeat of Athens was caused primarily by her own moral and spiritual errors—by her failure to assume the obligations of leadership in the unification of Greece and her repudiation of all values and ideals higher than her own aggrandizement.

The reasons for the catastrophe, and their close relationship with the general intellectual climate, were made unmistakably clear by Thucydides, who, in exile from his native Athens, set out to analyze the war with the same rationalistic objectivity that the philosophers had displayed in the study of nature. The first historian to explain events consistently and convincingly in terms of natural causes,[2] he left no doubt about his verdict, though, apart from an occasional grim and laconic comment, he allowed the heartbreaking events that he narrated to speak for themselves. The war itself, he declared, resulted from the growing power of Athens and the consequent fear of Sparta, and was thus a necessary consequence of the division of Greece into separate city-states. But he made it plain that the defeat of the Athenians was by no means necessary, but was caused by their unrestrained pursuit of power as an end in itself, and hence was a consequence of their general view of life.

Of all the episodes recorded by Thucydides, the most poignant and the most revealing was the conflict between the Athenians and the inhabitants of the Aegean island of Melos. Descended from Dorian colonists related to the Spartans, the Melians had never belonged to the Delian League, and, regarding it as dishonorable to fight against their kinsmen, had resolved to remain neutral in the war. In the year 416, however, the Athenians decided to coerce them into joining their empire and sent envoys to collect tribute. According to Thucydides, Athens justified her demands by an appeal to natural law. "Of the gods we believe, and of men we know," her representatives told the Melians, "that by a law of their nature wherever they can rule they will. This law was not made by us, and we are not the first who have acted upon it; we did but inherit it, and shall bequeath it to all time, and we know that you and all mankind, if you were as strong as we are, would do as we do. . . . We both alike know that into the discussion of human affairs the question of justice only enters where the pressure of necessity is equal, and that the powerful exact what they can

---

[2] Like Herodotus, Thucydides believed in the law of *hybris-nemesis,* but whereas Herodotus regarded this as simply a general principle of life, for Thucydides it was actually inherent in sequences of events. In the narrative of Herodotus, the final *nemesis* often has no verifiable connection with the original *hybris.* Thucydides, on the other hand, always shows in concrete detail how each item in a causal chain leads necessarily to the next. The difference between the two men shows how rapidly rationalism had advanced.

Properly to appreciate Thucydides, one may contrast the *History of the Peloponnesian War* with the Book of Kings. Each book records how catastrophe overwhelmed a city, and each book attempts to explain why. Chronologically, the two books were separated by only about two hundred years, but in attitude they are light-years apart.

and the weak grant what they must. . . . Surely you cannot dream
of flying to that false sense of honor which has been the ruin of so
many when death and dishonor were staring them in the face.
Many men with their eyes still open to the consequences have
found the word 'honor' too much for them, and have suffered a
mere name to lure them on, until it has drawn down upon them
real and irretrievable calamities." When the Melians refused to accept this reasoning, and continued to insist that it would be dishonorable for them to surrender their neutrality, the Athenians
besieged their city, forced them to surrender, and (according to
the brief and unadorned conclusion of Thucydides) "put to death
all who were of military age, and made slaves of the women and
children. They then colonised the island, sending thither five hundred settlers of their own." [3]

How could a people capable of such an action have appreciated
the humane idealism of the Funeral Speech and the tragic drama?
In fairness to the Athenians, it should be recorded that during most
of the war years they were still willing to permit dissenters to express their convictions with a freedom that would not be tolerated
in any modern community under similar conditions. Aristophanes
was able to ridicule the leaders of the war party and plead for
peace, and Euripides expressed his feelings about the Melian episode by producing in the following year that bitter and pathetic
denunciation of military brutality, the *Trojan Women*. Except
for a few brief intervals, Athens never lost her respect for intelligence. While her moral degeneration was caused largely by the
pressures of the war, it was, in fact, justified, as the debate with
the Melians makes plain, by means of philosophical ideas. For
fifth-century Greek thought, once it had cut loose from its moor-
ings in the traditional religion, had failed to maintain any adequate
standards of justice and had developed a view of life in which
the pursuit of power seemed the only reality. By repudiating the
mythical preconceptions that had still pervaded the thinking of
the Ionians and of Aeschylus, and by carrying rationalistic individualism to its logical limits, fifth-century Greece reached an intellectual and moral verge. This was perhaps the most brilliant
period in the entire history of human culture. It also provided a

---

[3] Thucydides, V, 105, 89, 111, 116.

convincing demonstration of the inadequacy of rationalism alone as a guide for human life.

Speculative thought had originated in the intuition of the Milesians that the world was a unity governed not by the actions of gods and demons, but by uniform laws of causation. Yet in spite of their scientific bent, the Milesians had inherited the original Homeric faith that nature was infused with divinity, and had regarded natural law as the manifestation of a cosmic justice and hence as normative for human society. Their fifth-century successors, on the other hand, displaying a more consistently scientific attitude, began to interpret the universe as simply a complex of material forces, governed solely by brute necessity, and no longer giving support to moral and political values. Thus, natural law became descriptive of natural processes and ceased to serve as a unifying social myth. Three men, the Italian Empedocles and the Thracians Anaxagoras and Democritus, most clearly represented the direct line of descent from Thales. All of them searched for some comprehensive hypothesis that would account for all natural processes, and all of them asserted the universality of scientific laws of causation; as Democritus declared, "all things happen by virtue of necessity." [4] Only scattered fragments of their writings have been preserved, but these relics still convey something of the sense of adventure with which they explored ideas that had never before been propounded by any human mind. For the first time in history, thinking was free from religious and political inhibitions, and men could follow the course of logic wherever it might lead them.

Empedocles of Agrigentum was a complex and ambiguous character, remembered by posterity not only for his philosophy, but also for his fanatical leadership of the democratic forces in his native city and for his claims to miraculous powers (according to legend, he ended his life by jumping into the crater of Mount Etna in the hope that men would believe he had been snatched up into heaven). He wrote poems in which he analyzed the world into four basic elements, earth, water, air, and fire, and two basic forces, attraction and repulsion. Anaxagoras of Klazomenae spent most of his mature life at Athens, where he was a friend of Pericles and one of the masters of Euripides. He suggested

---

[4] Milton C. Nahm: *Selections from Early Greek Philosophy,* p. 165.

that the universe originated as a mass of seeds or germs that were originally undifferentiated from each other but were set in motion by a pervasive force, "infinite and self-powerful and mixed with nothing," [5] which he defined as mind. Both these cosmologies, however, raised more problems than they solved and failed to satisfy the monistic impulse that characterized all the thinking of this period. The climax of scientific simplification was represented by Democritus of Abdera, of whose life we know almost nothing, but who was apparently born about the year 460. With Democritus, for the first time, we encounter a complete and consistent materialism. The universe, he declared, was infinite in both time and extent, and consisted of nothing but empty space and of atoms perpetually in motion, and all the processes both of nature and of the human mind could be interpreted as resulting from the constant redistribution of atoms into new combinations.

Democritus was fully aware of the moral implications of materialism. He wrote extensively on psychological problems, and adopted a thoroughgoing individualism that had no place either for the sense of aesthetic irradiation from which the traditional Olympian religion had derived so much of its vitality or for any concept of ethical obligation. Discussing sensory perception, he argued that all perceptible things were simply arrangements of atoms differing only in size and shape, and that the aesthetic qualities that men ascribed to nature therefore had no objective existence. "We really perceive nothing strictly true, but only what changes with the condition of our being or the influences going toward it or resisting it. . . . By convention, there is sweet; by convention, bitter; by convention, hot; by convention, cold; by convention, color; but in truth there exist atoms and the void." Thus, the experience of beauty was merely an illusion of the human mind, not an insight into reality. The ethics of Democritus was in conformity with his denial of objective values, and foreshadowed what later became known as Epicureanism. Basing his view of good and evil simply on what produced the maximum of satisfaction and the minimum of pain for the individual, he recommended emotional tranquillity. "Men attain cheerfulness through moderation in pleasure and equalness of life. Excess and want are ever alternating and causing

---

[5] Fairbanks: op. cit., p. 239.

great disturbance in the soul. Souls that are shifting from extreme to extreme are neither steadfast nor cheerful. You should, therefore, fix your mind upon what is possible and be content with what you have." As a later commentator summarized his doctrine, "the end of action is tranquillity, which is not identical with pleasure, as some by a false interpretation have understood, but a state in which the soul continues calm and strong, undisturbed by any fear or superstition or any other emotion." [6]

This materialist cosmology was, of course, a hypothesis about the constitution of the universe, not a generalization from observed phenomena. The atomic theory has proved in modern times to be a useful intellectual tool for exploring certain aspects of nature (though it does not cover other aspects, such as the behavior of organisms); but the original atomism of Democritus was not supported by experimental verification. As was pointed out by a contemporary critic of this type of reasoning, either the great physician Hippocrates or one of his disciples, it was a deduction from certain mental postulates, not from experience, and therefore should be considered as literature rather than as science. "Postulates are admissible in dealing with insoluble mysteries: for example, things in the sky or below the earth. If a man were to pronounce on them neither he himself nor any of his audience could tell whether he was speaking the truth. For there is no test the application of which would give certainty." [7] These postulates, moreover, can be regarded as reflections of the general climate of opinion. It was the growing individualism of fifth-century Greek society, its impatience with all collective restraints, and its sense of the limitless possibilities of human action, that impelled philosophers to interpret nature

---

[6] Nahm: op. cit., pp. 165, 166, 209, 218.

[7] "Certain physicians and philosophers assert that nobody can know medicine who is ignorant what man is: he who would treat his patients properly must, they say, learn this. But the question they raise is one for philosophy; it is the province of those who, like Empedocles, have written on natural science, what man is from the beginning, how he came into being at first, and from what elements he was originally constructed. But my view is, first, that all that philosophers or physicians have written on natural science pertains less to medicine than to literature. I also hold that clear knowledge about the nature of man can be acquired from medicine and from no other source." Quoted from *Ancient Medicine,* a fifth-century treatise written by a member of the Hippocratic school, by Benjamin Farrington: *Greek Science,* pp. 71, 74.

in terms simply of atoms in motion, undirected by any cosmic pattern of justice, and to declare that the universe was infinite. In the Europe of the Renaissance two thousand years later similar social tendencies resulted in a similar cosmology.[8] The significant, and genuinely scientific, aspect of this natural philosophy, however, was the exclusion of all value judgments. For the first time men were attempting to formulate a plausible interpretation of natural processes without demanding corroboration for human ideals of justice. Cosmological speculation had ceased to be mythical and become purely rationalistic. And because the whole Greek way of life had been based on faith in the divinity of nature, this intellectual development had cataclysmic effects.

The social implications of the new cosmologies were explored in the Sophistic movement, whose leading representatives were Protagoras, Gorgias, and Hippias. As we know them mainly through the diatribes of Plato, it is difficult to judge them fairly, and the word "Sophist," which originally meant simply a man who pursued wisdom, has never lost the unsavory connotations that Plato succeeded in pinning on it. In actuality the Sophists were a group of thinkers engaged in grappling with the central problem confronting any rationalistic society: the problem of establishing moral and political values without any support either from religious belief or from nature. They also represented a new development in education. With the growth of democracy, middle-class citizens wanted

---

[8] Whether the universe is finite or infinite is, of course, unknowable, either conception being equally beyond the scope of the human mind and imagination. How human beings choose to regard the universe depends on the sensibility of age rather than on any process of strictly scientific reasoning. The change from the finite universe of the Middle Ages to the infinite universe of post-Renaissance astronomy was a reflection of the dissolution of the feudal social system and the growth of individualism; it was given expression by the fifteenth-century philosopher Nicholas of Cusa long before it acquired scientific formulation, and was a product of the spirit that resulted, on another plane, in the voyages of discovery.

This spirit became manifest in the development of the visual arts at an even earlier period. According to Sir Kenneth Clark (*Landscape into Art*, Chapter 1), this occurred about A.D. 1420. "In a very extended sense of the term, this new way of thinking about the world may be called scientific, for it involved the sense of relation and comparison, as well as the measurement on which science is based. But it antedates the real rise of science by almost two hundred years, and we find it in the work of artists who do not seem to have been troubled by the mathematics of perspective, in the Blessed Angelico and the manuscript illuminators of the North."

a training that would fit them for political leadership and enable
them to compete oratorically with the members of the aristocratic
families who, like Pericles at Athens, had largely continued to
dominate popular debates. The Sophists were professional teachers
who undertook to make their pupils into statesmen, and who therefore emphasized such studies as grammar, rhetoric, and dialectic.
Much of the hostility expressed so violently in the Platonic dialogues was a simple expression of class prejudice. As Plato never
grew tired of complaining, the Sophists actually charged money for
their lessons instead of being gentlemen of leisure interested in
wisdom for its own sake; and they taught their pupils argumentative cleverness and facility in words instead of inculcating the
traditional standards of virtue and wisdom.

One aspect of the Sophistic view of life was represented by the
formula of Protagoras: "Man is the measure of all things, of the
existence of things that are, and of the non-existence of things that
are not." [9] This tantalizing fragment suggests a whole revolution
in human thought. In its epistemological applications it meant
that men could attribute reality only to what they perceived, and
that as different individuals had different perceptions, one must
conclude that truth was not absolute, but relative to the observer.
Presumably it meant also that there were no absolute values, and
that all rules of behavior should be tested by the standard of human needs. It was thus the slogan of an anti-religious, libertarian,
relativist, and pragmatic view of life. Implicit in the Protagorean
formula was the doctrine that man must create his own institutions
without guidance from any form of authority. Whether the gods
existed or not was, according to Protagoras, unknowable. Plato
directly challenged him in the *Laws* by declaring that God was the
measure of all things.

The main emphasis of Sophistic thinking, however, appears to
have been placed on the distinction between *physis* and *nomos,*
nature and convention. In the ages of confidence, when social
thinking still moves within the framework of mythical postulates,
nature and convention always appear as essentially harmonious,
the laws and mores of society and its artistic forms being assumed

---

[9] Nahm: op. cit., p. 242.

to be in accord with the structure of the cosmos. Such had been the case in the Athens of Aeschylus and Phidias.[1] The emphasis on conflict is always the mark of an age of disintegration when a growing individualism is in revolt against the established order. Pointing to the differences in the customs and institutions of different states, and speculating about the origins of civilization, the Sophists arrived at a contractual theory of society. For the sake of mutual preservation, they supposed, men had agreed with each other to set up governments and make rules of behavior, all of which were therefore conventional rather than natural, and should be judged by the standard of practical utility. As Plato summarizes Sophistic doctrine in the *Laws,* "These people would say that the good exists not by nature but by art, and by the laws of states, which are different in different places, according to the agreement of those who make them; and that the honorable is one thing by nature and another thing by law, and that the principles of justice have no existence at all in nature, but that mankind are always disputing about them and altering them, and that the alterations which are made by art and by law have no basis in nature, but are of authority for the moment and at the time for which they are made." [2]

The weakness of any contractual theory, apart from its obvious lack of historicity, is that it fails to account for the sense of moral obligation which is an inherent element in man's gregarious self. One group of Sophists, represented chiefly by Hippias and Antiphon, continued, however, to give a mythical connotation to nature, regarding it as a source of standards that men were obligated to obey, and arrived at doctrines tending to undermine the whole

---

[1] Thus, for Shakespeare, speaking through the mouth of Ulysses in *Troilus and Cressida* (I, iii), the social hierarchy of the Renaissance state was a reflection of the order of the natural universe. Polixenes expressed an allied idea in *The Winter's Tale* (IV, iv): "Nature is made better by no mean but nature makes that mean; so, over that art which you say adds to nature, is an art that nature makes." Similarly, nineteenth-century economists (and some of their modern disciples, such as F. A. Hayek) regarded the competitive laissez-faire system (even including such complicated and obviously man-made devices as the gold standard) as essentially "natural." Karl Polanyi, in *The Great Transformation,* has examined the mythical elements in this view of "nature."

[2] *Laws,* translated by Benjamin Jowett, 889–90.

structure of Greek political and social life. The distinctions between Greeks and foreigners, free citizens and slaves, and the loyalties and institutions of the different Greek cities were merely
conventional, and therefore had no particular claim to respect.
What was natural was, on the one hand, the independence of the
individual and, on the other hand, the unity of the human race and
the moral principles respected by all human beings. This view of
nature was to have an immense influence, since it was afterwards
developed into the Stoic doctrine of natural law and transmitted
through Stoic writings to post-Renaissance Europe, whence it became the main intellectual foundation of Western liberalism. It
should, of course, be recognized that this system of natural rights
and obligations, being a statement of values and not of facts, is
connected only by name with the natural law of rationalistic science.

Most of the disciples of the Sophists appear, however, to have
followed rationalistic thinking to its logical conclusion, the inevitable result being an emphasis on power as the ultimate determi-
nant in human affairs. In the form of the thesis that Plato attributes
in the first book of the *Republic* to Thrasymachus (whom we know
from other sources as a teacher of rhetoric), the intent seems to
have been primarily descriptive. There were no objective or universal standards of justice; rules of justice were made by men for
their own advantage, and in any particular community they would
always reflect the interests of the strongest group, varying according to whether power belonged to a tyrant, the upper class, or the
masses. In spite of the contempt with which Thrasymachus is
treated by his auditors in the dialogue, his argument is, of course,
when considered simply as a statement of realities, quite irrefu-
table, and Socrates does not, in fact, refute it, but evades the issue
first by some verbal legerdemain and then by shifting the discussion to a wholly different subject.

But as men are incapable of thinking about what *is* without also
asking what *ought to be,* they must always deduce normative conclusions from any description of social processes (this is why any
purely rationalistic system of thought, without mythical ingredients,
must end in contradictions). If all values are merely reflections of
somebody's will to power, then it is right to pursue power, the
denial of all moral standards becoming itself a morality and being

justified as in accord with nature.³ As Plato pointed out in the *Laws*, Sophistic teaching was interpreted as meaning that "the highest right is might, and in this way the young fall into impieties, under the idea that the gods are not such as the law bids them imagine; and hence arise factions, the philosophers inviting them to lead a true life according to nature, that is, to live in real dominion over others, and not in legal subjection to them." ⁴ This paradoxical, though inevitable, conclusion is expounded by Callicles in Plato's *Gorgias*. Proclaiming a Nietzschean will to power as the rule of justice, Callicles argues that moral restraints are inventions of the mass of weak human beings who wish to protect themselves from the superior few, and that the strong men should refuse to be bound by them. "Nature herself intimates that it is just for the better to have more than the worse, the more powerful than the weaker; and in many ways she shows, among men as among animals, and indeed among whole cities and races, that justice consists in the superior ruling over and having more than the inferior. . . . These are the men who act according to nature; yes, by Heaven, and according to the law of nature; not, perhaps, according to that artificial law, which we invent and impose upon our fellows, of whom we take the best and strongest from their youth upwards, and tame them like young lions—charming them with the sound of the voice, and saying to them, that with equality they must be content, and that the equal is the honorable and the just. But if there were a man who had sufficient force, he would shake off and break through, and escape from all this; he would trample underfoot all our formulas and spells and charms, and all our laws which are against nature." ⁵

Greek history during the Peloponnesian War was a demonstration of the practical effects of this morality of power. On one level

³ The philosophy of Nietzsche is a significant example of the inability of the human mind, when dealing with moral questions, to remain on a purely descriptive plane. Repudiating all objective standards of value, Nietzsche constantly insists that all human attitudes are products of the universal drive for power; thus, the "slave morality" of Christianity is a device by which the masses assert power over the strong few. If all forms of morality reflect a will to power, then, of course, none of them can be objectively advocated or condemned. Nietzsche, however, goes on to attribute an objective value to strength, which leads him to condemn "slave morality" and declare that the few need to protect themselves from the envy and moral sickness of the masses. All forms of amoralism result in similar paradoxes.

⁴ *Laws,* 890.
⁵ *Gorgias,* 483.

this was illustrated by the brutality of the Athenian war party, who justified their behavior (according at least to Thucydides' account of the debate with the Melians) by appealing to the law of nature. But once men have moved beyond tribalistic modes of thinking, no denial of universal standards of justice can be restricted to inter-state rivalries; it must lead also to the erosion of state loyalties, and can end only in the war of each against all. The war period saw a revival of murderous class conflicts between oligarchical and democratic groups. As Thucydides declared, "revolution gave birth to every form of wickedness in Hellas. The simplicity which is so large an element in a noble nature was laughed to scorn and disap-peared. An attitude of perfidious antagonism everywhere prevailed; for there was no word binding enough, nor oath terrible enough to reconcile enemies. Each man was strong only in the conviction that nothing was secure; he must look to his own safety, and could not afford to trust others." [6] Meanwhile, dissolute adventurers set out to gain power for themselves with a frank contempt for all religious and political restraints and all traditional concepts of shame and honor. The debacle of Greek civilization was most fully exemplified in the career of Alcibiades, the most brilliant and most dissolute character of the age, who fought alternately for the Athenians and the Spartans, but always primarily for his own aggrandizement.

Thus, political and intellectual trends followed the same course, the catastrophe of Greek political life through state and class war-fare being closely connected with the dilemmas reached by Greek intellectual life in the Sophistic movement. In such a process of constant mutual interaction, it is always impossible to assign causal priority to either the movement of events or the movement of ideas. Each of them is actually a manifestation of something deeper and more intangible, the general spirit of society; and this always finds its fullest and truest record in artistic creation. One of the world's major writers lived through the age of Athenian greatness and decline, and his works give direct expression to that self-confident individualism which was ultimately responsible for both the So-phistic movement and the destruction of Athenian power. By link-ing it with the Homeric ethos, and even with certain aspects of the

---

[6] Thucydides, III, 83.

old chthonian religion, he presents it as an inherent element in Greek culture from its origins.

Sophocles, who was born about the year 495 and died in 406, has probably been the most persistently misunderstood of all great writers.[7] Critics have conspired to represent him as the apostle of temperance, moderation, and self-control, the virtues that the Greeks were always talking about but rarely practiced. This illusion is fostered by the classic artistry of his style and plots, but is primarily due to the misleading *harmartia* theory of Aristotle. Most of Sophocles' admirers have supposed that his heroes come to grief because of their own errors, in particular because they are guilty of the sin of pride. It is true that Sophocles expresses a profound reverence for divine powers and denounces Sophistic rationalism. The plot of *Oedipus Rex* shows that, contrary to all rational expectation, the predictions of the gods must eventually be fulfilled.[8] But the religion of Sophocles, like that of Homer, is imbued with the old aristocratic ethos. The strong individual who can endure misfortune without being broken by it is the favorite of the gods. If one forgets Aristotle and studies what actually happens in the plays of Sophocles, it becomes plain that his sympathies are wholly with his suffering heroes, whom he admires for their very lack of restraint. The plays portray a series of characters of the most extraordinary strength, arrogance, stubbornness, and volcanic passion. These embodiments of heroic individualism come into conflict with the demands of society, which are likely to be expressed by some political leader with mediocre abilities and ignoble motives. The outcome is sometimes tragic and sometimes happy, but it is made evident that the polis needs the hero whom it misunderstands and tries unsuccessfully to discipline and control, and that by continuing to display his individual *arete* in spite of his sufferings he can become the savior of his people and may even earn deification. The supposition that Sophoclean characters come to misfortune because of their own moral flaws or errors leads to a most fantastic misreading of the plays. For Sophocles, unlike Aes-

---

[7] Cedric H. Whitman: *Sophocles* is the best study in English. Though emphasizing Sophocles' confidence in human power, Whitman does not accept any parallelism between the Sopho- clean idealization and the Alcibiadean reality.

[8] See Bernard M. W. Knox: *Oedipus at Thebes.*

chylus, the destiny of the individual is determined mainly by his own character and actions rather than by some family curse or by the will of Zeus; but his sufferings are not a punishment for any *hamartia*, but an ordeal that enables him to display his strength even more nobly.[9]

Four of the seven extant plays of Sophocles have unhappy endings, but in none of them can the misfortune of the central character be regarded as a punishment for error. Ajax is brought to disgrace by Pallas Athene (who—significantly, in view of her close association with the institutions of the Athenian polis—is portrayed in a somewhat unsympathetic light) and by Odysseus, who, as the man who gained his ends by cleverness rather than by valor, had become a standard symbol of the democratic politician; and, being dominated by an Achillean compulsion to win glory, he can finally maintain his honor only by suicide. The last four hundred lines of the play (usually dismissed by exponents of the *hamartia* theory as irrelevant) make its meaning plain, for they show how Ajax's friends successfully asserted his right to burial as a hero. Antigone, insisting that the unwritten laws of the old chthonian deities are more worthy of respect than the regulations of the polis, as represented by the well-meaning but blundering and unimaginative Creon, dies a noble death, while Creon is reduced to misery by the loss of his wife and child. Oedipus, having innocently violated the most sacred of all taboos, shows his virtue by resolutely uncovering the truth and accepting the consequences. Only Deianeira, the heroine of the *Trachiniae*, who is brought to ruin by the intensity of her love for her undeserving husband, seems to lack any vindication. In each of these plays critics have made

---

[9] What little we know about the personal life of Sophocles suggests that he was by no means a practitioner of the *sophrosyne* that the critics have insisted on reading into his plays. An aristocrat in both his political sympathies and his way of living, he was notoriously under the domination of Eros, especially in its homosexual forms. The best-authenticated anecdote about him depicts him, while serving as a general of the Athenian forces, giving a demonstration of his skill in "strategy" by stealing a kiss from a beautiful boy. Plato quotes him as welcoming old age because it diminished the power of Eros. In his final years (according to late and not wholly reliable sources) he is said to have become infatuated with a celebrated courtesan and to have been sued by his son for bequeathing his property to his illegitimate children, but to have convinced an Athenian jury that he was still *compos mentis* by reciting choruses from the play on which he was currently at work.

every effort to discover conventional moral meanings, blaming Ajax for insolence to Pallas Athene, Antigone for self-will, Oedipus for arrogance, and Deianeira for not being a sufficiently submissive wife; and in each play it is obvious that it is precisely the unbending quality of his heroes and heroines that Sophocles especially wishes to present in a favorable light.

Sophocles' view of life is displayed even more clearly in the three plays of his final period, the central characters of which continue to display an obstinate determination to go their own ways in defiance of all social pressures, and end not in catastrophe, but in triumph. Agamemnon's daughter Electra is rewarded for her stubborn fidelity to her father's memory by the advent of Orestes and his successful killing of Clytemnestra and Aegisthus. Unlike the *Choephori* of Aeschylus, the *Electra* ends in victory; Orestes is not pursued by any Furies, and does not require any civic law court to restore him to sanity. The *Philoctetes* shows the Greek leaders in need of the hero whom they have shamefully mistreated, and Odysseus attempts to secure his services by deceit; the trickery is exposed, but after a divine intervention Philoctetes agrees to give the Greeks the aid without which they cannot capture Troy. Finally, in *Oedipus at Colonus,* Sophocles' crowning work, apparently written close to his ninetieth year, the old hero, still arrogant and passionate in spite of all the horrors he has experienced, earns divine honors; and in accord with the beliefs of the old chthonian religion, his tomb in the soil of Attica becomes a lasting source of blessings for the Athenian people.

Fusing elements from both the Homeric and the chthonian traditions in order to glorify the *arete* of the strong individual, the plays of Sophocles can be regarded as expressions of a triumphant humanism. No writer in world literature has affirmed a more vigorous faith in man. But in contrasting an Antigone with a Creon, an Ajax or a Philoctetes with the leaders of the Greek army, Sophocles is also recording a loss of faith in the justice of the polis. His work registers the failure of the Aeschylean attempt to give a religious sanction to the Athenian form of government. Whereas Aeschylus had found a harmony of freedom and order in the rule of law, Sophocles sees a conflict which can properly be ended, as in the *Philoctetes,* only by the vindication of the individual hero. Thus, if he is placed in his context in fifth-century Athens, he becomes a less inspiring and more ambiguous figure. And while a writer cannot be held morally responsible for the forces of corruption in the society whose spirit is reflected in his work, there was at least one moment in history when the idealized individualism glorified in the Sophoclean drama became unmistakably linked with the anarchical amoralism that was bringing Greek culture to destruction. For in 411 Alcibiades, who four years earlier had fled from Athens to avoid indictment for profaning sacred rites, was again made general of the Athenian forces, after negotiations on the Aegean island of Samos, and in the following year the Athenians won a great naval victory at a place close to the site of Troy. And in 409 Sophocles produced his *Philoctetes,* in which the hero, abandoned on the Aegean island of Lemnos for ten years because his incurable wound has caused a profanation of sacred rites, is ordered by the god Heracles to forget his resentment, join the Greek forces at Troy, and thereby assure them of victory.

Such an overt parallelism with contemporary events is rare in Sophocles, who was primarily an artist rather than a social commentator. When we turn to the works of his leading competitor, on the other hand, we find a much more direct expression of political and philosophical issues. Euripides, born about a dozen years after Sophocles and dying one year before him, was a disciple of the natural philosophers and the Sophists, and his plays are filled with the clash of ideas, with expressions of religious skepticism, and with affirmations of faith in the Athens that stood for freedom and the protection of the oppressed, mingled with diatribes against the power-hungry politicians who were betraying her great ideals. To understand Euripides, one must make constant reference to his intellectual milieu, whereas the works of Sophocles seem, by contrast, to be timeless; and while Sophocles glorifies the individualism that was leading to anarchy on the political plane, the more humane and more sophisticated Euripides is aware of all its sinister implications. Yet precisely for these reasons Euripides has less social significance. The writer is always a product of his age and milieu, and when he is concerned simply with the artistic projection of his own emotional attitudes, ignoring all superficial and transitory currents of opinion, he tells us more about his society than when he gives explicit reflection to its political and philosophical conflicts. Euripides exhibits the intellectual climate of fifth-century

Athens, but the plays of Sophocles give a deeper understanding of its underlying spirit.[1]

Euripidean tragedy, nevertheless, indicates the direction in which Greek society was moving. The chief impression conveyed by his nineteen extant plays is that the world is chaotic. His work is a mass of fragments, many of them extraordinary for their lyric splendor, their intellectual acuteness, or their insight into human character, but not bound together by any coherent system of beliefs. He is sensitive to a wider range of impressions than either of his predecessors; but the firm outlines of the Aeschylean or Sophoclean view of life have been dissolved. Whereas Aeschylus sees man as the instrument of a beneficent divine will and Sophocles affirms his ability to rise superior to all misfortunes, Euripides portrays him as the helpless victim either of collective injustice or of demonic and irresponsible powers of nature. The forces that control human life have no moral meaning or purpose and cannot be rationally explained. For this reason Euripides is unable to give his plays the formal aesthetic unity characteristic of the work of his predecessors. If life is a series of accidents, it can no longer be presented through the logical development of coherent plots. A typical Euripidean tragedy is a sequence of episodes illustrating different aspects of human suffering, the causes being described in the Prologue or the Choruses but not integrated into the dramatic action. While some of the plays of Euripides are held in shape by romantically melodramatic plots that cannot be taken seriously, others are almost formless, abounding in abrupt changes of mood and subject, and sometimes culminating in impossible denouements consummated through the tongue-in-cheek device of a *deus ex machina*.

Euripides was the product of an age when the religious myths that had given Hellenic civilization its sense of unity had lost their efficacy. Instead of refining and spiritualizing them in order to express the consciousness of a new age, as Aeschylus had done, he was frankly a rationalist and a realist, portraying not the ideal norms that earlier generations had seen behind natural appearances, but human beings and the human predicament as they actually were. His gods are often depicted as explicitly fraudulent

---

[1] H. D. F. Kitto: *Greek Tragedy* gives the most convincing interpretation of Euripides.

or immoral (like Apollo in the *Ion*), or are presented under such improbable circumstances that belief is impossible. In dealing with the heroic figures bequeathed by the epic age, he seeks chiefly to reduce them to the human scale, presenting male characters (like Admetus and Jason) notable chiefly for a cowardly egoism, while his women are either unhappy victims of masculine brutality (like Alcestis and Hecuba) or (like Medea) strong-willed and amoral adventuresses. But, apart from occasional assertions that the universe is animated by a spiritual power and that the gods are good and therefore incapable of the wicked deeds that men attribute to them, he can present no new unifying mythology to replace that of the Olympians. The religious intuitions that were expressed in the worship of the traditional gods are, in fact, still present in his work, in baffling and significant contrast to its generally rationalistic spirit. For the early Greeks, as for all primitive peoples, those irruptions of demonic force that, whether for good or for evil, elevated human life above its normal tenor were manifestations of divinity. Probably the most moving of the extant plays of Euripides are the *Hippolytus* and the *Bacchae;* and each of them presents a demonic power, wholly destructive in its effects but explicitly identified with one of the gods. In the *Hippolytus* the central character, having dedicated himself to chastity, is brought to disgrace and death by the jealous anger of Aphrodite, while in the *Bacchae* Dionysus sweeps away all who refuse to share in the frenzy of his worship. Rationalism had not wholly eroded the sense of the numinous; and what survived of the traditional religious faith was its most primitive ingredient.

Achieving relatively little popularity in his lifetime, Euripides became the favorite tragedian of the Hellenistic and Roman periods. His work was, in fact, prophetic of the development of sensibility. During the age of imperialisms following the dissolution of the city-state system, men could see no meaning in the course of events and attributed everything to the power of chance, which was worshipped as a divinity. The traditional myths were treated as amusing fictions, and vital religious belief survived only in the form of mystical and orgiastic salvation cults. Euripides' general pessimism, as expressed especially in anti-war plays like the *Hecuba* and the *Trojan Women*, foreshadowed the spirit of the Hellenistic age, while in such tragic-comic melodramas as the *Ion* and the

Orestes he was a pioneer in the rationalistic treatment of myth, and in the tumultuous force and frenzy of the *Bacchae* he affirmed the continuing power of religious ecstasy.

While the tragedians gave expression to the main emotional currents of their society, it was the function of comedy to pass judgment upon them; and the final word belongs to Aristophanes. Born more than a generation later than Euripides, he produced his first play in 427, four years after the outbreak of the war, and his last in 388, sixteen years after it had concluded. No writer provides stronger evidence of the vigor and resilience of the Athenian character during the great age, as manifested not only in his irrepressible awareness of the comic incongruity between man's pretensions and his inescapable physiological needs, but also in the fact that some of the liveliest and most outspoken of his plays were written during the gloomiest periods of the war. A society that could appreciate Aristophanes still had extraordinary reserves of psychic health. His chief significance, however, is that while he deplored nearly everything that was happening in the Greece of his time, his condemnation was based on feeling, not on any reasoned view of life. Taking as his standard the simple unreflecting conservatism of the average farmer, and glorifying the Athens that had won the Persian wars, he was an enemy of all forms of rationalism, whether manifested in the imperialism of the war party, the amoralism of the philosophers, or the realistic character-portrayals of Euripides. But his conservatism was not supported by any system of beliefs; he could scarcely have used the gods as material for comedy (in the *Birds* and the *Frogs*) if he had had any strong conviction of their reality. His judgment of the tendencies of his time was largely sound, but in order to counteract them, he could appeal only to habit and prejudice. The *Clouds,* in fact, in which Socrates is presented as both impractical and morally subversive, is a classic expression of anti-intellectualism.

5

The Platonic Reaction

The end of the fifth century marks the great turning-point in the history of Hellenic civilization when it began to lose its creative vitality and succumb to a failure of nerve. This change was reflected in the philosophy of Plato. Dismissing the phenomenal world as a world of imperfection, illusion, and contingency, and affirming that genuine goodness, beauty, and truth could be found only in a transcendental realm of abstract ideas, Platonism was a comprehensive attack on the values of individual freedom, artistic creation, and empirical scientific investigation. Repudiating every progressive element in human society, it created an impasse from which later Greek thought never succeeded in escaping.[1]

With the aid of hindsight one can always account for any historical change so convincingly as to make it appear inevitable, and it is easy to argue that Platonism was the necessary next step in Greek intellectual development. After the Sophistic movement and the Peloponnesian War there had to be a new beginning, and perhaps this could only take the form of a reaction against both the naturalism of the philosophers and the democracy of the Athenian polis. Yet it was by no means inevitable that Plato should have carried this reaction to such extreme conclusions or should have presented them with such logical ingenuity or such eloquence and persuasiveness. Incomparably the most influential figure in the en-

---

[1] A number of anti-Platonic books have been written in recent years. Two lively examples are Warner Fite: *The Platonic Legend,* and K. R. Popper: *The Open Society and Its Enemies.* R. B. Levinson: *In Defense of Plato* is a comprehensive reply.

tire history of European philosophy, he has continued for nearly twenty-five hundred years to charm his readers into sympathy with moral asceticism, political authoritarianism, repudiation of the sensuous world as a realm of shadows, and concentration on an unchanging and eternal world of ideas as the only proper object of all human knowledge and desire. These doctrines are built into a coherent intellectual system and presented as logical deductions from necessary premises; yet it is easy to trace their origins in Plato's own heritage and experience. How differently the European philosophical tradition might have developed if Plato had not been prejudiced by his aristocratic background against all forms of liberalism, precluded by his sexual attitudes from any understanding of normal love, and disposed by the historical events that he had witnessed to seek an escape from the world of space and time!

Born a citizen of Athens while it was still animated by Periclean ideals, Plato may be said to have enjoyed advantages to which he was not properly entitled. For his lasting influence on the European mind has been due not only to the specific doctrines presented in his dialogues, but also to the social atmosphere they portray. The leisurely open-air conversations in the agora and the gymnasium; the long drinking parties, with their uninhibited discussion of every subject of interest to human beings; the lack of dogmatism and the willingness to follow an argument wherever it may appear to lead; the admiration for both physical beauty and philosophy, for athletic success as well as for the arts; the warm personal friendships; and the total absence of any form of sexual puritanism or hypocrisy—all this is conveyed by Plato with immense literary skill, and the impression is thereby created that the Platonic philosophy is somehow a consummation of the Greek spirit. We need not doubt that discussions like that recorded in the *Symposium* actually took place in fifth-century Athens; no other society in history has shown such enthusiasm for the analysis of ideas or has so harmoniously combined high culture with individual freedom of speech, admiration for intellectual achievement with an absence of moralistic inhibitions. But it should not be forgotten that Plato was a bitter enemy of everything that Pericles had stood for, and that the whole tenor of his philosophy was to repudiate that happy confidence in man's natural vitality which had been responsible for the major achievements of Greek civilization. Any application of Platonic principles would have destroyed the social milieu that had made such dialogues possible. There could have been no Socratic discussions in the authoritarian state envisaged in the *Republic* and the *Laws*.

The central theme of the Platonic dialogues can be stated quite simply. By interpreting the universe in materialistic terms, and by arguing that all laws and mores were conventional rather than natural, fifth-century Greek thought had undermined the belief in values and moral obligations. Socrates is represented as reasserting this belief by finding new sanctions for it within the human spirit. The earlier Greek myth of a cosmic justice manifested in natural law had become untenable, but Socrates declares that men have an intuitive knowledge of justice which can be made explicit by dialectical processes. This new approach to philosophy represented a double shift—from the study of the external world of nature and society to emphasis on the human soul, and from concentration on empirical data to the examination of human thought.

The problems raised in the dialogues are, of course, those which confront any society that has repudiated the guidance of religious tradition and adopted a rationalistic view of nature, and any attempt to answer them must proceed along somewhat similar lines. The belief in values is a necessity of the human spirit, not a deduction from the processes of the natural universe. Plato's enduring importance in the history of human thought is due to the fact that he asked all the right questions. But instead of declaring that values were realized during the normal processes of natural living, and thereby re-establishing the original Greek confidence in nature in a more sophisticated form, Plato went on to postulate a separate ideal realm that transcended the material world and could be reached only by repudiating it. He exhibited in an extreme form the major weaknesses of Greek thought—its conception of ideals as static and unchanging, and its denial of the reality of time; and, unlike most of his predecessors, he considered ideals not as immanent in nature, but as existing independently of it. In consequence, virtue for Plato consisted largely of the repression of natural appetites, while justice meant the imposition upon human society of a static and geometrical scheme of utopian perfection. His philosophy was pervaded by a compulsive demand for order of a most rigidly regimented kind, and by a conviction that all change was intrinsically evil. Its spirit is vividly exemplified in the argument in the last book of the *Laws,* probably written at the end of his life, that the stars must be divine beings precisely because they always followed the same fixed courses; "If they had been things without soul, and had no mind, they could never have moved according to such exact calculations." [2] This rejection of freedom and spontaneity, primarily caused, no doubt, by temperamental and political factors, was supported by reasoning based on two fallacious habits of thought: he assumed that if something was known, it must exist, from which he deduced the real existence of his realm of values and ideas; and he supposed that in so far as objects moved or changed, they were unknowable and hence mere shadows, the only real knowledge being a knowledge of what was static and eternal.

How far these Platonic doctrines were taught by Socrates is an unanswerable question. Some scholars have argued that the dialogues were essentially reports of actual discussions, but others have maintained that Plato was a writer of fiction who fabricated not only Socrates' speeches, but even the personality attributed to him. We are not, however, wholly dependent on the evidence of the dialogues, as we have the variant descriptions given by Xenophon and Aristophanes; we are informed by Aristotle that the Platonic doctrine of ideas was not held by Socrates; and—more significantly—we know that he was claimed as their master by certain other philosophers who by no means accepted Plato's ethical and political conclusions, notably by the individualistic Cynics and the hedonistic Cyrenaics. Whether Socrates anticipated all of

---

[2] *Laws,* XII, 967; Jowett's translation.

Jowett made the most readable English version of the dialogues, but he should be used with caution owing to his strong propensity to tone down statements that would be unpalatable to English audiences in their literal form. Some of his mistranslations seem to be almost fraudulent. In the *Symposium,* 211, for example, his version speaks of the educative value of "true love." What Plato says is not simply "true love," but *to orthos paiderastein,* "the right kind of boy-love." Most other English Platonists have shown a similar tendency to give their master a Protestant middle-class coloration. A. E. Taylor, the leading Platonic scholar of the twentieth century, even denies that the *Symposium* "is meant to deal with the sexual passion. . . . We must remember that Eros, in whose honor the speeches of the dialogues are delivered, was a cosmogonic figure whose significance is hopelessly obscured by any identification with the principle of 'sex' " (*Plato the Man and His Work,* 209).

Plato's attitudes or not, there can be no doubt that during the
later years of the fifth century he was giving a new direction to
philosophy at Athens by emphasizing the importance of man's inner life, turning from cosmological speculation to the analysis of
human thought and thereby trying to arrive at definitions of virtue
and justice which could not be undermined by Sophistic rationalism. While Plato may have misrepresented some of his master's
doctrines, at least in the later dialogues, he was probably an accurate reporter of the characteristic argumentative technique by
which Socrates pretended to be ignorant and then compelled his
opponents to admit their mental confusion by adroit questioning.
The dialogues, moreover, are likely to give a reliable portrayal of
the outstanding features of Socrates' personality: his passion for
philosophical argument, his disinterest in material comfort and
success, his physical toughness and moral courage, and his mystical
belief in some kind of divine guidance.

It should be added that the picture of Socrates in the dialogues
is not wholly pleasing, at least by non-Platonic standards. We see
him as an elderly man, of middle-class background (his trade was
that of a stonemason, though Plato nowhere shows him practicing
it), surrounded by a coterie consisting largely of aristocratic youths
who liked to sneer at the traders and artisans who enjoyed political
rights in the Athenian democracy without even knowing how to
dress elegantly.[3] These members of the *jeunesse dorée* were entertained by the argumentative virtuosity with which Socrates made
his opponents look foolish (often by mere verbal quibbling, not to
say bullying), and welcomed his constant insistence that just as
the care of the body belonged to a doctor and the management of
a ship to a sea captain, so the guidance of the state should be entrusted not to democratic politicians, but to experts in wisdom.
They made a cult of pederasty, which they considered a mark of
sensitivity and refinement, and Socrates pretended to share their

---

[3] "Such are the two characters, Theo-
dorus," says Socrates in the *Theaetetus*
(175); "the one of the philosopher or
gentleman, who may be excused for
appearing simple and useless when he
has to perform some menial office, such
as packing up a bag, or flavouring a
sauce or fawning speech; the other,
of the man who is able to do every
kind of service smartly and neatly, but
knows not how to wear his cloak like
a gentleman; still less does he acquire
the music of speech, or hymn the true
life which is lived by immortals or
men blessed of heaven."

excitement at the sight of a beautiful male body, though they regarded him as a paragon of self-control because he did not respond to sexual propositions.[4] His wife and children remain somewhere in the background; Xanthippe, who has gone down in history with the reputation of a shrew, makes only one appearance in the dialogues, visiting Socrates in prison shortly before his death and being quickly dismissed by him lest she should disturb his discussion of immortality by a feminine outbreak of weeping.

Possibly Socrates' fondness for young aristocrats was exaggerated by Plato, but his teaching certainly tended to give aid and comfort to the enemies of democracy. Otherwise one cannot account for his execution, which can only have been due to political motivations. In 404, when the Peloponnesian War ended, Athens was placed under the rule of thirty members of the aristocratic party who were willing to act as Spartan quislings. These men conducted a bloody reign of terror against the democrats, and were said to have killed more of their fellow citizens in eight months than the Spartans had in ten years. In the following year the democracy was restored, and with most unusual liberality it was agreed that there should be an amnesty for all political offenses. Many democrats, however, were understandably fearful of another swing of the political pendulum, and wanted to stop the propagation of aristocratic doctrines. Although Socrates had not approved of the rule of the Thirty, some of them had been among his close friends and disciples. Prohibited from attacking him directly on political

---

[4] The nobility of homosexual love and the vulgarity of heterosexuality are discussed by Pausanias in the *Symposium* (180–5). In the *Charmides,* Socrates meets the reigning beauty among the young men; Charmides sits down beside him, whereupon Socrates catches "sight of the inwards of his garment" and declares that he is "overcome by a sort of wild-beast appetite" (*Charmides,* 155). This lovely boy afterwards became one of the thirty quislings who governed Athens as Spartan agents at the end of the Peloponnesian War. In the *Symposium* (219) Alcibiades describes how he once spent a night with Socrates in his arms, but, owing to Socrates' "haughty virtue . . . nothing more happened." "I could not help wondering at his natural temperance and self-restraint and manliness," Alcibiades adds.

The pervasively homosexual atmosphere of the Platonic dialogues has given modern readers an erroneous impression of Greek sexual attitudes. Homosexuality was frequent at Sparta and Thebes; elsewhere it was merely a cult among some aristocratic families. If Plato is omitted, there is less homosexuality in classical Greek literature than in modern French literature or in American literature since World War II. There is none at all in Homer or the tragedians, and relatively little in the historians, while Aristophanes regards it as an aberration and strongly disapproves of it.

grounds, his opponents charged him with teaching disrespect for the official gods of the city and with corrupting the young, probably hoping either to silence him or to drive him away from Athens. Socrates, however, regarding such accusations as preposterous, took the offensive against his enemies with an uncompromising defense of his whole way of life (in the course of which he insisted on his political impartiality), and refused to escape into exile after he had been sentenced to death. His death in the year 399 was certainly a martyrdom, and the simplest explanation is that Socrates was martyred for insisting on his right to speak what he believed to be the truth. The writings in which Plato described his trial and last days, the *Apology, Crito,* and *Phaedo,* are among the greatest masterpieces of Greek literature, and have become the classic accounts of how a philosopher meets death rather than surrender his principles. It should be remembered, however (if Plato is a reliable witness), that Socrates did not believe in any general right of free speech, having (according to the *Republic*) only contempt for the city in which "a man may say and do as he likes," [5] and that the particular "truth" which seems to have brought about his prosecution, and to which he bore witness by the manner of his death, was that a city should be governed not by the will of its citizens, but by experts in wisdom.

Twenty-nine years old at the time of the death of Socrates, Plato spent the next dozen years abroad, and then returned to Athens to establish and preside over an institution of learning called the Academy. This was probably planned as a school for statesmen, but the Athenians showed no inclination to abandon their democracy and adopt the doctrines of Plato and his disciples. Plato's only attempt to make a practical application of his philosophy took place at Syracuse, which he visited twice in the illusory hope of persuading its young tyrant Dionysius to assume the role of the ideal philosopher-king. His lasting influence was exercised not through statesmanship, but through the dialogues in which he purported to expound the teaching of Socrates, though it appears that certain more esoteric doctrines were never published, but were communicated orally to students at the Academy.

The Socratic emphasis on the human soul and its innate knowl-

---

[5] *Republic,* VIII, 557.

 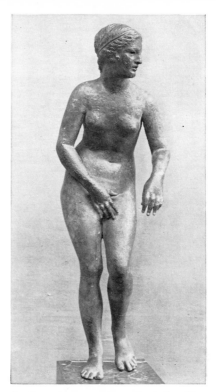

7. *a. Bronze statuette of Har-*
   marchos from the third cen-
   tury B.C.

b. Bronze statuette of Aphrodite
   from the third or second cen-
   tury B.C.

c. Relief from the altar of Zeus at Pergamum, 180 B.C.

Hellenistic sculpture emphasized naturalistic and sensuous portraiture
and scenes of struggle and violent emotion.

8. Roman wall paintings from Boscoreale, dating from the early empire.

edge of virtue was Plato's main starting-point, but his belief in a transcendent spiritual realm was partially derived from earlier philosophers. Greek thought during the sixth and fifth centuries had been predominantly naturalistic and empiricist, but there had always been an influential counter-tendency toward philosophical idealism and the repudiation of nature. Orphic mysticism had originally represented this impulse of flight from the material world, though it seems to have largely degenerated into a vulgar thaumaturgy. More important were the doctrines of the Pythagoreans and the Eleatics. Both these schools displayed the belief that men could somehow arrive at the knowledge of ultimate reality by thought processes alone, and that this reality was immaterial and unchanging. The type of reasoning upon which it was based can fairly be described as magical. It represented the same kind of confusion between thoughts and things, the same assumption that something conceived or imagined must have an objective reality, that had led to the imitative rituals of primitive man. Though totally lacking in practical efficacy, it has continued throughout the history of Western civilization to stimulate intellectual ingenuity and provide emotional consolation for philosophic minds of the introverted type. Its political implications have been of lasting importance: both in its original Greek form and in its modern Hegelian restatement, it has been the main intellectual support for authoritarianism.

Pythagoras, who was born on the Ionian island of Samos and moved to the Italian city of Croton about 532 B.C., founded an ascetic cult directed both to the moral purification of its adherents and to political leadership. He was important in the history of thought chiefly because of his belief that the reality underlying all phenomena was essentially mathematical. The world was built of numbers, which were somehow more real than the objects to which they referred, and men could thereby understand the universe simply by following the processes of mathematical reasoning. This intoxicating concept, with its promise of escape from the world of sensuous experience into a world of pure thought, seems to have been largely due to the discovery that the intervals in the musical scale could be expressed by means of arithmetical ratios; numbers were harmonious, and men could find salvation through union with the music of the cosmos. Plato was deeply influenced by this mathematical mysticism, especially in his later dialogues, and learned from it to regard the study of arithmetic and geometry as man's main means of access to the spiritual world.

The main contribution of the Eleatic school was its attempt to deny change and movement. Named after the Italian city of Elea, it was initiated by Xenophanes, an emigrant from Ionia, and was developed chiefly by Parmenides and his disciple Zeno, the author of the paradoxes of motion. By processes of pure logic, wholly divorced from experience, the Eleatics attempted to demonstrate that diversity and movement were illusions and that being in its essence was an indivisible and static whole. In the words of Parmenides, "there is left but this single path to tell thee of: namely, that being is. And in this path there are many proofs that being is without beginning and indestructible; it is universal, existing alone, unmovable and without end; nor ever was it nor will it be, since it now is, all together, one and continuous." The heart of the Eleatic philosophy was a mystical vision of a divine reality transcending sense experience, and this was defended by arguments intended to demonstrate that all empirical knowledge was necessarily fallacious. In so far as objects moved and changed, they were unknowable; and as the Eleatics identified knowledge and being (according to Parmenides, "thinking and that by reason of which thought exists are one and the same"), this meant that they did not really exist.[6] Plato always spoke of Parmenides with the utmost reverence, and, while not denying the existence of change, he adopted the Eleatic argument that it was not the true object of human knowledge.

Plato's earlier dialogues are largely concerned with the definition of specific forms of goodness. Socrates is represented as declaring that the soul is the most important part of the human being, and that just as health is the well-being of the body, so virtue is the well-being of the soul. Throughout these discussions he assumes that virtue depends on correct knowledge, that the different forms of virtue are aspects of a single state of spiritual well-being, and that this well-being means happiness. This leads him to the apparently paradoxical conclusion, repeated on a number of occasions, that it is better to suffer injustice than to do it. "He who does well must of necessity be happy and blessed, and the evil

---

[6] Fairbanks: op. cit., pp. 93, 97

man who does evil, miserable." In fact, "no evil can happen to a good man, either in life or after death." [7] Socrates' insistence that happiness depends on inner security, not on outward circumstances, represents a new emphasis in Greek thought, but his argument is still linked with the naturalism of Greek tradition in that moral goodness, like physical health, is regarded as a realization of man's inherent nature.

Throughout the earlier dialogues, however, Socrates never actually presents any concrete definition of the goodness that manifests itself in happiness; and when he makes his first serious attempt to do so, in the *Republic,* it turns out that what he means chiefly is self-control. The physical appetites should be under the mastery of reason. This is, no doubt, sound advice for adolescents, especially when they belong to the *jeunesse dorée,* but as a general moral principle its applicability is limited and can easily be over-estimated. What it has to do with one's duty to one's neighbor, and how it provides a standard of political and social justice, Socrates never explains. The general Platonic tendency is to consider the control of appetite not as a means to higher objectives, but as good in itself, and it gradually becomes manifest that this implies a dualist view of human nature, the soul being considered as somehow separate from the body and in need of liberation from it. As Socrates declares in the *Phaedo,* "each pleasure and pain is a sort of nail which nails and rivets the soul to the body, until she becomes like the body, and believes that to be true which the body affirms to be true; and from agreeing with the body and having the same delights she is obliged to have the same habits and haunts, and is not likely ever to be pure at her departure to the world below, but is always infected by the body." [8] The soul is, in fact, immortal, and will probably be rewarded or punished in an afterlife according to its deserts. Plato discusses this doctrine on several occasions, and, though apparently not wholly convinced of its truth, plainly regards it as a socially desirable belief. In complete contradiction of the original Socratic argument that goodness means happiness, he concludes that men must be frightened into virtue by the fear of punishment in the next world.

This dualism develops into the repudiation of the physical world

---

[7] *Gorgias,* 507. *Apology,* 41.   [8] *Phaedo,* 83.

which becomes fully explicit in the doctrine of ideas of the *Republic* and the later dialogues. The doctrine of ideas is primarily a theory of knowledge, but for Plato the knowledge of truth and the practice of virtue are always inseparably connected. Socrates now argues that the only genuine knowledge is the knowledge of abstract ideas existing in an unchanging and immaterial world; this world is like a cave in which man can see only shadows of the divine forms that really exist elsewhere. Plato seems to have arrived at this doctrine by way of the mathematical mysticism he derived from the Pythagoreans. Geometrical knowledge is a knowledge of ideal shapes never wholly realized in actuality. That the square of the hypotenuse of a right-angled triangle is equal to the combined squares of the two other sides is true of the ideal right-angled triangle which one can never exactly reproduce on paper, and of which all existing right-angled triangles may be regarded as imperfect copies. Assuming that all knowledge must be knowledge of something existent, Plato supposes that this ideal triangle really exists in some eternal and incorporeal realm, and then extends this assumption to all other forms of knowing. The whole material world consists merely of imperfect copies of eternal and unchanging ideas, and the only true knowledge is a knowledge of the ideas. The study of material things necessarily partakes of their unreality and imperfection, and is therefore mere opinion and delusion. Such an attitude, of course, means the total rejection of empirical science, a conclusion that Plato frankly and explicitly accepts. In one of the more curious passages in the *Republic*, Socrates declares that the astronomer should study "the true motions of absolute swiftness and absolute slowness," which are to be "apprehended by reason and intelligence, but not by sight," instead of wasting his time investigating the actual movements of the stars. "We should employ problems, and let the heavens alone if we would approach the subject in the right way and so make the natural gift of reason to be of any real use." [9]

Whenever Plato discusses his realm of ideas, he is likely to engage in an outburst of metaphysical lyricism. In the *Phaedrus*, for example, it is "the very being with which true knowledge is concerned; the colorless, formless, intangible essence, visible only

---

[9] *Republic*, VII, 529, 530. Socrates' auditor sagely replies that this is "a work infinitely beyond our present astronomers."

to mind, the pilot of the soul . . . Justice and temperance and knowledge absolute, not in the form of generation or of relation, which men call existence, but knowledge absolute in existence absolute." [1] Yet when one leaves the field of mathematics and extends the doctrine to other areas of knowledge, it soon becomes impossible to attach any intelligible meaning to it. It may be permissible to argue that any particular man or horse is an imperfect copy of the ideal representative of the species. But it is absurd to declare (as Socrates declares in the *Republic*) that all existing beds are imperfect copies of the ideal bed "existing in nature, which is made by God." [2] The doctrine becomes even more meaningless when it is extended from concrete objects to values and one is asked to withdraw one's mind from the imperfect justice and beauty manifested in the natural world and learn to apprehend these values in their ideal essence. Yet the love and contemplation of absolute goodness, abstracted from all material embodiments, is Plato's formula for salvation. This cannot be described as religious mysticism, which is always an emotional experience, the participant feeling a sense of unity with a spiritual power. Plato may have been a mystic in his esoteric teaching, but the doctrine of the dialogues is not emotional union with a personal God, but the intellectual contemplation of abstract ideas. Most of his readers have been too overwhelmed by the eloquence of his verbiage to inquire what is meant by beauty, justice, and goodness in their abstract essence. It is significant that whenever Plato tries to give a more specific content to his doctrine, he finds it necessary to return to mathematics. In the *Republic,* Socrates declares that the study of arithmetic, "if pursued in the spirit of a philosopher, and not of a shopkeeper," is the easiest way for the soul "to pass from becoming to truth and being, . . . compelling the soul to reason about abstract number, and rebelling against the introduction of visible or tangible objects into the argument." In fact, "the true use of it is simply to draw the soul toward being," its practical utility in trade being an unfortunate misapplication. In the *Philebus,* the forms of geometry are actually equated with ideal beauty. "Understand me to mean straight lines and circles," says Socrates, "or the plane or solid figures which are formed out of them by turning lathes and rulers

---

[1] *Phaedrus*, 247.   [2] *Republic*, IX, 597.

and measurers of angles; for these I affirm to be not only relatively beautiful, like other things, but they are eternally and absolutely beautiful." [3]

In the later dialogues, especially in the *Timaeus,* the doctrine of ideas is developed into a cosmology. Plato envisages the universe as composed of three basic factors: the primal matrix, which was originally a formless and chaotic flux; the formative energy of divine power; and the ideas used by God as patterns in ordering the world. The imperfections of the universe are due to the recalcitrance of the primal "necessity," with its "elements of violence and injustice," [4] which God could not completely shape in accord with the ideas. The *Timaeus* deals largely with astronomy and physiology, describing the universe in geocentric terms, arguing that the stars and planets are spiritual beings, and presenting a long and fanciful account of God's ethical objectives in designing the human body. God is primarily a mathematician, and most natural objects are composed of geometrical shapes, especially triangles.

Throughout this dialogue, Plato's main motivation was to provide a cosmological foundation for his views of human society. Assuming (like all pre-scientific thinkers) that political and ethical doctrines must be deduced from the structure of the universe, and wishing to prove the validity of authoritarianism and asceticism, he found it necessary to insist that the stars and planets moved in uniform circular courses around the earth. Thus, these spiritual beings displayed that undeviating conformity with an ideal order which Plato required, and deplored the lack of, in men and women. This reliance on astronomical theory as a support for earthly authority was shared by all Greek conservatives, having originated with Pythagoras. The fact that the stars and, more especially, the planets did not actually move in these uniform circular courses was a scandal that it was believed should be kept hidden (this was, no doubt, why Socrates in the *Republic* urged astronomers to "employ problems and let the heavens alone"). This political use of astronomy continued during the Hellenistic period, preventing acceptance of the heliocentric theory in spite of the evidence in its favor, and was inherited by the Christian Church. It did not disappear until the seventeenth century of our era. Throughout these two thou-

---

[3] *Republic,* VI, 523, 526. *Philebus,*   [4] *Statesman,* 273.
51.

sand years the *Timaeus* remained the chief source of cosmological opinion in the Western world, its prestige being one of the main obstacles to the growth of science.[5]

The importance of the doctrine of ideas lies, of course, in the practical conclusions that Plato used it to support, and these carry us back from lofty cosmological speculations to the moral and political realities of Plato's own life in fourth-century Athens. Having located values not within the natural world but outside it, he went on to argue that they could be realized only in so far as nature was mastered and surmounted.

There are two kinds of human experience by which physical forms become charged with a value transcending rationalistic explanation: the experience of love and the experience of art. While these may be taken as indications that the full meaning of human life cannot be comprehended in scientific terms, they derive their significance precisely from the fact that the feeling of transcendence is conveyed through a sensuous embodiment, thus suggesting that values are always immanent in the natural world, though becoming visible only in moments of irradiation. This sense of epiphany had been beautifully expressed in the Olympian religion, with its worship of divine beings whose presence was felt not in miracles and other supernatural interventions, but in any natural human experience of high intensity. But for Plato, nature and value belonged to different realms. It is significant that he was hostile to the whole Homeric mythology, complaining that its tales about the gods were immoral and degrading.

The transcendental significance of sexual love is the main theme of the *Symposium* and of part of the *Phaedrus,* love for a beautiful person being represented as an aspect of the love for beauty in general, and also of the desire for immortality, and hence as a method for the purification of the soul. The function of Eros is to act as mediator between gods and men. There are, however, two peculiarities about Plato's treatment of the subject, and both of

---

[5] Shakespeare's Ulysses, for example, appeals to astronomy in his plea for obedience to royal authority.
"The heavens themselves, the planets, and this center
Observe degree, priority and place,
Insisture, course, proportion, season, form,
Office, and custom, in all line of order."

(*Troilus and Cressida,* I, iii, 85–8)

them are directly related to the fact that he attributed religious meaning only to pederasty. Toward heterosexuality his attitude was always brutally utilitarian: regarding it as simply a means for breeding children and for satisfying masculine appetites, he advocated state regulation without the slightest recognition that important emotions might be involved.

The first peculiarity of Platonic love is that the loved object is simply a means to the appreciation of beauty in the abstract, and ceases to be loved when this has been attained. As the *Symposium* declares, "he who would proceed aright in this matter should begin in youth to visit beautiful forms; and first, if he be guided by his instructor aright, to love one such form only—out of that he should create fair thoughts; and soon he will of himself perceive that the beauty of one form is akin to the beauty of another; and then if beauty of form in general is his pursuit, how foolish would he be not to recognize that the beauty of every form is one and the same. And when he perceives this he will abate his violent love of the one, which he will despise and deem a small thing, and will become a lover of all beautiful forms. . . . The true order of going . . . is to begin from the beauties of earth and mount upwards for the sake of that other beauty, using these as steps only." [6] This consideration of the loved object as simply an educational instrument, a stepping-stone toward spirituality, is, of course, in accord with Plato's whole philosophy, but his lack of true personal feeling is due to the fact that he is thinking exclusively of desire for a beautiful boy, not of love for a wife or mistress or even for a man of his own age. The other peculiarity of Plato's doctrine is that (according to the *Phaedrus*) he believes that love is noblest, and best fulfills its educative function, when it is not physically consummated. The real reason for this curious and pathological attitude, as the discussions in the *Phaedrus* and the *Laws* make unmistakably plain, is that, in spite of his homosexual propensities, Plato is at the same time convinced that they are "unnatural." [7] In the *Laws*, written in his old age, homosexual love is explicitly prohibited. The whole concept of Platonic love is, in fact, a perversion, not merely because it is boy-love and not the love of women,

---

[6] *Symposium*, 210.   [7] See *Phaedrus*, 250, 256; *Laws*, I, 636; VIII, 836–41.

but for the profounder reason that it involves denial of the true meaning and purpose of sexual love in any of its forms.[8]

While Plato recognizes a spiritual element in love, though insisting that this is not expressed in carnal desire but must be liberated from it, he attributes to art no transcendental significance whatever. His attitude toward artistic creativity is, in fact, marked by such intense and persistent hostility that one must suspect a political motivation. Was he influenced by the close association of so many great artists with the Periclean democracy? One might have expected him to accept the more abstract and less representational forms of art as revelations of the ideas. This conclusion was actually reached in the Neo-Platonic philosophy of the third century of our era; according to Plotinus, architecture and music were the highest art forms because they were based on geometrical and mathematical principles and hence were direct expressions of the divine reality.[9] Plato, on the other hand, living in an age when most art forms copied nature, assumes that all art is necessarily representational (even music, which he regards as a representation of human emotions). This means that art is even farther removed from reality than are the objects it depicts; nature is an inferior copy of the ideas, and art is an inferior copy of nature. But while art has no religious significance, it has important educational functions because it tends to mold human character; it must therefore be rigidly supervised by the government, which should allow only ennobling emotions to be portrayed and should prohibit degrading conceptions either of the gods or of human beings. As Socrates declares in the *Republic*, "we must remain firm in our conviction that hymns to the gods and praises of famous men are the only poetry which ought to be admitted into our state." The arts have, in fact, such influence on human attitudes that no innovation whatever should be permitted, poets and composers being compelled by law to conform to the traditional styles. "When modes of music

---

[8] The function of the Platonic Eros was to elevate men from earth to heaven. The immense popularity of Platonic love (mostly in heterosexual forms) during the European Renaissance nearly two thousand years later was caused by an opposite movement. The European mind was swinging from religious transcendentalism back to naturalism, and Platonism justified the love of natural beauty by giving it a religious significance. Once the movement had been completed, men no longer needed the Platonic rationalization.

[9] Plotinus: *Enneads*, V, ix, 11.

change, the fundamental laws of the state always change with them." [1]

The full meaning and purpose of the Platonic philosophy, however, becomes apparent only in its political applications. The *Republic* and the *Laws* are much the longest of the dialogues, and the aristocratic and authoritarian form of government they prescribe must be regarded as the end toward which all of Plato's thinking is ultimately directed. The ideal state of the *Republic* may be described as the Spartan system covered with a veneer of metaphysics; the *Laws* is Sparta almost undisguised.

The problems raised in the two dialogues are, of course, the necessary starting-points of any discussion of political theory. What makes a government legitimate, so that it will exercise "voluntary rule over voluntary subjects"? [2] What kind of social order will men freely and spontaneously accept and support? What is meant by the just man, and what basic standard of justice can be applied to the reform of existing political and economic systems? These are the fundamental questions that confront, and in some form must be answered by, any rationalistic non-traditional society. Different societies at different periods of history have answered them in different ways; and any answer, like the initial postulates that form the starting-points of Euclidian geometry, must consist of an ethical affirmation, not of a demonstrable truth. Thus, liberalism begins by asserting the rights of the individual personality, which are regarded as incommensurate with all other social objectives and hence as of infinite value, while conservatism postulates a belief in the organic order and unity of society. These must be recognized as hypotheses, not as dogmas or facts, and the only possible test of their validity is operational. Any refusal to recognize this necessary uncertainty by insisting that the rightness of some particular system can be rationally demonstrated leads to intolerance and persecution—a conclusion fully exemplified by Plato and all Platonists.

Plato's alleged purpose having been to deduce the nature of the ideal state from rational first principles, it would perhaps be unfair to complain of his failure to provide a practical program for his contemporaries, but one may legitimately expect a philosopher to

---

[1] *Republic,* X, 607; IV, 424.   [2] *Laws,* VIII, 832.

show some real understanding of the problems of his own age. The underlying cause of the difficulties confronting Greece during Plato's lifetime was that, owing to the double movement of universalism and rationalistic individualism, the city-state had ceased to be a viable institution. What Greece needed was political leadership capable of foreseeing and guiding the transfer of loyalties to some larger political unity. But what Plato's ideal state actually represented was a reaction back to the narrow tribalism of an earlier epoch. Hating everything represented by Periclean Athens, he was hostile to trade, industry, and maritime enterprise; he assumed that the small independent city-state was the only possible political form, at least for Greeks; and though he wished to moderate the destructiveness of interstate warfare, he supposed that such warfare would continue and was, in fact, an ennobling activity. His model community was the small agricultural state, dominated by a privileged warrior class, which had existed in Greece before the advent of commerce and democracy and was still, on the whole, exemplified by Sparta. Despite the playful tone of the *Republic,* there can be little doubt that Plato actually hoped that such a state could be re-created under the leadership of some philosopher-king, and could then be prevented from degenerating by means of an all-embracing regimentation of the thoughts and activities of its citizens. The Platonic ideal was, of course, wholly static, and once it had come into being, any change whatever meant corruption. In the *Laws* Plato actually wishes to prohibit innovations not only in the arts, but even in children's games; if people are allowed to play new games when they are young, they will become revolutionaries when they grow up.[3]

The *Republic* begins by attempting to define the just man. After dismissing the argument that justice reflects the will of the strongest and is therefore merely conventional, Socrates shifts the discussion to a definition of the just state. A brief statement of the various specialized occupations needed in an organized community quickly leads to a recognition that the state needs soldiers, who also ought to constitute a specialized professional class. Socrates then abruptly plunges into a long description of the type of education which the soldier class ought to receive. This remains the central

---

[3] *Laws,* VII, 797.

theme throughout most of the rest of the dialogue; the original questions—the nature of the just man and of the just state—reappear only briefly and at rare intervals, and the fact that the soldier class is to constitute an aristocracy is slipped into the discussion without any argument whatever. The dialogue is, in fact, an extraordinarily skillful and ingenious piece of obfuscation, the main purpose of which is to deceive the unwary reader into accepting the most unpalatable conclusions by avoiding direct argument about them, and at the same time distracting his attention from what is really going on by keeping him interested in a program for an ideal education.[4]

It is assumed (without argument) that the state is like the individual and is therefore an organic whole composed of subordinate parts. The welfare of the state is the only concern of the statesman, any question of individual rights being wholly ignored (Socrates explains that his purpose is the happiness of the state as a whole, not that of its individual members). It is also assumed (again without argument) that each individual should devote himself to his own specialized function and not meddle with matters outside his own sphere; the cobbler should cobble, the soldier should fight, and the ruler should rule. This leads to the conclusion that there should be a separate group of rulers, who should be chosen from the more gifted and disciplined members of the soldier class and given an additional education. After expatiating on these arrangements, Socrates suddenly discovers that this is the meaning of justice. Justice in the individual means order and self-control, appetites and desires being guided by reason, and, similarly, the just state is the state in which each class maintains the harmony of the whole by concentrating on its own special tasks, government being entrusted to rulers who perform in the body politic the role that reason plays in the individual personality. Justice means "that one man should practise one thing only, the thing to which his nature was best adapted."[5] Thus, the central thesis of the *Republic* is a direct attack on the humanistic and democratic ideals of universal versatility and popular participa-

---

[4] Most English translators of the *Republic* have aided and abetted Plato by calling his ruling class "guardians." The Greek word is *phylakes*, which means "guards" and has definitely military connotations.

[5] *Republic*, IV, 433.

tion in government which had been proclaimed by Pericles in the Funeral Speech.[6]

After Socrates begins to describe the education of the soldier class, the mass of farmers, craftsmen, and traders who comprise the main body of the population quickly disappears from view and is scarcely mentioned again. Its only function in the Platonic scheme is like that of the Spartan helots: to provide economic support for the aristocracy. Plato's main concern is to describe an ideal ruling class, and he feels that the chief danger to be avoided is a growth of individualism. He therefore proposes that, in the process of welding the soldier and ruling classes into a unified group devoted to the defense of the established order, they should not merely be given a prolonged education composed of gymnastics, carefully censored forms of poetry and music, and (for the rulers) mathematics and dialectics, but should also be denied the rights of private property and private marriage. Their economic needs will be met out of the taxes paid by the mass of the population; their mating will be controlled by the state authorities with a view to maintaining high eugenic standards, especially courageous soldiers being rewarded with more sexual opportunities. Both the educational program and the economic and sexual communism of the *Republic* apply, of course, exclusively to the warrior and ruling classes (a fact that Plato, no doubt deliberately, fails to emphasize, so that unwary readers often overlook it), and their main object is not to promote anybody's happiness or welfare, but to create a disciplined body of automata who will maintain order and prevent innovation.[7]

---

[6] There are two significant references to Pericles in the dialogues. In the *Gorgias* (516) he is described as "the first who gave the people pay, and made them idle and cowardly, and encouraged them in the love of talk and of money." This is an allusion to the fact that among the democratic reforms for which Pericles was responsible was the adoption of payment for service on juries. In the *Menexenus*, Socrates insinuates that the Funeral Speech was really composed by Pericles' mistress Aspasia, and then recites a rather labored parody, also allegedly written by Aspasia, which may be described as a funeral speech to end all funeral speeches.

[7] Plato has won much credit for including women in his ruling classes. This was probably due to a recognition that the breeding arrangements could not be worked out on any other basis. The compliments paid to women in the *Republic* are not echoed elsewhere in the dialogues, Plato's usual opinion of them being (as one would expect) extremely low. In the *Timaeus* he suggests that "all those creatures generated as men who proved themselves cowardly and spent their lives in wrongdoing were transformed, at their second incarnation, into women" (*Timaeus*, 90).

Plato, of course, insists on the benevolence of his upper classes; as he repeatedly explains, they will be like sheep dogs who protect their own flock and use their teeth only against marauding wolves. But though he guards against the corrupting influences of the desire for wealth by denying them the right of private property, he shows no recognition of the dangers of the desire for power. No legal restrictions on their authority are proposed. Plato, in fact, regards the rule of law as necessary only in an imperfect society. In the *Statesman* he compares the law to "an obstinate and ignorant tyrant," and declares that "the best thing of all is not that the law should rule, but that a man should rule, supposing him to have wisdom and royal power." And though he hopes that the benevolence of the rulers will ensure the willing submission of the mass of the population, he proposes to rely also on force and propaganda. The soldiers should choose for their permanent encampment a place "whence they can best suppress insurrection." The rulers, moreover, should invent and propagate a myth to the effect that God has made some men out of gold or silver and others out of brass and iron, and "the species will generally be preserved in the children." Plato recognizes that some children of gold or silver parents may need to be demoted to the brass-and-iron category, and that farmers and artisans may occasionally have sons worthy of elevation to the warrior and ruling classes—an admission that has enabled his liberal admirers to claim that he believed in equality of opportunity. But in view of his emphasis on eugenic breeding among the warrior class, and in view also of the fact that the distinctive training and education of the upper classes are to begin at birth, it does not seem likely that the crossing of class lines would be a frequent occurrence.[8]

This rigid and hierarchical system, which seems (if its real intent and meaning are kept in mind) to be at the same time a throwback to the barbaric Greece of the Achaean conquerors and a foreshadowing of the one-party totalitarian state of the twentieth century, is, according to Plato, the one true commonwealth existing in the realm of values, all actual communities being perver-

---

[8] *Statesman*, 294; *Republic*, III, 415.

sions and corruptions of it.[9] Measuring existing republics by this ideal standard (near the end of the dialogue), Socrates finds, of course, that Sparta ranks closest to it, erring chiefly in being governed by its soldiers rather than by a ruling class trained in philosophy. Athens is near the bottom of the scale, the only worse system being the tyranny into which every democracy must finally degenerate. But although the ideal state does not at present exist on earth, "in heaven . . . there is laid up a pattern of it, methinks, which he who desires may behold, and beholding may set his own house in order. But whether such a one exists, or ever will exist in fact, is no matter; for he will live after the manner of the city, having nothing to do with any other": a statement that seems to imply a repudiation of allegiance to the democratic polis of which Plato was actually a citizen.[1]

After the deceptive fascination of the *Republic*, it is almost with relief that one turns to the final work of Plato's old age, the *Laws*, which is totally lacking in literary charm and consists largely of a rambling and disorganized collection of legislative proposals, but which spells out an authoritarian system of government much more frankly and in fuller detail. Abandoning the hope of realizing his ideal republic, Plato describes what he now regards as the best practicable alternative, envisaging a small agricultural community, remote from the sea with its commercial temptations, and governed by magistrates whose main purpose is to maintain strict moral discipline and prevent any innovations. Religious beliefs are to be prescribed by law, and any heretics are to be sentenced to prison. This emphasis on a kind of inquisition, to be exercised by a "nocturnal council" of censors who are to have the chief authority, has shocked many of Plato's admirers. Yet the main difference between the Plato of the *Republic* and the Plato of the *Laws* is that in the former he was hopeful that his aristocratic system could be maintained by deceiving the mass of the people into accepting it as "justice," whereas when he

---

[9] Aristotle points out that Plato's ideal republic would consist of "two states in one, each hostile to the other. . . . He makes the guards into a mere occupying garrison, while the husbandmen and artisans and the rest are the real citizens" (*Politics*, 1264a). With his experience of Greek political life, Aristotle understood Plato's intention much more clearly than most of his modern admirers.

[1] *Republic*, IX, 592.

came to write the *Laws* he recognized that it could be maintained only by repression.

Considered in relation to his own time and milieu, Plato registers the onset of decadence in Greek civilization. Men had lost faith in the gods and institutions of the polis, and were incapable of moving forward to some broader form of social integration. Under such circumstances, individuals always display a sense of alienation from their society, looking for private modes of salvation and indulging in utopian fantasies, while the need for order is met partly by outright force and repression and partly by a reaction back to the attitudes of some earlier period. All these tendencies are clearly exemplified in the Platonic philosophy.

Socrates (according to the *Crito*) felt that he owed allegiance to the laws of Athens even when the result was his own execution, but the Socratic emphasis on the inner life marked the beginning of a withdrawal from society which became increasingly emphatic in later philosophic movements. Plato's whole system was based on the repudiation of the world in which he physically existed; its practical implications were underlined by the affirmation in the *Republic* that the philosopher would live after the manner of the heavenly city, "having nothing to do with any other." This statement affirmed the decadence of the polis and the failure of the Greek world to develop any alternative institutional organism.

Plato's ideal republic was presented as a timeless pattern of perfection, applicable to the future as well as to the past, but its implications were, of course, reactionary. In actuality, however, any return to the polis of two or three centuries earlier was impossible, and the past institution to which the Greek world finally reverted was the theocratic monarchy of the Near East. The decadence of Greek civilization was accompanied by an influx of Eastern beliefs, particularly the concept of the deified king as the focus of political order. Of this orientalization of the Greek world Plato may be regarded as the unconscious forerunner. His specific references to the Near Eastern civilizations were mostly laudatory. He admired Egypt because of its frozen resistance to change, its preservation through thousands of years of the same art styles, its rigid class divisions, and its respect for priest-philosophers; much of his mathematical and astronomical mysticism, including particularly his belief in the divinity of the stars and in the magical

importance of certain time cycles, was borrowed from Mesopotamia. More generally, his conception of a static and eternal model
of perfection and his denial of the reality of history strongly resembled the attitudes of the theocratic age of the fourth millennium B.C. and pointed to the same political conclusion: obedience
to an inspired priest- or philosopher-king who would establish
this model of perfection upon earth.

During the period of the decadence, Platonism was challenged
by a number of rival schools, and relatively few individuals accepted it completely. Platonic ways of thinking, nevertheless, had
a pervasive and inescapable influence on all later Greek culture.
Hellenic philosophy never regained the liberalism and the naturalism of the great age; its bias henceforth was ascetic, pessimistic,
anti-democratic, and anti-scientific. Not until the advent of
Christianity, which combined an affirmation of individual freedom
and the goodness of nature with a religious universalism, did the
Hellenic world make a new intellectual beginning with new
premises. And even Christianity was deeply corrupted by Platonism during the centuries in which it was rising to dominance.

Plato's later influence on the civilization of the Western world
is another story. Stimulated by the questions raised in the dialogues and by their extraordinary dialectical richness and subtlety,
many of his readers have taken from him only what they needed.
In spite of his contempt for empirical observation, his emphasis on
the value of mathematics helped to promote the scientific development of the sixteenth and seventeenth centuries. His mystical
sense of the unreality of the world of space and time has been
echoed by a long series of poets and philosophers who have by no
means accepted all his forbidding conclusions. But his chief importance has been to provide philosophical support for the belief
that order requires the denial of freedom. He was the great enemy
of the faith in a natural harmony expressed in some universal
standard of justice which the Western world derived partly from
the Jewish Messianic hope and partly from the earlier Greek concept of the divinity of nature. For Plato there could be no harmony
except through the suppression of all forms of natural vitality,
and justice meant the total subordination of the individual to the
state. Thus, Platonism in its various forms has been the main
intellectual source of corruption in the Western heritage. The first

of those great system-builders who (like Calvin and Hegel and Marx in modern times) have erected imposing intellectual structures on foundations of personal prejudice, he was the archetype of all the ideologues, both radical and reactionary, who have wished to create some mathematical model of utopian perfection at the expense of human freedom and vitality.

6

Aristotle and Alexander

I n the fourth century B.C., Mediterranean society entered a new
phase of development which was to last for the next five
hundred years. The unity that the Greek city-states were incapable of achieving by their own efforts was finally imposed by the
armed force of Macedon. This was followed by an epoch of empire-building, initiated by Alexander and his generals and continued by Rome, which ended in the unification of the entire
Mediterranean world. Both the Macedonians and the Romans regarded themselves as the inheritors and sponsors of Hellenism,
and their conquests were accompanied by the diffusion of Hellenic
culture and the Hellenic polis. This movement of political and
cultural imperialism did not finally lose its impetus and begin to
recede until the third century of our era.

The Hellenism that spread through the Mediterranean world,
however, was no longer a living culture, but a closed and petrified
system of ideas. The period of high creativity in Greek civilization
ended in the fourth century. Unable to find solutions for its intellectual and political problems, the Greek mind turned back to
the past and devoted itself to the conservation and imitation of
the achievements of earlier generations. The creative artist and
thinker gave place to the scholar who commented on the works
of his predecessors and the rhetorician who specialized in the
graceful expression of commonplaces. Culture became divorced
from political and economic realities; and while order depended
henceforth mainly on force, mitigated only by the Oriental principle of worship of the god-king, intellectuals continued to culti-

vate the attitudes and beliefs associated with the free self-governing polis of the Periclean age. Thus, the Hellenistic and Roman
empires, so impressive in their material achievements, were aes-
thetically and spiritually far less productive than the city-state
society whose way of life they sought to imitate. This disharmony
between culture and social conditions could be ended only by the
adoption of a new view of life derived from new premises. Christianity, with its faith in a universal God and in the brotherhood
of man, may be regarded as a response to the problems that the
Hellenism of the fourth century had failed to solve.

Confronted by the dissolution of objective standards of truth
and justice, the disintegrating effects of individualism, and the
need for some broader principle of political integration, fourth-
century Greeks continued to cling to the small self-governing polis
as the only possible focus of loyalty. So deeply had the city-state
culture been impressed upon their minds and spirits that they
were incapable of the necessary transfer of allegiance to new
ideals, insisting instead that the solution for every political difficulty was to return to some earlier phase in Greek development.
Few people displayed this reactionary tendency as violently as
Plato, but there was a widespread inclination to condemn democracy and commercialism and to idealize the aristocratic and
agrarian society of earlier epochs. It is significant that this period
produced no poetry or drama worthy of survival, the extant literature consisting wholly of history, philosophy, and political and
legal oratory. Meanwhile, interstate warfare continued as before,
the Athenians building and losing a second maritime empire, until
all the Greek cities lost their liberties as a result of the victory of
Philip of Macedon at Chaeronea in 338.

The three leading figures of fourth-century Athens, Demosthenes, Isocrates, and Aristotle, all exemplified in different ways
this failure of creativity and contributed to the petrifaction of culture during the epoch of imperialism. Demosthenes, whose ideals
were Periclean rather than aristocratic, spent his mature years in
a long and futile effort to persuade his fellow citizens to show
enough courage and foresight to resist the growing power of
Macedon. The most eloquent of Greek orators, he proved by the
sublimity and passion of his speeches that the spirit that had inspired Aeschylus and Phidias had not yet wholly lost its vitality.

Yet the whole object of his career was to preserve the particularism of the city-state, and in his determination to prevent the unification of Greece by Macedonian power, he was even willing to seek help from Persia; devoted to freedom and republicanism, he saw no way of maintaining them except through the independence of the polis. The rhetoricians of later ages continued to echo his praises of the Athenian commonwealth, while owing the security that enabled them to practice rhetoric to the despotic rule of god-kings.

For Demosthenes the ideals of Hellenism were inseparable from the independence of the polis. Isocrates, on the other hand, recognized that the polis was no longer a viable institution and tried to separate Hellenic culture from the political roots that gave it nourishment. A teacher of oratory and a political pamphleteer, he advocated the unity of Greece and called for a crusade in the name of the Hellenic ideal against the Persian Empire. In his early life he hoped for Athenian leadership, though he distrusted democracy and favored a restoration of aristocratic rule; in his later years he supported the hegemony of Macedon. Hellenism, for Isocrates, meant primarily intellectual culture, and could therefore be imparted to non-Greek peoples. Yet in trying to transcend the particularism of the city-state and the opposition between the Greek and the barbarian, he ended with a theory of culture that was remarkably sterile and uncreative. He depicted it as a kind of intellectual gymnastic, a series of mental games paralleling the training of the body in athletics, appropriate only to a leisured wealthy class and serving no deeper social or religious purpose. "Our ancestors," he declared, "assigned to each a type of training suitable to his wealth. Those who had less property they put to farming and trade. . . . Those who had sufficient property they compelled to engage in riding, gymnastic, hunting and intellectual exercise, seeing that these pursuits make some men distinguished and keep others from most kinds of wickedness." [1] The main element in the culture of Isocrates was rhetoric, skill in the use of words, which he regarded as the essential quality distinguishing men from animals and as the foundation of all civilization. Rhetoric should therefore take the place of philosophy and the sciences

---

[1] Quoted by Werner Jaeger: *Paideia,* translated by Gilbert Highet, III, 121.

as the center of education. "Those who busy themselves with ethical education would be better men if they became ambitious to speak well and fell in love with the art of persuasion." [2] Isocrates exemplified his own principles by writing a prose that was uniformly smooth, lucid, and euphonious, though it lacked energy and originality. It was essentially the culture of Isocrates, with its concern for the skillful deployment of words rather than the knowledge of realities and its appeal to leisure-class snobbery, that spread through the Mediterranean world under the rule of Rome. The classicism that became the main basis of upper-class education in the Europe of the Renaissance was partly vitiated by the same weaknesses.

The most significant examples of the loss of intellectual creativity, however, are to be found in the work of Aristotle. A temperamental empiricist who nevertheless spent twenty years imbibing idealism at Plato's Academy, a rationalist with strong mystical and religious inclinations to which he attempted to give a scientific coloration, he was a very complex and, in some ways, inconsistent thinker; and because he covered all fields of knowledge with an encyclopedic scope that no other philosopher has ever equaled, his view of life cannot be summarized in any simple formula. But there can be no doubt that in his philosophy (as distinct from his scientific researches) he was primarily a conserver of the values of the past, making no attempt to look beyond the established Hellenic ethos. His main philosophic purpose was to systematize the traditional view of life by finding formulas that would resolve the doubts and bridge the contradictions suggested by his predecessors. This work of restoration resulted in one of the most imposing intellectual syntheses in all Western history, but its main effect was to close lines of inquiry rather than to open them, to end speculation instead of stimulating it. Although Aristotle (unlike Plato) located the ideal forms within nature and not outside it, he followed Plato in regarding them as the only objects of true knowledge, the material world being subject to contingency and hence partially unknowable. Such an attitude blocked all progress in the physical sciences. Aristotle showed, moreover, much of the tendency to regard culture as the adorn-

---

[2] Jaeger: op. cit., III, 150.

ment of a leisure class and identify it with the mechanical imitation of established models that was so conspicuous in Isocrates.

It is ironical that Aristotle should have been for three years the tutor of Alexander of Macedon, for their relationship was a reversal of the more usual difference between the man of thought and the man of action. Whereas Aristotle saw only the past, Alexander intuited the future. During the same decade in which Aristotle was giving final expression to the Greek way of life, his pupil was proclaiming the new political principles that would dominate the Mediterranean world for the next five hundred years. We do not know in what ways Alexander was influenced by his teacher, but certainly he did not learn from him to build an empire in which all races and religions would be unified under the rule of a god-king.

Born in 384, Aristotle spent his young manhood at the Academy, and his early writings, which have not survived, seem to have been largely Platonic. His later intellectual biography, as far as it can be reconstructed, apparently consisted of a gradual emancipation from Platonic ways of thinking and an increasing respect for scientific observation. After Plato's death in 347, he spent a dozen years in Asia Minor and in Macedon, and then returned to Athens to found a new school, the Lyceum, where he continued to expound his own "peripatetic" doctrines almost until his death in 322. All his extant writings seem to date from this final period of his life. His own system of thought, largely worked out in a kind of implicit dialogue between his acquired Platonism and his own scientific temperament, may be regarded as an attempt to reconcile the two discordant tendencies in Greek thought, the empiricist and the idealist.

Hellenism had been founded on the faith that the norms and values expressed in the life of the polis were derived from nature. By the fourth century this faith had apparently become untenable. According to such empiricists as Democritus and Protagoras, values could not be found in nature and hence were merely conventional, and Plato had responded by removing them to an ideal and eternal realm and dismissing the whole phenomenal world as a world of shadows. Closely allied to the problem of values was the problem of knowledge. The empiricist assumption that all knowledge was derived from sense impressions apparently led to a universal relativism, as it was observed that sensuous appearances varied from moment to moment and between one individual and another. The Platonic answer was to dismiss all observation as necessarily fallacious and declare that the only true knowledge was a knowledge of unchanging forms and ideas innate in the human soul. Thus Greek thought confronted an apparently unbridgeable dichotomy between matter and spirit, the outer world of objective experience and the inner world of subjective affirmation. This is perhaps the most fundamental of the perennial dilemmas of philosophy, and any reconciliation can be found only through imaginative symbols transcending man's capacity for intellectual explanation. For the Greeks the two worlds had once been unified through the myths of the Olympian religion, expressed not in intellectual formulas, but in works of the creative imagination. But by the fourth century most educated persons no longer regarded the Olympian gods as more than entertaining fictions or hypostasizations of civic loyalty; and if they could not accept the mystery cults, they were left wholly dependent on the rationalizations of philosophy.

Aristotle sought an intellectual solution to these problems by interpreting the world in terms derived from biology. He was the son of a doctor, and his whole view of life was strongly influenced by the Greek medical tradition, with its conception of health as natural harmony and its insistence that the function of human art was to supplement nature's efforts. Just as the empiricists had arrived at moral relativism by applying to human life the concepts of physics, and the absolutism of Plato had been deduced from the immutable laws of geometry, so Aristotle was able to replace values in nature by generalizing from the facts of organic life. Every organism went through a process of growth in order to realize all the potentialities of its nature; the matter of which it was composed was shaped and molded by an inherent form, and the final achievement of maturity was implicit in its origins. From these biological conceptions Aristotle derived the basic formulas with which he built his metaphysical system: the view of every object as an indissoluble union of matter and form; the interpretation of all movement and change as the actualization of potentiality; the fourfold system of causation—material, efficient, formal, and final; and the assumption that all natural processes must be regarded teleologically. Above all, the biological approach enabled him to present ethical and political values as natural, avoiding both the Sophistic doctrine that they were merely conventional and the Platonic retreat into eternity. Every living creature, man included, sought to realize its own kind of perfection, achieving *arete* in proportion as the inherent form became actualized in matter. To live well was to live in accord with the purposes of nature. Thus Aristotle surmounted the Sophistic dichotomy between nature and civilization; his concept of nature included organized human society, instead of being contrasted with it.[3]

Although Aristotle did not endow nature with personality or identify it with God, he constantly used metaphors implying that natural processes showed planning and foresight. Nature is "like a good housekeeper"; it "does nothing in vain," and "behaves as if it foresaw the future." Aristotle's concept of nature, though expressed in apparently rationalistic terms, went, in fact, far beyond valid induction; this was mythology masquerading as science. And it is significant—and typical of the intellectualism that he exemplified—that in thus trying to disguise the fact that man can attribute values to nature only by means of a religious affirmation, he lost the realistic insights embodied in religious belief. The recognition of the intrinsically tragic and irrational quality of human life, which had been promoted by the worship of the Olympian gods, ceased to be possible as soon as nature was envisaged as a tidy and prudent housewife.

Aristotle's epistemology was similarly derived from biology. Forms and ideas really existed and could be known by the human mind, but—contrary to the doctrine of Plato—they existed only in material embodiments and were apprehended not innately, but through an effort of intellectual abstraction. By considering, for example, different specimens of men or horses, one could reach a conception of the form common to the whole species and, by a further process of abstraction, could advance from the typical man or horse to the nature of all animal life. The method by which the human mind proceeded from the observation of particular phe-

[3] The Sophistic view of civilization as conventional, not natural, was revived in the eighteenth century in the Romantic movement. The core of Romanticism was the assertion that man had a natural virtue that civilization was likely to corrupt. This conception has pervaded almost all American imaginative literature, both serious and popular, down to the present day.

nomena to the understanding of universals resembled the rally of defeated soldiers, a stand made at one point in the line being gradually communicated to the whole army. Thus, the progress of scientific knowledge involved a constant movement from the particular to the universal and back again to the particular. Believing in the reality of both the empirical fact and the general idea, Aristotle went on to analyze their relationship, and this led him to make the studies of logic that formed a general introduction to his whole system. The two main methods of intellectual advance that he analyzed were the syllogism, by which one deduced a particular fact from a general principle, and induction, by which one reached general principles from the accumulation of particulars. This was a valid conception of knowledge as long as science was regarded, in terms more appropriate to the biologist than to the chemist or physicist, as a kind of inventory of descriptions. The purpose of Aristotelian logic was to describe nature, not to experiment with it or devise ways of changing it.

Aristotle applied these epistemological principles in the detailed studies of animal life which were apparently made during the last years of his life. He described some five hundred different species and, having by this time liberated himself from the Platonic contempt for empirical observation, was not above using his hands and actually engaging in dissection. Probably he made a greater contribution to the knowledge of biology than any other individual in history, and this remains his truest title to greatness. The spirit in which he undertook his researches is well exemplified in a passage from his *Parts of Animals*. "Though there are animals which have no attractiveness for the senses; yet for the eye of science, for the student who is naturally of a philosophic spirit and can discern the causes of things, Nature which fashioned them provides joys which cannot be measured. . . . We ought not to hesitate nor to be abashed, but boldly to enter upon our researches concerning animals of every sort and kind, knowing that in not one of them is Nature or Beauty lacking. I add 'Beauty' because in the works of Nature purpose and not accident is predominant; and the purpose or end for the sake of which those works have been constructed or formed has its place among what is beautiful." [4]

---

[4] *Parts of Animals,* translated by A. L. Peck, 645a.

As soon as Aristotle moved outside the field of biology, however, his thinking ceased to be genuinely scientific and became largely an attempt to provide philosophic justification for the aristocratic government and ethos of the traditional Hellenic polis. Both in social studies and in physics and astronomy it was no longer scientifically meaningful to consider all movement and change as the actualization of inherent potentialities or to interpret them teleologically and attribute them to formal and final as well as to material and efficient causes. The assumption that nature was always purposive, which was so fruitful in the analysis of organisms, led in other fields of knowledge to *a priori* theorizing that often took the place of observation and was generally used to support rigidly conservative conclusions. For Aristotle the purposes of nature did not change and had been fully realized in the aristocratic type of polis. His world was static and had no room for any conception of progress. Thus, the Hellenic way of life, no longer supported by the symbolisms of a vital religious belief, was now summed up in intellectual formulas allowing for no further development.

Cosmology usually reflects sociology, attitudes about human relationships being projected into the structure of the universe; and Aristotle's conception of the nature of the physical world, like that of Plato, can best be understood by relating it to his writings on ethics and politics. In astronomy, as in society, he envisaged a closed, finite, and unprogressive system, hierarchically organized, with activity eternally subordinated to philosophic contemplation. Based on teleological assumptions, this system was almost as unscientific as that set forth in Plato's *Timaeus*, from which, indeed, it was largely derived. The earth was the center of the universe, and around it revolved fifty-five concentric spheres carrying with them the heavenly bodies.[5] Change and imperfection were possible only below the moon, and were due to the recalcitrance of the matter from which all terrestrial objects were composed. The heavenly bodies, on the other hand, were made not of the four terrestrial elements, but of a fifth element, the ether, which was perfectly shaped by the cosmic form and purpose,

---

[5] This explanation of the movements of the stars and planets had originally been worked out during Aristotle's lifetime by the mathematician Eudoxus of Cnidus, who had, however, postulated only twenty-seven spheres.

and the mark of their perfection was that they moved eternally in circles. The ultimate cause of all natural processes, the unmoved mover, was a God who did not guide or participate in earthly affairs, but drew all things toward himself by the attraction of his divine perfection, and hence was the form of forms, the final purpose, of the entire cosmos.[6] Because he was the complete realization of all potentialities, the only activity which could be attributed to him was contemplative; he was thought perpetually thinking itself. Thus, the differences between the stars and sublunar beings represented a hierarchy of values; the higher one ascended in the cosmic scale, the more static everything became; and the apex of the cosmic pyramid was a self-sufficient philosophic deity absorbed solely in leisurely meditation about his own perfections.

Like all Greeks, Aristotle regarded ethics and politics as aspects of the same subject, and deduced his political ideals from ethical premises. "The virtue of the good man is necessarily the same as the virtue of the citizen of the perfect state." [7] His main assumption was that the norms of moral excellence were provided by nature, so that by achieving the kind of excellence appropriate to his own temperament, the individual would become happy. "That which is proper to each thing is by nature best and most pleasant for each thing." [8] In accordance with the traditional Hellenic emphasis on *sophrosyne,* he interpreted each specific form of virtue as a mean between opposite extremes. All his thinking on social questions, however, was permeated by the belief in human inequality. Greeks were naturally superior to all non-Greeks (they were both high-spirited like the Northern barbarians and intelligent like the Asiatics, and if united could rule the world); and some Greeks were superior to others. Nature in-

---

[6] In accordance with the static preconceptions of all Greek thought, Aristotle supposed that all movement required the continuous intervention of a mover. In order to account for the motion in the universe, it was therefore necessary to assume the existence of God. By the laws of motion of modern physics, on the other hand, as foreshadowed by late medieval nominalism and fully formulated in the seventeenth century, a moving object continues to move in a straight line until it is checked or deflected by another force. Thus, movement no longer requires a mover, and the main Aristotelian proof of the existence of God has become invalid.

[7] *Politics,* translated by B. Jowett and W. D. Ross, 1288a.

[8] *Ethics,* translated by W. D. Ross, 1178a.

tended that the lesser should serve the greater. Somewhat inconsistently, Aristotle regarded two different types as most completely
embodying nature's purposes. One was the magnificent or great-
souled man, who lived on a grand scale and devoted himself to
the pursuit of a noble glory, and the other was the philosopher
engaged in the life of contemplation. The magnificent man was
the fullest example of a humanistic *arete,* and represented the
ideal of aristocratic individualism that was so deeply rooted in the
Hellenic ethos and had been portrayed by so many writers from
Homer down to Sophocles; but the philosopher cultivated the
reason that was man's highest and most distinctive quality and
hence fulfilled even more completely the particular end for which
man had presumably been created. In celebrating the contemplative life, Aristotle displayed a mystical tendency at variance with
his general view of the universe. Reason was divine, and by living
for the sake of reason man could become like God, thought thinking itself. "We must not follow those who advise us, being men,
to think of human beings, and, being mortal, of mortal things,
but must, so far as we can, make ourselves immortal, and strain
every nerve to live in accordance with the best thing in us." "The
activity of God, which surpasses all others in blessedness, must be
contemplative; and of human activities, therefore, that which is
most akin to this must be most of the nature of happiness." [9]

Having established his system of values, Aristotle applied it to
the study of social organization on the assumption that the state
was a creation of nature and that its purpose was to promote
virtue. Governments should be judged by this objective ethical
standard, not by the extent to which they protected the general
welfare or satisfied popular wishes. "Political society exists for the
sake of noble actions." This objective could be attained only in a
small community where all the citizens knew each other. "If the
citizens of a state are to judge and distribute office according to
merit, then they must know each other's characters; where they

---

[9] *Ethics,* 1177b, 1178b.

This double morality was inherited
by the scholastic philosophy of the
medieval Church. According to St.
Thomas (*Summa Theologica,* II–I–
109–2), man needs grace for two different reasons: first, that he may be
healed of sin and achieve natural good;
second, that he may achieve supernatural good. The first of these reasons
implies a humanistic ethos; the second
implies an ethos of asceticism and
renunciation of the material world.

do not possess this knowledge, both the election to office and the decision of lawsuits will go wrong. Where the population is very large they are manifestly settled at haphazard, which clearly ought not to be. . . . Clearly then the best limit of the population of a state is the largest number which suffices for the purposes of life, and can be taken in at a single view." Living at a time when his pupil Alexander was merging the Greek cities into a world empire, Aristotle still accepted the polis as the only proper unit of government.[1]

A large part of Aristotle's *Politics* consisted of empirical observations, with much acute analysis of the causes of revolutions. He distinguished between governments according to whether they promoted the welfare of the whole community or solely the interests of the rulers (this was the basic difference between the three good forms—monarchy, aristocracy, and democracy—and the three perversions—tyranny, oligarchy, and mob rule), and concluded that a mixture of aristocracy and democracy usually made the most satisfactory constitution.[2] But alongside these generalizations made by Aristotle the scientist, Aristotle the philosopher developed his own conservative view of society. Because the state existed for moral ends, it should be ruled by those whose *arete* was most pre-eminent. If, for example, one man excelled all his fellow citizens, he should be made a king (the only alternative would be to banish him, for such a man "can no longer be regarded as part of a state [and] . . . may truly be deemed a god among men. . . . For men of pre-eminent virtue there is no law—they are themselves a law"). But the highest forms of *arete* —magnificence and the contemplative life—could be achieved only by leisured gentlemen supported by the labor of other people. "No man can practise virtue who is living the life of a mechanic or laborer," for which reason "the best form of state will not admit them to citizenship." Aristotle, in fact, regarded slavery as more in accord with nature's purposes than wage labor; the slave was better able to share his master's *arete*, and would therefore be happier. "The slave shares in his master's life; the artisan is less closely connected with him, and only attains excellence in

---

[1] *Politics*, 1281a, 1326b.
[2] By Aristotle's definitions, representative government, in which decisions are made not directly by the people but by elected officials, would be considered as a form of aristocracy.

proportion as he becomes a slave. The meaner sort of mechanic has a special and separate slavery; and whereas the slave exists by nature, not so the shoemaker and other artisans." [3] Like Plato, Aristotle derived his political standards from the polis of an earlier epoch in which a landowning aristocracy had ruled a subject population of peasants and slaves. Because he believed that every organism had an inherent tendency to actualize its own kind of perfection, Aristotle did not share Plato's authoritarianism; the harmony of the individual and the group in the ideal state would be achieved by conforming with nature's purposes, so that it would be unnecessary to resort to force or indoctrination or to invent fictions about the origins of human inequality. But the ideal state which Aristotle regarded as natural differed only in details from Plato's utopia.

One other Aristotelian treatise has had a lasting influence, though it exemplified the conservatism of the teleological approach even more sharply than the *Politics*. In his *Poetics*, which was apparently left unfinished, Aristotle dealt chiefly with tragedy, analyzing the works of the fifth-century Athenian dramatists on the assumption that they were perfect specimens of the art and that no new development was possible. "Tragedy," he declared, "gradually evolved as men developed each element that came to light and after going through many changes, it stopped when it had found its natural form." [4] Just as the norms of politics were to be found in the aristocratic polis, so aesthetic standards were perfectly exemplified in the three great Attic tragedians. Even more clearly than Isocrates' theory of culture, Aristotle's *Poetics* marked the point at which the living classical tradition began to harden into classicism, the mechanical imitation of earlier masterpieces. The treatise can fairly be described as a handbook for the guidance of would-be tragedians.

The chief aesthetic theories stated in the *Poetics* should probably be interpreted as replies to Plato. In the *Republic* all poems except hymns to the gods and praises of famous men had been prohibited on the grounds that they aroused disturbing and subversive emotions and that, being mere imitations of phenomena that were themselves imperfect imitations of ideas, they did not present

---

[3] *Politics*, 1284a, 1278a, 1260a. [4] *Poetics*, translated by W. Hamilton Fyfe, 1448a.

philosophical truths. Aristotle replied that the purpose of poetry
was to allay rather than to arouse emotion; tragedy, for example,
purged its auditors of pity and terror (this theory of "catharsis"
was a metaphor from medicine). Poetry, moreover, was more
philosophical and more serious than history, being concerned
with general truths rather than particular facts. Regarding catharsis
as the main function of tragedy, Aristotle was primarily concerned
with plot, and found it most purgative when a good man suffered
catastrophe because he had committed some *hamartia*. Aristotle's
remark about catharsis has evoked a vast quantity of critical com-
mentary, on the assumption that he must have meant something
very profound by it. Yet it is plain that he believed too strongly
in the rationality of all natural processes to be capable of any real
understanding of tragedy; nor is there in the *Poetics* any sufficient
recognition of the essential differences between the great writer
and the talented imitator.[5] In fact, the whole catharsis theory, with
its conception of literature as supplying an outlet for undesirable
emotions, really applies to the escapism of popular fiction
rather than to the great works that heighten our understanding of
human experience.

It was Aristotle's misfortune that he influenced posterity chiefly
through his least valuable works. His remarkable biological studies
were never fully appreciated until modern times. On the other
hand, his cosmology, after being somewhat modified by the work
of Alexandrian scientists, was generally accepted throughout the
Western world until the Renaissance, while his political and
ethical theories, combined with those of Plato, have helped to
provide an intellectual foundation for European conservatism.
Generally regarded by the ancients as inferior to Plato, he achieved
his greatest influence during the Middle Ages, when his philosophy
was accepted by the Catholic Church and fused with Christian
theology in the system of Thomas Aquinas. Subsequently he was
regarded by the founders of modern physics as the great obstacle
to scientific thinking, while political and aesthetic innovators were
similarly impeded by the prestige of his social and critical theories.

---

[5] Those qualities of sensitivity and
perceptiveness which especially distinguish the great writer are revealed by
the analysis of style rather than of
plot. The earliest surviving recognition
of this fact is in the treatise *On the
Sublime*, which bears the name of
Longinus and was probably written in
the first century of our era.

9. *Reliefs from the Ara Pacis, erected in Rome to celebrate the achievements of Augustus.*

10. *a. Statue of the Emperor Augustus.*   *b. Bust of the Emperor Caracalla.*

c. A Roman sarcophagus from the second century, depicting a musical contest between the Muses and the Sirens.

The Aristotelian philosophy, in spite of its almost consistently rationalistic intent, was in fact well calculated to block all further progress. His characteristic formulas—form and matter, potentiality and actuality, the fourfold system of causation—became, when applied not to biology but to the physical sciences, a series of meaningless incantations which gave the illusion of understanding while blocking all experimental investigation. His teleological interpretation of politics and ethics tended, in practice, to justify a narrow authoritarianism. Once nature's purposes in the formation of the human personality and human society had been fully defined, then no deviation from those purposes might be permitted.[6]

When considered in relation to his own time, Aristotle is chiefly significant as exemplifying the failure of the Hellenic mind to achieve adaptation to new conditions. Witnessing the beginning of a new phase of social development, he could only turn back to the past and restate the principles embodied in the polis of an earlier epoch. Yet in one aspect of his thinking—and it is significant that he expressed it in a tone of emotional exhortation not usually present in his writing—he foreshadowed a future trend. The highest type of life, he declared, was to be found not, as the Greeks of earlier epochs would have assumed, in participation in the affairs of the polis, but in the practice of a contemplation by which men could achieve a kind of divinity. During the epoch of imperialism following the breakdown of the polis, philosophers more and more insistently were to preach withdrawal from earthly affairs and retreat into the self. This was the highest wisdom of the ancient world prior to the advent of a faith in a God who, instead of contemplating his own perfections, had shared the sufferings of mankind, and of an ethic not of aristocratic aloofness but of active charity.

---

[6] The Catholic attitude to sex provides a good example of the Aristotelian type of thinking. The natural purpose of sexual intercourse is to propagate children; any attempt to frustrate this purpose must therefore be regarded as sinful.

There is much truth in the verdict of Léon Robin (*Greek Thought*, p. 308): "He was a skillful and tricky dialectician, but was neither deep nor original. The invention which is most clearly his consists in well-tried formulas, verbal distinctions which are easy to handle. He set up a machine whose works, once set in motion, give the illusion of penetrating reflection and real knowledge. . . . So he for a long time turned science away from paths in which it might fairly soon have made decisive progress."

This world in which philosophers could not feel at home was largely the construction of Aristotle's pupil Alexander. Dying at the age of thirty-three after a reign of only thirteen years, he changed the shape of human affairs more decisively than any other figure in Western history. Most great men of action have been primarily instruments of social forces and have achieved success by giving form and direction to tendencies that were clearly already inevitable. Alexander, on the other hand, aided by his good fortune in inheriting power and opportunity when he was still a boy, displayed the kind of dazzling creative initiative characteristic of a poet rather than of a general or a statesman.[7]

Alexander's education had included the Homeric poems, and the most obvious facet of his character was his Achillean compulsion to win immortal glory. He was the last and greatest embodiment of the individualistic ethos of the *Iliad*. His devotion to Homer was, no doubt, due partly to the fact that social conditions in the Macedon of his childhood were similar to those described in the epics. The Macedonians were still a rural people, consisting mainly of peasants and landowning nobles; and the king, like Agamemnon, was a war leader rather than a despot and was expected to take counsel with his peers before embarking on any new enterprise. After many centuries of quiescence and isolation, Macedon had become a strong military power under the rule of King Philip, who resembled the Russian Peter the Great in his driving ambition, his program of introducing the techniques of more advanced peoples, and the brutality and sensuality of his personal character. But Alexander did not inherit his father's less attractive qualities. Although (like all Macedonians) he drank immoderately, his private life was remarkably pure; and though the barbarism of his Macedonian background was never far below the surface of his personality, so that he was sometimes guilty of the most savage violence when his will was thwarted, he was true to his model in his essential magnanimity. He could be extraordinarily generous to his friends; and while he resembled Achilles in his frenetic rages, he was capable also of treating his enemies with the gentle courtesy with which Achilles had given hospitality to Priam.

---

[7] The most useful biography is W. W. Tarn: *Alexander the Great*.

After Philip had made himself master of the whole Greek mainland, he had planned to invade Asia Minor in order to end Persian rule over the Greek cities of Ionia and other provinces (these cities, liberated by Athens in the fifth century, had again lost their independence after the Peloponnesian War, with the disgraceful connivance of the Spartans). He proposed to unify the whole Hellenic world, and—as Isocrates had recognized—unity could be maintained only through a war against a foreign power. But when Alexander succeeded to the throne on Philip's death in 336, he developed these war plans on a scale that neither Isocrates nor Philip had ever contemplated, and ended by merging the idea of Hellenic unity into the much bolder and more comprehensive idea of world empire. Embarking in 334 for the conquest of Asia with an army of some forty thousand men, he landed near the site of Troy, where he sacrificed to Pallas Athene and poured libations at the alleged tomb of Achilles. According to Plutarch, he told his friends how fortunate Achilles had been in that his glorious deeds had been recorded for posterity by a great poet.

Achillean traits were dominant for the next ten years, although Alexander displayed extraordinary abilities as well as an insatiable ambition. It had been proved on earlier occasions that Greek armies, with their superior weapons, discipline, and morale, could usually defeat the large but relatively untrained levies called into service by the Persian kings; but the apparent ease with which Alexander won his victories was due also to his careful planning, his brilliant leadership in battle, and—above all—to the amazing speed with which he moved. Alexander won the Battle of the Granicus, liberated the Greeks of Ionia, defeated the Persians again at Issus at the southeastern corner of Asia Minor, conquered Syria after a three-month siege of Tyre, took possession of Egypt, won a final and decisive victory over the Persian king at Gaugamela in Mesopotamia, subdued the militant tribesmen of Persia's eastern provinces, crossed the passes of the Hindu Kush into the Indus Valley (where he had apparently expected to find himself close to the end of the world), and, after his men finally refused to go farther, returned to Babylon after a most difficult march across the deserts bordering the Indian Ocean. During the last year of his life he set about organizing the empire he had conquered in accord with ideas that had no precedent in earlier political practice. He now showed that he was capable of constructive planning as well as of a mere lust for glory.

Alexander regarded himself as the apostle of Hellenism, and Hellenism meant the polis. Throughout the conquered territories he had planted cities intended to be centers of Greek culture and the Greek way of life (as represented by such institutions as the gymnasium, the theater, and the worship of Olympian gods). Later chroniclers attributed no less than seventy-five cities to him (probably with some exaggeration); many of them quickly disappeared, but others, particularly Alexandria in Egypt, were more enduring. By this means he sought to bring about the Hellenization of the Orient, and thereby to establish his empire on a firm foundation. But although the Alexandrian polis copied the cultural institutions of its Greek exemplar and was given rights of self-government in its internal affairs, it did not enjoy full political independence. Alexander's intentions did not become wholly clear, but they can be gauged from his treatment of the mainland and Ionian cities. In accord with the policy already adopted by Philip, the mainland cities were governed by oligarchies willing to support Macedonian domination. In Ionia, Alexander established democratic governments, but only because the Ionian democrats were traditionally pro-Hellenic, whereas the oligarchies had accepted Persian rule. Thus, the polis of the empire represented only the culture of Hellenism, divorced from the political freedom that had originally made cultural development possible.

What Alexander ultimately envisioned, however, was not Greek domination of the conquered provinces, but a genuine world empire based on an equality of races. Relatively early in his career of conquest he had begun to wear the costume of a Persian king and to appoint Persians to high administrative positions, thereby provoking some angry complaints from his Macedonian veterans. During the last year of his life he tried to promote a true union of East and West. In a festival at the old Persian capital of Susa, he celebrated the marriages of eighty of his officers and ten thousand of his soldiers with Persian women. A few months later at Opis, he presided at a feast for men of both races, nine thousand in all, and after pouring a libation from a silver bowl that had belonged to the Persian kings, he made a speech appealing for *homonoia,* unity of spirit. *Homonoia* had been a favorite concept of Isocrates, but he had applied it only to the Greek world. Alexander was the first to envisage a *homonoia* that transcended racial and religious differences. Even more remarkably, he declared that all men were brothers; all men were children of the same God, although some of them (he added) were favored more particularly than others. This was the first affirmation in all history of the brotherhood of man, and—ironically—it came from the lips of a military conqueror.

How could *homonoia* be established? How was such a vast conglomeration of different peoples to be unified? Alexander's solution was the old Oriental principle of the god-king. Apparently this concept had first been suggested to him in Egypt, where he had visited the desert shrine of Amon-Re and, as the king of Egypt and heir of the Pharaohs, had been greeted by the priests as the son of the god. The Greeks identified Amon-Re with Zeus, and this episode led to stories that Alexander was actually the son of Zeus, who was said to have visited his mother Olympias in the form of a snake. Belief in human deification, however, was not exclusively Oriental: although faith in the Olympians had declined, the chthonian element in the old Greek religion still had considerable vitality, and the chthonian rituals had included worship at the tombs of dead heroes who had earned divinity. Even in the Olympian religion, though not in its Homeric form, some individuals, most notably Heracles, had apparently risen from mortal to immortal status through their services to mankind. Alexander therefore decided that he should be considered a god, and sent orders from Susa that the Greek cities should pay him divine honors. There is no evidence that he actually supposed himself to be endowed with any supernatural powers, though his extraordinary achievements undoubtedly gave him the feeling that he was especially favored by God. He seems to have regarded deification primarily as a useful political formula. According to the Hellenic view of life, every man was naturally a member of some particular political community, and nobody could exist in isolation without losing his humanity. But Alexander proposed to transcend all communities, being a member of each of them and at the same time representing in his own person the ideal of universal *homonoia.* This made him more than a man, and the only status that could be attributed to him was that of a god.[8]

These three principles—the diffusion of Hellenic culture through the foundation of cities, the unity of all races in a common citizenship, and the worship of the god-king as the embodiment of *homonoia*—indicated the direction of political development in Mediterranean society for the next five hundred years. They represented man's first attempt in the Western world to pass beyond tribalism and realize a universalist ideal. The creation of a universal empire, though by no means inevitable, could, of course, be regarded as the logical conclusion of the growth of commercial relations and political conflicts among the different Mediterranean states. More significantly, universalism was implicit in all the new views of life promulgated during the Axial Period. Yet before the advent of Alexander no people had actually succeeded in transcending tribalistic loyalties. Although the Greeks had developed the concept of universal laws of nature, they had continued to regard their superiority to all "barbarians" as axiomatic; and although the Jews had believed in a universal deity, they still considered themselves his chosen people, set apart from the gentiles by their obedience to the Mosaic law. Among empire-builders the Persians had come closest to the practice of racial and religious tolerance, but the peoples whom they had conquered were still treated as subjects and not admitted to full equality. Alexander was the first man to proclaim universalism not merely as an abstract theory, but as a working principle of government.

The epoch that Alexander inaugurated was characterized, nevertheless, by the decay of cultural vitality, by the brutal oppression of the masses by a fortunate few, and by a growing pessimism about the whole meaning of human existence. The surface of life in the Hellenistic and Roman empires had a material splendor far surpassing that of any earlier epoch, but wherever one can penetrate more deeply into the sensibility of the age, one finds chiefly either

---

[8] Did Alexander remember the passage in the *Politics* in which Aristotle declared that the man of pre-eminent *arete,* being himself a law, must be considered as a god among men? In view of the inconsistency of this idea with Aristotle's general political and religious views, it seems more probable that it originated with Alexander and that Aristotle wrote the passage with his pupil in mind.

cynicism or a profound and pervasive sadness. It was an age whose highest wisdom was expressed in the ideals of *autarkeia*, individual self-sufficiency, and *ataraxia*, freedom from all disturbing emotions. This was the inevitable result of a universalism based not on any system of beliefs, but on a military power that meant the loss of all political freedom. Hellenism had failed to develop new loyalties and institutions to replace those of the polis, and instead of moving forward to some new principle of order, the Mediterranean world turned back to the theocratic despotisms of the fourth millennium.

7

The Hellenistic Era

Although the universalism envisaged by Alexander was implicit in the development of Mediterranean society, it was for a long time understood only by a few philosophers, not by practical men. During the early Hellenistic period, the breakdown of all traditional forms of social integration was much more conspicuous than the growth of any new institutions. Alexander left no heir capable of taking his place (his only son was born posthumously), and his death in 323 left the whole of the Near East in a state of flux. This was a time when all the normal rules of behavior were suspended, and nothing seemed beyond the scope of an adventurer who was sufficiently bold, crafty, and unscrupulous. No longer restricted to the narrow confines of their native peninsula, the Greeks had an empire to play with, and dazzling material rewards went to those who knew how to seize their opportunities.

Alexander's leading generals began almost immediately to carve out kingdoms for themselves, and for the half-century following his death there was almost incessant fighting among different Macedonian families. Eventually three new dynasties established their control over major slices of the empire, although warfare about boundary lines continued until the final unification imposed by Rome in the first century B.C. The Antigonids became kings of Macedon; the Ptolemies ruled Egypt; and the Seleucids held Syria and for a long time were also masters of most of Asia Minor and of Mesopotamia. The eastern provinces of the old Persian Empire soon reverted to the rule of native chieftains and did not remain part of the Hellenistic world. Greece was still split into small states, although their powers of self-government were usually limited by the Macedonian kings.[1] As before the rise of Persia, however, the most flourishing centers of Greek civilization were now to be found in Asia Minor, where Hellenic enterprise could make use of supplies of servile labor and rich natural resources. Such cities as Rhodes and Ephesus developed into wealthy commercial communities, and in the second century B.C. a new ruling dynasty, the Attalids, built Pergamum into a prosperous kingdom.

The Macedonian chieftains who had become masters of most of the Near East remained true to their Homeric background in their barbaric lust for glory and their driving energy and self-confidence, and though some of them ended their careers on battlefields or in captivity, others proved capable of holding and organizing kingdoms as well as of conquering them. They were capably seconded by their women, who were startlingly different from the secluded, submissive females of the Greek city-states. Throughout the Hellenistic period an extraordinary series of Macedonian queens and princesses, most of them named Arsinoë, Berenice, or Cleopatra, intrigued and fought for power, governed kingdoms, quelled insurrections, led armies into battle, changed husbands, and made unblushing use of their sexual attractions in order to achieve political ambitions.

The rule of the Macedonian dynasties opened new opportunities to the whole Greek people. Their native peninsula, with its meager natural resources, had long been overcrowded, and one of the reasons for the interminable interstate warfare had been the cessation of overseas colonization after the rise of the Persian Empire. Now the Hellenistic kingdoms needed officials, secretaries, engineers, architects, sea captains, doctors, and mercenary soldiers, and the opening of the Orient led to the expansion of trade and industry. Greeks began to migrate in vast numbers to the new Hellenistic cities, especially to Alexandria in Egypt and Antioch in Syria, and became the dominant race throughout the whole Near East. The population of the Greek peninsula soon began to decline; and although Athens retained its pre-eminence as the main center

---

[1] Two groups of mainland states came together in federations, known as the Achaian and Aetolian leagues, but these attempts to solve the problem of disunity came too late to have much practical importance. Greek experiments with federalism were studied by Madison and other makers of the American Constitution two thousand years later.

of philosophical studies, the old Greek cities no longer had much political or economic importance.

Once the Hellenistic world had achieved some kind of political order, its rulers could settle down to the systematic exploitation of its economic resources. In Egypt the Ptolemies inherited and intensified the theocratic state socialism originally created by the early pharaohs; and by imposing a fixed annual tribute upon every peasant family and by operating most branches of industry and commerce as government monopolies, they were soon extracting an immense revenue from the native population. Elsewhere the main feature of Hellenistic economy was the growth of large capitalistic enterprises. Huge slave factories in Asia Minor and Syria soon controlled the market for manufactured goods, turning out cheaply produced pottery and textiles with which independent artisans could not compete, while merchants and bankers conducted operations on a much bigger scale than their predecessors in Periclean Athens. The accumulation of wealth was reflected in the growth of immense urban areas, the largest of which, Alexandria, had by the first century B.C. a population exceeding one million.

By materialistic standards Hellenistic civilization appeared, in fact, to have progressed far beyond the Greece of the Periclean age, where life, even for the upper classes, had always been simple and remarkably unluxurious. Its economic growth was most clearly demonstrated in the splendor of its urban architecture. Most of the new Hellenistic cities were designed according to the same general plan, which afterwards spread to the western provinces of the Roman Empire and has remained characteristic of Mediterranean civilization to this day. The center of the city was usually a broad open market place surrounded by pillared colonnades where citizens could meet for business while shaded from the sun. Near by were such public buildings as the town hall, the most important temples, the theater, and the gymnasium. The street plan was rectangular, with two main thoroughfares, at right angles to each other, crossing at the market place. The adornment of cities opened a large market for sculpture, and the vast majority of the surviving Greek works of art date from the Hellenistic period.

But though the rulers of the Hellenistic world enjoyed a luxury and magnificence that had been unknown in classical Greece, few of the benefits of economic development appear to have percolated down to the masses of the population. Although class struggles between rich and poor continued in some places, especially in the Greek peninsula, most of the Hellenistic cities were wholly undemocratic: some of them, like Alexandria and Pergamum, were directly ruled by kings; others were controlled by small mercantile oligarchies. Slavery had become a more important feature of the economy, and the slave population was relatively larger than in the fifth century, and included many Greeks as well as barbarians. The incessant wars and the growth of piracy made life highly uncertain, and even well-educated citizens of civilized communities sometimes suffered the misfortune of being sold into servitude in a foreign country. It was indicative of the whole moral deterioration of Greek society that the island of Delos, which had formerly been sacred to Apollo and had been the original center of the league formed by Athens to liberate Ionia, had become the chief slave market of the eastern Mediterranean, boasting that it could handle ten thousand sales a day.

It must be remembered, moreover, that the Hellenistic cities were essentially outposts of Greek civilization in potentially hostile territory. In most areas the aims of Alexander—the Hellenization of the East and the creation of *homonoia* between Greeks and Orientals—were never realized. The Ptolemies, controlling Egypt from Alexandria with the aid of a mercenary army and surpassing even the most oppressive of the pharaohs in their merciless extraction of its wealth, seem to have been always regarded as aliens by the native population, although resentment could show itself only in occasional labor strikes and in the flight of peasant families from tribute-collectors. The Seleucids, who adopted more humane economic policies and followed the example of Alexander in founding Greek cities throughout their dominions, won considerable support in Mesopotamia, where their rule produced a renaissance of the traditional culture. But they could not overcome the hostility of the old temple cities of Syria, some of which had probably been governed for thousands of years by the same priestly families, or of the feudal landowners with their serfs and the nomadic shepherd peoples of the rural areas. Only in parts of Asia Minor was there a genuine fusion of East and West, as was shown by the worship of the Great Mother Cybele, the traditional peasant goddess, in cities like Pergamum and Ephesus. Possibly it was for this reason that natives of Asia Minor made such important contributions to the formulation of new views of life, particularly of Stoicism and Christianity. Elsewhere there remained a fundamental conflict of values between the Hellenistic cities and the Oriental countryside. Believing that divinity was immanent in all natural processes, Hellenism remained humanistic, its characteristic symbols being the lecture hall and the gymnasium, while the Orient still worshipped powers that transcended nature. The resurgence of the Orient after the shock of Alexander's conquests began in the second century B.C. with the rise of the kingdom of the Parthians in western Iran, followed by their conquest of Mesopotamia from the Seleucids. In Syria and Egypt the resistance of the peasant population to the values of Hellenism continued for many generations, one of its earlier manifestations being the Jewish rebellion against Antiochus Epiphanes under the leadership of the Maccabees. This Oriental opposition to Greek humanism found expression after the rise of Christianity in theological movements refusing to accept the orthodox doctrine that Christ represented the union of humanity and divinity in one person, and finally eased the way for the Mohammedan conquest of the sixth century of our era.

Under such conditions, how could power be legitimized? For the Hellenistic monarchies, as for Alexander, the only solution was to consider the king as endowed with divine powers. The Ptolemies, as heirs of the pharaohs, almost immediately made claims to godhood, also sometimes adopting the pharaonic custom of brother-and-sister marriage. The Seleucids and other dynasties were more modest, but did not generally discourage their subjects from worshipping them, and it was generally assumed that kings became gods after death. Deification was not merely a device adopted by the monarchies for political reasons; it was the expression of a real popular craving, and was by no means confined only to Orientals. The Hellenistic dynasties, in fact, linked themselves with the Olympians, the Seleucids claiming descent from Apollo and the Ptolemies from Heracles and Dionysus. Soon after Alexander's death, the Antigonid Demetrius Poliorcetes was hailed as a god by the people of Athens (although he subsequently lost popular favor by desecrating the Parthenon with his ceaseless and insatiable amours). During the chaos following the break-up of Alexander's empire, the ordinary citizen could hope for security only by relying on the power of some strong leader, and he turned to the kings as divine saviors and benefactors partly because he had lost faith in other gods. The popular song with which the Athenians appealed for the protection of Demetrius declared: "The other gods either are not, or are far away; either they hear not, or they give no heed; but thou art here, and we can see thee, not in wood or stone, but in very truth." [2] Thus, king-worship was not, as in the time of the early theocratic civilizations, a symbol of faith in the divine order of the universe, but, on the contrary, an expression of despair in a world that seemed wholly irrational and anarchical.

The real attitudes of Hellenistic civilization were fatalistic. Man could discern no moral or rational meaning in the course of events and could not hope to control them. Having lost his sense of participation in any political community, the individual felt isolated and helpless as he confronted a universality that seemed to be governed not by the gods, but by pure chance. In the third century, when Macedonian chieftains were conquering and losing kingdoms with bewildering rapidity, men began to worship the goddess Tyche (fortune). Tyche seemed to be the most powerful of all the deities, and perhaps by propitiating her one could ensure her favor. Certain prosperous individuals and communities had their own special guardian spirits, or geniuses, which could guarantee continued success. After the Hellenistic dynasties had become established, the worship of luck began to change into the worship of destiny. The future was predetermined, and man had no power to change it. This resulted in attempts to foretell the future, particularly through astrology. The stars, moving in fixed circles in a realm where everything was certain, were worshipped as gods and were believed to control the future. The astral mysticism that had been developed in Mesopotamia, and to which both Plato and Aristotle had given some support, had an enormous vogue in later Hellenistic society and was perhaps the most popular of all its pseudo-religions.

How could the individual circumvent the decrees of fortune or

---

[2] W. W. Tarn: *Hellenistic Civilization*, p. 53.

of destiny? The cities maintained public religious observances, but real belief in the Olympians scarcely survived the freedom of the polis. On the other hand, private religious cults continued to flourish, providing initiates with communal ties and associations, and promising them salvation. The mysteries of Dionysus and of Eleusis still assured their devotees a happy immortality. Cybele was still worshipped by eunuch priests with anointed hair and whitened faces who danced to the music of timbrels and boxwood flutes and slashed themselves with knives in states of orgiastic ecstasy. Isis, the queen of heaven and the underworld, remained a promise of divine protection, and was now linked with a new husband, the god Sarapis, who appears to have been deliberately manufactured by the Ptolemies in order to replace the native Egyptian deity Osiris. These and other cults, along with a wide variety of magical practices, spread through the Hellenistic cities and provided consolation for the masses of the oppressed. Thus, with the decay of the official Greek religion, more primeval and more irrational beliefs gained new strength.

Such a climate of opinion was not favorable to science and the arts, in spite of the fact that cultural activity was now subsidized by the ruling classes on a much more generous scale than had been possible at earlier periods. It is true that some substantial achievements stand to the credit of Hellenistic civilization, but most of them occurred within the first hundred years after the death of Alexander and were plainly owing to a prolongation of the intellectual tendencies of the classical age. When this impetus had exhausted itself, Hellenistic society ceased to display any further creativity and produced only scholars and academicians.

The most promising scientific developments took place at the Lyceum under the direction of Aristotle's two immediate successors, Theophrastus and Strato. Continuing the emphasis on exact observation which Aristotle had shown in the biological studies of his later years, and repudiating Platonic idealism much more consistently than Aristotle had done, these two men came closer than any other figures in ancient history to a full understanding of scientific method. Theophrastus' specialty was the study of botany, though he also ranged over the whole field of knowledge and was the author of a delightful volume of character-sketches. He is especially significant, however, in that he tried to disentangle

science from the theological prepossessions that had been so conspicuous in the physics and metaphysics of Aristotle. Arguing that
movement was an inherent quality of natural objects, he suggested
that it was unnecessary to invoke any divine power in order to account for the motions of the stars, and he expressed skepticism
about the purposiveness of nature. "With regard to the view that
all things are for the sake of an end and nothing is in vain, the
assignment of ends is in general not easy, as it is usually stated
to be. . . . We must try to set a limit to the assigning of final
causes. This is the prerequisite of all scientific inquiry into the
universe." [3]

Strato, who seems to have been primarily a physicist, went even
farther. More fully than any other ancient scientist, he understood
the meaning and importance not only of observation, but also of
experiment, as is shown by some beautiful examples in the surviving
fragments of his writings. That he wholly separated science from
theology is indicated by the description of his position given by
Cicero. "Strato of Lampsacus gives God a dispensation from his
arduous task, opining that if the priests of the gods get holidays
it is only fair that the gods should have them too. He says he does
not use the help of the gods to make the world. Everything that
exists, he says, is the work of nature. . . . He himself goes
through the parts of the universe one by one and proves that
whatever exists or comes to be has been made or is made by
purely natural forces and movements." [4]

Under appropriate social conditions the work of the Lyceum
might have been the beginning of a real scientific revolution comparable to that of seventeenth-century Europe. But the intellectual
atmosphere of the Hellenistic world was not conducive to the
rationalistic exploration of nature. Nor was scientific development
sufficiently stimulated by practical needs; in an economy increasingly based on slavery there was little inducement to search for
technological improvements. Athens, moreover, having lost its
political and economic pre-eminence, soon surrendered its intellectual leadership to Alexandria, where the Ptolemies were able to
attract men of learning by lavish patronage but where full intel-

---

[3] B. Farrington: *Greek Science*, pp.
162–3.

[4] B. Farrington: op. cit., pp. 182–3.
See also Marshall Clagett: *Greek
Science in Antiquity*, pp. 68–74.

lectual freedom was impossible. After the death of Strato in 269, the Lyceum ceased to produce important original work, and became chiefly a center for education in rhetoric and ethics. Nearly two thousand years passed before Western scientists arrived again at any comparable understanding of scientific method.

The Ptolemies subsidized learning on a scale never surpassed until the American millionaire foundations of the twentieth century. The Museum of Alexandria employed a staff of one hundred scholars and scientists; its library included the whole corpus of Greek literature and thought and eventually contained no less than seven hundred thousand rolls; it also included an observatory, dissecting-rooms, and zoological and botanical gardens. That its atmosphere was not wholly favorable to original thought is suggested by the Cynic philosopher Timon's description of its professorial employees as "fatted fowls in a coop." In addition to promoting the arts and sciences, they were expected to make themselves useful to the reigning dynasty by their contributions to military engineering and by devising mechanical tricks that could be passed off as miraculous and employed in the worship of the new deity Sarapis. A more serious impediment to freedom of inquiry was the conflict, especially in astronomy, between the scientific attitude and the accepted socio-theological view of the universe.

The astronomical data gathered both by the Mesopotamians and by the Greeks already indicated that the geocentric hypothesis might be untenable, and sometime during the third century one of the Alexandrian mathematicians, Aristarchus of Samos, suggested that the phenomena could more plausibly be explained on the assumption that the sun and the stars were motionless while the earth and the planets revolved around the sun. According to what was then known about physics, there seemed to be valid scientific objections to such a theory, but it failed to win acceptance partly because it ran counter to the whole Hellenistic climate of opinion. Religious belief seemed to depend on the assumption, maintained so emphatically by both Plato and Aristotle, that the universe was a finite sphere with the earth at its center, that the stars were divine, and that the chief mark of their divinity was that they moved eternally in perfect circles. Aristarchus was accused of impiety, and only one other ancient astronomer, the Babylonian

Seleucus, ventured to adopt the heliocentric conception. During the second century B.C., Hipparchus, possibly the greatest of Alexandrian scientists, displayed a misdirected genius in working out a cosmology that appeared to account for the phenomena in geocentric terms. As restated and improved by Ptolemy in the second century A.D., his theories were not disputed until the Renaissance, and continued to provide cosmic support for social hierarchy.

In spite of social and ideological obstacles, the third century B.C. added considerably to knowledge, especially in mathematics (with the works of Euclid, Archimedes, and Apollonius), in mathematical geography (with Eratosthenes), and in medicine. Scientists like Archimedes also displayed considerable ingenuity in devising technological inventions for use in warfare, hydraulics, and other fields of concern to governments (though it is also recorded of Archimedes that he regarded "the work of an engineer and everything that ministers to the needs of life as ignoble and vulgar" [5] and remained a Platonist in insisting that the deductive reasoning of pure mathematics was the highest form of truth). But it is significant that almost all the important men associated with the Museum went to Alexandria from elsewhere, being natives of Greek city-states, and that the impetus given to research by the munificence of the Ptolemies did not retain its strength for more than two or three generations. The decline of the polis was followed by the cessation of original scientific activity, which could not establish any lasting roots in the authoritarian atmosphere of Alexandria. Hipparchus was the only major scientist of the second century. The first century was empty of important discoveries, as was the whole of the Roman period.

The decline of creativity was equally conspicuous in literature and art, although this was owing to deeper factors than the growth of authoritarian governments and irrational beliefs. It was a product of changes of sensibility which had already become manifest during the later classical period, especially in the work of Euripides. What kinds of art can be produced in a society no longer unified by any collective religious affirmation about the meaning of human life and man's place in the universe? What attitudes will be expressed by writers and artists spiritually alienated from the world

---

[5] Quoted from Plutarch by Marshall Clagett: op. cit., p. 60.

around them? Alexandrianism remains the stock example of such an aesthetic situation. Whenever comparable conditions have developed during the subsequent history of the Western world, the arts have acquired similar qualities.

No longer regarded as an expression of spiritual truths, art became primarily a form of entertainment. Its purpose was to provide aesthetic pleasure or excitement. But because artists had ceased to perform any recognizably important social function, they could no longer always appeal to large popular audiences, being often compelled to address themselves mainly to the cultivated few who had leisure for discriminating appreciation. We cannot measure the extent to which the fifth-century Athenian populace could understand the tragedies of Aeschylus, but certainly it had participated in their presentation with religious seriousness as a duty to the state and to the gods. The poets of Alexandria, on the other hand, wrote primarily for an elite. Much of their work was sophisticated, subtle, ironical, learned, and overweighted with recondite allusions.

During the Hellenistic period the most important areas of human experience were no longer amenable to aesthetic treatment. No longer believing that the universe was directed by powers akin and intelligible to man, poets could no longer place their characters within any cosmic framework. And as they lived in a civilization not animated by any collective ideal of justice, they could not relate their characters to any concepts of political and social order. Hellenistic literature turned for its subject matter mainly to the private life of the individual. In some areas, especially in the exploration of personal emotion and in the realistic depiction of social types (often with the intent of producing moral or aesthetic shocks), it went beyond the work of the classical period. But it was significantly unable to present whole human beings capable of positive and constructive action. When the world in which men live is felt to be anarchical, the human personality loses its standards of order and tends to become fragmented into its component emotional drives; the organic unity of the individual self is dependent on the sense of a unity in society and in the cosmos. In Hellenistic literature, the separate emotion, especially the emotion of sexual desire, usually has more reality than the man or woman who succumbs to it.

For the same reason, writers were now confronted with the problem of form. Experience now presented itself as chaotic; how could it be shaped and integrated into aesthetic wholes? The kind of single vision that had been reflected in the unity of the Homeric epos and of Athenian tragedy before Euripides had become impossible. Much Hellenistic writing was frankly episodic, without any attempt at structural organization. Much of it, on the other hand, was highly formalized, but form had now become simply a conscious technical artifice (as in the well-made plots of the New Comedy), a device for providing aesthetic entertainment rather than the expression of a belief in the intrinsic unity of human experience.

For the subsequent history of Western literature and art, nevertheless, the work of the Hellenistic age is more important than that of the classical period. The Romans found their artistic models in Alexandria rather than in Athens, and through Latin imitations the Alexandrians set the standards for the Europe of the Renaissance. This was partly because, being self-conscious craftsmen for whom aesthetic pleasure was its own fulfillment, they developed forms and techniques that could easily be copied, whereas Homer and Aeschylus were inimitable. In consequence, Alexandrianism has been an obstacle to the true understanding of Hellenism; our impressions of Greek mythology having been derived mainly from Ovid, and indirectly from his master Callimachus, both of whom regarded it simply as a storehouse of entertaining fictions, we can never wholly recapture the religious awe that the Olympians inspired in early Greece.[6] Yet without the work of Alexandrian scholars we might know relatively little of the classical writers. One of the most useful tasks performed at the Museum was to assemble the corpus of Greek literature and establish accurate texts.

The most important of the Alexandrian poets were Callimachus, Apollonius Rhodius, and Theocritus, all of whom flourished during the early decades of the third century. Callimachus, who was apparently the literary dictator of the Museum, wrote a number of

---

[6] Modern conceptions of Greek mythology are typified by the conventional portrayals of Parnassus, as exemplified by Raphael's picture in the Vatican. This shows a gentle acclivity on the top of which Apollo is playing a lute to an audience of Muses and some twenty male and female poets. The real Parnassus is an immense mountain, snow-capped through much of the year, with precipitous slopes that make it almost inaccessible to human beings.

short poems, the most ambitious of which were hymns to the
Olympians. Loaded with an immense theological erudition and
displaying a polished perfection of style and form, they have a
chilly magnificence that exemplifies both the impeccable good taste
of the Alexandrian literati and their lack of real belief in the
subjects they regarded as appropriate for poetic celebration. The
work that most fully typifies the Alexandrian spirit, however, is the
Argonautica of Apollonius, which was written in defiance of Callimachus' theory that long poems were no longer possible. This
narrative of the adventures of Jason and the crew of the *Argo* in
quest of the golden fleece tells an exciting story and is filled with
vivid descriptions. It is Alexandrian in its romantic emphasis on
outlandish people and places and its display of recondite mythological and geographical learning (much of the latter being de-
liriously wrong). For the classical Greeks, beauty had been inherent in the here-and-now, but the Alexandrians found poetry
only by escaping to imaginary worlds and could handle contemporary subjects only in the form of a vulgar realism. Even more
significantly, the *Argonautica* is Alexandrian in that it conveys no
feeling of organic energy in either its structure or its characters.
The poem is simply a string of episodes which might have been
prolonged indefinitely if the author had not grown tired of it, with
none of that capacity to impose form and order upon diverse materials which one feels so vigorously at work in Homer. As for
Jason, he is not an epic hero, but an Alexandrian intellectual.
Repeatedly described as *amechanos,* "without resources," he is incapable of initiative (except with women), gives way to despair before every obstacle, and succeeds in his mission only because he
is aided by several goddesses and by the Princess Medea. Constantly propelled by external circumstances, he is not a man of
action, but a man to whom things happen. The most memorable
feature of the poem is the detailed and moving account of the
love of Medea. Imitated by Virgil in his portrait of Dido, this has influenced half the imaginative literature of the Western world. The
analysis of individual emotion, especially in its more destructive
forms, was what the Alexandrians could do best.

The impulse of escape was equally conspicuous in Theocritus.
It is not surprising that the growth of a sophisticated megalopolitan
society should have been followed by the idealization of nature

and the simple life, and Theocritus supplied the need with his poems about Sicilian herdsmen. Since the pastoral developed into the most tediously artificial of all poetic genres, it is difficult to be fair to its inventor; but while one cannot take seriously the loves and song contests of Theocritus' rustic characters, he knew his subject matter from personal experience, and his country environment was authentic, if the people who lived in it were not. His capacity for exact observation is shown in the most memorable of his non-pastoral works, his account of two middle-class Alexandrian housewives going to a religious festival. With his disciple Virgil, on the other hand, who transferred the locale from Sicily to Arcadia (previously known only as the most uncivilized part of Greece), and with a long line of Renaissance writers, the pastoral ceased to bear any relationship to the realities of rural life and became simply a device by which poets constructed a fantasy world free from most of man's normal obligations and anxieties. The Arcadia of literature was inhabited solely by lovers and musicians, the sheep and goats being merely unconvincing stage properties.[7]

The other leading literary invention of this period was equally artificial and has been even more influential. Late in the fourth century, Athens developed the New Comedy, whose chief representative was Menander. The drama, like other art forms, could no longer present religious or political affirmations, and now turned for its material to the private lives of individuals, especially to the amorous experiences of young people. Menander deployed a well-established collection of stock characters—the *jeune premier*, the irascible father, the resourceful slave, the elderly miser, and so on—and depended for his effects mainly on witty dialogue and on ingeniously constructed plots with neat surprise endings and a heavy reliance on coincidence. The New Comedy never rose above the level of sophisticated entertainment, but through its Latin adaptations by Plautus and Terence it set the standards for the European comedy of the Renaissance and has continued indirectly to influence the Western theater down to the present day. Aristoph-

---

[7] For obscure reasons, city people always sentimentalize the herdsman rather than the agriculturalist, regarding him as a carefree individual addicted to singing songs of his own composition. The modern equivalent of the pastoral poem is the cowboy story.

anes was possible only in fifth-century Athens, but every well-made comedy on the modern stage is still likely to employ some of the conventions devised by Menander.

After the third century, literature, like science, seems to have withered away. Certainly little was produced that later generations thought worthy of preservation. Such fragments of imaginative literature as have been preserved show a continuing preoccupation either with private emotion or with the realistic depiction of social types, the former being exemplified in the love poems of Meleager, of the Palestinian city of Gadara, and the latter in the mimes of Herodes, which dealt chiefly with bawds, brothels, and female lasciviousness. The only major writer of the later Hellenistic period was the historian Polybius, an Arcadian Greek who found an inspiring subject in describing the rise of the Roman Empire. But although he made a serious attempt to achieve factual accuracy, he was typical of his milieu in his inability to present any theory of historical causation. His work was a disorganized mass of details, unified only by his conviction that all earthly affairs were governed by chance and hence that the chief moral lesson to be learned from history was that one should always be ready for the unexpected and the accidental. Although he was occasionally compelled to recognize that the Romans owed their empire to their own virtues, his more usual view was that it was "the finest and most beneficent of the performances of Fortune." [8]

The social disintegration of the Hellenistic age was similarly mirrored in its art, considerable quantities of which have been preserved. Much of it consisted of idealized divine figures that no longer inspired any religious reverence. Alongside this escapist art there was also an emphasis on the realistic portrayal of human suffering, showing man as the victim of forces that he could not hope to control.

The disappearance of religious awe from the depiction of the gods was already apparent in the sculpture of the fourth century. In the works of Praxiteles, the Olympians became merely handsome men and women, divine only in their immunity from suffering and in their enjoyment of a euphoria that had become mindless and irresponsible. The *Hermes* found at Olympia, the earliest sur-

---

[8] Polybius: *Histories,* translated by W. R. Paton, I, 4. See also I, 64.

viving Greek statue of identifiable authorship, has a cloying and sentimental beauty that makes it far less expressive than the *kouroi* of the archaic period, in spite of its more masterly craftsmanship. Praxiteles' most popular work was a portrayal of Aphrodite, modeled after his mistress, the famous Athenian prostitute Phryne, and this was repeatedly imitated, with minor variations, through the Hellenistic period. The Hellenistic Aphrodite was a desirable woman intended to suggest sensuous titillation rather than reverence for the mysterious powers of sexuality. Divested of the clothing that she had retained in classical representations, she was portrayed as making a gesture of mock modesty with hands that called attention to what they pretended to conceal.

More indicative of the actual spirit of the age were the naturalistic renderings of human types, many of them ugly or grotesque, and the interest in the depiction of pain. The latter tendency showed itself in the fourth century in the work of Scopas. It was especially manifested at Pergamum, which developed under the patronage of the Attalids into the most impressive art center of the Hellenistic world. The finest surviving examples, the reliefs of the colossal altar of Zeus, depicted the battle of the gods and the giants, thus conforming with classical precedents in subject matter; but the tortured and writhing figures were in sharp contrast with the calm self-assurance displayed by the Olympians in classical renderings of the same theme. The latest and best-known masterpiece of Hellenistic art, the representation of Laocoön and his sons in desperate struggle with the snakes that were about to strangle them, was typical of its whole tone. It saw man as the victim of an unfriendly chance or destiny. For this reason it showed a new interest in his environment. Classical reliefs had portrayed only universalized human forms, abstracted from time and place, but the artists of the Hellenistic period began to locate their figures against specific backgrounds and show them responding or recoiling.

Eventually art patrons became unwilling to contemplate any further explorations of men in agony, and art relapsed into the academic imitation of earlier models. The Neo-Attic style of the first century, which owed its vogue largely to the eagerness of wealthy Romans to decorate their homes with tasteful *objets d'art,* was a chilly and lifeless imitation of the work of the classical period. Greek literature and art still had a long career ahead of them; but the capacity of the classical writers and sculptors to fuse the ideal and the actual could not be recaptured.[9]

The most characteristic intellectual products of the Hellenistic age were not its works of science or of art, but its ethical philosophies. Whereas the thinkers of the great age had aspired to find a rational interpretation of all nature and society, their Hellenistic successors mostly concentrated on less ambitious and more immediate objectives. The universe now seemed incomprehensible, and man's capacity to arrive at any certain knowledge of things outside himself was limited and uncertain. The function of philosophy was therefore to provide the individual with a guide for living, based on what man knew about himself. Hellenistic thinking reflected the breakdown of the political community and began with the isolated individual. In so far as it still recognized man's sense of moral obligation, this was attached not to the city or the state, but to the universe as a whole. Between the individual and the universe there was no mediating community. But, for the most part, Hellenistic philosophy sought primarily not to unite the individual with spiritual forces outside himself, but to make him morally independent of the society in which he lived. In a world that was anarchical and mostly evil, he could rely only on his own inner capacity for resistance. *Autarkeia* and *ataraxia* were the ideals of the Hellenistic age. Pessimism about the value of human life could scarcely go farther.

The earliest of the new schools, that of the Cynics, antedated the loss of political freedom and represented a fusion of Socratic and Sophistic doctrine. Its founder, Antisthenes, was contemporary with Plato, though its best-known representative was Diogenes, of

---

[9] Although political conditions in the twentieth-century United States are markedly different from those in the Hellenistic kingdoms, the aesthetic situation is in many ways similar. Modern American literature therefore displays a number of Alexandrian qualities. One might mention the differentiation between sophisticated and popular art; the conception of art as superior entertainment rather than as a revelation of truth; the preference for social realism; the concentration on the private lives of individuals rather than on the political and religious ideals animating the social organism; the tendency to regard experience as inherently chaotic and, in consequence, either to present it as such or to impose an artificial form with little relation to the content; and the inability to present whole human beings capable of constructive action. The modern American novel often resembles the *Argonautica* in being a string of disconnected episodes, with a central character who is the victim of external forces.

whom legend records that he lived in a tub, carried a lantern in order to search for an honest man, and, on being asked by Alexander what favor he would like to receive, asked him merely to stop blocking the sunlight. Combining the Socratic emphasis on the inner life with Sophistic skepticism and the Sophistic distinction between nature and convention, the Cynics denied all the values of civilization. The wise man lived according to nature, repudiating glory, knowledge, and pleasure as illusions, and was a citizen of the world. Throughout the Hellenistic and Roman periods, Cynic philosophers, wearing only short cloaks and carrying only staffs and wallets, wandered from town to town living by begging and preaching open-air sermons ("diatribes") against the follies of civilization. Carrying the assertion of individual independence and the repudiation of social life to the farthest possible conclusions, the Cynics curiously foreshadowed the itinerant preachers of Christianity.

Much the same attitude was represented by the Skeptics, although their denial of civilization was less churlish and intolerant and their appeal was to more cultured social groups. Their founder, Pyrrhon, a younger contemporary of Aristotle, denied the possibility of attaining reliable knowledge about anything, and went on to declare that pleasures and pains were illusions and that wisdom meant a complete tranquillity of mind which would be superior to all disturbing emotions. Dying about the year 275 at the age of ninety, he wrote nothing, but impressed his contemporaries by the completeness with which he realized his own ideal of renunciation. Later representatives of the Skeptical school were important chiefly because of their effective criticism of all forms of dogmatism and their respect for scientific method.

Much the most influential of the new schools, however, were the Epicureans and the Stoics. To the Academy of Plato and the Lyceum of Aristotle were added the Garden of Epicurus and the Porch (*stoa*) of Zeno. These four, all of them established in Athens, remained the most important schools of philosophy throughout the Hellenistic and Roman periods, though in the first century of our era there was also a revival of Pythagoreanism.

Like Socrates and Pyrrhon, Epicurus aroused the enthusiasm of his disciples by the sanctity of his personal character. After teaching in Athens for some thirty-five years, he died in 270, having endured a painful disease with a cheerfulness that was the best proof of the value of his doctrines. After his death his disciples worshipped him as a god and founded a kind of semi-religious sect, with organized groups in most of the leading cities. In contrast with the complete egoism and individualism apparently implied by Epicurean doctrine, Epicurean practice asserted the values of friendship and taught its devotees, while withdrawing completely from political activity, to assist each other in cultivating the virtues of tranquillity. As Epicurus declared, "the wise man when he has accommodated himself to straits knows better how to give than to receive: so great is the treasure of self-sufficiency which he has discovered." "Of all the things which wisdom acquires to produce the blessedness of the complete life, far the greatest is the possession of friendship." "Friendship goes dancing round the world proclaiming to us all to awake to the praises of a happy life." [1]

Epicurean doctrine was based on the materialistic atomism of Democritus. The universe consisted simply of particles of matter in space which came together and fell apart in different combinations. Epicurus, however, had no real interest in science, and his purpose in adopting these views of physics was to deny any moral meaning in the course of events or any reason to fear death or the gods. The gods existed, but, being examples of the ideal of complete tranquillity, they had no concern for earthly affairs. Man should therefore emancipate himself from all superstitious fears and recognize that, as an isolated piece of matter, he was under no moral obligation to any spiritual power and that the enjoyment of pleasure was the only rational purpose of his existence. Epicurus' conception of pleasure, however, was severely ascetic. It meant primarily the mastery of fear and pain, and could be achieved only by limiting desire rather than by satisfying it. The truly wise man would retire from the world, find pleasure in the simplest possible way of life, and control his body so completely that he could remain cheerful even while suffering the most acute physical pain.

Whereas Epicurus represented the pole of complete individualism, Zeno and the Stoics preached an absolute universalism. Equally in-

---

[1] Translation by Cyril Bailey. Reprinted in W. J. Oates (ed.): *The Stoic* *and Epicurean Philosophers*, pp. 37, 42, 43.

sistent on self-control and the renunciation of desire, they derived their ethical doctrines from man's sense of moral obligation rather than from a rationalistic calculation of pains and pleasures. Judged by intellectual standards, much of their teaching appears naïve, confused, and contradictory, possibly because none of their writings has survived and we know them only from secondhand accounts. The core of their doctrine was an intuition about the oneness of the universe, religious rather than philosophical in quality, which they never wholly succeeded in rationalizing. This element of mysticism made Stoicism the most vital and the most long-lived of all the Hellenistic philosophies. Its appeal owed more to the integrity of character displayed by its adherents than to the cogency of their arguments. Its founder, Zeno, who began teaching about the year 300, was honored at his death by the city of Athens in one of the nicest tributes ever paid to a philosopher. "He made his life a pattern to all," declared the official decree, "for he followed his own teaching." Many of the long line of philosophers who adopted and developed his doctrines seem to have been equally worthy of such an encomium.

Of Asiatic origin, being apparently of Phoenician descent, Zeno constructed his system out of material borrowed from earlier Greek thinkers; yet much of its underlying spirit was Oriental. He was deeply influenced by Babylonian fatalism and by the whole religious consciousness of the Near East. His physics was materialistic, being largely derived from Heraclitus. Brushing aside the epistemological doubts raised by Plato and the idealists, he accepted the validity of sense impressions and regarded the universe as governed by deterministic laws and as moving in cycles. It was periodically destroyed by fire and afterwards reconstituted in an infinite series of repetitions. The Stoics, however, like the Epicureans, were not concerned with scientific investigation, and their philosophy was, in fact, an obstacle to its development. Zeno supposed that the astrology of the Babylonians was a valid way of predicting the future. His central doctrine was the affirmation that the whole cosmic system was permeated by a divine reason (*logos*). All events were necessary and predetermined, but were the work not of blind chance or destiny, but of all-pervading deity. Like all the Hellenistic philosophies, Stoicism taught men to renounce their desires, control their passions, and become reconciled to circumstances, but it elevated fate into providence and represented submission to it as a moral duty.

Logically, Stoicism should have resulted in an Oriental passivity and quiescence; yet, like some other doctrines of divine predestination, it actually promoted a moral strength and vigor that found expression in political action. Its emphasis on the oneness of the universe and on its permeation by the divine *logos* led to the reaffirmation of the Greek belief in a normative law of nature and to the use of this concept of universal law for the reform of existing institutions. Even more significantly, the belief in natural law led to the assertion of the equality and brotherhood of man. These implications of Zeno's doctrines were developed more fully by philosophers of later generations, especially by Panaetius, who took Stoicism to Rome during the second century, and by Posidonius of Rhodes, the most learned and influential teacher of the early first century. Thus Zeno's Oriental religious fatalism, fused with Hellenic rationalism, became a medium by which the most important of Greek concepts was preserved and transmitted to later ages. The Stoic doctrine of natural law had a most important influence on the development of Roman jurisprudence, of Christian theology, and of the whole political tradition of the Western world.

The practical effects of Stoicism were, of course, limited. Basing its ethics solely on resignation to fate and obedience to natural law, not on love or sympathy, it was accepted only by a small elite and had no popular appeal. Stoic sages sought moral freedom by repressing all natural appetites and emotions, and demonstrated their sanctity by noble moral gestures that were likely to be somewhat theatrical. Although most Stoics were theoretical republicans, they could promote reforms only by acquiring influence with kings and ruling classes, not by more democratic methods. Interpreting and justifying popular beliefs as symbols of higher truths, they did little to check the increase of magical and religious superstitions. In spite of their doctrine of human brotherhood, they made no attack on slavery, remaining content with the affirmation that if a slave practiced the Stoic virtues, he was, by Stoic standards, the equal of a king and could enjoy a moral freedom far more important than mere physical freedom. Yet during the centuries between the decline of the polis and the rise of

Christianity, Stoicism was the one movement that stood, on the whole, for political and social idealism. Unlike the philosophies of Plato and Aristotle, it looked forward rather than backward, its doctrine of man's natural equality making a sharp contrast with almost all previous political and social theory. This doctrine, however often denied in practice, became a permanent part of the Western cultural heritage.

8

The Rise of Rome

According to those historians who propound cyclic theories of history, the unification of the Mediterranean world was a necessary and inevitable process. Such words can rarely be applied to the development of human society, and should probably be restricted to the physical sciences. Yet it can be said that during the Hellenistic period, the weakening of local allegiances, the growth of individualist and universalist attitudes, the expansion of commerce, and the incessant and senseless wars among the reigning dynasties were creating conditions that made unification possible, provided that some power existed which was capable of taking advantage of them. Such a power emerged in central Italy, on the periphery of Hellenic civilization. A pragmatic and utilitarian people, primarily concerned with the most efficient means of achieving material strength and deficient in intellectual curiosity and aesthetic imagination, the Romans could not revive the spiritual vitality of classical civilization, but they had the talent for political organization which the Greeks so notably lacked. By the middle of the third century B.C., Rome was the mistress of most of the Italian peninsula and was ready for imperial expansion overseas.

What were the causes of Rome's success? Why did this city alone, among all the innumerable political units in the Mediterranean world, prove capable of building a durable empire? The explanation can be found only in her early history and institutions, but unfortunately we know relatively little about these subjects owing to the paucity of literary and artistic records. According to tradition, Rome was founded about the middle of the eighth century, but it was not until more than five hundred years later that any of her citizens began to display any serious interest in aesthetic expression. And by the time that Roman society emerged into the light of history, it had become morally and politically corrupt; if we are to judge Rome by the Romans of the second and first centuries, then her rise to power becomes inexplicable. The most important period in Rome's development was the period, known only in bare outline, during which she laid the foundations of her empire by making herself the ruler of Italy. In the course of this achievement she acquired the moral discipline, military strength, and political shrewdness that were afterwards applied to the domination of the whole Mediterranean world.

The Roman way of life originated in conditions similar to those which had shaped the early development of both Judaism and Hellenism. Probably at about the time when the Achaeans were taking possession of Greece, other groups of Aryan herdsmen, carrying with them similar patriarchal institutions, were moving into the Italian peninsula. Among these were the Latin peoples who settled in the foothills of the Apennines south of the river Tiber, where they continued for many centuries to maintain a primitive pastoral and agricultural society. They were divided into a number of small village communities, but the strongest social unit was the patriarchal family in which the father had virtually absolute powers over his wife, children, and dependent servants. Their religion consisted of simple rituals in honor of the great Aryan sky god known to the Latins as Jupiter, of the tutelary war gods of the different communities, and of the numinous powers responsible for family continuity and prosperity. Rome, which was apparently founded by individuals who had seceded from other communities, shared these Latin institutions, which formed the original bases of her moral character.

Rome would not have risen to greatness, however, if she had not become conscious of the value of her way of life and deliberately resolved to maintain it. Crucial in her early development was an effort of self-definition by which she differentiated herself from alien cultures and affirmed her own spiritual identity. Like Israel, although with very different results, Rome created her own character by defending her patriarchal tradition in opposition to worshippers of the mother goddess. Like both Israel and Greece, she asserted ethical values and a view of life reflecting the belief

in man's capacity to shape and dominate biological forces instead
of submitting to them in a mystical abnegation of the will. The
precipitating factor in this process appears to have been the conflict between the Latins and the Etruscans.[1]

The Etruscans have remained a mysterious people, known only
through their artistic remains, not through written records; but it
is generally agreed that they went to Italy by sea from the East,
probably from Asia Minor. Halfway through the first millennium,
Etruscan ruling classes were in control of most of western Italy
north of the Tiber. Their religion and institutions were typical
products of the Mediterranean world before the advent of the
Aryans and the new doctrines of the Axial Period. Their rules of
inheritance were probably matrilineal, and their religious rituals
included both sexual orgies and human sacrifices. Worshipping
dark chthonian spirits of blood and soil, fertility and death, they
deified the biological powers of reproduction, whether embodied
in women or in bulls and other horned animals. It was perhaps
this sense of man's inextricable involvement in nature that caused
them to believe so firmly in the possibility of predicting future
events by the observation of such natural phenomena as the flight
of birds, thunder and lightning, and the livers of sacrificial animals; this practice of augury had presumably been learned in the
East, through contact with the Babylonians. Etruscan art gave expression to an enjoyment of sensuous phenomena and to an exuberant gaiety very different from the prosaic solemnity of the
Romans, but it also reflected a fascination with cruelty and death
that was equally characteristic of chthonian religion. The gladiatorial conflicts that disgraced the Roman people after they had become decadent originated among the Etruscans as rituals in honor
of the dead. Something of this Etruscan spirit, including both
the reverence for sexual fertility and the obsession with images of
bloodshed, may have remained as a lasting part of the Italian cultural heritage. Two thousand years later the same qualities became
manifest in the art of the Renaissance, which first developed in
precisely those regions of Italy where the Etruscans had established
themselves.

---

[1] This interpretation of the Etruscan impact is largely derived from
Franz Altheim: *A History of Roman*
Religion. W. Warde Fowler: *The Re-*
ligious Experience of the Roman Peo-
ple is the best survey of the subject.

11. *a. Reliefs from the Column of Trajan, showing Roman soldiers engaging in various activities during a campaign against German barbarians.*

b. Relief from the Column of Marcus Aurelius, showing the miraculous rainstorm that saved the Roman army. The religious emotionalism of this relief makes a sharp contrast with the serene self-assurance conveyed by the Column of Trajan a half-century earlier.

12. *The interior of the Pantheon. From a painting made in the eighteenth century by Giovanni Paolo Panini.*

We know almost nothing about the early relations between the Latins and the Etruscans, but it is probable that Rome, built on hills overlooking the Tiber, was originally a Latin outpost guarding the frontier. The Latins did not always maintain their spiritual independence, and Etruscan influences, including the practice of augury and the worship of certain gods, spread south of the Tiber. During the sixth century, Rome herself seems to have lost her autonomy and come under the rule of an Etruscan dynasty, the Tarquins. The decisive events in early Roman history were the expulsion of these foreign kings and the establishment of the republic, which apparently occurred in 509. This was followed by the reassertion of the native Latin tradition and the elimination of those Etruscan elements that could not be incorporated into it. During the next two hundred years, in fact, the Romans admitted few foreign deities and customs, and had little contact with alien cultures. Rejecting both the mysticism and the savagery of chthonian ritualism, they maintained their own simple observances in honor of their traditional gods, the *di indigetes,* who were associated with a strict, even puritanical, family discipline and did not countenance sexual orgies or human sacrifices. By the standards of the time, early Roman religion was surprisingly free from degrading rituals. In this respect, the unknown legislators who established Roman institutions after the expulsion of the Tarquins performed a work analogous to that of Moses among the Jews and Homer among the Greeks.

The patriarchal family remained the foundation of Roman society, and from it the Romans acquired the unquestioning devotion to the state and the respect for ancestral custom (*mos maiorum*) and for the authority (*auctoritas*) of elder statesmen which made them for a long time the most cohesive and disciplined of ancient peoples. A special group of deities had charge of the family; and though they were considered as less powerful than the divine powers worshipped by the state, they were more deeply cherished and more intimately associated with Roman ways of living. The Genius who represented the virility of the paterfamilias; Vesta, the spirit of the undying hearthfire; the Lares who ensured the productivity of the family farm; and the Penates who were located in the family storeroom—these were the especial guardians of the private household, and every family sought by means of appropriate rituals to maintain their vigor and ensure their continued protection. The family was regarded as a continuing organism, each individual paterfamilias being merely the trustee of the tradition. The wealthier and more distinguished families preserved masks of their ancestors, and these were worn by living persons at funerals and other ceremonies, thus giving the impression that all the successive representatives of the family were alive and watching the conduct of their descendants.

Women fully shared the responsibility for the transmission of family discipline. In spite of the legal emphasis on paternal authority, the Roman family was always a partnership, and women actually acquired a much higher status than in Greece or in the Orient. As in all patriarchal societies, they were expected to be chaste (according to legend, the assault on Lucretia by an Etruscan prince caused the rebellion against foreign rule), but, as can be seen in the plays of Plautus, they were by no means submissive to their husbands. The ideal Roman matron, visualized as training her sons for service to the state and sending them into battle without tears, was a most important element in the Roman's image of his society.

Rome owed her stability mainly to this family piety, but neither the religion of the family nor that of the state ever evolved beyond a primitive level. Reflecting the attitudes of the unsophisticated peasant farmers and herdsmen of Latium, it never acquired much intellectual or aesthetic content. The Romans were totally lacking in the myth-making imagination of the Greeks, and to describe their objects of worship as gods would, in fact, be somewhat misleading. Roman deities were not beings, but numinous forces who manifested their wills by means of material phenomena, especially in ominous events that ran counter to normal expectation. They were not personalized or pictured in physical forms. Many of the innumerable minor deities who had to be placated in the various exigencies of daily life were known only through their actions, and could therefore be defined by verbs better than by nouns.[2] The relationship between the Romans and their deities was

---

[2] As we learn from the sarcastic accounts of Roman mythology given by such Christian writers as Tertullian and Augustine, at each stage in the process of sexual intercourse the Roman paterfamilias could, if necessary, evoke the help of a different deity.

conceived largely in contractual terms: as long as men performed the prescribed rituals, they could count on divine aid against natural catastrophes and against hostile states. The task of defining the *jus divinum,* comprising the duties that men owed to the divine powers, was assumed by the civic authorities, especially the colleges of the pontifices and the augurs, and citizens who adhered to the rules that these authorities prescribed needed to feel no religious anxiety.

In these religious attitudes, in spite of their peasant simplicity, one can discern the qualities that made the Romans an imperial people. The deities of the Greeks had represented the universal and unchanging processes of nature, divinity being inherent in the material universe; those of Rome, on the other hand, were forces with specific plans which would be worked out in historic events and which men must discover and obey. The Etruscan practice of augury was adopted by the Roman state as a means not of foretelling the future, but of finding out what the gods wished their worshippers to do. The Romans, in fact, retained a pervasive sense of supernatural guidance long after they had ceased to believe in the reality of their original deities; like the Jews, they had a religion of history rather than of nature, and came to regard themselves as a chosen people whose rise to empire had been decreed by whatever divine power governed the universe. What was central in the Romans' attitude to life was their conviction that men prospered not by conforming with natural processes, but by resisting them and mastering them. Life consisted essentially of duties, which were imposed by the gods and by the state and were necessarily unpleasant, and enjoyment was possible only in moments of irresponsibility.

The best indexes of the character of a people are the heroes whom its popular mythology presents as models for imitation. The early Romans appear to have invented no stories about their gods, but they preserved the memory of certain of their citizens who had exhibited an extraordinary fortitude and sense of duty. Horatius guarding the bridge and Cincinnatus returning to his plow; Regulus, who ensured the victory of his army by offering his own life in sacrifice to the gods; Curtius, who gave himself up to the enemy to be tortured and put to death in fulfillment of his pledged word; Torquatus, who won a battle, but afterwards submitted to execution for disobeying his father's orders—such men were the embodiments of what the Romans meant by *virtus*. Nothing could be more different from the *arete* that for the early Greeks had been exemplified in Achilles and Odysseus. The Romans were concerned not with individual glory, but with the greatness of the republic, and the citizen was honored not for his achievements, but for displaying in adversity the qualities of the Roman character. These were summed up in the untranslatable word *pietas*, which meant an attitude of seriousness (*gravitas*) and reverence, obedience to all legally constituted authority, readiness to do one's duty both to the gods and to the state.

Piety and a sense of duty, however, had been strongly developed in some of the Greek communities, especially among the Spartans. To these tribalistic attitudes the Romans added another and most essential virtue: strict good faith (*fides*) in the execution of treaties, agreements, and promises. Their belief that states and individuals were bound by contractual obligations pervaded their whole view of life, and led to the practice of an elementary honesty that may be regarded as the basic Roman contribution to human development. This was the quality that especially differentiated the Romans from all their rivals and made it possible for them not only to conquer an empire, but also to organize it. Unlike their Greek and Near Eastern competitors, the Romans could trust each other and could inspire confidence in foreign peoples. Institutionalized in the Roman legal system, the Roman emphasis on the performance of contracts became through this medium an essential part of the Western tradition.[3]

The character of the Romans, acquired as a necessity for survival while they were still a weak and struggling people, deteriorated

---

[3] It was the honesty of the Romans that especially impressed the first historian to describe their rise to power, the Greek Polybius. In Polybius' opinion, it was a result of the fear of the gods inculcated by the Roman state religion. In Greece, he declared, "members of the government, if they are entrusted with no more than a talent, though they have ten copyists and as many seals and twice as many witnesses, cannot keep their faith; whereas among the Romans those who as magistrates and legates are dealing with large sums of money maintain correct conduct just because they have pledged their faith by oath. Whereas elsewhere it is a rare thing to find a man who keeps his hands off public money, and whose record is clean in this respect, among the Romans one rarely comes across a man who has been detected in such conduct." Polybius: *Histories*, translated by W. R. Paton, VI, 56.

after they became successful. As long as there were enemies to be conquered, the incessant emphasis on discipline continued to make them invincible. But after they had built their empire, there were no higher goals to be achieved, and the tension could no longer be maintained. Their simple peasant religion offered no support for man's spiritual aspirations and no answers to his metaphysical questions, and could no longer sustain the state after its citizens had become rich and cultivated. The final results were a moral collapse and a conviction of cosmic futility. Yet the Romans never wholly lost their respect for personal integrity and the consequent sense of mutual trust. For this reason Roman political and social life differed in its whole tone and atmosphere from that of Greece, and is much more nearly intelligible to the modern West.

The history of the early republic was often stormy, but the welfare of the state took precedence over individual and class interests, and for nearly three hundred years Rome was remarkably successful in avoiding the murderous civil wars and the anarchic individualism characteristic of so many Greek cities. The republic had a mixed form of government, combining an aristocratic senate with a democratic popular assembly, and much of its early history consisted of prolonged struggles between the patricians and the plebs. Yet Rome continued to be governed mainly by those families whose ancient lineage or large landholdings entitled them to patrician status. Trained from infancy in the traditions of the state, and acquiring a kind of hereditary shrewdness, sagacity, and sense of responsibility, their members continued, generation after generation, to be elected consuls and to fill the senate. Such a ruling class always displays a stability and a capacity for long-range views which cannot be attained by either a monarchy or a democracy.

The discipline of the Roman people, displayed in a long series of wars during the two and a half centuries following the expulsion of the Etruscans, made them the dominant power, first of Latium, and afterwards of most of Italy. But the real genius of Rome was displayed not so much in her military victories as in the prudence and moderation with which her ruling class made use of them and in its scrupulous respect for treaty obligations. Dependent Italian states were not held by force or required to pay tribute: they were bound to Rome by a network of agreements under which they retained self-government and were obligated only to provide

troops for the Roman army. Roman or Latin colonies were planted
at key points, and various grades of citizenship were offered as
rewards for fidelity. A confederation under Roman leadership
rather than an empire, confusing and illogical in its broad outline
but shrewdly realistic in its detailed application, this arrangement
proved to be the answer to the problem the Athenians had so
catastrophically failed to solve in the Delian League. It was possible only because the Roman patrician families were schooled in
self-control and relatively free from individual greed and desire
for glory and because they were guided by practical expediency
rather than by logic. The political success of the Romans, like that
of the British, was largely owing to the fact that they were an
unphilosophical people, uninterested in general ideas, who were
willing to wait on the course of events and felt no compulsion to
rationalize and systematize their institutions.

Once Rome had unified the Italian states, the pressure of
events led her to the building of a Mediterranean empire, not from
any deliberate intent but because each step forward led inexorably
to the next. The methods that had been applied in Italy, however,
could not be extended to many of the overseas possessions. In
some areas Rome continued the policy of holding the support of
dependent kings and republics by making alliances with them,
and the Hellenic cities retained autonomous rights under their
local oligarchies; but most of the new provinces were placed under
the direct rule of Roman officials and required to pay tribute.
Under such conditions, the imperialism of Rome became increasingly predatory, and as her citizens became richer and their greed
more unrestrained, she lost most of the qualities that had originally made her strong.

The later years of the third century B.C. were filled with a struggle with Carthage for the mastery of the western Mediterranean.
Hannibal invaded Italy and inflicted a series of catastrophic defeats
on Roman armies, but the Roman ruling class refused to despair
of the republic and finally ended the war victoriously in the year
202 by a direct attack on Carthage's home territory. This Second
Punic War was the most prolonged and exhausting struggle in
which Rome was ever engaged, and she never fully recovered from
its devastating effects. But it gave her control over much of Spain,
southern Gaul, and northern Africa, and made her so much the

strongest power in the whole Mediterranean world that her involvement in the affairs of Greece and the Hellenistic kingdoms was almost unavoidable. The establishment of her power in the East began in the year 201, when she entered a coalition of Hellenic states against Hannibal's ally, the king of Macedon. The process continued for about a century and a half, culminating in the sixties when Pompey organized Roman rule over Asia Minor and the former Seleucid kingdom of Syria. Of the Hellenistic kingdoms, Egypt alone, under the descendants of the Ptolemies, retained a precarious independence until the year 30. The Roman ruling class was often reluctant to extend its responsibilities, but Rome continued to acquire new provinces because the security of her existing dominions seemed to require it and because there was no other Mediterranean power strong enough to resist her. It is not surprising that when men began to reflect about the building of the empire, they should have attributed it to the will of heaven, which worked through the activities of human beings even in despite of their conscious wishes.

Meanwhile, Rome was becoming Hellenized. Even during the early republican period, commercial contacts with the Greek cities of southern Italy had led to the introduction of a number of Greek deities and rituals. In the end the whole Roman religious system was fused with that of Greece, in spite of the sharp differences in the views of life which they represented. During the third century, Rome acquired a theater and Greek games, and poems and plays, most of them closely copied from Greek originals, began to be written in Latin. After the Punic War, a number of patrician statesmen became enthusiastic devotees of Hellenic culture. The reproduction of works of art and their sale to Roman aristocrats became a major source of revenue for Greek merchants, and young Romans made a practice of visiting Athens or Rhodes to study rhetoric and philosophy. Eventually, in fact, Hellenism spread through the whole empire and became its main bond of spiritual unity; Rome claimed the allegiance of the provincials not merely because she imposed peace and order, but also because she sponsored the propagation of the highest culture known to man. Unfortunately, the Hellenism of the Roman period (Stoicism excepted) was a closed system of ideas which had lost the power of growth. What it meant was an educational system emphasizing the study of earlier masterpieces and the practice of rhetoric, a collection of fanciful tales about gods who had ceased to be objects of religious belief, and several ethical philosophies promising happiness to individuals. Stoicism, which became popular with the best of the Roman aristocrats, helped to maintain a sense of moral obligation and contributed eventually to the growth of a less exploitive form of government. Otherwise Hellenism promoted only an empty sophistication leading neither to the advancement of knowledge nor to political reform. It undermined the traditional Roman tribalism and offered no broader form of integration capable of replacing it.

By the end of the second century, in fact, the old Roman religion had almost ceased to have any moral efficacy, except among the peasants. The civic authorities continued the mechanical performance of the traditional rituals, but these, being based mainly on the agricultural calendar, had become meaningless to most of the urban population. The augurs still interpreted omens and examined the livers of animals, but the ruling class frankly manipulated such findings for their own political purposes. And while most members of the aristocracy had grown openly cynical about the gods, the poorer classes were becoming ripe for more emotional religious practices. The first of the Oriental cults to enter Rome was the worship of Cybele, the Phrygian Great Mother, which was introduced by the Senate as a device for allaying popular hysteria during the war with Hannibal. Conveyed by boat from Pessinus in the form of a black stone, presumably a meteorite, Cybele was received at the seaport of Ostia by the leading Roman general, Scipio, carried to the city in the arms of aristocratic matrons, and housed in a temple on the Palatine. Apparently the senate had been unaware of the nauseating character of her rituals, for it subsequently decreed that no Roman could become one of her priests. Under the republic, in fact, no other Oriental cult received official sanction, but private citizens began to worship Isis and several Asiatic deities.

With the erosion of moral restraints, the empire degenerated into a vast system of exploitation, especially after the acquisition of the wealthy Hellenistic provinces with their servile populations. It became customary for proconsuls to engage in the systematic looting of their dominions and carry immense fortunes back to

Rome. They were aided and abetted by the growing Roman middle class of merchants and bankers, the *equites*,[4] many of them recruited from the Italian provinces or from overseas, who became wealthy by organizing the trade of the empire, lending money at exorbitant rates of interest to dependent Eastern kings and city-states, and acquiring contracts to farm the taxes of the provinces. Thus, the whole Mediterranean world was drained of its surplus wealth to enrich the Roman aristocratic and equestrian families. The provincials, held in subjection by the Roman army, were helpless to resist, but the system was inherently unstable because of growing conflicts within Rome herself. The simple institutions of a peasant republic could not be successfully adapted to the rule of an empire.

Office-holding was still restricted mainly to the old ruling families (the *optimates*), along with a few of equestrian origin. In fact, during the period of imperial expansion the aristocracy assumed broader powers at the expense both of the Roman poorer classes and of the Italian provincials. But as its members competed for office, they lost their original cohesiveness and sense of duty. During the last age of the republic a handful of patrician families were engaging in murderous struggles for the control of the empire, with the immense opportunities for enrichment which it afforded. Some of them professed allegiance to the tradition of aristocratic rule and affirmed their devotion to republican liberty, while others (the *populares*) sought the support of the populace by advocating democratic reforms; but the importance of such ideological differences can easily be exaggerated. In their private enjoyments the Roman aristocrats were equally unrestrained. Marriage was rarely permanent, and became little more than a device for cementing temporary family alliances, and patrician women changed husbands and lovers as easily as the men took mistresses.

The independent peasant class, which had been the original foundation of Rome's military strength, was rapidly disappearing. Much of the money that poured into the city was invested in land, and rural Italy was becoming a region of big estates owned by

---

[4] This word, which means "horsemen" and is often translated "knights," originated with the conscript army of the early republic; citizens were classified according to their wealth, and upper groups, being presumed to own horses, were required to serve in the cavalry.

absentee landlords and cultivated by slaves or tenants. As the
peasantry decreased, the army ceased to represent the Roman
people and became a body of professional soldiers, recruited for
long-term service from the overseas provinces as well as from Italy
and loyal only to those individual generals who could win their
confidence. Instead of peasants, Rome acquired an impoverished
and degraded urban proletariat willing to support any political
adventurer who would provide them with doles of food and extravagant spectacles. The era of bread and circuses had arrived.
And though some forms of Roman pageantry had originated in
the early days of the republic, especially the "triumph" in which
a victorious general, his face daubed with red pigments, led a
parade of soldiers and captives up to the temple of Jupiter on the
Capitol, other spectacles were products of degeneration. The Roman mob expected to be shown pantomimes depicting realistically the amours of the Olympians, bloody combats of gladiators,
and criminals being clawed to death by wild animals.

The death agony of the republic began in 133 B.C., with the
tribuneship of Tiberius Gracchus, and lasted for a little over a
century. The first phase opened with the attempt of the Gracchus
brothers to introduce political and agrarian reforms for the benefit
of the Roman proletariat, and ended in the massacre of several
thousand of the reformers by the *optimates*. An interval of calm
was followed in the nineties and eighties by a murderous conflict
between rival generals, the democratic Marius and the aristocratic
Sulla. This was accompanied by a slave rebellion and by a revolt
of the Italian provincials against Roman domination, the former
being ended by the crucifixion of thousands of the rebels, whose
hanging corpses adorned the roads leading out of Rome for many
years afterwards, the latter leading to the grant of full Roman
citizenship to all Italians. In 78, after proscriptions by which most
of the leaders of the *populares* were slaughtered without trials,
Sulla restored the republic. This endured precariously for another
generation, though it was soon overshadowed by two new rival
generals, Pompey and Caesar. It was increasingly obvious that anybody who could win the support of the army and the mob could
make himself master of the state.

How could the empire be stabilized? A solution could be found
only through the imposition of order under the rule of a dictator,

the enlargement of the privileged class by the admission of provincials, and the spread of a unifying culture; in other words, by the transcendence of the disintegrating tribalism of the republic. But such remedies required the destruction of the Roman aristocracy, with its insistence on a republican liberty that meant, in practice, the liberty of Roman patricians to fight each other and loot the provinces. In the end the logic of events would bring about the fulfillment of the program of Alexander: the rule of a god-king, the equality of races, and the propagation of the Hellenic way of life through the medium of the autonomous city. But the full realization of such a program meant the end of the political and moral tradition that had given the Roman people their distinctive character, and its replacement not by a dynamic faith in universalism, but by a petrified Hellenism. Its achievement gave the ancient world a long period of peace and material prosperity, but it left a spiritual void that could be filled finally only by the adoption of an alien religion.

The last age of the republic, known to us in intimate detail through the writings of Cicero and other contemporary sources, had an extraordinary brilliance and corruption. The dissolution of a system of moral and political order, like the splitting of the atom, always releases energies that are normally blocked and inhibited by social discipline; thus, it produces a corruscating display of individual force and talent, though with ultimately destructive effects. This was a time not only of incessant political violence and of the most extravagant luxury and sensuality, but also of intellectual achievement.

Latin literature, for the first time, now acquired genuine originality. The works of two major poets, Lucretius and Catullus, have survived; and though Lucretius derived his subject matter from the physics of Democritus and the ethics of Epicurus, and Catullus was an imitator of Callimachus, each of them had a splendor of language and an emotional force peculiarly his own. Lucretius, who apparently lived in retirement as befitted an Epicurean, preached liberation from religious fear in an isolated masterpiece, the *De Rerum Natura,* which seems to have found few professed admirers. Catullus, on the other hand, belonged peculiarly to his age. A provincial from northern Italy who plunged into the life of the capital and became involved with the most notoriously dissolute of patrician women (known in his writings as Lesbia), he displayed in his love poems and political invectives a naked and bitter intensity of feeling possible only in a society that had repudiated all moral standards and inhibitions. His main subject was the destructiveness of sexual desire; and while this pervaded his apostrophes to Lesbia, with their fusion of love and hate, it was conveyed even more terrifyingly in his greatest poem: his description of Attis aroused to frenzy by the power of the Great Mother Cybele and driven by the pitiless goddess to self-emasculation. Catullus' premature death at the age of thirty prefigured that of the Roman aristocracy whose passions and excesses he had shared and expressed.

Three men, Cato, Cicero, and Caesar, epitomized the political tendencies of the age, the first embodying the old aristocratic tradition, the second attempting vainly to reform it, and the third representing the future.

A man of austere integrity, Cato showed that the tradition had not wholly lost its virtue, but his stubborn conservatism and his contempt for equestrians and provincials served to block the reforms needed to preserve it. Later generations honored him for committing suicide after the fall of the republic and idealized him as a symbol of Roman virtue, forgetting his unbending class arrogance and his total lack of realistic statesmanship.

Cicero, who also aspired to lead the conservatives, suffered from the disadvantage of being a *novus homo*. A provincial equestrian who achieved membership in the ruling class by his oratorical talents, he hoped that the republic could be preserved through an alliance of the *nobiles* and the equestrians against the *populares*, the enforcement of higher standards of honesty in provincial government, and the restoration of Rome's traditional moral standards. His speeches were filled with rhetorical appeals to the old ideals, to the *auctoritas* and *gravitas* of aristocratic statesmen, and to ancestral custom, religion and piety, law and good faith. Without Cicero we should have a much scantier conception of the self-image of the Roman citizen. But while he denounced the misdeeds of individuals with a scathing brilliance that often overshot its mark, he had no insight into the deeper forces that were destroying the republic. And though his conservatism was the expression of a genuine preference, not merely of snobbery and self-interest, he was too conflicted and insecure a character, and was the product of too complex an age, to be himself an exemplar of aristocratic *virtus*. His private letters reveal his waverings and time-servings, his moods of cynicism, his inordinate and incessant vanity. The words of Yeats, "The good lack all conviction, while the bad are filled with passionate intensity," sum up the political character of all ages of disintegration, and Cicero, in spite of his manifold faults, was one of the good. The same brilliant super-ficiality, the same inability to achieve convictions that were ex-pressions of his total self and not merely intellectual attitudes, were displayed in his philosophical writings. These had great his-torical importance both in making the Latin language into a vehicle for the expression of abstract concepts and in restating the Greek doctrine of natural law and applying it to Roman imperialism. They were the chief sources of the belief that Roman administra-tion should be inspired by universal principles of justice, which was afterwards restated by Virgil and which guided the best of the early emperors. But Cicero's ideas were wholly derived from Greek originals, chiefly the Stoics and the Platonists, and much of his writing was mere translation. Lacking any philosophical per-sonality of his own, moreover, he borrowed eclectically from dif-ferent schools with little regard for intellectual consistency.

Caesar was in all respects Cicero's antithesis. His outstanding qualities were a superbly realistic intelligence, a spirit of adventure, a refreshing sense of humor, and a calm self-assurance that no crisis or danger could ever disturb. In his speeches and writings, and indeed in his whole style of living, he showed a contempt for rhetoric and a capacity to see his objectives and proceed directly to them. Yet his motivations remain an enigma. How far did he de-liberately aim at supreme power? To what extent was he guided by an understanding of the deeper forces that were shaping the course of history? These are unanswerable questions. Until past the age of forty he seemed to differ from other Roman aristocrats only in that his political methods were even more unscrupulous and his private life even more dissolute. Then he spent eight years in the conquest of Gaul, where he created an army willing to support him in the overthrow of the republic. In the year 49 he led his troops into Italy, assumed dictatorial powers, and crushed his rival Pompey, who had the reluctant support of Cato and most of the aristocracy. During the five years that remained to him, most of them occupied with further campaigning against Pompeians and republicans, Caesar was emperor in all but name. It was during this period that he established his strongest claims to statesmanship.

Unlike earlier dictators, he pardoned his opponents and sought their support instead of murdering them and seizing their property. And while seeking harmony among Romans, he instituted reforms that foreshadowed the whole future development of the empire. He extended citizenship rights to many provincials, even added provincials to the Roman Senate, and founded cities in almost all regions of the empire and gave them rights of self-government. Becoming dictator for life, he was worshipped as a god, and a temple was consecrated to him within the city of Rome. This was Alexander's program, though there is no evidence that Caesar was influenced by his precursor or guided by anything deeper than a clear-sighted understanding of contemporary needs. But though Caesar anticipated the trends of history, he failed to recognize the importance of sentiment and tradition in human affairs. Offending so many of the ancient customs and prejudices of Rome, he would not, in spite of his generosity, end the opposition of the old ruling families. It is not surprising that, in the year 44, he should have been assassinated by a group of patricians in the name of republican liberty. Their leader, Marcus Brutus, descended from a family that had belonged to the governing class ever since the expulsion of the Tarquins nearly half a millennium earlier, was Cato's son-in-law and a disciple of the Stoics, and was universally admired for his integrity of character. It is also of interest, as an indication of the meaning of republican liberty, that Brutus had lent money to a community in Cyprus at the usurious rate of forty-eight per cent.[5]

---

[5] Shakespeare's three Roman plays, although often inaccurate in detail, are extraordinarily true to the general spirit of Roman politics. Just as a paleontologist is able to reconstruct a prehistoric animal from a few bones, so Shakespeare, guided only by the *Parallel Lives* of Plutarch, was able to reconstruct a whole society. The problem of legitimacy is basic to Shakespeare's political thinking; but whereas in his English historical plays divine-right monarchy is presented as the only legitimate authority, in the Roman plays the republic represents legitimacy. It is astonishing that a citizen of Tudor England should have understood this so clearly.

Shakespeare also had remarkable insight into the inner springs of the

Because the Caesareans retained the support of both the army and the urban populace, the liberators were unable to re-establish effective republican government, and Caesar's death was followed by a struggle for his political inheritance, the leading contenders being his former lieutenant Mark Antony and his grand-nephew Octavian. In 43 and 42 Antony and Octavian temporarily joined forces, murdered thousands of their opponents (including Cicero) in another bloody proscription, and in the Battle of Philippi crushed what remained of the republican aristocracy. They then divided most of the empire between them, Antony taking the East and Octavian Italy and the West. The inevitable conflict was postponed only for a few years. In 31 Antony and his ally and wife, Cleopatra of Egypt, were defeated by Octavian's forces in the naval battle of Actium. By 29, both Antony and Cleopatra having committed suicide, Octavian was master of the whole empire. He ruled it until his death forty-three years later.

Vindictive, superstitious, hypochondriac, lacking in physical courage, and cold-bloodedly intent from boyhood on the acquisition of power, Octavian (better known by his later title of Augustus) had none of the more attractive qualities of his uncle. Yet, unlike Caesar, he succeeded in living to a ripe old age and in transmitting his position to his chosen heir. After more than a century of political murders and civil wars, the empire had at last found a leader who could maintain order. While this was partly due to the virtual annihilation of the republican leaders in the proscriptions and at Philippi and to the universal desire for security and peace, a more fundamental reason was that Augustus linked his regime with the old Roman way of life. Instead of dissolving the Roman tradition in an Alexandrian universalism, as seemed to be the intent of Caesar's legislation, he set out to re-establish the old loyalties and adapt them to the service of the empire. Unlike the rationalistic Caesar, he appealed to sentiment and prejudice, partly, no doubt, because of his own superstitious temperament and intellectual

---

Roman upper-class character, as he showed in *Coriolanus*. Coriolanus' relationship to Volumnia is a suggestive study of maternal domination. The role of the Roman mother in shaping the Roman character is a subject that might repay psychological investigation, particularly as several Latin poets display an intense resentment against women and present them as destructive forces. This is most evident in Catullus and Juvenal. In Virgil's *Aeneid*, Dido, though treated sympathetically, plays a destructive part, and the maternal role is divided between the kindly Venus and the hostile Juno.

limitations. His regime may be regarded as a compromise by which
the old tribalistic ethos of Rome was incongruously combined with
the new universalism. In consequence, he was able to create a
system of government which remained effective for two hundred
years and permitted movement toward the Alexandrian program
by a slow and gradual evolution.

The power of the aristocracy was now definitely broken. Most
of its surviving members accepted the new order. Meanwhile, the
old families were failing to reproduce themselves, and within a
century almost all of them had become extinct. The main support
for the Augustan regime came from the businessmen of the
equestrian order and from Italian provincials, privilege being
henceforth based on money rather than on birth. Romanism was,
in fact, expanded into a kind of Italian nationalism. It was significant that Augustus himself, allied to Caesar and the aristocracy
only through his grandmother, came from a provincial banking
family, and that his leading general, Agrippa, was of peasant stock,
and his chief civilian minister, Maecenas, was an Etruscan. But
the empire was still controlled by a dominant oligarchy, though
no longer narrowly Roman, and Augustus endeavored to imbue
this group with Roman loyalties and ideas. Although he retained
personal control of the army and of a number of key provinces,
including Egypt with its immense revenues, he professed to have
restored the republic, and was known officially not as the emperor
of the Romans but merely as the *princeps,* the first senator. Unlike
Caesar, he did not claim divine honors from the Romans, although
he was expected to become a god after his death and was worshipped during his lifetime in the Hellenistic provinces. The Senate
and the consuls continued to go through the motions of government, and the Roman populace, to the number of no less than
200,000, were placated with free food and the customary spectacles. Augustus devoted much time and money, moreover, to an
attempt to revive the old Roman religion and enforce the old
morality. He built or restored an immense number of temples,
showed an antiquarian zeal in reconstructing all the ancient rituals
and arranging for their continued performance, prohibited any
public worship of Oriental deities within the city limits of Rome,
and made laws for the protection of marriage and the family. His
own favorite deity was Apollo, the Olympian lawgiver who had

always stood for moderation, self-control, and upper-class rule. Augustus, in fact, represented the principate as the embodiment of the best elements in the whole Helleno-Roman heritage and actually succeeded in identifying himself with all the great men of Roman history, including not only Caesar but also Cato and the Pompeians.[6]

These aspects of the Augustan system were dramatized during the struggle with Antony, which was portrayed as a conflict between Hellenism and the Orient. In actuality, Cleopatra was a pure-blooded Macedonian, and although Antony had sought popular support in the Hellenistic world by identifying himself with the salvation cults and posing as the embodiment of Heracles and Dionysus, he had not ceased to be a Roman. Their marriage seems to have resulted more from political expediency than from sexual passion, Antony hoping to get control of the riches of Egypt, Cleopatra being intent on keeping and enlarging her kingdom. Yet, according to Augustan propaganda, Antony was supposed to have betrayed his ancestry by succumbing to the wiles of an Oriental queen—a fabrication out of which afterwards developed one of the world's great love stories—and their victory would have meant the destruction of Western humanism and its replacement by the degraded mysticism of the ancient East. Virgil gave classic expression to the official interpretation in his description of the Battle of Actium as portrayed on the shield of Aeneas. "Here Augustus Caesar, leading Italians to strife, with peers and people, and the great gods of the Penates, stands on the lofty stern; his joyous brows pour forth a double flame, and on his head dawns his father's star. . . . Here Antonius with barbaric might and varied arms, victor from the nations of the dawn and from the ruddy sea, brings with him Egypt and the strength of the East and utmost Bactra; and there follows him (O Shame!) his Egyptian wife. . . . Monstrous gods of every form and barking Anubis wield weapons against Neptune and Venus and against Minerva. . . . Actian Apollo saw the sight, and from above was bending his bow; at that terror all Egypt and India, all Arabians, all Sabaeans turned to flee." [7] Thus Augustus' victory was attributed

---

[6] This interpretation of the Augustan program is derived mainly from Ronald Syme: *The Roman Revolution*.

[7] *Aeneid*, translated by H. R. Fairclough, VIII, 677–706.

to the Olympians and to the old household deities of the Roman family, who had protected the Western world from the animal-worship of Egypt and the Orient.

It is easy to be cynical about the Augustan compromise. An anachronistic religious and moral tradition cannot be revitalized by legislative fiat. But the old beliefs were not wholly dead, at least among the provincial Italians, and Augustus was partially success-ful in fusing them with reverence for the greatness of Rome and her mission of order and civilization and with gratitude to himself for putting an end to the civil wars. His attempt to legitimize his rule by giving it an ethical and mythological foundation was politically effective for two hundred years. Not until the third century of our era did the empire cease to be a principate and become an outright military despotism. But although the compromise could maintain order, it could not inspire creativity; the faith by which it was animated was too shallow and too artificial. It is true that the reign of Augustus was distinguished by great literary achievements, but all its major writers except Ovid were products of the republic, and while they glorified the Augustan program, they also expressed a deep underlying disillusionment and failure of vitality that were prophetic of the Roman decadence.

Always a materialistic people, the Romans contributed little to the literature that bears their name. Of all the surviving writers, only Caesar among the historians and possibly Lucretius among the poets were actually Roman. Every other Roman writer came from the Italian provinces or—in later ages—from Spain or North Africa. Rome, however, supplied her language, which had de-veloped largely as a medium for legal and political formulas and was extraordinarily terse without any lack of precision. Handled by a craftsman who could make full use of its potentialities, espe-cially of its unrivaled capacity for conveying different emphases by means of variations in word order, Latin was superbly adapted for that compression and fusion of meanings which is an essential quality of all great poetry. And although none of the Augustan writers was Roman, they gave expression to the Roman spirit, to its harsh realism (which found expression in satire, the only literary genre in which the Romans could claim to have excelled the Greeks), and to its sense of duty, of divine guidance, and of an imperial destiny.

The leading Augustans reached manhood before the establishment of the empire and initially turned to literature in response to the same forces as had influenced their predecessors of the last age of the republic. It was the function of Maecenas to win their support for Augustus and persuade them to adopt political and religious themes. His attempts to press literature into the service of the state had little success with Propertius, who preferred to continue writing about love with some of the neurotic intensity of Catullus, or with the smoother and feebler Tibullus. But three more important writers, the historian Livy and the poets Horace and Virgil, were more receptive.

Livy's long prose history celebrated the rise to greatness of the Roman people. Although he displayed Pompeian and republican sympathies, these were not regarded as necessarily subversive by a regime that was seeking to identify itself with the whole Roman tradition; Augustus was portrayed by his propagandists as the re-embodiment of all great Romans since the founding of the city by Romulus. Livy's work, however, was wholly backward-looking and showed no sense of history as a movement. He wrote in order to provide his contemporaries with a series of models for imitation, on the assumption that the moral qualities that had led to greatness in the early peasant republic were still valid for the new era. This unrealistic nostalgia for the banished past remained characteristic of Roman culture throughout the whole history of the principate.

Horace was an ex-republican who had fought on the losing side at Philippi and subsequently become a clerk in a government office. Rescued from drudgery by Maecenas and presented with a country estate where he could enjoy comfort and leisure, he had strong personal motives for celebrating the new order, but he had too much artistic conscience to write simply to please his patrons. Though he duly professed his reverence for the ancient gods and his admiration for the victories of Augustus, his poems actually reflect the underlying spirit of the age rather than its official doctrines. After the violence of the republic, men wanted tranquillity; they accepted Augustus not because of any positive belief in empire, but because his rule meant peace and safety. Horace was the poet of disillusionment, and his characteristic quality was his repudiation of all intense emotion. Political partisanship, Catullan passions, eagerness for wealth and power or for greatness in any form—all this led only to disappointment and destruction. The wise man preferred to live in retirement and enjoy modest pleasures. This philosophy of moderation was conveyed in impeccably polished verses that made full use of the capacity of the Latin language for concentrated statement. Horace's *Odes, Epistles,* and *Satires* have survived because of their perfection of form and style and because they gave classic expression to the attitudes of middle age. But the decline of energy and enthusiasm which they reflected was characteristic not merely of the poet, but also of the whole Augustan epoch.

Disillusionment, along with a pervasive sense of pity for the sufferings of human beings, was also a strong underlying tone in the work of Virgil. His main purposes, nevertheless, were to justify the building of the empire and the rule of Augustus and, at the same time, to infuse them with a higher moral and religious idealism. Himself a countryman from northern Italy, he adopted Romanism as his religion, chiefly in the hope that it was bringing peace and order to the whole Mediterranean world, and gave expression in his poetry to the whole Roman spirit and tradition.

Virgil's first book, the *Eclogues,* was a series of five-finger exercises in imitation of Theocritus, though it also affirmed his admiration for the policies of Augustus and (in the famous fourth *Eclogue*) his longing for a utopia of peace and harmony. The *Eclogues* already conveyed that crepuscular and autumnal mood, so different from the sunlit vividness of its exemplar's Sicilian idylls, which became one of the main hallmarks of Virgil's poetry. Possibly at the suggestion of Augustus and Maecenas, whose program included the revival of Italian agriculture, he then produced the *Georgics,* which took the form of a didactic poem about farming but which derived its poetic quality mainly from its intense devotion to the natural beauty and fertility of the Italian motherland.[8] Meanwhile, he had promised a poem dealing directly with Augustus, and this developed finally into the *Aeneid,* the epic history of the Trojan refugee who—according to legends that had been current for several centuries—was the principal ancestor of the Roman people, and more particularly of the Caesarean family,

---

[8] The love for nature exemplified in the *Georgics* and in much other Latin poetry was a new literary theme. Greek poetry, like Greek art, had been concerned almost exclusively with man.

and the model of Roman statesmanship and Roman virtue. Recounting Aeneas' escape from Troy, his arrival at Carthage and involvement with Dido, and his struggle to secure a home for himself and his people in Italy, Virgil traced a process of personal development paralleling the course of the action. Through the first five books, Aeneas had not fully accepted his destiny; he continued to look back at Troy, and was tempted to unite himself permanently with Dido. In the sixth book he visited the underworld of the dead and the not-yet-born and saw the Roman heroes of the future awaiting incarnation—an experience suggestive of the initiation ritual of a mystery religion with its enactment of death and rebirth. In the second half of the poem, Aeneas faced the future and met his Italian opponents with a bold and energetic self-confidence that he had lacked, finally killing his principal enemy, Turnus, in single combat.

Virgil's greatness was largely a product of the immense range of human experience which he was able to concentrate and synthesize. He was a learned poet, familiar with the whole work of his Hellenic and Latin predecessors, and his writing was filled with literary echoes and allusions, references to Homer, to Apollonius Rhodius, and to the early Roman poets being especially frequent. He had studied the philosophers, having spent some years in an Epicurean school at Naples, and had finally adopted a form of Platonism, believing (according to the sixth book of the *Aeneid*) in the immortality and ultimate purification of the soul and regarding its confinement in the body as the source of its corruption. He was acquainted, moreover, with the early history and religious customs of Italy, and many details of the *Aeneid* that one might suppose to have been invented have actually had archaeological corroboration. Yet, though he was master of all the culture of his time, he also retained the countryman's sense of dependence on mysterious natural powers. The *Aeneid* was more sophisticated than the Homeric epos, but it was at the same time closer to the primitive mentality, displaying a much stronger and more pervasive sense of religious fear and of the constant irruption of divine forces into human affairs.

Homer had glorified the *arete* of the hero. Human destiny was ultimately determined by the fates, whose decisions were inscrutable and without moral meaning, but within these limits men could

display skill and courage, thereby winning glory and achieving a
sense of unity with the Olympians. In the *Aeneid,* on the other
hand, human beings were merely the puppets of the gods, instruments for the fulfillment of divine purposes, and although they
were free to obey or disobey the will of heaven and might sometimes misinterpret it, they had no real power of initiative. This
emphasis on divine guidance was the most characteristically Roman feature of the poem. Jupiter, whose will was identical with
fate, had decreed that Aeneas should go to Italy, in order that his
descendants might afterwards create a world empire. It was the
duty of Aeneas to perform the task assigned to him, at whatever
sacrifice of personal happiness. He was aided by his divine mother
Venus, but was repeatedly thwarted by Juno, symbol of unregener-
ate nature, who created storms and other natural obstacles and instigated the hostility of Turnus and his Italian allies. Thus, all the
actions of the poem originated in heaven, in the purposes of
Jupiter and the conflict between the two goddesses. The decisions
of the gods, moreover, were made manifest through omens and
portents, usually of a frightening character: thunder, earthquakes,
and falling stars; the snakes strangling Laocoön and his sons; the
blazing hair of Aeneas' son Iulus and his Italian bride Lavinia;
the Bacchic madness of the queen Amato.

Although Virgil, in imitation of Homer, occasionally allowed
his characters to engage in feasting and in boat races and other
athletic exercises, there was no joy in the *Aeneid.* Life was essentially stern and harsh, and pleasure must always be subordinated to the performance of duty. Aeneas repeatedly complained
of the cruelty of his destiny and, unlike any Homeric hero, even
longed for death; but he continued to obey the gods. This Roman severity was incompatible with any delicate regard for the
rights and sensibilities of other people; and as Jupiter had determined that the Romans should build an empire, Aeneas must
abandon Dido, steal the bride of Turnus, avenge the death of his
friend Pallas by slaughtering four captives as human sacrifices, and
conquer a home in Italy. As with the Israelite invasion of Palestine,
all this was justified as a fulfillment of the will of heaven. While
the *Aeneid* glorified Roman imperialism, it also strongly reaffirmed
the old family morality that had been the original foundation of
Roman society. As Aeneas repeated on every suitable occasion, he

had brought with him from Troy his family gods, the Penates, adorned with fillets, along with Vesta, the undying fire of the family hearth. His references to these primeval symbols of family continuity had a tone of intimate warmth and affection lacking in his appeals to the Olympians. Virgil's treatment of women was, moreover, thoroughly Roman in its emphasis on chastity. Unlike Homer, who did not hold Helen responsible for the catastrophic effects of her beauty, Virgil represented her as definitely a wicked woman, and though he attributed no blame to Aeneas for what happened at Carthage, he explicitly condemned Dido for sexual misconduct.[9] The functions of women in Roman society were to perform their marital obligations and to inspire and encourage their sons in the fulfillment of civic tasks—a concept that seems often to have resulted in a marked degree of maternal domination. In the *Aeneid* this role was assigned—somewhat incongruously— to the goddess Venus, who was transformed by Virgil from the patroness of sexual love into an ideal Roman mother.

Roman *virtus* was exemplified particularly in the person of Aeneas, more especially in the Aeneas of the last six books, after he had learned in the underworld fully to understand and accept his destiny and had put aside his doubts and complaints. In the struggle with Turnus he displayed all the qualities of the ideal Roman general and statesman—strength and courage in battle, skill and foresight in making plans, constant attention to the welfare of his men. His moral traits—his religious reverence, seriousness, and sense of duty—were summarized in the untranslatable word *pius,* which was attached to his name throughout the poem. In his portrayal of Aeneas, how far was Virgil thinking not only of the past leaders of the Roman people, but also of their contemporary representative? In the callousness with which Aeneas fled from Dido and his cruelty toward his Italian captives, in his constant anxieties and his total incapacity for exuberance and enjoyment—in all the qualities, in fact, that made him perhaps the least likable of all poetic heroes—Aeneas might have been modeled after Augustus. But although Virgil honored his imperial patron for the restoration of peace and attributed his achievements to divine guidance, he cannot have been blind to Augustus' egoism

---

[9] *Aeneid,* IV, 172.

and love of power. Aeneas should probably be regarded as a portrait not of what Augustus actually was, but of what Virgil hoped he might become, a leader who subordinated human feelings not to his own ambition, but to the necessities of statesmanship and to his duty to the state.

One feels throughout the *Aeneid,* in fact, a constant tension between the Roman concept of imperial destiny and Virgil's own humanity and sense of pity. He attempted to reconcile them through the affirmation that Roman rule would mean peace and justice. Rome's mission was not merely to rule the nations, but "to crown peace with law, to spare the humbled and to tame in war the proud." "Then shall wars cease and the rough ages soften; hoary Faith and Vesta, Quirinus with his brother Remus, shall give laws. The gates of war, grim with iron and close-fitting bars, shall be closed; within impious Rage, sitting on savage arms, his hands fast bound behind with a hundred brazen knots, shall roar in the ghastliness of blood-stained lips." [1] Thus Virgil, accepting the whole Roman past, sought to legitimize the empire on the basis not only of the divine will but also of a humane idealism, and to elevate it to a higher moral level. It is perhaps not wholly fanciful to suppose that these Virgilian doctrines may have contributed to the higher standards of administration that marked the early empire, and that the transformation of the vindictive and unscrupulous young Octavian into the more tolerant and enlightened Augustus of later years may have been due, in some measure, to Virgil's influence.

The final effect of the *Aeneid,* however, was one of sadness. The gods imposed intolerable burdens upon human beings, the heaviest of them being the task of conquering and governing an empire. Virgil might teach the Romans to spare the humble and war only against the proud, but he also reflected the sense of disillusionment and the decay of animal vitality that characterized the age of Augustus and became even more conspicuous in later generations. The *Aeneid* was a product of decadence, foreshadowing the ultimate disappearance of Helleno-Roman civilization and the submergence of Hellenic rationalism in a new religion. It has survived largely because of the splendor of its language, with its

---

[1] *Aeneid,* VI, 852–3; I, 291–6.

richly colored imagery, its unfailing euphony, and its extraordinary concentration of meanings. More often, perhaps, than any other writer, Virgil displayed the power of verbal magic which is the poet's most essential gift. By means of apparently simple statements (usually depending for much of their effect on the deep-rolling em sounds that were so frequent in Latin) he could somehow impose a sense of inexplicable profundities. Most of these famous Virgilian sentences conveyed the feeling of autumnal melancholy which was his most characteristic tone.[2]

---

[2] Probably the most familiar of these Virgilian sentences are the two lines from the first book which summarize the whole mood of the poem: *tantae molis erat Romanam condere gentem* (I, 33); *sunt lacrimae rerum et mentem mortalia tangunt* (I, 462). More incomprehensibly moving are such passages as the epitaph on Marcellus:

manibus date lilia plenis,
purpureos spargam flores animamque
  nepotis
his saltem accumulem donis et fungar
  inani munere (VI, 883–6).

The quality of such passages can be defined only in terms of their physiological effects; typically, a sensation in the pit of the stomach, or a cold shudder.

9

The Principate

By materialistic standards the Augustan compromise appeared for a long time to be brilliantly successful. The two centuries of the principate, extending from the Battle of Actium in 31 B.C. to the death of Marcus Aurelius, A.D. 180, were an epoch of extraordinary prosperity for the whole of the Mediterranean world. This was, in fact, the longest period of order and security in the whole history of Western civilization. Subsequent developments made it evident that the spiritual problems of classical society had been evaded rather than answered, that the empire was culturally sterile, and that society must either disintegrate or renew itself through a total spiritual transformation, but the deep inner malaise of Roman civilization did not produce overt effects until the third century.

The Augustan compromise had one obvious political weakness: its failure to adopt adequate rules of succession. In theory the choice of a new emperor was to be made by the Senate, which lacked the independence for the effective exercise of this responsibility; in practice, the succession became largely hereditary. During the first century of our era, the advent of several mentally unbalanced rulers caused some intervals of disorder. But there was serious misgovernment during only three reigns, those of Caligula, Nero (excluding his first five years), and Domitian, totaling only twenty-eight years; and only in the year 69, following the assassination of Nero, was there any outbreak of civil war. Even the bad emperors, moreover, did not seriously interfere with the government of the provinces, the chief victims of imperial paranoia being the surviving members of the old Roman aristocracy. In the second century the problem of the succession was temporarily solved through the adoption by each emperor of a suitable heir, a method that produced a sequence of four conscientious and efficient rulers, Trajan, Hadrian, Pius Antoninus, and Marcus Aurelius Antoninus, covering a period of eighty-two years.

Nor did the empire face any serious threat from foreign enemies. Two frontiers required constant vigilance: the line of the Rhine and the Danube, which guarded the Mediterranean world from the barbarian tribes of northern Europe, and the fluctuating boundary line between the West and the Orient which Rome had inherited from the Seleucid kings of Syria. But until the third century Rome could hold her own against both the Germans and the Parthians. After the establishment of the principate there was little further expansion in the boundaries of the empire, but the administration was able to maintain control over the Mediterranean world and its outlying provinces, and Roman institutions and Hellenic culture were diffused over the whole vast area from Britain and Gaul in the west to Syria, Asia Minor, and Egypt in the east.

Popular impressions of the history of the early empire have been derived mainly from the works of Tacitus, an aristocratic conservative who was obsessed with the more lurid aspects of life among the Roman upper class during the periods of misrule— with the loss of freedom, the moral degeneration, and the prevalence of spying, informing, and judicial robbery and murder. Neither Tacitus nor any other Roman writer paid much attention to the government of the provinces. Yet it is evident that the reforms of Augustus had put an end to the kind of exploitation that had prevailed under the later republic. The high administrative officials of the early empire continued to punish lawbreakers and crush rebellions with a merciless brutality, but they no longer regarded Roman rule as merely an instrument for personal or national aggrandizement. With political stabilization came the development of a sense of responsibility and of *esprit de corps*. The old Roman belief in duty, fused with Hellenic culture, with Stoic universalism, and with the Virgilian doctrine of a divine mission, was apparently producing a new concept of empire. For the best of the imperial officials it meant order and justice for all, the expansion of civilization, the equality and ultimately the fusion of races, and a growing *homonoia*.

The most significant expression of this attitude was in law. Reflecting the emphasis on the sanctity of contracts and on adherence to precedents that had characterized the Roman people since the early republic, the Roman legal system had already had a long evolution. As Rome became the center of an empire, legal theorists expanded its traditional civil law by developing the concept of a *ius gentium,* a law shared by all peoples. This was then rationalized and idealized by identification with the Greek philosophic doctrine of a *ius naturale,* a law of nature. Under the empire the process of universalization continued under the influence of Stoic philosophy. To a steadily increasing extent the Roman judicial system was infused with the belief that all men should be considered as legally equal and as endowed with rights entitled to protection. The Greeks, with their conception of the polis as a closely knit unity in which every aspect of human life found expression, had never developed the concept of private rights, with the result that in political conflicts individuals who belonged to the losing party could have no security of person or property. But the legislation of the early principate, for the first time in history, marked out an area in which individuals were protected against the state, private rights of life, liberty, and property being immune from political interference no matter what party might be in control of the government.

Thus, the imperial administration ceased to be based on racial privilege and became the expression of a concept of civilization that could be imparted to all peoples. The provinces were Romanized and Hellenized and could ultimately expect full participation in all the benefits of the empire. The spirit of Roman imperialism was exemplified in a speech that, according to Tacitus, was delivered in the year 69 by a Roman general to a group of Gauls whose loyalty was uncertain. "In common with the citizens of Rome," Tacitus represented him as saying, "you share every benefit. Our legions are often commanded by you. You govern your own provinces, and even others subject to the empire. All positions of honor are open to you. Nothing is debarred." [1] Augustus had made the empire Italian rather than Roman; later rulers continued

---

[1] Tacitus: *Histories,* translated by C. H. Moore, IV, 73–4.

to extend citizenship rights to provincials and to appoint them to the administration. The final step, the grant of full citizenship to all the inhabitants of the empire, was taken in 212. As early as the second century, provincials were even rising to the supreme position: Trajan and Hadrian came from Spain, Pius Antoninus from Gaul. Among the later emperors were natives of Africa, Illyricum, Thrace, Syria, and Arabia. Some regions of the empire, notably southwestern Gaul with its rich agricultural lands, seem to have become more prosperous than Italy itself. Thus, the universalism envisaged by Alexander and probably by Caesar was finally achieved, not by such an immediate obliteration of ethnic differences as would have destroyed moral and cultural traditions, but by the gradual assimilation of the provincials into the Helleno-Roman way of life.

The chief beneficiaries of the empire were the business classes. With the establishment of political stability, commerce rather than war or politics became the main avenue to privilege, and the members of the old Roman ruling-class families gave place to *nouveau-riche* merchants and landowners, the more successful of whom were the founders of a new senatorial aristocracy. Almost all the individuals about whom we have any information seem to have been remarkably wealthy: it is interesting, for example, that the younger Pliny, a man of letters and imperial official who was by no means regarded as one of the rich men of his time, was the owner of no less than five country estates in different parts of Italy. The luxury enjoyed by the fortunate few was, of course, made possible by the labors of the vast majority of the population— slaves, peasant freeholders, tenant farmers, and urban workmen. Although slavery decreased as a result of extensive manumissions, coupled with the decrease of the foreign wars which had formerly been the chief source of supply, the system of big estates continued to expand in both Italy and the provinces, and many free farmers were reduced to tenancy. Yet, in spite of the sharp and increasing economic inequalities, the lower classes shared in the benefits of peace and orderly government. Class lines, moreover, remained remarkably fluid, and men of ability, even including slaves, had plenty of opportunities for advancement. A number of the millionaires and high imperial officials of the first and second centuries were provincials, often of Asiatic origin, who had been sold into slavery as children and won their freedom through services to their masters.

The most remarkable achievement of the early empire was the growth of cities. Having fully identified itself with Hellenism, the Roman administration regarded the city as the essential unit of civilization and as a means for its diffusion among the provincials. In accordance with the Hellenic and Hellenistic tradition, cities were endowed with extensive rights of self-government and had their own senates and elected officials; they were mostly dominated by local oligarchies of landowners and businessmen, but the crafts-men and retail tradesmen of the lower classes were frequently en-titled to vote in municipal elections. All the western provinces— Gaul, Spain, Britain, and north Africa—were soon covered with flourishing cities modeled after those of the Hellenistic East and displaying a comparable architectural splendor. It became custo-mary for wealthy men to seek prestige and enduring commemora-tion by endowing their native cities with public buildings and cultural institutions; lavish generosity was, in fact, required of candidates for municipal office, and many men of ambition must have almost bankrupted themselves in their efforts to win popu-lar favor. Never before or since, not even in modern America, has the practice of devoting private wealth to public purposes been so well established. By this means a city would gradually acquire a central colonnaded market place, temples in honor of deified emperors and of local gods (who were identified with members of the Olympian pantheon), a triumphal arch, an aqueduct for the provision of fresh water, public baths, a gymnasium, a school of rhetoric, a primary school, a public library, a theater, and an arena for the combats of gladiators and wild animals.[2]

---

[2] The Hellenic concept of the city has been preserved by Mediterranean peoples down to modern times, and was transmitted by the Spaniards to Latin America. The founders of the Spanish Empire built cities at key points as soon as they had taken pos-session of an area; these were endowed with certain rights of self-government, and were intended to serve as centers for the diffusion of Spanish civilization. With their central colonnaded market places, rectangular street-plans, and im-pressive public buildings, the cities of Latin America recall those of the Ro-man Empire and of the Hellenistic kingdoms even in their physical ap-pearance. The English, on the other hand, regarded cities merely as places of business, not as moral organisms. In consequence, the cities of the United States mostly grew up with little planning, and even today have not acquired full self-government, the

Thus, Rome appeared to have solved the problem that had
eluded the Greeks, combining unity with local autonomy, order
with individual freedom. This was the theme of a panegyric delivered at Rome in 143 by a Greek orator, Aelius Aristides. The Romans, he declared, through their genius for government had created the universal harmony, based on justice and freedom, which
the Greeks had dreamed of but had been unable to achieve. "A
civil community of the World has been established as a Free Republic under one, the best, ruler and teacher of order; and all come
together as into a common civic center, in order to achieve each
man his due." The Romans had "organized all the civilized world,
as it were, into one family. . . . A clear and universal freedom
from all fear has been granted both to the world and to those who
live in it." "For of all who have ever gained empire you alone rule
over men who are free. . . . There is an abundant and beautiful
equality of the humble with the great and of the obscure with the
illustrious, and, above all, of the poor man with the rich and of
the commoner with the noble." "As on holiday the whole civilized world lays down the arms which were its ancient burden and
has turned to adornment and all glad thoughts with power to
realize them. All the other rivalries have left the cities, and this
one contention holds them all, how each city may appear most
beautiful and attractive. All localities are full of gymnasia, foun-
tains, monumental approaches, temples, workshops, schools, and
one may say that the civilized world, which had been sick from the
beginning, as it were, has been brought by the right knowledge to
a state of health. . . . Cities gleam with radiance and charm, and
the whole earth has been beautified like a garden." [3]

A professional speaker dependent for his livelihood on public
favor, Aristides undoubtedly set out to flatter his Roman audience.
Yet his panegyric, however exaggerated and one-sided, gave expression to what many citizens of the empire must sincerely have
believed, especially in the halcyon period of the second century.
Yet this epoch of apparent general prosperity was followed within
a few generations by political disorders and economic decline, by a

powers of municipal authorities being
restricted by state legislatures. The feeling that the city represents moral degeneration rather than civilization is
deeply rooted in the Anglo-American
tradition.

[3] Aelius Aristides: *The Roman Ora-
tion,* translated by J. H. Oliver, 60,
102, 104, 36, 39, 97, 99.

reorganization of the whole imperial system along new lines, by a general repudiation of the naturalistic values of the Helleno-Roman tradition, and by a search for religious salvation. What were the causes of this failure of vitality and revolution of values? Why did the beneficiaries of Roman civilization fail to believe in it sufficiently to preserve it?

Part of the answer is implicit in the remarks of Aristides. A civilization that believes that it has finally solved the problem of government and that mankind has nothing before it but the enjoyment of "glad thoughts" has plainly lost the capacity for responding creatively to new challenges, and is ripe for decadence. The civilization of the empire was not infused with any dynamic religious belief about the meaning and purpose of man's existence or with any humanitarian drive toward the improvement of social conditions. As long as the organization of human life continued to function smoothly and effectively, there were no further goals to be achieved, no higher ideals to be embodied in institutions. The ultimate weakness of the Romans, as of all peoples who pride themselves on their efficiency and practicality, was that they were exclusively concerned with means, not with ends. Peace, order, security, the equitable administration of justice—these they could provide, and those persons who were content with the pursuit of material wealth and fortunate in its acquisition could indeed enjoy "glad thoughts." But in all the intellectual and aesthetic products of the empire there was an inescapable sense of oppression, of weariness and ultimate futility. This was a civilization that could serve the means of living by building superb roads and bridges, but when it tried to express its ideals, it could produce only an art that was massively insensitive and, for the most part, derivative. It provided its citizens with leisure, but its favorite entertainments, which spread to virtually every city of the empire, were gladiatorial combats and the spectacle of criminals being slaughtered by wild animals. The ultimate verdict on Roman civilization was pronounced in the sixth century by Pope Gregory the Great: "There was long life and health, material prosperity, growth of population and the tranquillity of daily peace, yet while the world was still flourishing in itself, in their hearts it had already withered." [4]

---

[4] Quoted by C. Dawson (ed.): *Monument to St. Augustine,* p. 25.

The early empire was, in fact, culturally barren. According to narrowly economic interpretations of history, this should have been a period of intellectual efflorescence. Enjoying peace, security, and material welfare, the upper classes might have been expected to use their leisure for the promotion of the arts and sciences. Yet this was one of the least creative periods in all Western history. Even the long-established intellectual centers in Italy and the East produced nothing of major importance and extremely little of smaller value. As for the flourishing cities of the western provinces, most of them eventually vanished from the earth without making a single significant contribution to man's intellectual and aesthetic heritage. Such sterility, among a people enjoying leisure and security, must be regarded as symptomatic of a profound spiritual malaise.

A political and social transformation requires a corresponding change in values and beliefs. But the transition from the tribalism of the city-state to the universalism of the empire had not been accompanied by any new philosophy of life which could legitimize the new institutions and infuse them with creative vitality, and the Roman belief in duty and administrative efficiency was no adequate substitute. The sense of weariness and self-pity with which Virgil's Aeneas undertook his imperial mission was prophetic of the whole history of the principate. For its cultural and religious values the empire was dependent on the Hellenism of the past— not the living Hellenism of the great age, but the petrified and sterile Hellenism of the Greek decadence.

In the political sphere this meant a deep disharmony between the accepted values of society and its actual institutions. Hellenism was a product of city-state republicanism and could not be reconciled with a system of one-man rule. Although every emperor was the subject of innumerable panegyrics during his lifetime and was deified after death, the principate was never convincingly rationalized and justified in religious and philosophical terms, but remained a mere expedient that men accepted because of the failure of the republic. The Augustan compromise, by which the emperors were represented as fulfilling the whole Roman tradition, was too much at variance with actualities to inspire real belief. According to political and legal theorists throughout the whole imperial period, the will of the Roman people was the ultimate source of all authority; power was merely delegated to the emperors, though the grant was unlimited and irrevocable. Philosophers and other intellectuals continued, in fact, to cherish republican ideals while recognizing that they were no longer capable of application; they regarded the principate not as a positive good, but merely as a necessity and, like Tacitus, attributed it to the wickedness of men and the anger of the gods. Thus, in spite of the dazzling material achievements of the principate, it was based not on any dynamic faith, but on a negation, and hence could not inspire the loyalty needed for survival.

The spiritual sickness of Roman civilization, however, was caused not only by the fact that the political values men professed to believe had ceased to have any practical meaning, but also by a fundamental weakness in the whole view of life. With Plato and Aristotle, Hellenic thought had lost its creativity and reached an impasse. Both the Platonic doctrine of ideas and the Aristotelian doctrine of forms meant that human beings and institutions must always be copies of the same eternal models of perfection, unaffected by the movement of time. Discrepancies between the model and the actualization were caused by the corrupting influences of matter. This view of life denied all meaning both to the processes of history and to human individuality, for the same unchanging ideals applied to all phases of social development and to all human beings, and it led to a fatalistic acceptance of evil, which was attributed to matter and hence was inherent in the natural world. And as men could not hope to surpass the greatest of their predecessors in the attempt to realize ideals, the chief practical result was the frigid and mechanical imitation of the past. In politics it was recognized that, by Hellenic standards, the principate was a time of degeneration, but individuals could still copy earlier heroes in the conduct of their personal lives, and learning and the arts could preserve the Hellenic inheritance. Thus, the culture of the early empire was wholly backward-looking and offered no hope for the future. Whenever its aesthetic expressions ceased to be merely imitative and acquired some degree of originality, one finds in it a nostalgia for earlier idealisms, a desire to escape into some world of pure fantasy, and a profound sadness.

The cultural sterility of imperial society was strikingly exemplified in its educational system. There was no lack of respect for intellectual attainment. Education was widely diffused, and received considerable financial support from the government, and academic success was a qualification for appointment to high administrative positions. Never in European history, in fact, has it been more highly rewarded, and rarely has it been less worthy of such reward. The basis of education was the kind of mental gymnastic, divorced from practical realities, that had first been recommended in the writings of Isocrates. The four great schools of philosophy continued to flourish, though with a total lack of new developments, but the chief subject taught in institutions of learning was rhetoric, the skillful deployment of words. All over the empire, boys from wealthy families learned to make speeches, the whole emphasis being placed not on content, but on form. The good pupil acquired a flowery diction, an epigrammatic style, and an impassioned delivery. Listening to speeches by professional orators was, in fact, the favorite entertainment of the cultured classes, and the tropes and figures, forms of sentence construction, gestures and vocal effects of virtuoso performers were analyzed and appraised in the most minute detail. No form of mental discipline could have been better calculated to stifle original and realistic thought and promote a complacent conservatism. It is illustrative of the divorce between culture and actuality that any historical subjects assigned to students in the schools of rhetoric appear to have been taken exclusively from the republican era. A young orator was required to compose the kind of speech which might have been delivered by some ancient champion of political liberty in Periclean Athens or in the Rome of Cicero and Cato. With no apparent sense of incongruity, he would at the same time eulogize the reigning emperor as the guide and protector of his subjects.[5]

Science could not flourish in such an intellectual atmosphere. Late Hellenic philosophy, which asserted that the ideal forms were the only true subjects of knowledge and that all sublunar objects were subject to chance, was, in fact, wholly incompatible with true science. The scientific productions of the empire consisted,

---

[5] The low intellectual standards resulting from this exclusive concentration on rhetoric are exemplified by the fact that St. Augustine, who had the usual higher education of his time and adopted an academic career, could not even read Greek with any facility. It is also interesting that in Augustine's time all reading was normally done aloud. Augustine was amazed when he found St. Ambrose reading a book in silence (*Confessions,* II).

therefore, almost wholly of restatements of the work of earlier epochs. A few names have seemed important because they summarized what had been discovered by their predecessors and hence provided starting-points for man's next scientific advance fifteen hundred years later. What we know of ancient medicine comes largely from Galen, of astronomy from Ptolemy, of mechanics from Hero, of geography from Strabo, of natural history from the elder Pliny, and of architecture and engineering from Vitruvius and Frontinus. These half-dozen figures preserved some of the genuinely scientific spirit of the great age, but they added little of much importance. Along with the third-century Alexandrian mathematician Diophantos, who did original work in algebra, apparently based on early Mesopotamian sources,[6] they comprise virtually the whole scientific achievement of the imperial period. There was a similar lack of technological advance; in fact, the decrease of slave labor seems to have resulted in technological retrogression.

Most of the literary production of the empire was florid, empty, and derivative. Roman gentlemen composed frigid epic poems in imitation of the *Aeneid;* Greek orators published collections of speeches modeled after those of Isocrates. Critical standards were set by the rhetoricians, who demanded a brilliantly epigrammatic style and were uninterested in content. Amid the pervasive mediocrity, about a dozen figures achieved some individual distinction. If one counts as imperial writers only those who reached maturity after the final destruction of the republic, then the roster begins with Ovid in the later Augustan period. Seneca, Lucan, and Petronius wrote during the reign of Nero, all of them eventually displeasing the Emperor and committing suicide in order to avoid execution. Tacitus and Juvenal belonged to the era of Trajan, and Lucius Apuleius to that of Marcus Aurelius. A few lesser names might be added to the list. Greek literature, apparently moribund for many generations, revived during the early second century, its chief representatives being Plutarch and Lucian. Much of what these men produced can be classified under the general heading of escapism. If they presented ideas, they either condemned imperial society by the standards of an obsolete republicanism or took refuge in some form of private salvation. Unlike Virgil, none of

---

[6] See B. L. Van Der Waerden: *Science Awakening,* translated by Arnold Dresden, pp. 278–86.

them presented any constructive interpretation of the society in which they lived.

The prince of the escapists was Ovid. The favorite writer of that sophisticated leisure-class Roman society which Augustus had vainly attempted to moralize, he found his subject matter in the celebration of a lighthearted sexuality and in the fairy-tale world of Greek mythology, which he used simply as a source of entertaining stories without making even a pretense of religious belief. A master of brilliantly colored imagery and swift narrative, writing in a style that was polished, ironical, and unfailingly picturesque, he had all the qualities of a great poet except the capacity for ethical and religious seriousness. His masterpiece was the *Metamorphoses,* a series of tales about the gods loosely bound together by the general theme of miraculous changes of shape. This became the favorite source of mythological information for the poets and painters of the Renaissance, and has remained one of the most purely delightful books ever written.

Later storytellers turned mostly to prose romance, which became the favorite art form of the decadence. The only surviving Latin examples are the *Satyricon* of Petronius and the *Golden Ass* of Lucius Apuleius. Writing about the escapades of rascally fortune-hunters with a Roman realism and an energy and exuberance all his own, Petronius produced a portrait of the more unsavory aspects of imperial society which can be called decadent only in its refusal to pass any moral judgments. Apuleius, on the other hand, introduced his readers to a world of magic and witchcraft, heavily spiced with sex, and ended with an ecstatic celebration of the power and benignity of the goddess Isis. The escapist tendency was more conspicuous in the numerous Greek romances, mostly written in the second and third centuries. Books like the *Chaereas and Callirhoe* of Chariton, the *Aethiopica* of Heliodorus, the *Daphnis and Chloe* of Longus, and the *Leucippe and Clitophon* of Achilles Tatius carried pairs of lovers through complicated and improbable adventures, filled with kidnappings by brigands or pirates, attempted rapes, hairbreadth avoidances of death, and denouements based on coincidence or divine intervention, with much emphasis on the preservation of the heroine's virginity up to the point when she was finally united with the hero. As Moses Hadas has pointed out, they closely resemble the modern cinema in their plot structure and their social and moral assumptions.[7]

The rejection of actuality, however, was not confined to the literature of entertainment. The more serious writers of the empire were equally incapable of coming to terms with their society, and could only condemn it by standards that had no contemporary relevance. The greatest energy was displayed by those Latin writers who still clung to the tribalistic traditions of the republic and hated the principate not only because of its suppression of Roman liberties, but also because of its universalist tendencies. Idealizing the past, they would have liked to see the empire still governed by the old patrician families. Their inability to find any positive values in the principate was a striking example of the dependence of the whole classical ethos on the political system of the city-state and of the ultimate failure of the Virgilian and Augustan attempt to legitimize the empire in moral and religious terms. But because they recognized that one-man rule, however evil, was also inevitable, their attachment to the past had no practical efficacy and could only waste itself in a savage and futile indignation. Thus, Lucan, in his epic poem about the wars of Caesar and Pompey, presented Cato, the leader of the doomed republican aristocracy, as the only real hero of the conflict. Seneca also, in his moral essays, considered Cato a model of all the virtues. Tacitus, writing the history of the empire from the death of Augustus to that of Domitian, produced a portrait gallery of monsters, etched with unforgettable epigrammatic bitterness, but the violence of his hatred prevented him from recognizing the benefits enjoyed by the provincials and from seeing the principate as anything but a curse inflicted on the Romans by divine anger. His contemporary, Juvenal, satirized the corruption of Roman society with a comparable brilliance and an even greater lack of discrimination. Idealizing the mores of the old peasant republic, he regarded any change as degeneration, deploring the influx of Hellenic and Ori-

---

[7] "Among ourselves the art form which has the largest popular following is the cinema, and the techniques and social and moral premises of the cinema story find their closest parallel in the Greek romance. The Greek experience of some 1,500 years which we have surveyed is so broad as to provide analogy, close or labored, for any new situation. Does it mark a rise in our own spiritual stature and institutions that we find ourselves spiritually at home in the dreariest centuries of those 1,500 years?" Moses Hadas: *A History of Greek Literature* (Columbia University Press), p. 298.

ental immigrants no less than the luxury and avarice of the rich, and castigating women with intellectual interests almost in the same breath with those who murdered their husbands or had affairs with gladiators.

Romans who wanted a philosophy of life continued to prefer Stoicism; its stern ethical discipline and its republican associations had little relevance to the society of the principate, but it promised a spiritual escape from an evil world. Seneca, the chief literary exponent of Roman Stoicism, was an ambiguous and baffling figure who typified all the paradoxes of the Augustan compromise. The tutor and (for five years) the chief minister of Nero, and one of the richest men of his time, he defended the principate on the ground that it had preserved all the liberties of the republic except the liberty to perish, and interlarded his philosophical meditations with the grossest flattery of his imperial master.[8] Yet his essays were filled with subtle analyses of moral questions, based on the traditional Stoic doctrine that happiness depended wholly on inner fortitude, not on external circumstances, so that "nothing evil can happen to a good man." [9] His tragedies on Greek mythological themes, written in the inflated and epigrammatic style inculcated by the rhetoricians, exhibited the same confidence in man's capacity to achieve a mastery of all disturbing emotions; the noble gestures in which his characters indulged during moments of crisis were in sharp contrast with the sober realism of the Greek originals. Seneca went beyond earlier Stoic writers in asserting belief in a personal God who was the father of mankind, and this led Christians of a later age to claim him as a disciple of St. Paul, with whom he was alleged to have corresponded. But there was a profound difference between the Stoic ethic and that of Jesus. With its aristocratic confidence in human strength, Stoicism promised a godlike liberation from all forms of sorrow; even pity was a weakness, for the wise man never felt grief.[1] The Stoicism preached by such men as Seneca and his two second-century successors, the freed slave Epictetus and the Emperor Marcus Aurelius (both of whom wrote in Greek), may have served to strengthen the moral

---

[8] *"Ad summam libertatem nihil deest nisi pereundi libertas," De Clementia,* I, i, 8. For flattery of Nero, see *De Clementia,* I, i, 5–8; II, ii, 1–2.

[9] *"Nihil accidere bono viro mali potest," De Providentia,* II, 1.
[1] *De Clementia,* II, ii, 4; V, 1.

fiber of the ruling class, but it was too constricting and inhuman to stimulate any healthy cultural growth or provide any real fulfillment of man's spiritual needs, and its suppression of emotional spontaneity may have contributed to the aesthetic barrenness of Roman civilization. The *Meditations* of Marcus Aurelius are perhaps the noblest expression of classical moralism, but they have no joy or hope or warmth of feeling, and the virtue that the Emperor sought to achieve meant a kind of frozen perfection, devoid of individuality and derived from stern self-discipline and from resignation to destiny.[2]

After the feverish and tortured intensity of the Roman traditionalists, it is a relief to turn to the more placid and antiquarian nostalgia of the Greeks. Plutarch, though a close friend of the Emperor Hadrian, chose to spend his life in retirement in the little Boeotian town of Chaeronea, where he indulged his passion for ancient Hellenism by serving as a local magistrate and as priest of the old shrine of Apollo at Delphi. Amid such activities he seems almost to have succeeded in forgetting the contemporary world; only at very rare intervals do his writings refer to anything later than the fall of the Roman republic. His essays, which range over a wide variety of philosophical, scientific, and ethical questions, display him as a mediocre thinker—credulous, whimsical, and devoid of all intellectual discipline—but as a singularly attractive and morally enlightened human being. Though he preferred Plato to any subsequent philosopher, he did not imitate Plato's ethical severity or his aristocratic arrogance. This anachronistic Hellenist was, in fact, the only figure of the principate (except perhaps the Emperors Hadrian and Marcus Aurelius) for whom the modern reader can feel any real liking.

The most curious expression of Plutarch's antiquarianism was his defense of the old mythology. As a Platonist he believed in mono-

---

[2] Wisdom, wrote the Emperor, "consists in keeping the daemon within a man free from violence and unharmed, superior to pains and pleasures, doing nothing without a purpose, nor yet falsely and with hypocrisy, not feeling the need of another man's doing or not doing anything; and besides, accepting all that happens, and all that is allotted, as coming from thence, wherever it is, from where he himself came; and, finally, waiting for death with a cheerful mind, as being nothing else than a dissolution of the elements of which every living being is compounded." *Meditations,* translated by G. Long, II, 7.

theism and deplored the immorality of the Homeric legends, but as a Hellenist he was eager to rehabilitate the worship of the Olympians. He solved the dilemma by postulating the existence of a multitude of daemons intermediate between God and man, some of whom were evil and hence capable of performing the wicked deeds men had mistakenly attributed to Zeus and Apollo. Living chiefly on the moon, the daemons were not immortal (for abstruse Platonic reasons Plutarch calculated that they had a life span of 9,720 years), and some of those worshipped by the ancient Greeks might already be dead—a fact that perhaps accounted for the silence of so many of the ancient oracles of Hellas. Plutarch defended this theory with a story of a mysterious voice calling to a ship at sea that the great god Pan had died and of other voices heard weeping and lamenting when the sailors repeated the news elsewhere. The assertion that this had occurred during the reign of Tiberius, and hence during the lifetime of Jesus Christ, made it interesting to Christian theologians.

Plutarch's most influential achievement, however, was his *Parallel Lives*. Written primarily in order to demonstrate that Greece, in spite of her subjugation, had produced as many great men of action as Rome, this was pervaded with the spirit of antique republicanism. Plutarch's heroes were the statesmen of the Greek city-states and of early Rome; the founder of the principate, Julius Caesar, was condemned as a man of sinister ambition. No work of classical literature did as much to promote the cult of liberty in later ages. It was ironical that this gallery of models of republican virtue should have been written by the friend of an emperor nearly five hundred years after the Greek cities had lost their autonomy.

The other leading representative of the Hellenic renaissance, Lucian of Samosata (a town in Syria), was a man of much tougher intellectual fiber, but was equally anachronistic. A rationalist who devoted himself to satirizing all religious beliefs, both the traditional Olympianism and the new mystical cults of his own day, he seemed like a throwback to the age of the Sophists. A culture that could produce this Voltairean figure still had reserves of energy; no other Greek writer of any period was so sophisticated or so consistently amusing. But in laughing at religion Lucian was conducting a rear-guard action against the strongest emotional tendency of his time. He was, in fact, the last exponent of a thoroughgoing naturalism for more than a thousand years.

As in many other societies, the visual arts were the most accurate mirror of the Roman spirit, reflecting both its consummate practical efficiency and the poverty of its ultimate goals and values. The most satisfying Roman achievements were purely functional—the bridges and aqueducts that spanned the rivers, the roads proceeding directly to their objectives with masterful disregard of all natural obstacles. Many Romans would probably have agreed with the comment of Frontinus in his survey of the aqueducts of the capital city: "With such an array of indispensable structures carrying so many waters compare, if you will, the idle pyramids or the useless though famous works of the Greeks." [3] But Roman building was not merely utilitarian: it aspired to become decorative and to give expression to the values inherent in the civilization of the empire. In their technical skill Roman architects far surpassed those of classical Greece: they introduced the arch, the dome, and the vault from the Near East, made use of a great variety of building materials, erected structures of an extraordinary size and complexity, and planned their cities in order to provide long-range vistas. Yet the temples, palaces, baths, and triumphal arches that exhibited their power and wealth were lacking in that ultimate spiritual grace which the Greek builders, with their relative poverty of materials, had rarely failed to convey. As W. R. Lethaby declared, Roman works "stand for force, expansion, splendor, the art was official, self-satisfied, oppressive. It gives a voice to matter as Greece had expressed mind. Rome was lacking in the things of the spirit. There is little wonder—the first early wonder at mysteries—left in Roman art; the dew of the morning is dried up; it is the great Philistine style." [4]

Roman sculpture was mostly naturalistic, expressing both a respect for brute historic fact and an inability to transcend it and give it spiritual meaning. Vast quantities of it have survived the ravages of time: statues of Olympian deities in poses' crudely modeled after Hellenistic originals; sarcophagi with bas-reliefs depicting Bacchic revels and other mythological scenes of sensuous

---

[3] Quoted by B. Farrington: *Greek Science*, II, 265.   [4] W. R. Lethaby: *Architecture*, p. 99.

excitement; portrait statues and busts of emperors and generals equipped for battle in which the dominant impression, suggested by the insensitive brutality of the features, the massive size of the limbs and torso, and the elaborate carving of the breastplate, is an unquestioning confidence in the efficacy of physical force. Few spectacles are more depressing than a museum of Roman art, especially for those who can recall the tenderness and delicacy with which Greece had represented the human form.

For a brief period during the reign of Augustus art was partially infused with a sense of ideal values, at least in intention. The statues of the Emperor portray him, Aeneas-like, as a graceful and meditative but somewhat melancholy superman, while the Ara Pacis, dedicated in the year 9 B.C., conveys a Virgilian belief in Rome's divine mission and a Virgilian reverence for the fertility and beneficence of nature. Yet if one contrasts the friezes of the Ara Pacis with those of the Parthenon, the figures seem earth-bound and static, lacking the Greek sense of free movement, while the conventionality of the poses and the sense of complacency inescapably suggested by the whole composition make it a characteristic product of the Augustan compromise. Even this degree of idealization disappeared from later Roman sculpture. The portraits of emperors and the battle scenes depicted on their triumphal arches and columns often displayed a superb fidelity to fact. Perhaps the most effective example was the Column of Trajan, around which was carved in an ascending frieze a sequence of seventy-six episodes in the Emperor's wars with the German Barbarians. This technique of sculptural narrative reflected the Roman sense of history, by contrast with the timelessness of fifth-century Greek art, which had sought always to capture those moments when sensuous phenomena became infused with a divine perfection. But the only purpose of such a work was to show what had happened; it conveyed no emotional attitude and suggested no significance. When Roman sculpture turned away from naturalism, moreover, as happened for a period in the second century, especially during the reign of the Greek-loving Hadrian, the usual result was a florid, empty, and wearying ornateness.

Thanks to the eruption of Vesuvius which entombed and embalmed the cities of Pompeii and Herculaneum, we know something of the painting of the early empire. But the art of that section of southern Italy was probably Greek rather than Roman, and was the product of a long evolution of which the earlier stages have been totally lost. Although the Pompeian paintings were commercial products, they appear to have been copied, more or less accurately, from the works of original artists. Their renderings of mythological episodes, rituals from mystery cults, and imaginary buildings, many of them brilliantly colored and delicately executed, have a hauntingly fairy-tale quality that link them with Alexandria rather than with Rome, recalling in tone and mood the poetry of Ovid. They bear witness to the luxury and sophistication of the upper classes and to the divorce of Hellenic culture from actuality. If Trajan's Column was fact unilluminated by spirit, the Pompeian wall-paintings were fantasy that no longer recognized its obligations to reality.

Rome's aesthetic impulse was not strong enough for any wide diffusion, and the farther one went from the traditional centers of civilization, the coarser and cruder the arts and crafts were likely to become. To the western provinces Rome brought only a debased official style, vulgarly representational, which often marked a sharp deterioration from the standards achieved by barbarian society before the Roman conquest. Judging from the evidence of artistic history, Roman rule meant the destruction of vital sensibility and the imposition of a vulgar and brutal uniformity.[5] The Celtic tribes of Britain, for example, had developed a flourishing tradition of abstract art. But "with the Roman conquest" (declares a recent history of Roman Britain) "a rapid and disastrous change comes over the whole spirit of British craftsmanship. In taste, the standards of classical art in its degraded imperial form, and the com-

---

[5] "At the same time as industrial activity was becoming decentralized, the goods produced were gradually simplified and standardized, whether they were produced in large factories or in small shops. The sense of beauty which had been dominant in the industry of the Hellenistic period, and still prevailed in the first century A.D., gradually died out in the second. No new forms were created, no new ornamental principles introduced. The same sterility reigned in the domain of technique. . . . As the demand was for cheap, that is to say, standardized goods, the artisans of the small cities, unlike those of the Greek cities of the archaic period, did not produce original articles, which would have been too expensive to compete with imported wares. They simply reproduced the standardized articles by the methods they had learned in the larger factories." M. Rostovtzeff: *Social and Economic History of the Roman Empire* (Oxford, The Clarendon Press), pp. 166, 168.

mercialized provincial variety of that degredation, begin to dominate the minds of those who set the fashion. In manufacture, mass-
products take the place of individual design and execution. . . .
By the late second century, everything that meets the archaeologist's eye is infected with the uniform and sordid ugliness of drab
Roman-British daylight. . . . On any Roman-British site the impression that constantly haunts the archaeologist, like a bad smell
or a stickiness on the fingers, is that of an ugliness which pervades
the place like a London fog; not merely the common vulgar ugliness of the Roman empire, but a blinding, stupid ugliness that
cannot even rise to the level of that vulgarity." [6]

A civilization is not to be condemned solely because it fails to
produce any important art, but a lack of artistic creativity is likely
to indicate some more general failure of vitality. It is the function of
art to sharpen human perceptions and sensibilities, to communicate
an awareness of the values and significances inherent in human
experience, and thereby to enrich man's understanding and enhance his capacity for enjoyment. That a society has become incapable of original self-expression means that it is deficient both
in the apprehension of reality and in the power of appreciation.
A society without good art is likely to succumb to a pervasive
ennui and sense of futility and oppression, and to turn for stimulation to violent and morally shocking forms of entertainment. Only
a people devoid of aesthetic sensitivity could have developed such
a passion for watching gladiators. The strongest impression conveyed by the art of the early empire is that it was the product of an
immense boredom. This is the simplest explanation for the decline
of Roman civilization and may also be the truest.

[6] R. G. Collingwood and J. N. L.   *lish Settlements*, pp. 249–50.
Myres: *Roman Britain and the Eng-*

10

The End of Hellenism

W hen a society displays the weariness, spiritual inertia, and
flaccidity characteristic of the Helleno-Roman world during
the second century, how can its ideals be transformed and its
energies reinvigorated? How can fatalism be changed into hope,
passive acquiescence into dynamic activity? How is a new beginning possible? The metamorphosis of classical civilization during
the third and fourth centuries is the only example of such a situation
of which we have a full historical record.

Superficially this appears as a period of decay, and this is how it
has traditionally been interpreted. It was indeed marked by civil
wars and barbarian invasions, by a decline of city life and a decrease in the production of wealth. Yet these were symptoms
not only of death, but also of rebirth. What was dying was not
civilization as a whole, but Hellenism, and while the old order was
breaking up, new beliefs and new institutions were taking shape.
In spite of all the external manifestations of disintegration which
filled the third and fourth centuries, this period was incomparably
more creative in art, philosophy, and religion than the two centuries of the principate which had preceded it. What was happening was a revolution of sensibility, the most fundamental and comprehensive in the history of Western man, which expressed itself in
new views of life, new modes of art, and new social forms. The
transformation can be measured by the contrast between the Hagia
Sophia and the Parthenon, between the mosaics of Ravenna and
the Ara Pacis commissioned by Augustus, or between Plotinus'
Enneads or Augustine's *City of God* and the writings of Aristotle

or Cicero. The beginnings of this revolution can be traced back to the period of the principate, before there were any overt symptoms of social decline, and the disorders of the third century should properly be viewed as the consequences rather than the causes of the new spiritual attitude. The traditional Helleno-Roman civilization disintegrated because men had ceased to believe in the values on which it depended.

Western writers have customarily regarded this period as the beginning of the Dark Ages. But the whole concept of a Dark Age reflects a narrowly provincial view of history. It is true that the transformation of society came too late to preserve civilization in the western provinces of the empire. In the fifth century the imperial administration lost control of these areas, and they entered upon a period of slow cultural decline which was not fully arrested for six hundred years. But the eastern Mediterranean witnessed no comparable descent into barbarism. On the contrary, the tradition of culture in its new form was maintained in the Byzantine Empire, which was a direct continuation of that of Rome and which lasted for a thousand years, while such areas as Syria and Egypt, under Arabic rule, soon displayed a new impulse of creativity. Civilization was not obliterated; it receded from the western provinces, where it had been introduced only at a relatively late period and had never established deep roots, but it continued to flourish throughout its original Hellenic and Near Eastern habitats. From these centers, in the course of time, it was again transplanted into western Europe with firmer roots and a greater capacity for growth than during the age of Hellenism.

It is impossible to summarize this cultural revolution by means of any simple formula. In many of its aspects it appears as a regression. In their search for positive values men turned back to earlier religious beliefs and political forms. Revolting against the naturalistic ethos of the Hellenic tradition, they sought salvation by an ascetic repudiation of the world and the flesh, and a mystical union with a transcendent God. Much of the spiritual development of the epoch might be summarized as an affirmation of unity— a unity that in both politics and culture meant a denial of the variety and multiplicity of actual human life. By humanistic standards the Mediterranean world was less enlightened in many ways (though not in all) than the Greece of the classical period. Yet this regression appeared, in the perspective of history, as part of a process of rebirth, preliminary to a new advance. The central factor in the history of the epoch was the rise of Christianity. And while Christianity shared in the regression and has retained strong traces of it throughout its whole later history, it proclaimed a new ethic and a new cosmology that promoted the progress of civilization in all its aspects more effectively and more lastingly than Hellenism had done.

The regression has often been regarded as a process of orientalization by which the values, beliefs, and art forms of the Hellenic tradition were replaced by those of the Near East. Some historians have interpreted the change in ethnic terms, emphasizing the disappearance of the old Greek and Roman aristocratic families and the westward migration of Asiatics. Oriental attitudes are supposed to have been propagated throughout Italy and other provinces by slaves and merchants and other middle-class citizens from Asia Minor and Syria. The extent of this Oriental influence remains, however, an unsettled question. There can be no doubt that the new religious cults originated in the East, but they were largely reinterpreted in Hellenic terms and fused with what was still viable in the Hellenic tradition. The source of the new art styles has been the subject of violent controversy: while one school of thought sees everywhere the influences of Syria, Armenia, Iran, and areas even farther to the east, an opposing group insists that the City of Rome itself was the main center of aesthetic innovation, the whole Near Eastern area being artistically imitative and uncreative.[1] The whole question of origins, however, is not of major significance and can be left in uncertainty. Whether the intellectuals and artists of the empire were borrowing from elsewhere or themselves devising new styles, what is important is that they felt impelled to express a new sensibility. This would not have happened if the traditional Hellenic culture had retained its vitality and its capacity for assimilating alien immigrants and resisting or absorbing foreign influences.

The elements of regression and orientalization were perhaps

---

[1] The case for Oriental influence is argued soberly and moderately in C. R. Morey: *Early Christian Art,* and with obvious exaggeration in the writings of Josef Strzygowski. Emerson H. Swift: *Roman Sources of Christian Art* is a thoroughgoing reply.

most conspicuous in the sphere of political and economic life. The imposing façade of Roman imperialism began to show ominous cracks late in the second century. In the third century the whole system almost collapsed, and in the fourth it was reconstructed along such radically different lines that it no longer bore much resemblance to the city-state society in which it had originated.

The most obvious aspect of the third-century disorders was the dominance of the army. The immediate precipitating factor was the incompetence of Marcus Aurelius' son and successor Commodus (180–193), who was interested mainly in gladiatorial shows and actually liked to perform in the arena. After thirteen years of disorder and civil war, a new dynasty was founded by an African soldier, Septimius Severus. Although Severus professed to be restoring the Augustan system, his rule was based mainly on the support of the army, its spirit being fairly indicated by the advice he is alleged to have given to his sons: "Be united, enrich the soldiers and scorn the rest." The death of the last of the Severi in 235 was followed by thirty years of anarchy. The army, no longer submissive to any civil authority, set up emperors and then murdered them with bewildering rapidity; civil war was almost incessant; and various sections of the empire came under the rule of independent governments. At the same time the western provinces were ravaged by German raiders from across the Rhine, while Syria and Asia Minor were threatened by a revival of Iranian power under the Sassanid kings, who absorbed the Parthian kingdom and aspired to restore the glories of the Achaemenids. These disasters were accompanied by economic decay. The demands of the army resulted in crushing taxation and a ruinous inflation that destroyed the prosperity of the cities, while trade and industry were also disrupted by the wars and barbarian raids. The growth of city life, which had proceeded with few interruptions for over a thousand years, was now sharply reversed, especially in the western provinces, and there was widespread urban depopulation. Meanwhile, the wealthy landowners began to assume independent powers for the protection of their estates and their tenants—a development that marked the beginning of the feudalism that was to pervade western Europe for the next thousand years.

Ultimately order and unity were re-established by a series of soldier emperors from Illyricum and other Balkan provinces. The reorganization was completed by two remarkable statesmen, Diocletian (287–305) and Constantine (312–337), whose reforms maintained stability through most of the fourth century. The new empire, however, was based on Oriental rather than Helleno-Roman principles of legitimacy. No longer pretending to be merely the first citizen of the Roman republic, the emperor now claimed to be responsible to God alone, dramatizing his supremacy by surrounding himself with ritualistic splendors largely copied from the court of the Sassanids. Under this autocratic regime, the citizens of the empire no longer enjoyed the same civil rights as under the principate. In order to support the military and bureaucratic hierarchies, urban citizens continued to be subjected to crushing taxation, to such an extent that many of them began to fly to the country and even to take refuge among the barbarians. The government then set out to maintain tax-collections and essential economic services by decreeing an increasing number of urban occupations to be hereditary; men were compelled to follow the same trades or professions as their fathers and were prohibited from changing their places of residence, thus becoming the slaves of the state. Thus the new empire finally brought to an end freedoms that had first developed in the early Greek cities, and society began to crystallize into castes.

These changes can be regarded as a kind of social revolution. The decisive element in the situation was the transfer of power to the army from the wealthy bourgeois and administrative groups that had controlled the empire under the principate. The third-century army, however, including the officers, was composed mainly of men of peasant stock, most of whom came from the most backward and least Hellenized provinces of the empire, and in consequence had little understanding of, or sympathy with, the traditions of classical civilization. The legislation of the third- and fourth-century emperors reflected their peasant and military backgrounds. Such men had no compunction about ending the autonomy of the cities, establishing strict controls over industry and commerce, and taxing the wealthy bourgeoisie virtually out of existence. These policies constituted not only an economic but also a cultural attack on classical civilization, for Hellenism had always been rooted in the autonomous city; if the emperors had deliberately set out to destroy the social basis of Hellenism, they could not have accomplished this objective more fully and effectively.[2]

The ultimate causes of such a transformation can only have been cultural and spiritual. No dominant minority ever loses power as long as it retains the spiritual vitality and the faith in principles of social order by which its leadership is rationalized and justified. Why did the beneficiaries of classical civilization fail to display the energy and public spirit needed for its preservation? Why were the peasant soldiers of the third century, unlike those who had served under Julius Caesar and Augustus, unwilling to support traditional institutions? The Hellenism of the principate was no longer a faith capable of evoking any dynamic loyalty and enthusiasm. In the words of Pope Gregory, it had withered in men's hearts.[3]

The military emperors of the third century had, of course, no conscious intention of inaugurating a revolution. Although some of them displayed an outspoken contempt for the rich civilian bourgeoisie, their fiscal and economic policies were determined simply by the pressure of necessity, the main factor being the need for money with which to pacify the army. The ultimate result was by no means social equality; the disintegration of Roman rule in the western provinces left the wealthy landowners with increased powers, while in the east there developed a caste system dominated by a new hereditary bureaucracy. Yet it is significant that Roman law now began to show more concern for the poorer classes. The reigns of the Severi constituted one of the most fruitful periods of Roman jurisdiction, being notable for the reforms of such jurists as Papinian, Ulpian, and Paulus (the first two of whom were Asiatics). The chief effect of their work was to give greater protection to debtors at the expense of creditors, and to peasants and craftsmen at the expense of landlords and employers. Of similar

---

[2] This interpretation of the decline and revival of the empire is largely based on M. Rostovtzoff: *Social and Economic History of the Roman Empire.*

[3] Some historians have stressed biological rather than institutional factors, indulging in speculation (not supported by adequate evidence) about a possible decline in soil fertility or about the spread of malaria, or emphasizing the onset of several destructive pestilences, which apparently caused a sharp decline in population. But a vigorous society can always take such material catastrophes in its stride and make a rapid recovery, as western Europe did after the Black Death of the later Middle Ages and again after the two wars of the twentieth century.

significance was the law of 212, promulgated by Septimius' son Caracalla, which extended full Roman citizenship rights to the whole population. These humanitarian and leveling tendencies continued under the later empire. The late Roman and Byzantine states, while restricting individual freedom, showed much more responsibility than the principate for the welfare of the poor and unfortunate. The strongest expression of this new attitude was, of course, the ethical teaching of Christianity.

The most striking new tendency, however, was the religious reverence for the person of the emperor. His actual responsibilities were probably little greater than during the principate, but the accompanying attitudes were now Oriental rather than Helleno-Roman. Republicanism was obviously dead, having survived only as an academic pretense since the time of the first Caesar, and in their search for a legitimate source of power men regressed to the adoration of a divinely appointed autocrat. In spite of occasional rebellions and assassinations, this principle proved effective in maintaining unity, as was demonstrated throughout the long history of the Byzantine Empire. In order fully to understand the exaltation of the emperor, one must see it as one aspect of a more general affirmation of unity. The new autocracy paralleled and echoed the growth of monotheism in religion. The rule of the emperors was, in fact, regularly compared with that of God over the universe, and their public monuments and statues were infused with a spirit of religious reverence, the same techniques being employed in the portrayal of divine figures and their earthly representatives. Did men come to believe in divine oneness because they felt a necessity to centralize all political authority in a single superman, or did they come to believe in political autocracy because of their growing sense of the oneness of the cosmos? One can affirm only that religious and political thinking were closely connected, being products of the same underlying sensibility.

The whole revolution of sensibility was reflected in the transformation of the visual arts, which registered a sharp break with Helleno-Roman naturalism. Third- and fourth-century portrayals of the human figure appeared crude and clumsy when compared with those of earlier periods, but this was not because of a mere decrease in technical skill; artists were trying to find ways of conveying a different sense of reality. The new attitude finally found a fully adequate expression in the mosaics of the early Byzantine period. In architecture there was no regression at all, but a continuous progress from the building of the early Roman Empire to the climax and consummation of the early Byzantine spirit in the Hagia Sophia of the sixth century. If one were to consider simply the history of architectural styles in the main centers of civilization, the later empire would appear as a time not of decay and breakdown, but of uninterrupted development.

The change in aesthetic attitudes antedated the political changes, being already implied in the Column of Marcus Aurelius. The contrast between this Column and that of Trajan, erected some seventy or eighty years earlier, suggests that the transformation of human attitudes was already in process long before it received conceptual formulation or produced overt political consequence. Both Columns commemorated wars with German barbarians, but whereas the Trajanic sculptor was concerned simply to portray with a masterful and unemotional realism what had actually happened, his successor sought to give events a transcendental significance. On Trajan's Column the Emperor is shown participating with his troops in battle actions, and the victory of the Romans is assumed as natural; the Column of Marcus Aurelius, on the other hand, magnifies the figure of the Emperor, emphasizes the horrors of war and the miraculous rainstorm to which the Romans attributed their victory, and shows tendencies toward frontalism, immobility, and abstractionism in the presentation of groups. Art was beginning to move from naturalism to expressionism, and what it expressed foreshadowed both the revival of religious values and beliefs and the adoration for the emperor as the symbol of divine unity.

These tendencies were carried farther in the Arch of Severus, and may perhaps be said to have reached their goal in some of the reliefs on the Arch of Constantine, in spite of their unusually crude and hasty workmanship. In these and other late Roman sculptures most of the figures were shown frontally, without movement and with considerable distortion, and were isolated from each other, the central image of the emperor being the only unifying element. Constantine, no longer sharing the activities of his troops as in the portrayals of Trajan, became a divine form dominating the composition and giving his protection to the rows of grotesque mannequins ranged beside him. Thus, meaning and unity were no longer inherent in natural scenes and actions, as in the Helleno-Roman tradition, but could be found only by relating natural objects to a static and transcendental power. The same spirit was conveyed in the late Roman portrait busts and, perhaps even more clearly, in the art of Oriental outposts of the Helleno-Roman world like Dura on the Euphrates and the Syrian frontier city of Palmyra. Rejecting both the Greek preoccupation with physical beauty and the Roman preference for realistic portraiture, sculptors now attempted to express religious values by distorting the human figure, especially by enlarging the head and the pupils of the eyes and shrinking the body, and giving the face an expression of solemn concentration. The statues of some of the later emperors, it has been said, had "the remoteness, the intensity, the immutability of cult images." [4] Even more expressive of the new sensibility were some of the somber and ascetic faces of third-century Palmyra, in which the carving of the mouth seemed almost a deliberate repudiation of the smile that the Greeks had given to their portrayals of the Olympians.[5]

In architecture, the new attitudes found expression not in a departure from the styles of the principate, but in a further development of them. Roman builders and engineers had already made revolutionary innovations that could be adapted to the purpose of

---

[4] Roger Hinks: *Carolingian Art,* p. 37.

[5] "Thus over the dying empire the gods were resuming their indomitable sway, and what was dying with the empire was pagan art. Those smiling faces of Attica and Alexandria, those resolute faces of the Capitol, were as out of keeping with the desert, the forests and the Catacombs—with that oriental night-world of Blood and doom-fraught stars—as Plutarch was with Saint Augustine. For art was now seeking to break away from the human as obstinately as in Greece it had sought to attain the human. Smiles and movement disappeared; whatever moves—all that is fleeting—was no longer deemed worthy of the sculptor's art. The monstrous, elemental forms dear to the Orient and the nomads were reappearing; yet neither the un-moving, nor the inhuman was to be transmuted into the eternal without a struggle. Gallo-Roman art felt its way cautiously towards a break with Rome, while that of pre-Islamic Arabia, from the Druse country to Petra and perhaps to Sheba, abolished the Roman face with a frenzy soon to be that of the iconoclasts; replacing the nose by a trapezoid, and the mouth by a straight line. Why assume that the Zadkine before his time who carved such faces was incapable of making the nose less flat and of giving the lips their natural curves? The technique of realism was no more unknown to him than it is to modern artists; but like them he rejected it, though for different reasons." André Malraux: *The Voices of Silence,* translated by Stuart Gilbert (Doubleday and Co.), pp. 186–7.

the new religious consciousness. Exploring the potentialities of the vault and the dome, they had discovered how to produce new aesthetic experiences through the organization of inner space. A Greek temple had been planned primarily with a view to the external appearance, and its relation to the locality had always been an integral part of the aesthetic effect. But in the domed structures of the early empire, of which the second-century Pantheon in Rome was the most striking example, the exterior was unimportant, the dome often being scarcely visible from outside, and the whole purpose of the design was to create a strong internal effect. On entering the building the observer had the sensation of being abstracted from his environment and becoming absorbed into a new and different totality sharply separated from normal experience. This shaping of inner space, which from the aesthetic viewpoint represented perhaps the most significant new development in the entire history of architecture, could easily become a medium for conveying the sense of transcendent religious realities.

The Pantheon was a transitional building appropriate to the spirit of the principate. Bounded simply by a single round shell lit from a hole at the top, its inner space was clearly defined and brightly illuminated, so that the whole impression remained sensuous and concrete rather than mystical and transcendental. Later builders, however, began to work out complicated lighting effects, combined with the lavish use of brilliantly colored marbles and mosaics, which gave an impression of infinite vistas and vast complexity. The observer had a feeling both of his own individual insignificance and of immersion into a form that transcended spatial limitations and was beyond human understanding. This spirit was already apparent in the larger monuments of late Roman paganism, such as the Baths of Caracalla, the Baths of Diocletian, and the Temple of Minerva Medica. It was carried farther in the churches built by the early Christian emperors, especially in the Basilica of Constantine at Rome.

This new sensibility eventually found a full expression in a new religion that was both a summation of the tendencies of the age and an affirmation of new principles. But before the triumph of Christianity the traditional cults were being reinterpreted and transformed into vehicles for the new attitudes. The paganism of the third century had much more in common with its Christian competitor than with the religion of classical Greece and republican ·Rome.

Under the later empire, virtually all educated pagans believed in some form of monotheism and tried to reconcile this with the traditional myths and rituals by interpreting them allegorically. Between the divine unity and earthly multiplicity, however, there was a great gulf, and this was bridged by postulating the existence of inferior spirits emanating from God. Like Plutarch, many pagans made use of this theory of emanations in order to preserve the belief in the Olympians, though they rejected all the morally discreditable stories traditionally told about them. The theory was also invoked to justify the star-worship and the astrological determinism associated with it, perhaps the most widely prevalent cult of the imperial period.

Even more characteristic of the age was its pessimistic and ascetic repudiation of the natural world. Matter was now widely regarded as inherently evil. The soul of man was a fragment of divinity imprisoned in a corporeal envelope and could find salvation only in purification from fleshy taints and reabsorption into the divine matrix. For the more extreme ascetics of the later empire, sensuous enjoyment in all its forms, which Greece had once accepted as the gift of the Olympians, had become repellent, seemingly evoking a nausea that was almost physiological. Demanding a new way of life, such men apparently felt impelled to cleanse themselves of every trace of Hellenism by a total rejection of all that it had represented.

Outside the Christian Church, the highest expressions of the new attitude were to be found in revivals of the anti-naturalistic forms of Greek philosophy. Pythagoreanism and Platonism gave support to both the monotheism and the asceticism of the age. Less sophisticated persons looked for some divinely guided savior who would hold the evil of the world at bay and assure them of salvation. This resulted in the spread of the Oriental mystery religions, which were incorporated into the traditional paganism with little conflict or sense of incompatibility. The cults of Isis and Cybele had largely permeated the urban population of the Hellenistic world, especially the women, even before the Roman conquest. Along with a new cult originating in Asia Minor and derived indirectly from the

Zoroastrian dualism of Iran, that of Mithra, they began to spread to the western provinces during the second and third centuries. Mithraism, a masculine creed preaching a virile moral discipline, had an especially strong appeal to the peasant soldiers who guarded the frontiers of the empire. It is significant that the Severi, the real founders of the later empire, were the first emperors to break with the Roman traditionalism of Augustus and give official approval to the worship of these Oriental deities.

As far as we know, however, none of the new cults had much intellectual content or gave much stimulus to the arts. And in spite of their common emphasis on the repudiation of nature, all these systems of belief embodied elements of magic and thaumaturgy and other remnants of man's primitive mentality. Although the ascetic was dedicated to the contempt of worldly prosperity in all its forms, he was still the repository of a numinous power that could be exerted for the remedying of earthly ills. With the decay of the Hellenic confidence in rational thought, the whole primeval and Near Eastern heritage began to resume its sway over the human mind. The belief in magic and miracle, in prophetic inspiration and mystical union with divine powers, which had never disappeared from Hellenic society even during its most rationalistic periods, now became stronger and more nearly universal.

Perhaps the most characteristic document of the third-century mentality was the life of Apollonius of Tyana, written by the Greek Philostratus at the request of the Syrian wife of the Emperor Septimus Severus. According to his biographer, Apollonius was born in Asia Minor during the reign of Tiberius and became a follower of Pythagoras. Devoting himself from boyhood to ascetic practices, he remained celibate, abstained from meat and wine, never cut his hair or beard, and once spent five years without speaking. Eager to increase his knowledge of divine things, he traveled to India in order to learn the secrets of Brahmans, and subsequently visited Egypt, where already—even before the advent of Christian monasticism—a number of ascetics were living as hermits in the desert. Apollonius' life was spent in preaching, casting out devils, and performing other magical cures in different parts of the Roman Empire, and also in several acrimonious conflicts with rival sages and former disciples. Rebuking both Nero and Domitian for their misdeeds, he was imprisoned by both emperors, but was able to escape execution by making use of his miraculous powers. Apparently he regarded himself as a philosopher and a Hellenist and felt no need to divorce himself from the traditional religion, though he repudiated some of its rituals and beliefs, especially animal sacrifice; yet the whole tenor of his life, as reported by Philostratus, was utterly un-Hellenic. Some of his third-century admirers used his career as an argument against Christianity, claiming that his achievements were fully as remarkable as those attributed to Jesus. But Philostratus' biography, though a fascinating story of wanderings in different countries, does not show that he had any particular ethical or theological insights, most of the wise sayings recorded of him being remarkably platitudinous.[6]

One figure rose superior to the regression into primitive magic and thaumaturgy and gave expression to the new sensibility in its purest and most concentrated form. This was Plotinus, the chief spokesman of Neo-Platonism, who was born in Egypt in 205 and studied philosophy there, but spent most of his mature life in Rome. He ranks both as the last great philosopher of the Hellenic tradition and as the first great exponent of the mystical consciousness of the new era.

Gathering together all the threads of Greek philosophical idealism as represented by Pythagoras, Parmenides, and Plato, and rejecting everything in their thought that reflected the varied activities and tumultuous political conflicts of the fifth-century polis, Plotinus taught that men could find fulfillment only by turning away from the multiplicity of the world of sensuous experience as evil and unreal and becoming absorbed in the divine unity. God was the One, and this Oneness was so far above all experience that it was impossible to define it. "The One is, in truth, beyond all statement; whatever you say would limit it." "The Absolute is none of the things of which it is the source; its nature is that nothing can be affirmed of it—not existence, not essence, not life— It transcends all this." From this One emanated a divine mind and a divine spirit—a conception that influenced the Christian doctrine

---

[6] "To tell a lie is base, to tell the truth is noble." "Life is short for the man who does well, but for him that is unlucky it is long." "Most men are as apt to palliate their own offenses, as they are to condemn them in other people" (*Epistles* of Apollonius, translated by F. C. Conybeare, 83, 85, 88). These are typical.

of the Trinity. All the order, beauty, and goodness of the universe were derived from the One, while evil was simply its absence and hence could be defined as not-being. "If evil exists at all, it must be situated in the realm of non-being. By this non-being we are not to understand something that simply does not exist, but only something of an utterly different order from Authentic Being. Some conception of it would be reached by thinking of measurelessness as opposed to measure, the unshaped against a shaping principle, the ever-needing against the self-sufficing; while whatever participates in it and resembles it becomes evil, though not to the point of being evil absolute." In some sense, matter might be regarded as the principle of evil: "the soul becomes ugly by sinking itself into the alien, by a descent into body, into matter." Yet the matter of Plotinus had no positive existence and was an indefinable something that acquired reality only in so far as it acquired form and measure through the communication of divine being. From this conception of the universe, Plotinus derived an ethic that was uncompromisingly mystical and ascetic. The human soul was a fragment of the divine being, and therefore actually a part of God; it must put away all earthly interests and affections and find its way back to its source. "In this world itself, all is best when human interests and the memory of them have been put out of the way." "Passing on the upward way all that is other than God, each in the solitude of himself shall behold that solitary-dwelling Existence, the Apart, the Unmingled, the Pure, That from which all things depend, towards which all look, the Source of Life, of Intellection and of Being." "This is the life of Gods and of godlike and blessed men—liberation from the alien that besets us here, a life taking no pleasure in the things of earth,—a flight of the alone to the Alone." [7]

Displaying little interest in political, social, and scientific problems, Plotinus was more limited in scope than his master Plato; but he was a more disinterested philosopher, with a purer devotion to the truth, being refreshingly free from the reactionary political attitudes and dubious sexual emotions that had determined so much of Plato's thinking. Unlike Plato, moreover, he deduced his basic conceptions not from processes of intellectual argument,

[7] *Enneads,* translated by Stephen MacKenna, V, iii, 13; III, viii, 10; I, viii, 3; I, vi, 5; IV, iii, 32; I, vi, 7; VI, ix, 11.

but from an immediate personal experience which he attributed to the presence of God. Eliminating all desires, shutting out all thoughts and images of the material world, and sinking into the depths of his inner self, he felt himself united with the divine power that pervaded the entire universe. "Many times it has happened," he declared; "lifted out of the body into myself; becoming external to all other things; beholding a marvellous beauty; then, more than ever, assured of community with the loftiest order; living the noblest life, acquiring identity with the Divine; poised above whatsoever is less than the Supreme." [8] On four occasions, according to his biographer Porphyry, he reached the culminating and final stage of complete absorption into the divine Oneness. This mystical conviction was reflected in the sustained tone of spiritual ecstasy and exaltation which pervaded the *Enneads*.

No earlier Hellenic thinker appears to have described religious experience in these terms (how far Plotinus may have been influenced by Oriental thought is an unsettled question). Various emotional states and ethical imperatives had been attributed to divine influence, but the belief in the possibility of union with the godhead first entered the Western cultural tradition with Plotinus. All later Western mysticism has conformed substantially with Plotinus' description, in spite of the insistence of Christian theologians that the soul of man is a separate individual entity and therefore incapable of actual absorption into the divine being. During the past seventeen hundred years a long series of ecstatics, both Christian and Mohammedan, Catholic and Protestant, have given similar accounts of how they achieved communion with God and of the deep unshakable sense of peace, harmony, and spiritual security resulting from it. The emotional value of the experience is proved by its practical effects in the lives of mystics. But how far it can be regarded not only as a source of emotional strength but also as a means of valid knowledge either about man's ultimate being or about the nature of the universe in which he lives is a different and more debatable question. Perhaps the conviction of the mystics can be cited as an argument for believing in a spiritual reality underlying material appearances and in an ultimate harmony between human aspirations and the

---

[8] *Enneads,* IV, viii, 1.

external world, but any more detailed theological interpretations become highly speculative and are likely to vary in different cultural climates. Christians and Mohammedans have found in mysticism supports for their particular beliefs, while the Nirvana of Buddhism appears to be a similar experience divorced from theological doctrines of any kind and (at least in its original form) accompanied by a denial both of God and of human immortality.

Plotinus found in mysticism support for his belief in the Oneness of All. "This All is one universally comprehensive living being, encircling all the living beings within it, and having a soul, one Soul which extends to all its members; every separate thing is an integral part of this All by belonging to that total material fabric, while in so far as it has participation in the All-Soul, it possesses spiritual membership as well. Each several thing is affected none the less by all else in virtue of the common participation in All. This One-All, therefore, is a sympathetic total and stands as one living being." [9] Undoubtedly the belief in some kind of unity is common to all forms of mysticism, but Plotinus' extreme insistence on the Oneness of everything and his denial that the individual soul had any independent existence reflected the sensibility of the third-century empire, being paralleled in the transformation of the visual arts and closely related to political developments. His philosophy, in fact, can be regarded as a theological reflection of the growth of the imperial autocracy and the decline of individual freedom, just as his aesthetic theory, with its definition of beauty as formal unity emanating from the divine mind and its preference for abstract rather than representational art, corresponded to the new trends in the visual arts.[1] This was manifested, indeed, in Plotinus' occasional references to earthly monarchy as a symbol of divinity. "Before the great King in his progress, there comes first a minor train," he declared, speaking of how nature reflected the divine presence; "then rank by rank the greater and more exalted, closer to the king the kinglier; next

---

[9] *Enneads,* IV, iv, 32.

[1] Plotinus regarded architecture and music as the highest arts because they were the most abstract (*Enneads,* V, ix, 11). He also gave a philosophical justification to the changes in portraiture: "Why are the most living portraits the most beautiful, even if the others happen to be more symmetric? Why is the living ugly more attractive than the sculptured handsome?—Because there is soul there—because there is some glow of the light of the Good" (*Enneads,* VI, vii, 22).

his own honored company, until, last among these grandeurs, suddenly appears the Supreme Monarch Himself, and all prostrate
themselves and do Him reverence." In other passages monarchy
becomes symbolic of human virtue. "In the lowest human type
the man is a compost calling to mind some inferior political organization; in the commonplace man we have a citizenship in which
some better section sways a demotic constitution not out of control; in the superior type the life is aristocratic, emancipated from
what is base in humanity and tractable to the better; in the finest
type, where the man has brought himself to detachment, the ruler
is one only, and from this master principle order is imposed on
the rest." [2]

Ever since the first development of rationalistic thinking in the
sixth and fifth centuries B.C., Hellenism had been struggling with
man's perennial problem of unity and multiplicity. How could the
necessary moral unity of society be reconciled with the claim of
the individual to freedom of thought and action? How could a
political universalism be created which would transcend, without
destroying, the particularistic loyalties clustered around the self-
governing polis? Man can answer such questions only through
myths and symbols, affirming imaginative concepts that go beyond
rationalistic verification. But the religion of ancient Greece was
incapable of the necessary degree of spiritualization; of all its intellectual leaders, Aeschylus alone had seriously tried to transform
the cult of the Olympians into a vehicle for the expression of
higher political and moral ideals. Deriving little spiritual sustenance
from its official religion, and unable to find a rationalistic answer
to its dilemmas, the Greek world had finally been unified by force,
applied first by the Hellenistic monarchies and more successfully
by the pragmatic Romans. The spiritual death that is the inevitable
result of a force inspired by no positive idealism had been delayed
by the Augustan compromise, with its attempt to make use of the
traditional city-state ethos for the purposes of the new imperialism,
but had finally become manifest in the third century. Now thinkers
were again in search of a principle of spiritual unity, but were
tempted to find it in a total denial of individualism, a total submergence in the One-All of universalism. Plotinus believed in a

---

[2] *Enneads*, V, v, 3; IV, iv, 17.

harmony of freedom and order, but in his philosophy man could find genuine freedom only by suppressing all his desires and denying his own separate identity. The evil that had befallen human beings had its source "in self-will, in the entry into birth, in the desire for self-ownership." True freedom belonged only "to those who, through the activities of Mind, live above the states of the body. . . . The unembodied is the free. . . . Soul becomes free when, through Divine Mind, it strives unimpeded towards the Good; what it does in that spirit is its free act; Divine Mind is free in its own right." Only God, in other words, was free, the freedom demanded by human beings being an illusion. Thus, the Hellenic world seemed to be turning toward an Oriental quietism.[3]

The Neo-Platonic school retained its vitality for two hundred years, though its later spokesmen, such as Iamblichus and Proclus, were markedly less rational than Plotinus and combined their mysticism with a vivid belief in magic and in subordinate spiritual beings emanating from God and capable of influencing human life for both good and evil. But the significance of Plotinus cannot be measured by the number of his professed disciples. His philosophy reflected and summarized the dominant spiritual tendencies of the later empire and represented a view of life that continued to pervade the culture of the Western world for many centuries to come.

Meanwhile, a radically new view both of God and of man, associated with a new mythology and a new ethic, had been steadily gaining ground. Christianity was deeply influenced by the other religions and philosophies of the later empire, displaying a similar ascetic bias and contempt for physical welfare, a similar emphasis on a mystical oneness in which concrete objects lost all intrinsic meaning and value, a similar belief in magic and miracle. The religion that triumphed under Constantine was, in fact, perhaps closer to the *Enneads* than to the Gospel; and it was not until the Middle Ages, or even later, that men began to rediscover the full significance of its original doctrines. Yet Christianity never denied the separate existence of the individual soul, which was not a part of God but had been created by him as an independent being and endowed—at least initially—with free will; and it never taught that the physical world was essentially evil, in spite of its corruption,

---

[3] *Enneads,* V, v, 1; VI, viii, 4–7.

but declared that the human body and all other material things were capable of regeneration. Although these doctrines were for a long time overlaid by attitudes derived from Neo-Platonism and the mystery cults, Christian theology represented in its essence a new attempt, based on new mythical affirmations, to reconcile the universal with the particular, the order of the whole with the freedom of its individual members.

13. *a. Gravestone from Palmyra. The sculpture of this third-century Syrian frontier kingdom is infused with a spirit of
religious solemnity.*

b. Head of the Emperor Constantine.

*c. Relief from the Arch of Constantine. The Emperor (whose head has not
survived) is shown distributing money. The contrast in style and subject
matter with earlier reliefs illustrates the whole transformation of Heleno-
Roman society.*

14. *a. The Hagia Sophia, Constantinople, completed in 537. The minarets were added after the Mohammedan conquest.*

b. Painting from the catacomb of Pietro e Marcellino, Rome. Dating from the third century, this specimen of early Christian art shows Christ as the Good Shepherd, four believers in attitudes of prayer, and four scenes from the story of Jonah.

c. The Colossus of Barletta. This represents an emperor of the late fourth or early fifth century, possibly Valentinian or Marcian.

PART IV

CHRISTIANITY

The source of a new view of life could be found only among a group that had not been assimilated into Helleno-Roman culture. Such a group was the Jews, who, in spite of their absorption into the Roman Empire, had preserved their own special religious tradition. Christianity had its roots in the ethical monotheism and the Messianic expectation of Judaism. It began as an obscure Jewish sect, and only gradually broke its connections with the Jewish community and became transformed into a gentile religion.

Christianity grew and finally achieved dominance over pagan philosophy because it offered both a more optimistic and a more plausible interpretation of human life, being founded not on a body of ideas but on a personality and an experience. The man Jesus, who had actually lived under the early empire (A.D. 29 being the most probable date for the crucifixion), was regarded as a revelation of divinity and as a model of behavior. To become a Christian meant to undergo an emotional transformation centered in trust in Jesus Christ and in a resolution to imitate him. Christianity was based not on theory, but on faith—in other words, on affirmations that transcended human reason; and this faith resulted in the reorganization of the believer's whole personality and the adoption of new ways of behavior and new ethical responses. In the course of time Christianity acquired a body of theological dogmas, but these originated as attempts to explain the Christian experience and way of life. The transformation of the personality was primary; the theological rationalizations were derivative and not always adequate or convincing.

By the standards of Hellenic philosophy, the affirmations of the Christian gospel appeared to be paradoxical and rationally untenable. In particular, Christianity affirmed that man and God had been united in the person of Jesus and that, while God was omnipotent, man was nevertheless endowed with freedom. Proceeding from these affirmations as basic postulates, Christianity went on to create a new view of life presenting a way out of the impasse in which Hellenism had ended. It declared that man was morally responsible for his own destiny, that the whole of human nature was capable of regeneration, and that human society was progressing toward a final Messianic culmination. This confidence in humanity was confirmed in the personal experience of Christian converts and validated by their behavior.

373

In the course of time Christian thought absorbed much of the Hellenic philosophic tradition, but the differences between Christianity and the Hellenism of the empire were sharp and fundamental. They differed in their conceptions of good and evil, of the nature of God, and of the nature of man.

According to Platonic and post-Platonic philosophy, the source of all evil and imperfection was matter, which could never be perfectly shaped and molded by the ideal forms. This meant that evil was an inherent element in the universe. Man was not morally responsible for it: his essential self, being a spark of the divine spirit, was intrinsically good. On the other hand, he could not expect to overcome it, but could hope only to escape from it through union with God after death. The ideal forms belonged to a spiritual and eternal world, and there was therefore no meaning in the processes of history. This repudiation of human responsibility was accompanied by a general tendency toward fatalism, all events being supposedly predetermined by the workings of fortune or destiny or the movements of the stars. Such a view of life denied all possibility of social or political progress, and could result only in a hopeless resignation to the inevitable movement of events. The wise man must cultivate impassivity and learn to endure whatever his destiny had decreed, meanwhile looking forward to being released by death from the trammels of matter.

By contrast with this fatalistic pessimism, the Christian gospel affirmed human freedom and human responsibility. The whole material world, having been created by a beneficent God, had originally been not evil, but good. Man himself was the author of evil, having made a wrong use of the power of choice with which his Creator had endowed him. Instead of subordinating self-interest to the good of the whole, he had preferred to assert his own egoism, and this initial act of rebellion had caused the partial corruption of the material world. Thus, evil consisted not of matter, but of sin, and its source was the human will, which had misused its God-given freedom. But while this meant that man must carry a heavy burden of guilt, it also meant that by reversing his original error he could bring about the regeneration both of himself and of the world.

This doctrine of freedom was combined with the Jewish belief in divine omnipotence and, in later theology, with the Hellenic concept of an order of nature, so that Christianity embodied a central paradox incapable of intellectual clarification. Logically, it was impossible to reconcile human responsibility with God's government of the world, man's freedom of choice with natural law; but Christianity boldly affirmed that the truth transcended logic, and never lost its grasp of both horns of this intellectual dilemma. Implicit in all Christian thinking was a new conception of the divine will and hence of the meaning of history. God had created man and endowed him with freedom because he desired a voluntary obedience rather than the submission of automata; this had entailed the possibility of disobedience as a necessary consequence. In spite of its emphasis on human guilt, Christianity gave man a higher place in the universe than any previous religion, declaring that the realization of human freedom was the purpose of the whole historic process.

The Christian view of God was in even sharper contrast with Hellenic beliefs. For Hellenism the gods had always been free from sufferings and imperfections; as immortal creatures they had embodied the euphoria and impassivity that men could feel only at brief intervals and could never wholly achieve. To suggest that the supreme being could feel pity for men and women to the extent of putting aside his immortal nature and himself experiencing all their sufferings would have seemed to any Hellenic poet or philosopher a blasphemous denial of the dignity of the godhead. Christianity, on the other hand, presented the paradox of a God who had endured human labors and human sorrows and had actually endured the most painful and ignominious of human deaths. Jesus had felt hunger and weariness, fear and disappointment; and in the shortest and most pregnant sentence in the gospels was described as weeping for the death of a friend. Because men were free, they could be induced to obey the divine will only by persuasion, not by force; and God had therefore put on human flesh in order to regenerate them by the influence of his example and by himself paying the penalty for their misdeeds. According to Christian theology, Jesus was both wholly human and wholly divine, representing both God's love for man and man's potential deification and thereby giving a profound cosmic significance to the whole of human experience.

From this cosmology Christianity deduced a new conception of human destiny. According to Hellenic philosophy, man consisted of form and matter, or of a divine spark imprisoned in a body, which meant that he had no separate individuality and could look forward after death to reabsorption into the One-All. For Christianity, on the other hand, salvation consisted in the regeneration of the whole personality, body as well as spirit. Whereas Hellenism had believed in the immortality of the soul, Christianity promised the resurrection of the flesh. In the literal meaning that the early Christians attached to it, the doctrine of the resurrection was, of course, incompatible with any scientific understanding of nature, but as symbol and myth it was of immense importance because it conveyed the belief that every part of human nature, body as well as soul, was potentially good and could be restored to its original perfection. According to the Christian mythology, history was moving toward a final Messianic kingdom in which this perfection would be fully realized in society as well as in individuals, the order and harmony of the whole being combined with the freedom of the members. The unifying principle would be love, the love of men for God and for each other, and this became the foundation of Christian ethics. Whereas pagan morality had upheld the negative quality of impassivity as its highest ideal and had regarded pity as a weakness, the Christian showed a self-abnegating sympathy and charity for the sufferings of others.

By promising the total regeneration of human nature, Christianity transformed not only man's attitude toward the universe, but also his attitude toward himself. Pagan philosophy had no true concept of human personality; man's body after death would return to the elements, while his soul would be absorbed into divinity. For Christianity, however, each man was endowed with a separate individual existence both in this life and in the next. And whereas the pagan philosopher had assumed a role of impassivity and tried to suppress disturbing aspects of his personality, the Christian believed that true virtue meant the reintegration of the whole self and would express itself in spontaneous and positive love. The sense of sin and the consequent belief in the reality of hell were the most obvious features of the new Christian sensibility. The goal of Hellenic ethical philosophy had been human happiness, to be achieved by resignation to the decrees of fate, but Christianity emphasized man's obligations to his divine Father and Creator and his inevitable failure to fulfill those obligations. This was perhaps the sharpest distinction between the pagan and the Christian character. But the moral anxieties and soul-searchings induced by the Christian sensibility were the necessary accompaniments of its more elevated view of human potentialities. The result was that man, for the first time, began to look at himself as a totality, recognizing that he was sinful, but encouraged by this very recognition to a comprehensive self-examination from which nothing, however shameful, should be excluded. In the autobiographical literature of early Christianity we find complete human beings portrayed with a frankness and sincerity that had been impossible for paganism. The confessions of Marcus Aurelius, in spite of his moral earnestness and sensitivity, presented a series of noble poses; those of St. Augustine portrayed a man.

Thus, the essence of Christianity was a new affirmation—according to Christian believers, a new religious revelation—which promised to revolutionize every aspect of human life. But no new belief can become established unless it can appeal to habitual attitudes and expectations, and the new intuitions of Christianity were presented in a partially traditional framework and linked with some of man's oldest thought-patterns. Initially, in the teaching of Jesus and the apostles, the Christian gospel was associated with the Jewish Messianic expectation, which was believed to be on the verge of literal fulfillment. When it was adopted by gentile converts it became connected with ceremonies and myths that had originated long before the beginning of civilization and had been preserved in pagan religious cults. The central act of worship of the Christian community recalled the ritual of eating the god which had started among the paleolithic hunters; the crucifixion and resurrection of Jesus paralleled the death and rebirth of the vegetation deity in neolithic fertility rituals. Thus, the new religion was able to assimilate and transmit much of mankind's previous psychic experience, giving fulfillment in more spiritual forms to some of man's oldest and deepest wishes and expectations. Christians themselves were embarrassed by the parallels between paganism and their own religion, and found it necessary to argue that the devil had obtained foreknowledge of Christian practices and communicated it to his own adherents in order to confuse men's minds. For, unlike the pagan cults with which it was in competition, the

Church refused to concede any validity whatever to other forms of belief, insisting that its own system alone was true and that all others were forms of devil-worship. Yet if, as Christians believed, the incarnation of Jesus Christ was the central event upon which the whole meaning and purpose of history depended, then one would expect to find numerous foreshadowings of Christianity in earlier rituals and beliefs. And although Christianity may have borrowed from the pagan heritage, it borrowed only what it could integrate with its own basic doctrines and could profitably absorb and make use of. All its borrowings acquired new meanings in the new Christian synthesis.

Much more important in the early evolution of Christianity was the influence of the classical intellectual heritage. As men trained in Hellenic and Roman modes of thought became converted, they began to reinterpret the new doctrines in the terms to which they were accustomed. Thus, Christian theology was presented in the language of Greek philosophy and of Roman law. Much of the classical tradition was worthy of preservation and could be harmonized with the new religion. Especially significant was the assimilation by Christianity of the whole Greek concept of natural law, especially in its Stoic form. On the other hand, Christianity also became linked with the Platonic heritage, in spite of the sharp contrasts between the teaching of Jesus and that of Plato; and from this and other sources it gradually acquired a bias toward an ascetic denial of the world and the flesh which was not a part of the original gospel and which tended to obscure much of its original meaning. It can be argued that the Church never afterwards wholly freed itself from the alien influences that it absorbed from the Helleno-Roman decadence and that to this extent the full potentialities of the gospel of Jesus have remained unrealized.

Even more deeply corrupting was the effect of political and social changes. In the fourth century, by the action of Constantine, Christianity became linked with Roman imperialism, the dynamism engendered by the Messianic promise being harnessed to the mundane task of legitimizing traditional institutions. In the Hellenic East the Church passed under the control of the secular authority, and its teachings became mystical rather than ethical. In the Latin West it retained its independence, but with the breakdown of Roman authority in the fifth century and the onset of the barbarians its doctrines no longer had much relationship to social conditions. Christianity had developed in response to the spiritual needs of a world in which tribalistic loyalties had given place to attitudes of individualism and universalism and men had long been seeking for some corresponding system of beliefs that would give meaning and purpose to their lives. It could preserve little of its original ethic amid the resurgence of tribalism and other primitive ways of thinking during the Dark Ages.

The Messianic promise, however, was still enshrined in Christian theology, and was repeatedly rediscovered and reinterpreted by later generations. The ultimate goal of Christianity—the permeation of human society by the gospel ethic—remained unrealized. But the hope of achieving it was a constant stimulus to creative social action, and the affirmations of the Christian faith became the basic postulates of the Western view of life.

I

The Gospel of Jesus

How did the Christian gospel originate? How many of its beliefs and practices were derived from its Jewish matrix, and how far was it a new creation? We do not have enough information either about first-century Judaism or about the early history of the new religion to give any certain answers to such questions. The available authorities are so enigmatic and incomplete, and present so many problems and apparent contradictions, that any attempt to reconstruct the doctrines of Jesus and his first disciples must be based largely on guesswork. The existing evidence, however, suggests that early Christianity was more closely connected with Judaism than the adherents of either religion have usually liked to believe.

After the loss of its political independence in 63 B.C., Palestine was at first governed by puppet kings of the Hasmonaean and Herodian dynasties. These were willing to collaborate with Rome, and were supported by the small Sadducee aristocracy. Direct Roman rule was established over Judaea in A.D. 6, though Herodian princes continued to reign over other sections of Palestine for two more generations. But the main body of the Jewish nation never became reconciled to Roman imperialism or submitted to the processes of ethnic and cultural fusion which Rome promoted among most of the peoples of her empire. The Zealots, deriving their support largely from the peasants, continued to plan armed rebellion, while the religious tradition of Judaism was preserved mainly by the Pharisees, whose claims to intellectual leadership were accepted by most of the population. Though the Jerusalem Temple, controlled by the Sadducees, continued to be the official center of the national religion, loyalty to the Mosaic heritage was maintained mainly through the synagogues, where meetings were held every Sabbath for the reading and interpretation of the Law. These were especially important among the Jews of the Diaspora, who probably outnumbered those in Palestine. Thus, the Jews continued to be set apart from neighboring peoples by their dietary and other ritualistic requirements, their refusal to participate in pagan religious ceremonies, and their belief in their divine mission. This resistance to assimilation made it possible for them to engender, preserve, and transmit a radically new view of life.

The Jews were tolerated by the Roman government, which exempted them from the requirement to join in the worship of deified emperors; but their insistence on preserving their isolation and their refusal to pay their respects to other peoples' gods caused them to be regarded as an obstinately misanthropic people. Gentile society, moreover, seemed to have good reason for regarding them as grossly superstitious. In defiance of all reason and common sense, the Jews insisted that they were the peculiar people of the one omnipotent God, that their God had commanded them to obey a burdensome and largely meaningless code of ritualistic regulations, and that in his own good time he would send the Messiah and make them the rulers of the whole earth. Yet, in spite of the irrationality of the Messianic myth, its kernel was an intuition about the meaning of human life which was capable of counteracting the pessimism of Helleno-Roman culture. The Messianic expectation implied that evil was not an inherent element in the material world, but was caused by the abuse of human freedom, and hence could be overcome; that God expressed himself primarily not through natural forces, but through ethical imperatives; and that history was a meaningful process toward a coming kingdom of righteousness in which all men would freely obey the divine will. In the course of time, these affirmations were destined to permeate the whole of Western society.

Originally formulated by the prophets during the dark days of Assyrian and Babylonian imperialism, the Messianic hope had assumed either material or spiritual forms in accord with the trend of events. At all times the Jewish people remained confident that

Jehovah would ultimately demonstrate his omnipotence by giving them supremacy over the gentile world, but this belief varied between a narrow and militant nationalism and an enlightened universalism, and between reliance on physical force and trust in a miraculous divine intervention. In the time of Jesus the disillusioning outcome of the Maccabean wars of independence and the triumph of Rome had discouraged reliance on material means, and the coming of the Messiah was usually interpreted in spiritual and supernatural terms. The Messiah himself was envisaged as human and not divine—Jewish monotheism did not permit belief in any second or subordinate deity—and as a descendant of the house of David; but he would be endowed with supernatural power and would immediately bring about the overthrow of Rome and the establishment of the Jewish kingdom. The most widely accepted versions of the Messianic eschatology reconciled nationalist and universalist ideals by affirming that the end of the world would come about in two stages. The Messiah would first establish his kingdom on earth, and earlier generations of Jews would be raised from the dead in order that they might share in the glory of Israel. This nationalistic consummation would be followed, a thousand years later, by a universal resurrection depicted in imagery borrowed from the Zoroastrian religion of Iran: God and his angels would judge all men according to their deserts, the virtuous would go to heaven and the wicked to hell, and good would finally triumph over evil. According to the more spiritual interpretations of the Messianic myth, the Jews could not achieve their liberation from foreign rule until God chose to send the Messiah, but they could indirectly promote the fulfillment of the divine purpose by showing themselves worthy of it. By repenting of their sins and living righteously, they could hasten the day of their deliverance.

The most conspicuous feature of the Jewish ethos was its insistence on rigid obedience to the moral and ritual code attributed to Moses. In fact, even God himself was sometimes depicted as meditating about the books of the law and spending every Sabbath day reading them. Jewish morality was in many ways enlightened, in spite of its narrowly tribalistic emphasis, and its more liberal exponents followed the prophets in declaring that love and charity were more pleasing to God than obedience to the letter of the law. All the characteristic ethical doctrines of the gospel can be paralleled from non-Christian Jewish sources, although by directly attacking ritualism Jesus gave them a new emphasis and placed them in a different light. But strict adherence to ritualistic requirements, however burdensome and irrational, had become a necessity for ethnic survival, and there can be no doubt that the letter often took precedence over the spirit. The Pharisees, who were the chief exponents of Jewish piety, laid an excessive emphasis on rules about diet, clothing, and Sabbath-day observance, and their religion had acquired an unpleasantly self-righteous flavor. Believing in a direct relationship between man and God, they followed Ezekiel in declaring that God would protect not only the community but also the individual who obeyed his commands. This led them to interpret worldly misfortune as usually a punishment for sin.

The Pharisees represented the main line of Jewish development. After the destruction of the Jerusalem Temple by the Romans, A.D. 70, it was chiefly the Pharisees who kept Judaism alive, and later Judaism was based mainly on Pharisaic doctrine, all divergent tendencies being suppressed. Early first-century Judaism, however, was more complex and varied than would be suggested by a reading either of the Bible or of the orthodox Jewish authorities, comprising movements both toward philosophic rationalism and toward more extreme and mystical forms of piety. Some of these movements influenced early Christianity, possibly very substantially.

Among the Jews of the Diaspora, especially at such intellectual centers as Alexandria, contact with the gentile world led to reinterpretations of the national religion in terms derived from Hellenic philosophy. The Book of Ecclesiasticus, written about 200 B.C., had shown an inclination to rationalize Judaism by affirming that the world was pervaded with the Divine Wisdom, and this had been followed by a substantial body of "wisdom" literature. The most important of the philosophizing Jews was the Alexandrian Philo, who was contemporary with Jesus. Philo identified the Wisdom of Jehovah with the Platonic ideas and with the divine reason or *Logos* of the Stoics, represented the Jewish law as the highest expression of the *Logos,* and disposed of the more primitive and irrational of the actions attributed to Jehovah in the scriptures by interpreting them allegorically. This attempt to make Judaism acceptable to Hellenists did not represent any weakening of the national sense of mission: Philo's aim was not to fuse Judaism with Hellenism, but to restate it in language that Hellenists could understand. In fact, he even suggested that Moses had been the real founder of philosophy and that Plato had acquired his doctrines from Jewish sources. But his tendency to hypostasize the divine *Logos* by speaking of it as though it were an emanation from Jehovah rather than merely a part of his personality paralleled similar trends in gentile thinking and was inconsistent with the rigid monotheism of orthodox Judaism. The philosophizing movement represented by Philo and his predecessors does not seem to have influenced the teaching of Jesus, but it entered the stream of Christian thought by way of the gospel of John, which identified Jesus with the *Logos,* and had an enormous influence on the later development of theology, especially through its demonstration of the uses of allegorical interpretation.

Meanwhile, the mystical tendencies inherent in Judaism were causing other individuals to retire from the world both singly and in groups in order to devote themselves exclusively to religious observances. From Josephus and other early authorities we hear of the Essenes, who lived rigidly disciplined lives in monastic communities. It is probable, though by no means certain, that the Essenes were identical with the Sect of the New Covenant, known to us through the recently discovered Dead Sea scrolls. According to the scrolls, this sect had been founded, perhaps about a century before the birth of Jesus, by somebody known as the "Teacher of Righteousness," who was eventually put to death by the "Wicked Priest." Its members held all their property in common, for which reason they called themselves "the poor," isolated themselves from the rest of the Jewish community, and spent their time in prayer and ascetic exercises in expectation of the rapid coming of the Messiah. Their ethical doctrines displayed an even narrower intolerance and a stronger emphasis on ritualistic observances than those of the Pharisees. Professing a rigid dualism of good and evil, the members of the Sect were required "to separate themselves from the congregation of the perverse," to love only "the sons of light" (only each other, in other words), and "to hate all the sons of darkness, each according to his guilt by virtue of the vengeance of God." [1] The Sect's Manual of Discipline pre-scribed rigid Sabbath-day observance, even to the extent of for-bidding the rescue of a drowning man, and laid down an elaborate system of penalties for violators of the community's rules of be-havior. A member was required to live apart from the community for ten days if he gesticulated with his left hand, for thirty days if he laughed foolishly, for thirty days if he was guilty of spitting or falling asleep during a meeting of the "masters."

Thus, the ethical precepts of the scrolls exhibited in a most ex-treme form precisely those tendencies of Judaism that Jesus most vigorously condemned, for which reason any suggestion that the Sect can be more or less identified with the Christian Church must be dismissed as untenable. Nevertheless, there were a number of significant similarities between the two organizations. In fact, cer-tain basic Christian doctrines and rituals that have usually been regarded either as new creations or as borrowed from gentile sources appear to have been foreshadowed in some of the writings of the Sect. Like the Sect, the Church began as a brotherhood of disciples who held all property in common. Both organizations adopted as their central ritual the eating of a common meal at which the Messiah was regarded as mystically present, although, as far as we know, the Sect did not fully anticipate the Christian eucharist by identifying his body with the bread and wine. Some early Christian writings were clearly influenced by those of the Sect, employing the same phraseology and the same imagery; in fact, manuals of piety originally produced by the Sect appear to have been adopted by the early Church with only superficial revision. Above all, the Sect seems to have anticipated the most important and the most revolutionary of the doctrines of the gospel by visualizing the Messiah as suffering. The suggestion that the Messiah could fulfill his mission only by undergoing pain and humiliation and himself making atonement for the sins of others had been implied in the "Servant" passages of Deutero-Isaiah, though these had probably referred primarily to the whole people of Israel rather than to the person of the Messiah; but orthodox

---

[1] A. Dupont-Sommer: *The Dead Sea Scrolls,* pp. 46, 47, 50. Perhaps the best of the numerous books on the subject is Millar Burrows: *The Dead Sea Scrolls.*

Jewish thought had never accepted this apparently paradoxical conception. The Sect of the New Covenant, on the other hand, possibly influenced by the martyrdom of their own "Teacher of Righteousness," seems not to have expected the Messiah to be immediately triumphant and to have believed in a mystical concept of redemption as dependent upon suffering.

Were Jesus and his first disciples themselves originally members of the Sect who rebelled against its intolerance and its excessive ritualism but retained much else of its beliefs and practices? When Jesus commanded his followers to love each other as brothers and to sell all their possessions and give the money to "the poor," was he using the vocabulary of the Sect? Did the legalism to which the early Jewish Church reverted under the leadership of Jesus' brother James represent a return to the original Sectarian doctrine? These are tempting hypotheses, especially as they suggest explanations for some of the more puzzling aspects of early Christian development; but they are not supported by any evidence at present available. New discoveries may possibly revolutionize the whole traditional conception of the origin of Christianity. At this time, however, there is no proof of any direct contact between the Sect of the scrolls and the Church. Christianity may have acquired some of its distinctive doctrines from the Sect or, on the other hand, these doctrines may have been widely current in Jewish religious thought of the first century and perhaps shared by other sectarian groups of which no record has survived. The chief importance of the scrolls has been to demonstrate that pre-Christian Judaism was more varied and complex than had been realized, and hence to throw new emphasis on the Jewish sources of Christianity.

From any rationalistic viewpoint, the study of Jewish sectarianism must appear as a kind of historical slumming. How could any doctrines of permanent value and importance have originated with such ignorant, superstitious, and obscure eccentrics? How, indeed, could anything so preposterous as the Messianic expectation have engendered a faith destined to conquer the whole Western world? This paradox appears in its most acute form in the history of the early Christian Church. Belonging mainly to the laboring classes of the northern province of Galilee, where nationalistic loyalties were even more fanatical than in other parts of Palestine, the first

Christians surpassed even their Jewish neighbors in their credulity, their emotionalism, and their conviction of the rapid advent of the Messiah. Yet by repudiating Jewish ritualism and ethnic intolerance, and by reaffirming and developing the more idealistic elements in Jewish ethical thinking, the Christians created out of the basic intuitions of Judaism a new universal religion.[2]

The paradox began with the career of Jesus. He became the focus of Western man's religious experience primarily because he gave expression to a moral vision of human life with an incomparable force and vividness and at the same time demonstrated its meaning in concrete form by the manner of his life and death. Yet he was an uneducated Galilean artisan who shared most of the intellectual limitations of his milieu. He believed that he could cure diseases by exorcising the evil spirits responsible for them; he expected the establishment of the kingdom of heaven in the near future; and, according to evidence that cannot easily be dismissed as posthumous invention, he supposed himself to be the Messiah. His life apparently ended in a tragedy of disillusionment, without the supernatural vindication for which he may have hoped. His bitter words from the cross, "My God, my God, why hast thou forsaken me?" which cannot easily have been invented, imply that what he had looked forward to was not an ignominious death, but the triumph of a divine intervention.

Scarcely any incontrovertible facts about the life of Jesus have been preserved. We do not know when or where he was born, how he learned the doctrines he preached, when he began his mission or how long it lasted, or how he acquired his first disciples. Our earliest sources for the origins of Christianity are the letters of Paul, the most important of which were written during the decade of the fifties, probably about a generation after the death of Jesus; but these are concerned with the implications of Jesus' resurrection, not with the facts of his earthly career. For our knowledge of the life of Jesus we are primarily dependent on the three synoptic gospels, which were probably written during the last quarter of the first century, after Christianity had definitely emerged from its Jewish chrysalis. The gospel of John, which is

---

[2] Of the innumerable books on the origins of Christianity, C. Guignebert: *Jesus* and M. Goguel: *The Birth of* *Christianity* have seemed to me to be the most useful.

too strongly influenced by Jewish mystical thought to be his-
torically convincing, gives a narrative that frequently seems to
contradict that of the synoptics, and presents Jesus consistently not
as a human being but as the Son of God.[3]

All the gospels display a strong and palpable desire to dissociate
the new religion from Judaism, to demonstrate that it was never a
threat to Roman authority, and to blame the Jews rather than the
Roman officials for the crucifixion. At the same time they also include a number of statements and anecdotes implying, in contradiction to the main trend of the argument, that Jesus regarded himself not as the savior of all humanity but as a Jewish prophet and
believed in the fulfillment of the Jewish national hope. Such passages suggest that the career of Jesus may actually have had different meanings and purposes from those attributed to it by his
biographers, and that much of the original story was afterwards
suppressed, misunderstood, or forgotten. It is difficult to make sense
of certain items in the gospel narrative unless one supposes that the
followers of Jesus were more highly organized than is ever overtly
indicated, that Jesus conceived his objectives as in some fashion
political as well as religious, and that the authorities, Roman as
well as Jewish, had good reasons for regarding him as politically
subversive. The whole story of his triumphal entry into Jerusalem, his last week of preaching, and his arrest, trial, and execution is unintelligible in its surviving form; it is filled with contradictions and impossibilities, and at the same time includes a
number of details that sound like authentic memories but cannot
easily be reconciled with the accepted versions of Jesus' mission.
By the time the gospels were written, one must conclude, the
events leading up to the crucifixion had been revised in order to
remove from Christianity the stigma of Jewish nationalism. The
gospels reflect the attitude of the Church during the period when
it was divesting itself of its Jewish connections and transforming
itself into a wholly gentile organization.

Yet, in spite of their total unreliability on all questions of fact,
the synoptic writers present the impact of Jesus' personality with

---

[3] John has usually been dated a generation later than the synoptics. On
the basis of parallels with the Dead
Sea scrolls, scholars are now inclined to give it an earlier date.

astonishing clarity. The whole background is dark and misty, but the central figure stands out with a vividness unsurpassed in all literature. This was a new kind of biographical writing, displaying an impulse to tell the whole truth about a remarkable human being without artistic pretentiousness or falsification in a manner appropriate to the beginning of the new Christian view of human nature. The three writers adopt different approaches. Mark tells the story most simply and clearly, with emphasis on Jesus' more human qualities, and makes some effort to narrate events in what may have been their correct order. Matthew and Luke both make extensive use of Mark, but introduce much new material which is left in utter chronological confusion, and display various biases of their own. Matthew, who ranks with the author of the gospel of John as the main source of anti-Semitism, quotes frequently from the Old Testament in order to prove that Jesus fulfilled all the Messianic prophecies and hence that the Jews had no excuse for failing to acknowledge him, and includes many bitter denunciations of the scribes and Pharisees. He also records some miracle anecdotes which (like that of Peter finding his tribute money in a fish's mouth) can only be described as cheap. Luke has a fondness for picturesque stories, especially those reflecting credit on prostitutes, beggars, and other bohemian characters and showing rich and respectable citizens in an unfavorable light.

Yet, in spite of the numerous divergencies among the three synoptics and the even sharper differences between all the synoptics and the gospel of John, all of them are manifestly portraits of the same individual. The style of Jesus, as conveyed in parable, aphorism, or symbolic action, is always inimitable and unmistakable. A quick intuitive insight into the crux of any moral situation, dislike of any form of pretentiousness and a talent for deflating it, respect for the sincerity of simple people, the constant use of homely imagery to convey moral lessons, a fondness for humorous exaggeration, ability to escape from dialectical dilemmas and turn the tables on opponents by means of swift and effective repartee—these are the qualities most clearly portrayed in the gospels. It was primarily by the force and flavor of his personality, rather than by the doctrines that he preached or the remarkable actions he performed, that Jesus was able to dominate his disciples, influencing them so profoundly as to transform their lives and even cause them to believe in his survival after the crucifixion.

Jesus first appeared as a preacher and miracle-worker in Galilee, his main theme being the rapid approach of the Messianic age that the prophets had promised: in other words, of the kingdom of heaven. In order to fit themselves for membership in the kingdom, men must quickly repent of their sins and put aside worldly desires and ambitions. This gospel message was specifically directed only to Jews; Jesus did not preach to gentiles, and is recorded as reluctant even to cure the daughter of a gentile woman. We may assume that he accepted the current eschatology which divided the end of the world into two phases, the first phase being a Jewish kingdom. Predictions that the Messiah was at hand, coupled with threats of perdition for those who failed to repent in time, were by no means infrequent in the emotionally charged atmosphere of Palestine, especially among the unsophisticated peasants and artisans, and Jesus had had an immediate forerunner in John the Baptist. From the manner in which Jesus is described as calling his first disciples and some other indications, it would appear that he set out to assume the leadership of a sectarian group already in existence, whether founded by John the Baptist or by some earlier evangelist. The members of the group were apparently known as Nazarenes, which means "holy ones" and is occasionally applied in the New Testament to the early Christians without any plausible explanation of its origins.[4]

In performing miraculous cures Jesus was conforming to what was expected of a religious leader. Many diseases were attributed to possession by demons, who would necessarily obey a man en-

[4] According to Matthew, ii, 23, Jesus was called a Nazarene because he came from Nazareth. But this is a linguistically improbable derivation and is not supported by other Biblical references to the word. It can plausibly be argued that Jesus was supposed to have come from a town called Nazareth only because his biographers did not know the meaning of "Nazarene." There is no non-Christian evidence for the existence of such a place. Josephus does not mention it in his apparently exhaustive list of Galilean towns.

We hear in Acts, xix, 25, of a certain Apollos, who was regarded as a member of the Christian community in spite of the fact that he had known only "the Baptism of John." This implies that the community antedated the preaching of Jesus and was not founded by him.

dowed by God with spiritual power. Many of the maladies that Jesus is said to have cured can plausibly be regarded as psychic in origin, and hence as responsive, at least temporarily, to faith healing performed by a man of intense personal force. It is specifically stated, moreover, that Jesus could not cure individuals who lacked belief in his mission. By the time the gospels were written, Jesus was, of course, credited with power to control storms, feed thousands of people with a few loaves and fishes, and restore the dead to life. The growth of such legends was to be expected, and it is, on the whole, surprising that the New Testament does not lay more emphasis on them and preserves so much of what must have been the actual story.

If Jesus had been merely an eschatological prophet and miracle-worker, he would, of course, have been forgotten quickly. He was remembered because of the new moral content he gave to the Messianic promise. What he preached was based on the assumption that all human society was on the point of total transformation. He had little to say about political or economic or sexual problems, chiefly because he regarded them as no longer important. Because the kingdom of God was at hand, it was futile for human beings to make any elaborate plans for the morrow. The one thing needful was to be ready for the kingdom, and this meant the repudiation of worldly plans, love for others, purity of heart, and a childlike trust in God. It is easy to dismiss this gospel ethic as utterly impractical, being predicated on expectations that had no realistic basis. The Christian Church eventually learned not to take literally many of Jesus' statements, such as his advice to turn the other cheek to aggressors and his injunction to rich men to sell all their possessions and give the money to the poor. But in human affairs, as in the physical sciences, a hypothesis that is obviously a subjective invention, not supported by observed facts, may sometimes be a means of reaching new truths. The gospel can be dissociated from the Messianic expectation without losing its essential significance. The naïve eschatological hope of this Galilean carpenter was, in fact, a medium by which a new vision of the meaning of human life achieved expression and entered the stream of human thought.

What was meant by the Messianic kingdom? As envisaged by the prophets, especially by Jeremiah, it meant an ideal order in which all men would freely and spontaneously do the will of God, conflict and oppression would cease, and justice would be universal; mankind would thus regain the primal innocence it had lost by the sin of Adam. What was required of men if they were to become worthy of membership in the kingdom? Jesus recognized that the kingdom could not be brought about by the enforcement of rules and regulations, but only by a transformation of human nature itself. Men must repudiate all purely egocentric wishes, turn toward each other with feelings of love and charity, and treat each other as brothers. Thus the problem of justice would be transcended. The central problem of all human society has been to find an objective standard of justice which all men will be willing to accept even when it conflicts with their own interests. But in the brotherhood of the gospel kingdom, men would be guided by love for each other and rules of justice would become unnecessary. This was the meaning of Jesus' teaching about neighborly charity, forgiveness of injuries, and returning good for evil.

Such a change of human nature must extend not merely to men's behavior, but also to their underlying motives. Many of Jesus' most pungent sayings referred to the hypocrisy of those who performed good deeds not from love, but from the desire to make a good appearance. Men must be judged by their intentions as well as by their actions, and were not ready for the kingdom if they continued to feel aggressive and lustful desires. To wish to do evil, as Jesus repeatedly insisted, was the moral equivalent of doing it. Goodness was a matter of the heart, and meant a disinterested purity of motive rather than mere outward conformity to ethical ideals. This was possible only if men put away all worldly cares and fears and acquired an inner peace and security based on a childlike trust in divine goodness. Only men who were free from fear could turn toward each other with positive love.

One of Jesus' more remarkable psychological insights was his recognition that the love of man depended on belief in the fatherhood of God. The doctrine of divine fatherhood was important not only because it implied that all men were brothers, but also because it resulted in a general sense of security. It might be defined as the objective correlative of the psychological condition of release from anxiety. What it meant was an acceptance of life and of whatever the future might bring. It is significant that while Jesus gave imaginative expression to this doctrine by repeatedly insisting that God could be trusted to give good things to his children, he did not suggest that virtue would necessarily be rewarded with divine protection. On the contrary, he directly challenged traditional doctrines by denying that misfortune was a punishment for sin. Men put to death by Roman officials or killed in the fall of a tower should not be regarded as more sinful than their neighbors.[5] This repudiation of the primeval belief that obedience to God would result in material prosperity was one of the most significant aspects of the whole Christian gospel.

Thus, the moral teaching of Jesus meant revolutionary changes of emphasis from legal regulation to spontaneous love and from outward behavior to inner attitudes. The spirit of brotherhood would be the only principle of unity needed in the coming kingdom, and by genuinely loving each other men could enjoy the freedom of the sons of God. Under such conditions, ritualistic requirements would obviously lose their meaning, nor would there be any value in the mortification of the flesh. Unlike almost all other religious leaders in history, Jesus did not preach or practice asceticism. His manner of life, in fact, evoked criticism from those who assumed that a prophet must abstain from all forms of enjoyment. As he himself declared, he "came eating and drinking, and they say, Behold a man gluttonous, and a winebibber, a friend of publicans and sinners." [6]

Believing the kingdom to be close at hand, Jesus urged his auditors to put its principles into practice in their personal lives immediately. Thus, the Church began as an association of men and women endeavoring to live as though the kingdom was already a reality. Jesus' ethical insights, however, were inextricably entangled with the Messianic eschatology: the full realization of the kingdom was to be brought about not by human effort, but by some kind of divine intervention in the near future. Much of the early history of the Church consisted in a gradual adjustment to the disillusioning recognition that this divine intervention, usually envisaged as the Second Coming of Jesus, had been indefinitely

---

[5] Luke, xiii, 1–5.   [6] Matthew, xi, 19.

postponed. In consequence, the gospel ethic, which had been predicated on the rapid achievement of a perfect society in this world, eventually lost much of its concrete practical meaning and was transformed into a means of personal salvation after death. This distortion of Jesus' original teaching did not, however, prevent it from having a revolutionary impact on the whole cultural development of the Western world.

The vitality of Western civilization has always depended on belief in the possibility of an ideal unity and order regarded either as an eternal reality underlying material appearances or as the goal toward which history is moving. It was Jesus who most vividly gave expression to this belief and most clearly stated its implications for human attitudes and behavior. His doctrine of a coming kingdom of heaven became one of the central myths of Western society, giving meaning to the processes of history and serving as a standard for the judgment of all actual social organization. Jesus' emphasis on the fatherhood of God, coupled with the Jewish belief that the whole universe had come into existence by an act of divine creation, implied that goodness was natural, and this made it possible for Christian theology to absorb, and become fused with, the Greek concept of a normative order of nature. Western civilization found its standards in a union of the gospel ethic with natural law.

Is it possible to say more? Can we affirm that the moral teaching of Jesus is a wholly valid guide for human behavior? Implicit in the doctrines of the gospel is the belief that universal brotherhood is man's natural condition and that he fails to realize it only because he has been perverted by sin. In the last resort, Christianity must stand or fall with the proposition that human beings find their own proper emotional fulfillment in love and charity for each other, the practice of the gospel ethic being not an obligation but a means of self-realization. If universal brotherhood is actually an unnatural ideal, then the doctrines of non-resistance and the forgiveness of injuries must lead, in practice, not to the extirpation of aggressive impulses, but merely to a condition of neurotic repression. This means, however, that unity and concord are beyond the capacity of the human race. If an ideal order is possible, it can be brought about only through the application of the gospel ethic. The hope of achieving such an order, and thereby of creating conditions that would make the brotherhood of the gospel possible, has been the strongest dynamic force in Western civilization for the past two thousand years; and the Christian ethic of charity, with its corollary of the inestimable value of every individual, has been a constant stimulus to humanitarian activity and social reform. As Jesus himself predicted in a characteristically homely simile, belief in the kingdom of heaven has acted like a leaven put by a housewife into three measures of flour.

Jesus himself does not seem to have realized the full universalist implications of his teaching, though they quickly became apparent to some of his followers after his death. According to the gospels, he regarded himself as still faithful to the Mosaic law and tradition, though he insisted that the Judaism of his time exaggerated the importance of ritual and had come to regard it as an end instead of merely a means. Obedience to dietary, clothing, and Sabbath-day regulations had become more important than charity and purity of heart. Jesus denounced current attitudes by declaring that the Sabbath was made for man and not man for the Sabbath; men were corrupted not by what they ate and drank, but by their own words and deeds. God, in words which he quoted from the prophet Hosea, required loyal love and not sacrifice. As these implications of Jesus' teaching became apparent, he came into conflict with the Pharisees, especially when he attacked another of their favorite doctrines by asserting that misfortune was not necessarily a sign of divine anger. The hostility between Jesus and the Pharisees may have been exaggerated in the gospels, but there can be no doubt that most of them regarded his teaching as subversive of the Jewish tradition because of its lack of respect for ritual. In consequence, Jesus' activities soon began to evoke vigorous opposition, and his Galilean mission ended in failure. When he first began preaching he aroused wide popular interest and was invited to address synagogue audiences. After he had been denounced by the Pharisees, perhaps within a few weeks or months, he found it difficult to secure a hearing, was sometimes without food or shelter for the night, and could count on the support of only a small body of disciples. Under these circumstances he seems to have resolved to transfer his mission to Jerusalem.

What did he expect to accomplish at Jerusalem? According to the gospel narrative, he made a triumphal entry into the city in the role of a Messiah, plans to this effect having previously been made with secret sympathizers, and subsequently took it upon himself to expel the money-changers from the Temple by force. These were dramatic acts that can only have been designed to arouse popular excitement and support and which would obviously alarm both the Sadducee ruling class and the Roman authorities. Jesus' objectives at this point appear to have been partly political. It is significant that at least one of the disciples who were supposed to guard him during his vigil in Gethsemane carried a sword and that, according to Luke, this had Jesus' approval.[7] Did Jesus believe himself to be the Messiah, and did he expect some kind of supernatural aid in an attempt to start an insurrection? The gospels are unanimous in declaring that before setting out for Jerusalem, Jesus had revealed his Messiahship to his disciples. This revelation had taken place at Caesarea Philippi, in mountainous country east of the Jordan, where Jesus had apparently taken refuge from his Galilean opponents. But how Jesus envisaged his Messianic role remains obscure. Did he succumb to popular fantasies, in contradiction to the more idealistic implications of his own teaching, and look forward to an easy triumph with divine aid and the establishment of a political kingdom? Or had he learned from the Sect of the New Covenant or some other source of mystical thought that the Messiah must suffer and perhaps be put to death before the kingdom could be established? Did he deliberately invite arrest and execution at the hands of the Roman authorities in order that he might fulfill all the requirements of the Messianic role? Perhaps the best answer is that he did not know what form his Messiahship would assume. To judge from the synoptic narratives—and in spite of their ex-post-facto assertions that Jesus warned his disciples of his coming death, it is surprising how much they record of his state of mind—he went to Jerusalem in both hope and fear, expecting some kind of rapid climax to his mission but uncertain what this would be or what role he himself would be required to play. Once he had made public announcement of his Messiahship, his arrest was, of course,

---

[7] Luke, xxii, 38, 49–50.

a foregone conclusion. He was captured by agents of the Sadduces in a secret hiding-place at Gethsemane, the disciples supposed to guard him having fallen asleep, and was turned over to the Roman government and executed. The story that Pilate deemed him innocent and consented to his execution only under Jewish pressure can most plausibly be regarded as a later fabrication. Anybody who did what Jesus is recorded to have done in Jerusalem would have been regarded by a Roman governor as a dangerously subversive character.

Contrary to all reasonable expectation, the crucifixion proved to be not the end of Christianity, but its beginning. It was followed by a crucial and mysterious series of events which ensured the continuity of Jesus' influence. His disciples, who had all deserted him at the time of his arrest, seem to have given up their hope of seeing the kingdom of heaven and to have made their way back to their original homes in Galilee. Yet within a short time they had come to believe that Jesus was still alive. Our earliest record of the resurrection is in Paul's first letter to the Corinthians and contains none of the details about the empty tomb which were added in the gospels. Paul gives a list of six appearances of the risen Jesus: first to his closest adherent, Peter; then to the twelve apostles; then to a group of five hundred disciples; then to Jesus' brother James; again to the twelve apostles; and finally to Paul himself.[8] We know that Paul had a vision of Jesus on the road to Damascus and that this vision was not shared by his traveling-companions. Presumably the other appearances listed by Paul were of a similarly subjective quality. As all the gospels specifically declare that Jesus promised his disciples before his death to go before them into Galilee, we may suppose that these appearances took place after they had returned to their homes, and not in Jerusalem. The whole tomb story, which was apparently unknown to Paul and is not mentioned in the speeches recorded in the Acts of the Apostles, must have been a later development. That the unsophisticated peasants and fishermen who had followed Jesus should have seen visions of him, both individually and collectively, is indeed by no means surprising. What was extraordinary was the sense of conviction with which they

---

[8] I Corinthians, xv, 5–8.

affirmed the continued existence of his personality and made this henceforth the guiding principle of their lives.

The faith of the disciples in the resurrection was confirmed by the remarkable experience described in the second chapter of the Acts. According to the record, the apostles had returned to Jerusalem and were all assembled in an upper room when the Holy Spirit descended upon them. "Suddenly there came a sound from heaven as of a rushing mighty wind, and it filled all the house where they were sitting. And there appeared unto them cloven tongues like as of fire, and it sat upon each of them. And they were all filled with the Holy Ghost, and began to speak with other tongues, as the Spirit gave them utterance." [9] This state of collective ecstasy was attributed to divine influence and regarded as a proof that Jesus' disciples were still guided by his spirit and mystically united with him. Outbreaks of glossolalia, by which persons in a state of excitement are impelled to make unintelligible sounds, have been, of course, standard phenomena of religious revivalism. This initial manifestation and the accompanying sense of collective inspiration were regarded as the real beginnings of the Christian Church, and for a long time became standard experiences for new converts. In fact, individuals who did not undergo such experiences were considered as not yet fully incorporated into the brotherhood of the disciples. Thus, the Church began as a small sect of ecstatics distinguished by their belief that the kingdom of heaven was beginning, that they were still mystically guided by the spirit of the risen Jesus, and that states of ecstatic excitement were proofs of such guidance.

[9] Acts, ii, 2–4.

2

The Mission to the Gentiles

The emergence of the Church from its Jewish matrix was a slow and painful operation, not completed for half a century or more. The early stages of the process are charted in the Acts of the Apostles, although not always in consistency with statements made by Paul in his letters. What was at stake was whether Christianity would remain a small and obscure Jewish sect, comparable to the one described in the Dead Sea scrolls, or whether it would develop into the universal religion that had been implied, although not clearly stated, in the ethical teaching of Jesus. Liberalizing tendencies began to manifest themselves within a few years of the Crucifixion, but these were vehemently opposed by Christians who remained faithful to the full Mosaic code. Apart from a few brief and ineffectual attempts at repression, official Judaism was usually tolerant of the Christians as long as they conformed with the Mosaic law and remained within the Jewish community—a fact that seems to confirm the thesis that Pontius Pilate rather than the Jewish Sanhedrin was mainly responsible for the crucifixion.

The original group of apostles who had been attached to Jesus were not men of much ability or capacity for leadership, even Peter, the most prominent of them, being notably lacking in firmness of character. They seem at first to have taken it for granted that Christians would continue to adhere to the Jewish ritual code and that no gentiles would be admitted to the Church unless they became circumcised and accepted all the other obligations of Judaism. The members of the Christian community continued, therefore, to attend services in the Temple and the synagogues without much interference from the Jewish authorities. Their initial beliefs and practices cannot be determined with any certainty. If the speech attributed to Peter in the second chapter of the Acts can be regarded as reliable evidence, Jesus was at first regarded not as the Son of God, but as a man who had been elevated to heaven after his crucifixion. His disciples, mystically fused into a single body by the influx of the Spirit, composed the nucleus of the coming Messianic kingdom and endeavored to practice the ethics of the gospel. It is impossible to say whether the apostles supposed that the kingdom would be established by a second and triumphal coming of Jesus or simply by the continued workings of the Spirit, but certainly they expected it in the near future and assumed that it would be restricted to Jews and Jewish proselytes. In anticipation of the final realization of the kingdom, Christians were expected to sell their surplus possessions and give the money to the Church, though how fully the communal ownership of property was put into practice is uncertain: the Church apparently maintained out of its common fund those members who could not support themselves, but obviously most Christians must have continued to work at their normal occupations. The principal Christian rituals were baptism and a communal meal commemorating the last supper of Jesus and his disciples before his arrest.

The trend toward universalism developed among converts who seem not to have personally known Jesus and who belonged not to Palestine but to the Diaspora, though they were temporarily residing in Jerusalem. Under what circumstances such men were attracted to Christianity has not been recorded. Within a few years of the crucifixion, one of them, Stephen, was apparently maintaining that the gospel meant the abrogation of the Mosaic code. Haled before the Jewish Sanhedrin, he delivered a violent attack on official Judaism, declaring that throughout their entire history the Jews had always resisted the Holy Spirit, and so infuriated his auditors that he was promptly dragged out of the city and stoned to death, thus becoming the first Christian martyr. This was followed by a persecution not of the Jerusalem Church, which remained loyal to Judaism, but of the liberalizing Christians. These were compelled to seek refuge beyond the borders of Palestine, especially at Antioch, which now became the main center of

Christian activity. The Antioch leaders began not only to make gentile converts, but also to declare that gentile Christians need not undergo circumcision or comply with the other requirements of the Mosaic code. Critics were silenced by the argument that these gentile Christians had received the Holy Spirit: in other words, they had manifested glossolalia and other symptoms of religious ecstasy. The Antioch Church then began to send out missionaries to other provinces, the most prominent of them being Paul, a native of the Asiatic city of Tarsus who had at first been a violent opponent of Christianity, but had been abruptly converted to it, probably about the year 33, after seeing a vision of Jesus while traveling from Jerusalem to Damascus. Paul seems to have been the first Christian to preach a thoroughgoing universalism by which all distinctions between Jew and gentile would be obliterated. As he declared in his letter to the Romans, "there is no distinction between the Jew and the Greek: the same Lord is Lord of all and bestows his riches upon all who call upon him." [1] Between 48 and 58 Paul made a series of three missionary journeys through the leading cities of Asia Minor and Greece, preaching in Jewish synagogues wherever possible, but also appealing directly to gentiles, and founding a number of new branches of the Church. Thus Christianity began to spread through the eastern provinces of the Roman Empire. During the same period a small Christian community was also established in Rome itself.

These developments led to a series of conflicts between the Antioch Church and the Church at Jerusalem. Paul was the ablest and most vigorous spokesman of the liberals; the chief advocate of Jewish orthodoxy was Jesus' brother James, who had apparently brushed aside the apostles and assumed the leadership of the Jerusalem Church within twelve or fifteen years of the crucifixion. His authority was presumably based on some kind of hereditary right, possibly associated with claims to descent from the Davidian dynasty. James was a rigidly orthodox Jew, with none of Jesus' more liberal spirit. According to traditions recorded by the fourth-century historian Eusebius, he was an extreme ascetic who never bathed, drank wine, or cut his beard, and spent so much time

---

[1] Romans, x, 12, Revised Standard Version.

praying in the Temple that his knees became as hard as those of a camel.[2] If the Acts is to be accepted as reliable, then a conference, probably held in 49, agreed on a compromise settlement by which Jewish Christians must continue to adhere to the full Mosaic code, while its requirements were relaxed, though not wholly abrogated, for gentile Christians. But Paul's letters, which do not corroborate this story, show continued bitter antagonisms. Regarding himself as endowed with full authority by the Holy Spirit, in spite of the fact that he had never known Jesus, Paul was contemptuous of the Jerusalem leaders, men who "were reputed to be something," and especially of the vacillating Peter, who at first violated the ritual code by eating with gentile converts and then reverted to Jewish orthodoxy from fear of James and his supporters. Judaizing Christians continued to declare that all gentile converts ought to be circumcised, which evoked from Paul a series of angry comments to the effect that such "dogs" who insisted on "mutilating the flesh" deserved to be emasculated.[3] Somewhat inconsistently, Paul continued to obey the ritual code in his own personal life, apparently in the hope of conciliating his opponents, but the circumcision of gentiles he regarded not only as unnecessary, but also as actually wrong. He seems to have planned to exert economic pressure on the Jerusalem Church, which was in need of financial assistance: but when he visited Jerusalem in 58, bringing with him contributions from the churches in Asia Minor, he was arrested on charges of profaning the Temple. Rather than submit to trial by the official Jewish authorities, Paul appealed to the Roman government. After being held in prison for two years by a Roman official who was eager to please the Jews, he was shipped to Rome for examination, after which he disappears from the pages of history. According to legend, he was put to death by the Emperor Nero, who chose to blame the Christian community in Rome for the fire which destroyed a large part of the city.

---

[2] Eusebius also records a story that the Roman authorities became alarmed lest the family of Jesus, with their presumed Davidian descent, might become the representatives of Jewish nationalism. By orders from the Emperor Domitian, officials searched for any surviving members of the family, but could find only two ignorant and obviously harmless Galilean peasants, who were apparently grandsons of one of Jesus' brothers (*Ecclesiastical History*, II, 23; XIII, 20).

[3] Galatians, ii, 6, 11–12; v, 1–12; Philippians, iii, 2. The meaning of Galatians v, 12 is discreetly veiled in all official English translations.

15. *Mosaics from San Apollinare Nuovo, Ravenna, dating from the sixth century. Above: scenes from the life of Jesus. Below: part of the procession of virgins.*

16. *Mosaics from the Cathedral of Monreale, Sicily. This twelfth-century representation of Christ in the role of Pantocrator is a typical example of late Byzantine art.*

In the end, political developments negated any claim to leadership on the part of the Jerusalem Church. When the Jewish people revolted against Roman domination in the years 67–70, the Church remained aloof from the conflict, and its members took refuge in the mountains east of the Jordan. As Jerusalem was destroyed by the Romans, they were unable to return to their original headquarters after the war; and as the reorganized Judaism that survived the conflict excluded all Christians from its synagogues, apparently because of resentment against their neutral attitude during the war, they were deprived of their Jewish affiliations. Known to other Christians as "Ebionites," the Judaizers became steadily weaker and seem to have finally become extinct during the third century. Henceforth Christianity was mainly a gentile movement; and though it spread through considerable areas of the Near East and assumed various Oriental forms, the most important trend in Christian development was the fusion with Hellenism.[4]

After the disappearance of the Jerusalem Church, Christianity continued to spread without any central organization or official body of leaders, and the doctrines preached by the liberals were accepted as authoritative. Gentile Christians were able to abandon all obligations to obey the Jewish ritual code with the exception of Sabbath-day observance, which was included among the Ten Commandments (although there was a change from the last day of the week to the first, in commemoration of the resurrection). On the other hand, Jewish conceptions of morality were regarded, somewhat inconsistently, as still valid for the new religion. Christianity, in fact, continued to acknowledge its Jewish heritage, with results that were in some ways paradoxical. God, it was believed, had initially chosen the Jews as the recipients of revelation, and the whole of the Jewish scriptures had been dictated by divine inspiration. But the revelation made to Moses and the prophets had now been superseded by the preaching of Jesus; and after the Jews had forfeited their privileged position by failing to recognize him as the Messiah, the promises made to Abraham and Moses had

---

[4] Armenia became officially Christian near the end of the third century and Abyssinia about the middle of the fourth. Christian missionaries also made a number of converts in Iran and areas even farther east. There was considerable conflict between Hellenic and non-Hellenic Christians, especially in Egypt, where the native "Coptic" church of the peasants was hostile to the Hellenizing influences emanating from Alexandria.

been transferred to the Christian Church. By means of a considerable distortion of the writings of the prophets, Jesus was represented as having perfectly fulfilled all their predictions, and this alleged confirmation of prophecy by historic fact became one of the favorite arguments of Christian apologetics.

The inconsistencies resulting from this fusion of the Jewish national myth with religious universalism were most sharply illustrated in the Christian conception of the nature of Jesus. On the one hand, he was the Jewish Messiah and must therefore be of Davidian descent and born in David's native city of Bethlehem (in spite of the fact that Jesus himself had never claimed such ancestry, and had actually denied that the Messiah would be the son of David.) [5] Gentiles, on the other hand, quickly came to believe in Jesus' divinity, identifying him with the wisdom or *Logos* emanating from God with which Hellenic philosophy had made them familiar. Eventually Christian theology arrived at a definition of Jesus as a perfect union of God and man, but this required centuries of controversy. Within twenty years of the crucifixion, however, Jesus was being presented to gentile audiences as God's first-born son. Making an overliteral interpretation of this metaphorical expression and overlooking the doctrine of Christ's pre-existence, gentile Christianity then invented the notion of the virgin birth.[6] In the gospels of Matthew and Luke, the two variant conceptions of the nature of Christ were presented side by side without any recognition of their incompatibility. According to two detailed genealogies (quite different from each other), Jesus was descended from David through his earthly father Joseph, while at the same time he was not the son of Joseph at all, but of Mary and the Holy Spirit. The authors of the two gospels added a number of charming legends about Jesus' birth and infancy, thereby partially atoning for their misjudgment in establishing both Davidian descent and the virgin birth as Christian dogmas.

Of more urgent importance than the problem of the nature of

---

[5] This seems to be the meaning of the anecdote related in Matthew, xxii, 41, Mark, xii, 35, and Luke, xx, 41.

[6] The virgin birth was supported by a mistranslation of Isaiah, vii, 14. The original Hebrew said merely that a young woman would bear a son called Immanuel. The Greek version of the Old Testament, the Septuagint, erroneously spoke of a virgin bearing a son. When Jewish scholars pointed out this error, they were accused by Christians of tampering with the original Hebrew text.

Christ was the exploration of the meaning of the Christian experience and its elaboration into a general view of life. This was primarily the work of Paul, and was expounded in his letters to different branches of the Church. Somewhat variant doctrines were developed by a mystical group, probably located in Asia Minor, which was responsible for the gospel and letters attributed to John, but Paul was unquestionably the main author of the theology of gentile Christianity. In spite of his early education as a Pharisee, he was a Jew of the Diaspora who did not share the narrow nationalism of his Palestinian compatriots. Having a deep respect for Roman authority, which was exercised, he declared, only against wrongdoers, he was proud of both his Roman citizenship and his citizenship of Tarsus, and was willing to borrow phrases and conceptions from the pagan mystery cults in order to elucidate the meaning of Christianity. After his abrupt conversion, he devoted his life to the propagation of the gospel with a fervor that repeated mob attacks, beatings, imprisonments, shipwrecks, illnesses, and disappointments could never quench. His letters, which were dictated to amanuenses and were obviously poured out at white heat with little concern for formal organization, mingled theological argument and impassioned apostrophes to the love of God with personal reminiscence. Emotional and excitable, alternating between states of ecstasy and depression, utterly convinced of his guidance by the Spirit and given to boasting of his own achievements, a warm and tactful friend and a bitter and outspoken enemy, devoted above everything else to the spiritual welfare of the converts he had made, Paul revealed his whole personality with an astonishing candor and sincerity. His letters were the earliest example of that full acceptance of naked humanity not as it ought to be, but as it was, which was precluded by pagan philosophy and made possible by Christianity. They set forth, moreover, a general view of life which, though largely derived from Jewish sources, represented a remarkably bold and comprehensive attempt to formulate a theology for the new religion.

Although Paul endeavored to expound the intellectual meaning of Christianity, the gospel that he and other missionaries carried to the gentiles should not be regarded as a system of dogmas. Christianity began not as a theology, but as a new way of life associated with a new kind of sensitivity. The emotional attitude was primary, whereas the theological rationalizations that were used to explain it were derivative and not always satisfying. The basic experience by which a man or woman accepted membership in the Christian community cannot easily be described in words and has remained largely incommunicable. In Paul's terminology, it consisted essentially of faith, by which he meant an affirmation of the truth of the gospel and a decision to trust in the resurrected Jesus and unite oneself with him. But the Christian acquired faith not by an intellectual choice, but through an emotional transformation that was attributed to the operations of the Holy Spirit and of divine grace. Faith brought about a reorganization of the entire personality around new values, the love of God and of one's fellow men being thereafter paramount. This meant a repudiation of all those selfish impulses which Paul attributed to the flesh; the body must be mortified in order that the Christian might live in the Spirit. But the final result, as he repeatedly insisted, was a sense of liberation. The Christian was free from the domination of fate and fortune and evil spirits, free from bondage to his own carnal passions, free even from the feeling of compulsion to obey moral laws conflicting with his own wishes. Being purged of sin, united with the risen Jesus and transformed into his likeness, he no longer desired anything that conflicted with the will of God and the welfare of other human beings, and hence did good not from fear of divine anger, but freely and spontaneously. The Holy Spirit manifested itself in various ecstatic phenomena (Paul himself, as he told the Corinthians, excelled all his converts in glossolalia), but the one essential fruit of the Spirit was love. Even selling all one's goods to feed the poor or giving one's body to be burned was of no spiritual value, as Paul affirmed in the ecstatic thirteenth chapter of his first letter to the Corinthians, unless it was done in a spirit of love. The true Christian convert already belonged to the promised Messianic kingdom in which men would be united by love into a brotherhood, legal compulsions would become unnecessary, and the conflict between order and self-interest would be transcended. In reading Paul, one should never forget that his whole system of thought was predicated on the rapid realization of the kingdom of Jesus.

In some of his writings, especially in the letter to the Romans, which was apparently planned as a formal statement of his beliefs,

Paul went on to sketch the outlines of a cosmology. The enjoyment of the kingdom of heaven and of eternal life was man's proper destiny, according to the purposes of God and the nature of the world he had created. But the first man had abused the power of choice which God had given him by preferring his own selfish wishes to the will of God, and hence he and his descendants had forfeited their freedom and come under the domination of their own carnal passions, incurring death as the penalty of their sins. The God of Paul was the God of the Jewish prophets, the ruler of all mankind, but at the same time the especial deity of the Jews, whom he had chosen as the recipients of revelation; and the Mosaic law, now abrogated, was of divine origin. But God had also revealed himself to the gentiles indirectly through his works, and in the end both Jews and gentiles came under the same condemnation: all alike had failed to live in conformity with the divine order. Finally Jesus Christ, who was both the Messiah promised by the Jewish prophets and "the image of the invisible God, the firstborn of every creature," [7] had canceled the sin of Adam, paid the penalty of human guilt by his death on the cross, and made it possible for men to regain their primal perfection and the immortality associated with it. Paul's expectations for the future seem to have been largely derived from the traditional Jewish eschatology, though dissociated from Jewish nationalism. Unlike some other early theologians, especially the author of the gospel of John, he declared that Christ would physically return and establish a terrestrial millennium. Membership in his kingdom, having been forfeited by the Jews, would be the privilege of Christians. This would be followed at a later date by the end of the world, the resurrection of all men, and the day of judgment. A curious passage in the second letter to the Thessalonians suggests that Christ's second coming would be immediately preceded by a time of troubles in which the forces of evil would no longer be restrained by the beneficent authority of the Roman Empire.[8]

The Pauline vision of human destiny has been one of the decisive factors in the shaping of the Western mind. It was the principal medium by which the Messianic myth of the Jewish prophets was transmitted to the non-Jewish world and transformed

---

[7] Colossians, i, 15.   [8] II Thessalonians, ii, 7–8.

from a nationalistic aspiration into a promise for all humanity. Paul was a faithful follower of Jesus, and the core of his religion was his acceptance of the gospel ethic; but it is probable that Jesus' teachings would quickly have been forgotten if Paul had not given the gospel experience a cosmological foundation. Yet Paul's theology was replete with problems, and during the nineteen centuries that have elapsed since he wrote his letters, Christians have rarely ceased to argue about what he really meant. Armies of learned divines have compiled libraries of commentaries, and during the age of Luther and Calvin the peoples of the Western world actually became divided into hostile armed camps separated by variant interpretations. If salvation came by faith, then why should the Christian perform good works? If only those whom God had elected could be saved, then why should the individual make any effort on his own behalf? How could one reconcile Christian freedom with the obligations of morality, divine grace with human responsibility, the fatherhood of God with the dogma of predestination? Was it just that all men should inherit the sin of Adam, even infants being held guilty of rebellion against God? And why could sin be canceled only by the death of Christ on the cross? By suggesting such questions, the letters of Paul evoked a dreary and apparently interminable series of controversies, accompanied during the sixteenth and seventeenth centuries by wars and persecutions and all the evils of theological hatred. Yet if one remembers that Pauline theology began not with logic but with subjective experience, and that its primary intention was not to present a rational picture of the universe or to justify God's ways to man but to explain the meaning of the Christian attitude, then it is no longer difficult to understand.

In preaching that all men were sinners Paul was not trying to envelop all human life in a pall of gloom or expressing a vindictive and neurotic hatred of the world and the flesh; he was stating a psychological fact. Man was a divided creature, driven by egotistical passions that conflicted with his own moral principles, capable of envisaging ideals, but unable to realize them. Obviously he fell short of his proper perfection, and this failure was written large in the pages of history with their melancholy record of violence, lawlessness, treachery, and unnatural vice. For Paul, unlike the Hellenic philosophers, the misery of mankind was owing not merely to evil, but to sin; man was morally responsible for his own shortcomings. But this emphasis on human guilt was a necessary consequence of the Christian exaltation of human destiny. God had originally given man the power of achieving perfection, and man's failure resulted not from the nature of the world but from his own abuse of the freedom with which God had endowed him. The root of evil lay not in matter, as Hellenic philosophy had declared, but in the human will, and this was capable of regeneration. By what means the original sin of Adam had been transmitted to his descendants, and how this doctrine of inherited guilt could be reconciled with the justice and benevolence of God, were questions which perplexed a long succession of theologians, but with which Paul was not concerned.

All men deserved death for their sins, but Christians could enjoy eternal life because the penalty had been paid by the death of Jesus Christ. This doctrine of the atonement was briefly stated in several of Paul's letters, thus transforming the cross, which for all inhabitants of the Roman Empire had been a symbol of the utmost degradation, into the instrument of man's salvation. There have been many different attempts to explain the atonement, most of them fantastic and repugnant. Christ's death has been interpreted as a satisfaction of God's honor or of God's justice or even as the payment of a debt to the devil. According to the "mousetrap" theory developed by Latin theologians of the third and fourth centuries, the devil had acquired power over humanity, but was tricked by the crucifixion into relinquishing it, Christ's flesh serving as the bait of a trap. Christianity has, in fact, never succeeded in rationalizing the atonement; yet it has never found it possible to abandon it. The true *raison d'être* of the doctrine is to be found not in the nature of God, but in the nature of man. The sense of guilt is one of the most potent and destructive forces in the human psyche, and man cannot enjoy spiritual health and security unless he is purged of it. Primitive man had satisfied his sense of guilt by transferring it to a scapegoat who was put to death in atonement for the misdeeds of the community. The Christian could rest assured of the love of God only because of his conviction that Jesus Christ, a man who was himself without sin, had suffered death as a universal scapegoat for the sins of others.

If all men were corrupted from birth, then they could achieve salvation only through divine grace, not by any effort of their own. The initiative in the process of conversion must come from God, not from man's perverted will, and only those whom God had chosen could be saved. Later theologians expounded these doctrines of predestination and election as exercises in logic, thus making God appear a monster of cruelty. In the fulfillment of his own inscrutable purposes he had decreed that only a tiny fraction of mankind would enjoy salvation while the remainder would be condemned to eternal torment for sins they could not avoid committing. Once again it is necessary to turn from logic to psychology. The Pauline doctrine of election was a deduction from the subjective experience of conversion. A man became a Christian not by making a conscious decision, but by submitting to emotional forces that brought about a transformation of his entire personality and seemed to him to come from an external spiritual power—according to Paul, from divine grace. Paul's own acceptance of Christianity had been brought about by an emotional cataclysm in the form of a vision of the risen Jesus; and the feeling of being called by the Holy Spirit was shared by his converts. Thus, faith appeared as the gift of God to those whom he had chosen; and as the essence of faith was trust in Jesus and an acceptance of his ethical values, it was necessarily followed by good works. Paul occasionally found it advisable to explain that Christian freedom did not mean a repudiation of all morality, but there was no problem in his own mind about the relationship between faith and works. Because the Christian was guided by love, he would spontaneously display goodness. With the transformation of his personality he would no longer feel obligated to obey a legal or moral code, but the sense of moral duty had been transcended rather than abrogated.

In speaking about human sinfulness, Paul used the word "flesh," which he contrasted with the spirituality of the Christian. This terminology perhaps reflected the influence of Hellenic philosophy, but the Pauline dualism was very different from that of the Platonists. Paul insisted on the resurrection of the body, in sharp contrast to the Hellenic doctrine of the immortality of the soul, and made the bodily resurrection of Jesus the central theme of his preaching. The whole man, body as well as soul, was capable of regeneration and would participate in the kingdom of heaven. This meant an acceptance of every part of the human personality as potentially good; whereas Hellenic philosophy had ended by repudiating most of human nature as hopelessly imperfect because of man's involvement in matter, the Christian doctrine of original sin implied that everything natural could be redeemed.

Life in the coming kingdom does not seem to have been envisaged in any detail, but in advising his converts how to conduct themselves while waiting for it, Paul showed much common sense and was by no means puritanical or ascetic. While he did not share that capacity for enjoyment which was so marked a feature of Jesus' personality as described in the gospels, he had none of that morbid hatred of the flesh which became so conspicuous in the Christianity of the fourth and fifth centuries. Because the time was brief, unmarried persons might do well not to divert their attention from divine things by taking spouses; but if they had strong sexual drives they should be advised to marry. It was better to marry than to be inflamed with sexual desire. Husbands and wives should give each other sexual satisfaction, refraining only by mutual consent and for short periods. The approach of the kingdom should not be used as an excuse for avoiding responsibilities, and Christians should continue to work at their regular occupations. This was, of course, an interim morality, and the same consideration determined Paul's attitude to political and social questions. In the coming kingdom all earthly power would come to an end, but prior to its realization Christians should not attempt to change the established order. They should respect the authority of Rome, and slaves should obey their masters.

The essential elements of Paul's theology, being firmly grounded in his own religious experience, have stood the test of time. Starting from the Messianic myth in the modified form it had acquired from the teaching, crucifixion, and presumed resurrection of Jesus, he was able to present a general interpretation of the world which gave meaning and purpose to all human experience. Yet because he accepted the myth not merely as a spiritual affirmation but also as a concrete physical truth, he was unable to preserve any clear distinctions between the realm of fact and the realm of values. The kingdom of heaven was not only a vision of what

human life ought to be; it was also a coming reality in which men
would no longer be bound by the physical limitations of earthly
existence. Alongside their enlightened ethical doctrines, Paul's letters also display magical modes of thinking, reflecting a primitive
identification of the subjective image with the objective reality.
For Paul, as for all other early Christians, the ethical insights of
the gospel were entangled with primitive superstitions, some of
which survived as permanent articles of Christian belief.

The resurrected Christ was the foundation of the new religion,
not merely as a symbol of a continuing spiritual influence, but
also as an assurance that death had been conquered. Death had
originated as a punishment for the sin of Adam; this implied that
the obliteration of sin in the coming kingdom would bring it to
an end. Confidently awaiting the kingdom in the near future,
Paul's converts expected earthly immortality; and when some of
them died, Paul had to reassure the survivors that these would be
resurrected after the return of Jesus. This confusion of matter and
spirit manifested itself especially in the development of the Christian sacraments. The physical rite of baptism, it was supposed,
actually washed away sins and assured divine forgiveness. In consequence of this belief, Christians soon developed a tendency to
postpone baptism until they reached maturity or even old age, in
fear lest they commit post-baptismal sins that could not be washed
away.

The eucharist exhibited the same mode of thinking even more
strongly. How Christians came to believe that the bread and wine
were the actual body and blood of Jesus is an obscure question.
This was an echo of the faith of primitive man that he acquired
the qualities of his animal deities by physically devouring them,
but we do not know whether it reached the Christian Church by
way of Jewish mystical thought or of one of the pagan cults. The
earliest statement of the doctrine of the eucharist is to be found
in Paul's first letter to the Corinthians, and it may be significant
that Paul's native province of Cilicia was the original center of
the cult of Mithra. When the gospels came to be written, the doctrine was well established, and Christians believed that by par-
taking of the eucharist they became physically united with Christ,
acquiring his virtues and sharing in his resurrection. In the words
of Ignatius, written early in the second century, it was the "medi-

cine of immortality." [9] On the other hand, the eucharist could be deadly to those who partook of it unworthily. When some of the Corinthian Christians died and others fell ill, Paul suggested that they must have eaten the eucharist in an improper spirit.

The physical union of Christians with the body of Christ, moreover, led to some perplexing problems with reference to union with other bodies, as is shown by a number of discussions in Paul's letters. Consorting with a prostitute was incompatible with Christianity not only on ethical grounds, but more especially, according to Paul, because the convert who had become united with Christ could not afterwards become one flesh with an immoral woman.[1] More controversial was the question of whether Christians should eat meat from a pagan temple. In the ancient world, it should be realized, most animals were normally slaughtered in temples and the appropriate parts offered as sacrifices to the images of pagan gods before the meat was made available for distribution to human beings. Would such meat convey spiritual contamination to those Christians who ate it? Paul declared that the meat was harmless, on the ground that the images to which it had been offered were merely creatures of wood and stone, although he added that Christians ought to refrain from it if it gave offense to overscrupulous brethren. On the other hand, Christians could not participate in pagan rituals: the Hellenic gods actually existed, being really evil spirits, and "ye cannot be partakers of the Lord's table, and of the table of devils." [2]

These aspects of Paul's theology, along with the continued Christian belief in miracles, faith healing, angelical and diabolical powers, and divine inspiration, have been burdens and embarrassments for the Church of modern times. It should not be supposed, however, that the early preachers of the gospel were any more credulous than their pagan contemporaries or that the growth of Christianity produced a lowering of the general level of enlightenment. Helleno-Roman society had long since lost

[9] Quoted by A. C. McGiffert: *History of Christian Thought*, I, 43.

[1] On top of the acropolis which towered high above the city of Corinth was a temple of Aphrodite which preserved the primitive tradition of sacred prostitution. In writing to his Corinthian converts about their ethical problems, was Paul thinking of fornication as a pagan religious ritual by which man became united with an embodiment of the mother goddess?

[2] I Corinthians, x, 21.

the classical Greek recognition of scientific law, and even its intellectual elite was inclined to attribute all events to the benign
or malignant influences of fortune or spirits or the stars. The
pagan philosophy of the imperial period was deeply imbued with
the belief in all kinds of supernatural agencies. The irrational aspects of Christianity were products of the age in which it developed. The significant differences between Christianity and all
forms of non-Christian thinking were in its ethical principles and
its attitude of optimism.

Obviously, many of Paul's converts could not appreciate his
more abstruse theological affirmations. Few of them were persons of much education. Paul had not had much success in his
attempt at Athens to present Christianity in terms that would appeal to an audience trained in Hellenic philosophy, and, as he
himself said, "not many wise men after the flesh, not many mighty,
not many noble" accepted the new religion. "God hath chosen
the foolish things of the world to confound the wise." [3] Early
Christianity seems to have appealed chiefly to urban craftsmen
and tradespeople and to slaves. But although such persons had
little understanding of the new cosmology and interpreted the
promise of the kingdom of heaven in extremely literal and materialistic terms, they could accept Christianity as a new way of
life organized around a new ethic. Apart from the writings of
Paul and the gospels and Acts, early Christian literature was, in
fact, almost exclusively concerned with ethical exhortation. This
was true of the non-Pauline letters in the New Testament and of
such non-canonical documents as the letter of Clement, the *Didache,* and the *Shepherd of Hermas,* all of which were written
before the end of the first century or not long afterwards.

In these writings the level of spiritual insight was markedly
lower than in Paul's letters. Christianity was presented as primarily a system of ethical precepts, not a means of emotional
transformation, and those who obeyed these precepts, it was implied, would be rewarded after Christ's return by sharing in the
privileges of his kingdom. Very few early Christians seem to have
understood the concept of spiritual freedom which Paul had so
strongly emphasized. There was a strong tendency to emphasize

[3] I Corinthians, i, 26–7.

the material advantages promised to the faithful, and this showed itself in one book that was admitted to the canon of the New Testament—the Revelation attributed (erroneously) to the author of the gospel of John. This apocalyptic fantasy, unique among Christian writings in expressing hostility to the Roman Empire, was derived from Jewish sources that had been given a Christian coloration, the main purpose being to reassure converts during a time of persecution that they would eventually triumph over their enemies. The popularity of such a document showed that many Christians had no real appreciation of the meaning of the gospel, and this fact was even more strongly demonstrated by the apocryphal New Testament writings produced in the second and third centuries—gospels representing Jesus in his childhood abusing his miraculous powers for trivial or malicious purposes, and sentimental romances about the adventures of the apostles and the women whom they converted (as in the pagan romances of the same period, the virtues of virginity were strongly emphasized).

Yet in spite of the intellectual limitations of most Christian converts, there can be no doubt that they actually endeavored to live by Christian principles, for otherwise the steady growth and final triumph of the Church would be incomprehensible. The concrete meaning of early Christianity can perhaps be most clearly estimated not from any of the New Testament writings, but from the *Shepherd of Hermas,* a collection of visions and parables apparently written in Rome about the end of the first century. In this book Christianity is presented as primarily ethical, its theology being almost ignored; the qualities chiefly emphasized are charity, humility, and cheerfulness. The characteristics of the good Christian are "the assistance of widows, visiting orphans and the poor, ransoming God's servants in their difficulties, showing hospitality . . . non-resistance to anyone, being of a quiet disposition, being poorer than all men, honoring the aged, practicing justice, exercising fraternal charity, enduring insults, being long-suffering, abstaining from spite," and a number of similar virtues. This Christian mildness and equanimity were in sharp contrast with the violent emotions induced by the spirit of evil. "When violent anger comes over you, or bitterness, you can tell he is within you. Then there arises the craving for excessive action, extravagance in many things to eat and drink, numerous feasts, varied unnecessary dishes, the desire for women, covetousness, arrogance, boasting, and a host of similar related excesses." Especially important was the avoidance of melancholy. "Sorrow is more wicked than all spirits and most dangerous to servants of God. . . . Every cheerful man does good, has good thoughts, and despises melancholy. On the other hand, the melancholy man is always committing sin." [4]

There is a similar emphasis in the writings of Justin Martyr, the most voluminous Christian apologist of the middle decades of the second century. Justin began as a pupil of the philosophical schools and turned finally to the new religion as a more satisfying answer to his ethical needs. Christianity, according to Justin, meant chastity, love, charity, patience, and obedience to the civil authorities, with the promise that these virtues would be rewarded after Christ's return. "We who formerly used magical arts, dedicate ourselves to the good and unbegotten God; we who valued above all things the acquisition of wealth and possessions, now bring what we have into a common stock, and communicate to every one in need; we who hated and destroyed one another, and on account of their different manners would not live with men of different tribes, now, since the coming of Christ, live familiarly with them, and pray for our enemies, and endeavor to persuade those who hate us unjustly to live conformably to the good precepts of Christ." [5]

In its insistence on freedom from disturbing passions, Christianity resembled the Hellenistic ethical philosophies, especially Stoicism. It differed from all forms of pagan thought in offering its converts not merely the negative virtue of emotional tranquillity, but also a positive faith and hope, in preaching active love and charity for others, and in inculcating humility, meekness, and a peaceful disposition. Sharply separating itself from its pagan environment and devoting itself to the practice of the gospel ethic, the early Church appeared as the nucleus of a new kind of society in which conflict and oppression would give place to universal brotherhood. The belief of Christians in the coming of the Messianic kingdom was an illusion; but their sincerity was proved by

---

[4] *Shepherd of Hermas,* translated by J. M.-F. Marique, Sixth, Eighth, and Tenth Mandates.

[5] Justin Martyr: *First Apology,* translated by A. Roberts and J. Donaldson, p. 14.

their willingness to incur social ostracism and, when necessary, persecution at the hands of the Roman government.

The emperors were not willing to extend to Christians the toleration they had given to Jews. Denounced as atheists and haters of the human race, the Christians were considered enemies of the state because of their refusal to acknowledge the traditional pagan deities and to participate in emperor-worship and also because of their opposition to military service. Periods of active persecution were few, and the total number of martyrs was relatively small; but the Church did not enjoy any legal status and had to remain, for the most part, an underground organization. Even emperors as enlightened as Trajan and Marcus Aurelius believed that obstinate Christians must be treated as criminals, though they did not regard them as sufficiently influential to require any special attention. In spite of the fact that obedience to established authority was declared by almost all Christian spokesmen to be a religious duty, the empire and the early Church did, in fact, represent opposing ideals and ways of life, and Roman officials were right in viewing Christianity as potentially subversive and revolutionary. In place of the traditional civic and political gods, Christians now appealed to a higher authority, that of the individual conscience illuminated by the Spirit. Despising the material achievement of the Roman state and the military force on which it depended, they preached charity, non-resistance, and universal brotherhood.

Thus, all Christians lived in danger of being condemned to death and thrown to wild animals for the amusement of the Roman mob, although few of them actually incurred such a fate. The effect on the development of the Church was in some ways unhealthy. The threat of martyrdom brought about a stronger emphasis on the rewards of the righteous and the punishment of the wicked after the resurrection, and gave to the Christian faith a feverish, fanatical, and markedly masochistic flavor. During the periods of persecution, some lukewarm Christians reverted to paganism, but others actually welcomed death as a means of proving their loyalty to Jesus and winning the assurance of a happy immortality. Yet there can be no doubt that in the long run persecution strengthened the Church by testing the sincerity of its adherents and enabling them to demonstrate it to the pagan world.

The mood of exaltation with which a Christian could confront death is exhibited in the letters written early in the second century by Ignatius, a Christian leader in Asia, while he was being transported to Rome in the expectation of being flung to the lions in the Colosseum. "May I enjoy the wild beasts that are prepared for me; and I pray that they may be found eager to rush upon me, which also I will entice to devour me speedily. . . . But if they be unwilling to assail me, I will impel them to do so. . . . Suffer me to become food for the wild beasts, through whose instrumentality it will be granted to me to attain to God. I am the wheat of God, and am ground by the teeth of the wild beasts that they may become my tomb, and may leave nothing of my body. . . . Come fire and cross and grapplings with wild beasts, wrenching of bones, hacking limbs, crushing of my whole body. Come cruel tortures of the devil to assail me. Only be it mine to attain unto Jesus Christ. . . . The pangs of a new birth are upon me. Bear with me, brethren. Do not hinder me from living; do not desire my death. . . . Permit me to be an imitator of the passion of my God." [6]

[6] Ignatius: *Epistles to the Romans,*   aldson, IV, V.
translated by A. Roberts and J. Don-

3

The Triumph of the Church

To all appearances the second, third, and fourth centuries were a period of steady Christian expansion. The Church continued to win new converts and spread to new provinces; it built up appropriate institutions and an efficient organization; and it clarified and rationalized its system of beliefs. To an increasing extent it became the most vigorous spiritual and cultural force in Helleno-Roman society, as was proved not only by its official adoption by Constantine early in the fourth century but also by the imposing succession of Christian theologians and apologists. Men like Irenaeus, Tertullian, Origen, Cyprian, Ambrose, and Augustine far surpassed their pagan contemporaries in mental vigor, originality, and perspicuity. Whatever intellectual arguments might be used for or against the dogmas and moral doctrines of the new religion, the decisive factor in the situation was that Christianity had incomparably more vitality than all of the cults and philosophies of Hellenism. Its triumph meant losses as well as gains—it meant, in particular, the growth of a narrow and fanatical spirit of religious intolerance that had been altogether alien to paganism—but it gave its adherents a hopefulness and a self-confidence with which the defenders of the old beliefs found it impossible to compete.

Yet while Christianity was in process of conquering Helleno-Roman civilization, it was at the same time losing much of its initially revolutionary character. During the centuries in which it was rising to dominance, the main emphasis of its preaching shifted from the hope of a regenerated society in this world to the promise of individual salvation after death. At the same time it was deeply infected by the dualism between the spirit and the body that was so prevalent in the culture of the Hellenic decadence, and in consequence acquired an ascetic tendency that had been wholly absent from the teaching of Jesus. Christian thinking began to make a sharp separation between the existing order and the order that was to come during the millennium, and to regard the ethical teaching of the gospel as a prophecy of life in the next world rather than a means of transforming human behavior in this one. Insulated from social realities, the doctrines of Jesus lost much of their practical efficacy. As a result of this transformation, Constantine was able to make Jesus the guardian of the Roman state without recognizing any serious obligation to adopt his teaching as a guide to policy. Not until the fifth century, in the philosophy of St. Augustine, did Christian thought begin to make a meaningful relationship between the divine order and the existing order of society.

The change in the character of Christianity was a consequence, in large measure, of the irrational elements in the original gospel. Jesus had believed in the imminence of the Messianic kingdom, and it was this hope that had given meaning to his ethical doctrines. Recognizing that human society could be regenerated by the practice of brotherly love, he had supposed that the ideal order would come about not by human effort, but by a divine intervention. His disciples should live in accord with the gospel ethic not because they would thereby initiate a social transformation, but in order to be ready for the coming kingdom. Down to near the end of the first century Christians continued to expect the kingdom in the near future. But as generations went by, it became increasingly evident that the interim period would be much longer than had been supposed and that most Christians would never see the kingdom in the normal course of their lives, but would share in it only after their resurrection. Continuing to postpone to the promised second coming the hope of a regenerated society, the Church now began to regard the practice of the gospel ethic as a means not of establishing the kingdom of heaven on earth, but of assuring individuals of salvation after death. This change of motivation transformed the whole spirit of Christianity. The resurrection of the body continued to be a Christian dogma; but when its locale was transferred from earth to heaven it largely ceased to have even a symbolic meaning except as an assurance of continued individuality. By the fourth century, asceticism had become widely prevalent. Dismissing the material world as hopelessly corrupt, the true domain of the devil, many Christians began to abstain from all forms of physical enjoyment, to punish their bodies, and to repudiate all social responsibilities in the hope of thereby making sure of the promised rewards of the afterlife.

This transformation was accompanied by a loss of the original confidence in spiritual freedom and by a growth of clerical power. The early Church had not supposed any central authority to be necessary because it had believed that all true Christians were under the direct guidance of the same Holy Spirit. The Spirit, it was assumed, would not contradict itself. There were at first no professional clergy, and even the missionaries engaged in spreading the gospel mostly preferred to support themselves (Paul, for example, had worked as a tentmaker, though he had occasionally accepted financial help from some of his converts). It gradually became apparent, however, that not everybody who prophesied or spoke with tongues was truly inspired, and that some recognized body of men must be empowered to define orthodox beliefs and decide between truth and falsehood. The *Didache,* otherwise known as the *Teaching of the Twelve Apostles,* a handbook of Christian practice compiled about the middle of the second century, shows that the behavior of some of the itinerant missionaries was presenting problems. Rules were needed in order to test the sincerity of such men. Preachers, it was now conceded, were entitled to financial support if they were genuine mouthpieces of the Spirit. But any itinerant should be regarded with suspicion if he asked for food or money or stayed more than three days without working. Such a man should be offered employment; and a refusal to accept it was a proof that he was "trading on the name of Christ." [1] Once it had been recognized that rational tests had to be applied to ecstatic phenomena and that the devil could counterfeit the manifestations of the Spirit of God, trust in inspiration began to decline. During the second century the Church gradually ceased to encourage prophecy and glossolalia, Christian services

---

[1] *Didache,* translated by F. X. Glimm, XI.

became more orderly, and a distinct professional group of bishops began to emerge as spiritual directors. At this period Christians still regarded themselves as forerunners of the kingdom of heaven. Members of the different Christian communities still contributed their surplus possessions to a common stock for distribution among those who could not support themselves. Tertullian, writing early in the third century, declared that: "One in mind and soul, we do not hesitate to share our earthly goods with one another. All is common among us but our wives." [2] But with the growing differentiation between the clergy and the laity and the delegation to the clergy of the power to define belief, Christianity was becoming institutionalized.

The most representative spokesman of the new religion at this stage in its development was Irenaeus, a native of Asia Minor who became bishop of the church at Lyons, Gaul, about 180. Strongly asserting man's freedom to choose between good and evil, the union in Christ of deity and humanity, and the potential regeneration of the whole of human nature, body as well as soul, he displayed a clearer grasp of the essentials of the faith than any other Christian writer since Paul. But he had no understanding of Paul's view of conversion as an emotional transformation resulting in spiritual freedom; his concept of morality was essentially legalistic, fusing the Jewish doctrine of obedience to the divine will with the Stoic concept of natural law. His main importance in Christian history is that, in discussing the danger of false doctrine, he affirmed the authority of tradition and of the organized Church. The revelation of new truths by mouthpieces of the Holy Spirit, he declared, had ended with the apostolic era. Doctrines should be considered true only if they were in conformity with the teaching of the apostles and the books written by them or under their supervision and with the creed professed by the Christian community as a whole and expounded by bishops in regular succession from the apostles. Both in his theology and in his concept of authority Irenaeus may be regarded as the principal founder of Catholicism. His definition left open the possibility of conflict among different bishops and branches of the Church, but in practice the Church of Rome was already assuming a position of leader-

---

[2] Tertullian: *Apologeticus,* translated by A. Roberts and J. Donaldson, p. 29.

ship, largely because of its location in the capital city of the empire. Even before the end of the first century, in fact, the leader of the Roman Church, Clement, had taken the responsibility of guiding Christians elsewhere, as is shown by his letter to the Corinthians.

A further stage in the growth of clericalism was registered in the writings of Cyprian, Bishop of Carthage, in the middle of the third century. Faced with the problem presented by Christians who had temporarily denied their faith during a time of persecution, Cyprian declared that they could be readmitted only by bishops in regular succession to the apostles and that the bishops were responsible to God alone. It was Cyprian who first coined the momentous formula: "Outside the Church there is no salvation." The Church throughout the world was a single body, and only its regularly appointed clergy could validly administer the sacraments which were the means of redemption for all believers. It was still to be determined whether the ultimate authority belonged to the whole body of bishops collectively or solely to the Bishop of Rome, but it was plain that little remained of the original gospel promise that all men could share in the brotherhood of the kingdom as sons of God. The Church had become an authoritarian institution, ready for partnership with an authoritarian state. In view of the irrationality of the original apostolic reliance on spiritual inspiration, such an evolution was probably inevitable.

This trend did not develop without opposition. Early in the third century a mystic in Asia Minor by the name of Montanus called for a return to the Christianity of the apostolic era. Declaring that the Messianic kingdom was now finally close at hand, that all true believers should follow the direct guidance of the Holy Spirit, and that all earthly authority was about to be abolished, he won a considerable following not only in his native province but also in Gaul, Africa, and elsewhere. Montanism, however, was not a pure revival of the teaching of Jesus and Paul; it also contained alien elements. Its main center was on the Phrygian plateau, the especial home of the Great Mother Cybele and her orgiastic rituals, and Montanus himself was said to be a former priest of the goddess. It was possibly from the worship of Cybele, traditionally associated with emasculation, that the Montanists derived their belief in perpetual chastity. Writings in praise of virginity emanated from

Montanist sources, and some of them appear to have had a wide influence in orthodox circles. As we know Montanism chiefly from the writings of its opponents, we cannot judge it fairly. The movement seems to have been quickly discredited by the failure to achieve the promised millennium and by the disorderly behavior of its adherents, though it did not wholly disappear for several centuries. The tendencies that it represented, however, were written too deeply into the gospels and the letters of Paul to be permanently extirpated, and they reappeared from time to time during the later history of Christianity. In the later Middle Ages and again after the Reformation, heretical sects reaffirmed the original Christian belief in the approach of the millennium, the direct inspiration of the Holy Spirit, and the abolition of all earthly authority. Voicing the protests of exploited groups against social injustice and promising the realization of a mystical Kingdom of Freedom, they displayed aspirations and illusions which, after the substitution of a materialistic for a religious mythology, have found expression in the modern world in Marxist Communism.

Meanwhile, Christianity was absorbing much of pagan culture and being partially transformed by it. When men of education became converts it was inevitable that they should interpret their new faith by means of the categories to which they were already accustomed, often failing to recognize all its essential novelty. The fusion of Christianity and Hellenism was made possible by the doctrine of the *Logos,* according to which Christ was the embodiment of the divine reason that pervaded the visible world and was the source of natural law. Thus, the new revelation appeared as the fulfillment and consummation not only of the Jewish Messianic hope, but also of the philosophic quest for truth, and Socrates no less than Moses could be considered as a forerunner of the gospel. As Justin Martyr declared early in the second century, "whatever things were rightly said among all men are the property of us Christians. For next to God, we acknowledge and love the Word who is from the unbegotten and ineffable God. . . . . For all the writers were able to see realities darkly through the sowing of the implanted Word that was in them." [3] By no means all Christians were willing to grant any independent validity to pagan thought. In fact, even Justin followed Philo in asserting that Plato had

---

[3] Justin: *Second Apology,* translated by A. Roberts and J. Donaldson, p. 13.

learned his philosophy from Moses but had kept his indebtedness a secret through fear of sharing the fate of Socrates and being put to death for impiety. But Christian thinkers were increasingly disposed to appropriate the Hellenic heritage and make use of it for their own purposes.

How much of Hellenism could Christianity incorporate without losing its own fundamental character? As long as Christian thinkers continued to affirm that man was endowed with freedom to choose between good and evil, that the material world was God's creation and therefore good by nature and bad only because of human error, that the human soul was not a fragment of the divine spirit but an independent entity, and that salvation consisted not in escape from the trammels of the flesh but in the regeneration of human nature by the practice of the gospel ethic, they had a firm grasp on the fundamentals of their faith. These doctrines could be reconciled with much of the Stoic tradition, especially with the Stoic conception of natural law. But they were more sharply at variance with Platonism; and to the extent that Christianity became Platonized it became tainted with the decadence of its environment.

In general, the essentials of Christianity were preserved more fully in the Latin West than in the Hellenic East, a fact of great importance for the whole future development of European civilization. The theology of the Latin Church, in harmony with the Roman tradition, became predominantly legal and political. God was envisaged as the sovereign of the universe and morality as a code of laws that man was obligated to obey. The categories of Roman jurisprudence did not have room for the Pauline doctrine of Christian liberty, and it was chiefly the Latin theologians who were responsible for defining the concept of the Church in authoritarian terms. But their mode of thinking preserved the original Christian emphasis on ethics, on man's freedom of choice, and on the potential regeneration of nature.

North Africa was for a long time the main stronghold of Latin Christianity, and a native of Carthage was its first outstanding theologian. This was Tertullian, who was converted to the new religion about 195 after a career as a lawyer and who subsequently wrote forty books of Christian apologetics. A man of varied learning, wide interests, and complex and passionate temperament, fond of epigram and paradox, sometimes tender and sometimes vituperative, but always unrestrained, he was the greatest Latin writer of the third century and the greatest Latin Christian writer before Augustine. Owing chiefly to the malice of Edward Gibbon, he has acquired a sinister reputation as the man who promised his fellow converts that they would be able after the resurrection to watch their enemies tormented in the flames of hell. This display of vindictiveness occurs once in all his writings, in the last paragraph of his *De Spectaculis,* and seems almost forgivable if it is remembered that he wrote it to strengthen the faith of Christians at a time when they were being thrown to the lions for the entertainment of the Roman populace.[4]

In the history of theology Tertullian is remembered chiefly as an enemy of philosophy. He believed that Christianity was founded on paradoxes that transcended reason and were incapable of philosophical explanation. "What indeed has Athens to do with Jerusalem?" he demanded. "What concord is there between the Academy and the Church? . . . Our instruction comes from 'the porch of Solomon,' who had himself taught that 'the Lord should be sought in simplicity of heart.' Away with all attempts to produce a mottled Christianity of Stoic, Platonic and dialectic composition!"[5] The Christian faith, he exclaimed with characteristic hyperbole, "is wholly credible because it is foolish; it is certain because it is impossible."[6] It was possibly his suspicion of Hellenic rationalism that led him eventually to espouse the Montanist heresy, under the influence of which he spent much of his old age writing books urging widows to remain chaste instead of seeking second husbands. Tertullian's fear of philosophy, however, was actually a fear of Platonism, and did not extend to the whole of pagan culture. He himself, to a greater extent than he seems to have recognized, was influenced by Roman jurisprudence and by Stoicism. An ex-lawyer, he interpreted Christian morality as an obligation owed by man to the sovereign of the universe, and identified the

---

[4] Gibbon quotes almost the whole of the relevant passage from *De Spectaculis (Decline and Fall,* Chapter 15), and then deliberately misleads his audience by mendaciously adding that "the humanity of the reader will permit me to draw a veil over the rest of this infernal description, which the zealous African pursues in a long variety of affected and unfeeling witticisms."

[5] Quoted by H. A. Wolfson: *The Philosophy of the Church Fathers,* I, 102.

[6] *"Prorsus credibile est, quia ineptum est; certum est, quia impossibile est."* Wolfson: op. cit., p. 103.

law of God with the natural law of the Stoics. The Ten Commandments given to Moses were laws of nature, God having made known his will through direct revelation to the Jews and through nature to the gentiles. Man's soul, in fact, was "naturally Christian." Tertullian had some of the deficiencies of the Roman temperament: in particular, a tendency to think in crudely materialistic and literal terms, often shown in his discussions of the resurrection. But his idealization of nature as God's handiwork, derived from both Christian and Latin sources, led him to a recognition of physical beauty for which much can be forgiven him. "One flower of the hedgerow by itself, I think—I do not say a flower of the meadow; one shell of any sea you like—I do not say the Red Sea; one feather of a moor-fowl—to say nothing of the peacock— will they speak to you of a mean creator? . . . If I offer you a rose, you will not scorn its creator." [7] This appreciation of nature, precluded by a philosophy that found beauty only in abstract ideas, was made possible by the Christian doctrine of divine creation.

In the Hellenic East, on the other hand, the dominant modes of thought were philosophical and mystical rather than legal, and when Christianity was interpreted in these terms it almost lost its ethical content. Accustomed to consider reality as static rather than dynamic and to regard the soul as a spark of divinity imprisoned in matter, Hellenic converts could not easily accept either the Christian view of history as the progressive fulfillment of divine purposes or the Christian doctrine of the regeneration of the flesh. The attempt to combine Christianity with Hellenic philosophy produced a number of heretical movements that interpreted redemption as an escape from the material world, while supposedly orthodox theologians showed a strong tendency to nullify those Christian beliefs that could not be reconciled with Platonism by interpreting them allegorically. Greek Christianity was always inclined to attribute salvation to correct doctrine rather than to virtuous behavior, emphasizing *gnosis* (knowledge) more than *agape* (love), and in the end became almost lost in a maze of theological subtleties.

The main battleground of Hellenic Christianity was always the problem of the nature of Christ. The orthodox doctrine according to which he was both human and divine symbolized the Christian

---

[7] *Adversus Marcion*, I, 13.

conception of God's love for man and of the ultimate regeneration of the whole of human nature, as against the Platonic repudiation of the world and the flesh and the Platonic view of salvation as the reabsorption of the soul into the transcendent godhead. Platonists were unwilling to believe that the supreme being had become incarnate in a material body. Such a doctrine was contrary both to their picture of the universe as a hierarchy of forms, with a great gulf intervening between heaven and earth, and to their view of the material world as necessarily imperfect and corrupt. They could not accept a deity who had truly become flesh, truly suffered, and truly died on the cross, nor could they suppose that a being who had appeared in human form could actually be a manifestation of the eternal and unchanging godhead. They preferred to think of Jesus as neither divine nor human but as an intermediary between God and man, his function being to assist human beings in escaping from the corrupting influence of matter.

References in Paul's letters to the Colossians and the Ephesians show that some of his Hellenic converts were already denying Christ's humanity. By the end of the first century, docetism—the doctrine that Christ was a spirit who had merely seemed to be a man—was being widely taught, and the gospel of John, which accepted the Hellenic identification of Christ with the *Logos* but strongly insisted on his real corporeality, may have been written in order to confute it. The second century was the especial flowering-time of Gnostic heresies that attempted to fuse Christianity with pagan mysticism. The Gnostics declared the material world to be inherently evil and declared that man could escape from it by some form of esoteric knowledge. Many of them elaborated fantastic systems of aeons and emanations to bridge the gap which they supposed to exist between God and man. Irenaeus enumerated ten of these heretical sects and thirteen heretical leaders; Tertullian compiled a list of no less than twenty-nine such groups. Gnosticism undoubtedly meant the corruption of Christianity, but we need not believe the accusations of gross immorality in which orthodox spokesmen so freely indulged. Such controversial methods show that as Christianity gained in strength, it was also gaining in intolerance and in the spirit of theological hatred.

The Gnostic sects appear to have been short-lived. The same tendencies, however, reappeared in a more formidable and long-lived movement which apparently had its roots not in Platonism, but in the Zoroastrian dualism of Iran, though for a long time it had a strong appeal to Platonizing Hellenists. This was Manichaeanism, whose founder, Mani, was born in Babylonia in 216 and was crucified by order of the King of Persia in 277 for denying the official Zoroastrian religion. Mani elaborated an extraordinarily complicated mythology somewhat resembling the old Orphic mystery cult. The essence of his system was a dualism between good and evil, spirit and matter, light and darkness. The devil, representing the material world, had swallowed fragments of divinity, as a result of which souls had become imprisoned in flesh. Christ was the way of salvation, but had not truly become incarnate. Partial release from the flesh could be attained by complete chastity and other ascetic practices, including abstinence from meat foods, which contained more of the evil principle than did vegetables. But as the material world was inherently evil, man must fix all his hope on the life after death. From what we know of Manichaeanism, derived solely from the writings of its opponents, it is difficult to understand how so pessimistic a creed can have won so many supporters. Perhaps the main reason for its appeal was that it justified moral relaxation; if man could not achieve virtue as long as he remained in the flesh, he had no reason for ethical discipline. Manichaeanism had a wide vogue through the Roman Empire during the fourth century. It survived in Armenia and other eastern provinces for many centuries, and subsequently spread to Bulgaria, where it became identified with nationalistic resistance to Byzantine dominance. Reintroduced into western Europe during the twelfth century, it flourished in parts of southern France under the name of Albigensianism and was finally extirpated only by an intensive persecution conducted by the Catholic authorities.

As long as the impulse to escape from nature found expression only in heresies frankly hostile to orthodox Christianity, the Church could preserve its basic beliefs inviolate. But Platonism became a more dangerous threat to the Christian view of life when it was presented as in harmony with the gospel revelation by men who remained within the Christian community. During the second century a school of Christian philosophy was founded at Alexandria. The second and third of the leaders of the school, Clement and Origen, wrote extensively in defense of the new religion, but at the same time transformed much of its meaning by interpreting it in Platonic terms. It is significant that Origen had been a pupil of an Alexandrian mystic named Ammonius Saccas, who was also the principal teacher of Plotinus. The kind of speculative religion which Origen represented, and which became prevalent among Greek-speaking theologians, meant the loss of the dynamic and optimistic elements of gospel Christianity, and was really closer to the *Enneads* in its underlying implications.

Clement placed Hellenic philosophy on the same level as the Mosaic and prophetic revelation, as equally an expression of the divine reason and a pathway to Christianity. "By images and direct visions," he affirmed, "those Greeks who have philosophized accurately see God." [8] His *Paedagogus,* a guide to Christian living, contained little that could be regarded as specifically Christian, Clement's Christ being primarily a manifestation of the eternal *Logos* rather than a being who had actually lived in the flesh. This tendency was carried farther by Origen, who was head of the school from 202 until 220 and then retired to Palestine, where he died a martyr in 254. A man of immense learning and prodigious industry, Origen was the first Christian who was primarily a scholar. The author of six thousand rolls, which included Biblical commentaries, defenses of Christianity, and a critical edition of the text of the Old Testament, he kept busy a staff of seven amanuenses, who were provided by a wealthy admirer. Origen's main conviction was that the Christian religion was wholly rational, any apparent paradoxes being illusory ("It is of much importance to give our assent to doctrines on grounds of reason and wisdom rather than of faith only," he declared),[9] and by rational he meant Platonic. While he accepted the Bible as the word of God, he reconciled it with Platonism by interpreting difficult passages as allegorical, a method learned from Philo.

Christianity appeared in Origen's writings as primarily a philosophical system rather than a new way of life. Its goal was the mystical knowledge of the divine being rather than the love of one's fellow man. Origen was much concerned about the nature of the godhead and the relationship of Jesus Christ to God the Father, and engaged in lengthy attempts to elucidate these mys-

---

[8] Quoted by A. C. McGiffert: *History of Christian Thought,* I, 183. [9] Wolfson: op. cit., I, 106.

teries. Virtue, moreover, was to be achieved not by the regeneration of man's natural feelings, but by their suppression through
rigorous self-discipline. For Origen, as for the ethical philosophers
of paganism, it meant freedom from all disturbing emotions. In
spite of his nominal acceptance of the teaching of the gospel, he
displayed a strong tendency to regard matter rather than sin as the
source of evil and to interpret salvation as liberation from the flesh.
In accord with the static cosmology of Hellenism he argued that
the universe existed eternally, instead of being created by God in
time and moving toward a temporal culmination, and interpreted
the resurrection in wholly spiritual terms, with no terrestrial millennium. It seems significant, as an indication of Origen's temperamental bias toward the repudiation of the world of space and
time, that early in his life he sought to escape from carnal temptation by emasculating himself.

Some of Origen's doctrines were clearly heretical, though they
were not formally repudiated by the Church until after his death,
and he was, therefore, never accepted as an official exponent of
Christian theology. Yet few men have had a greater influence on
the development of Christianity, and no one has done more to
obscure the original meaning of the gospel. By emphasizing a
Platonic *gnosis* rather than the *agape* of Jesus and Paul, he transformed the whole meaning of the new religion. The full results became apparent in the fourth century, after Christianity became the
official religion of the Roman state. Origen's Christological speculations led to prolonged and bitter conflicts in which man's eternal
salvation seemingly became dependent not on the practice of the
gospel ethic but on the right choice of formulas to describe mysteries that were admittedly beyond human comprehension. During
the same period his conception of Christian ethics was exemplified
in the monastic movement, which was motivated by the hope of
achieving a mystical knowledge of God by the suppression of all
natural desires.

The fusion of Christianity with pagan philosophy distorted the
original meaning of the gospel, but did not wholly deprive it of its
revolutionary implications. In the fourth century, however, the
Church was exposed to a more deeply corrupting influence by its
elevation into partnership with the imperial government. By the
action of Constantine, the Galilean carpenter who had preached

love, humility, and peace took the place of Romulus and Mars as
the official guardian of the Roman state.

For the first two hundred years of its existence Christianity had
been too obscure to cause any serious concern to the imperial authorities. But by the third century it had become strong enough to
present political problems, and it became increasingly obvious that
the government must either destroy it or win its support. Two
periods of systematic persecution, one under Decius in the middle of the century and the other under Diocletian at its conclusion, failed to destroy it. The retirement of Diocletian in 305 was
followed by another interval of civil war which ended in the triumph of another soldier emperor of Balkan peasant descent, Constantine. Constantine had adopted the "labarum" (apparently a
form of the cross) as the standard with which he led his troops into
battle, and after experience had convinced him of its efficacy in
bringing victory, he gave official protection to the Church. By the
Edict of Milan of 313, Christianity was granted full toleration and
the traditional association of the state with the pagan gods came to
an end. Before his death in 337, Constantine had gone a long way
toward making Christianity into the official religion. Though he
did not prohibit pagan worship, he lavished privileges upon the
Church, authorizing it to hold property and receive gifts and
legacies and exempting the clergy from all civil obligations. He
also assumed broad powers of control over its affairs. He called
himself the thirteenth apostle, and himself presided over ecclesiastical councils and helped to formulate Christian dogmas.

Constantine's motives have remained uncertain. Was his adoption of Christianity a wholly political measure, designed to strengthen
the imperial government by winning the adherence of the strongest
organization within the empire? Certainly he was himself no model
of Christian virtue. He was guilty not only of the acts of brutality
and treachery that were to be expected of an emperor at this period
of Roman history, but also of murdering his wife and one of his sons.
Yet it is probable that he was sincerely convinced of the truth of
Christianity, although lacking in the faintest comprehension of its
real meaning. Jesus had demonstrated his power by building the
Church and preserving it from destruction. The empire should now
seek his patronage, in place of that of the old deities who had failed
to protect it. As Constantine declared in his profession of faith, "it

appears that those who faithfully discharge God's holy laws and shrink from the transgression of his commandments are rewarded with abundant blessings and endowed with well-grounded hope as well as ample power for the accomplishment of their undertakings." [1]

The hope of securing divine aid in the pursuit of material prosperity had been mankind's oldest and most deeply rooted motive for worshipping the gods. Some of the thinkers of the Axial Period, most notably the Jewish prophets, had affirmed more rational and more enlightened religious beliefs, and their doctrines had been restated by Jesus, who, while preaching the fatherhood of God, had explicitly denied any correlation between virtue and prosperity. But under the patronage of Constantine primitive attitudes were reinstated in Christian theology. With lamentable eagerness the bishops of the Church welcomed the protection of the Emperor and assured him that the worship of Jesus was indeed a guarantee of victory over all his enemies. The abrupt degeneration of Christianity under the impact of success is luridly illustrated in the biography of Constantine written by Eusebius, Bishop of Caesarea. The main theme of this nauseating eulogy was that Constantine had become the greatest ruler in history because of his devotion to God and the perfection of his personal character. Henceforth Christian apologists continued to affirm that worldly success would be the reward of piety, while misfortune was either a warning or a punishment for sin, and devoted much misguided ingenuity to elucidating the moral purposes of every catastrophe in history.[2] This primitive attitude has constantly reappeared through the later development of Christianity, especially during periods of general crisis or disaster.

The Church now extended its blessings to the whole Roman heritage. Christ had given supremacy to Rome in order to prepare the way for the teaching of his gospel, and monarchy was the only divinely ordained form of government, the emperor exercising authority by divine right. The Christian poet Prudentius echoed Virgil in affirming that Christ had given the Romans "power for everlasting in a supremacy that is from heaven. No bounds indeed

---

[1] Quoted by C. N. Cochrane: *Christianity and Classical Culture,* p. 184.

[2] Christians took especial pleasure in recounting in lurid detail how all the persecutors of the Church had been murdered or succumbed to horrible diseases. See, for example, the treatise of Lactantius, *De Mortibus Persecutorum.*

did he set, no limits of time did he lay down. Unending sway he taught, so that the valor of Rome should never grow old nor the glory she had won know age." [3] Unlike their pagan predecessors, Christian spokesmen affirmed a belief in progress, declaring that the adoption of the new religion was a sign of mankind's increasing enlightenment, and continued to look forward to a kingdom of heaven in which love would replace justice as the principle of unity and order. But this Messianic kingdom would not be realized until the end of the world, and during the interim period society could not be governed in accord with the ethical teachings of the gospel. Human sinfulness required the continued exercise of coercive power and the protection of class distinctions and property rights by the imperial government.

Lactantius, the principal Christian spokesman in the era of Constantine, continued to make an uncompromising distinction between the ethics of the Church and those of the world. In a work dedicated to the Emperor, he declared that Christian justice meant love, brotherhood, and equality, and hence was completely contrary to the existing social order with its class distinctions and its reliance on military force. But the Christian ideal could be achieved only in God's appointed time, after a final time of troubles in which the Roman Empire itself would be destroyed. [4] Lactantius did not suggest that the emperor should be guided by Christian doctrine in his government of the empire. Constantine's legislation did, in fact, show a mild Christian influence, most notably in giving more protection to women and slaves and restricting divorce; but the Christian emperors made no attempt to bring about a new social order. On the contrary, the destruction of the middle classes by excessive taxation, the enforcement of hereditary caste distinctions, and the exaltation of the military and bureaucratic hierarchies continued with increasing momentum.

Thus the Church and the empire, although henceforth allied with each other, continued to represent different ideals, and there was no fusion of values. The ethics of Christianity, projected into the millennium, had little practical applicability, and imperial policy showed little Christian influence. Nor did the empire gain new

---

[3] Prudentius: *Contra Orationem Symmachi*, translated by H. J. Thomson, pp. 539–43.

[4] See Lactantius: *The Divine Institutions*, especially V, 8, 16; VI, 6, 10, 11, 12; VII, 2, 4, 24, 25.

strength from its adoption of the new religion. Christians became loyal supporters of the imperial government, but they did not easily forget their original opposition to military service (Basil of Caesarea, writing late in the fourth century, declared that soldiers who had killed enemies in battle should be excluded from the sacraments for three years). The Church displayed little positive enthusiasm for the preservation of the established order. The uncompromising devaluation of all temporal institutions in the writings of Lactantius continued to represent the Christian attitude. During the fourth century, in fact, increasing numbers of Christians repudiated all civic responsibilities and sought personal salvation by withdrawing into monasteries and hermitages.

The final struggle between Christianity and paganism lasted through the fourth century. At the time of the Edict of Milan the Christians composed only a minority—possibly not more than one fifth—of the total population of the empire, but Constantine's victory made conversion politically advantageous, and most of the imperial officials now became at least nominal Christians and an increasing number of Christian bishops belonged to aristocratic or bureaucratic families. The new imperial capital that Constantine built on the hills overlooking the Bosporus was from the beginning a Christian city. Some members of the landowning aristocracy, especially in the City of Rome, remained loyal to the traditional religion, but they displayed little sense of conviction about the existence of the old gods. In opposition to the Christians, however, they insisted that the traditional myths and the rituals associated with them were still valid means of access to divine mysteries and that the piety and moralities dependent on them should not be wantonly destroyed. As Quintus Aurelius Symmachus, the last outstanding representative of Roman paganism, declared in a speech delivered in 384, "each nation has its own gods and peculiar rites. The Great Mystery cannot be approached by one avenue alone. But use and wont count for much in giving authority to religion. Leave us the symbol on which our oaths of allegiance have been sworn for so many generations. Leave us the system which has so long given prosperity to the State. A religion should be judged by its utility to the men who hold it." [5]

---

[5] Quoted by S. Dill: *Roman Society in the Last Century of the Western Empire*, p. 30.

Paganism was still capable of inspiring one enthusiastic champion, Constantine's nephew Julian, who occupied the throne in succession to his cousin Constantius from 361 to 363. It is impossible not to sympathize with this impractical young idealist, whose antagonism to the new religion seems to have been largely motivated by a revulsion against the corruption and hypocrisy of the imperial court. But although Julian wished to preserve the old rituals, he was by no means a conservative. He proposed to organize a new synthetic religion centered in the worship of the sun as symbolic of the divine unity and borrowing many of the institutions of Christianity; and, being an ardent Neo-Platonist, he was a fervent practitioner of ascetic disciplines. Julian had more in common with his Christian contemporaries than with the old Greek and Roman heroes whose memory he revered.

Much more typical of the old age of paganism was the devotion to tradition displayed by Symmachus and other members of the old Roman families. History offers few more striking examples of indurated resistance to change. The owner of three great houses in Rome itself, of fifteen country villas, and of large estates in southern Italy and northern Africa, Symmachus played the role of a Roman senator as though he were living in the age of Augustus. His letters, composed with scrupulous attention to the rules of rhetoric and carefully preserved for the admiration of posterity, are filled with accounts of the tedious and futile social rituals to which he devoted his life. In this age of decadence and universal transformation, only a generation before the capture of Rome by the Goths, it is extraordinary to find how much importance was still attached to the proper performance of public games. In celebration of his son's elevation to the office of praetor, Symmachus arranged for the importation of lions and crocodiles from Africa, dogs from Scotland, horses from Spain, and Saxon gladiators from Germany. It was a disaster of major proportions that the crocodiles refused to eat and had to be destroyed, the horses were disabled by their journey, and the gladiators escaped from the necessity of killing each other in the Colosseum by committing suicide. The blind traditionalism exhibited in such trivialities goes far to explain both the victory of Christianity over the old religion and the decline of Roman power.

After the premature death of Julian in war with the Persians there were no more pagan emperors, and the dominance of Christianity steadily increased. One after another of the old rituals was brought to an end, and temples were abandoned or transformed into churches. The sacred places of the old religion, Delphi and Eleusis and Olympia and other shrines that had been centers of devotion for a thousand years, were gradually deserted and left to the slow erosion of the elements. Although the official policy of the emperors was to preserve the more important images of the old gods as works of art, often by removing them from their original homes to the new city of Constantinople, many of them were destroyed by mob attacks. In 416 all public offices were closed to adherents of the old religion, and in 439 the government began to prohibit the performance of pagan rites. After the fifth century it is no longer possible to find in Greek or Roman literature any overt expressions of disbelief in Christianity. Apparently the last Latin writer who preserved some degree of religious skepticism was the poet Rutilius Namatianus; his *De Reditu Suo,* which affirmed the greatness of the Roman tradition and voiced contempt for Christian asceticism, was written in 416. The last important non-Christian philosopher, the Neo-Platonist Proclus, died in 485. The schools of philosophy at Athens, which had continued to teach Neo-Platonism rather than Christianity, were closed by imperial decree early in the sixth century.

In literature and philosophy, Christianity won a total victory. Not for more than a thousand years would it be possible for any citizen of a Christian state to advocate rejection of any of its basic doctrines. But on the popular level, especially in rural communities, the acceptance of Christianity had very different results. Traditional religious attitudes, instead of being destroyed, were incorporated into the new religion with only superficial modifications, and the neolithic heritage, which had already survived the imposition of Aryan gods in the second millennium B.C., was readapted to the worship of Jesus. This was made possible by the transformation of popular Christianity into a virtually polytheistic religion through the veneration of saints and martyrs and the elevation of the mother of Jesus into the status of a goddess in all but name. All over the empire the local deities worshipped by peasants since time immemorial were replaced by Christian saints or by the Virgin Mary, and these new recipients of popular devotion were honored

by some of the same rituals as their predecessors and credited with
similar miraculous powers. Few traces survived of the worship of
the Olympians, who had always been aristocratic and urban deities;
but the old chthonian religion associated with the processes of
agriculture maintained much of its vitality. Under new names the
peasants continued to revere a mother goddess, to mourn the killing
of a male deity, to celebrate his triumphant resurrection in the
spring as a token of the continued fertility of nature, and to honor
the spirits of the dead and bring offerings to their tombs. Nor was
this grafting of Christianity onto the neolithic tradition restricted to
the illiterate. It is interesting to find that Monnica, the mother of
Augustine, was in the habit of bringing cakes and wine to the
graves of martyrs, apparently without any awareness of the beliefs
in which this age-old ritual had originated.

The heroic deeds of the martyrs now became the favorite theme
of Christian writers. Thus a new mythology was elaborated to replace that of the vanished Olympians. It was equally replete with
miracles and other evidences of supernatural power, but it honored
very different values: the endurance of suffering rather than victory
in battle, ascetic self-mortification instead of the perfection of
nature. Far removed from the teaching of the gospel, it perpetu-
ated the sickly and masochistic tendencies that Christianity had acquired during its centuries of persecution. Men and women who
had been roasted on grids or torn with iron claws or thrown into
rivers with millstones around their necks or eaten by lions in the
arena—these were the official exemplars of the new dispensation.
Yet it is unlikely that this celebration of suffering exerted much influence on popular morality. The saints were honored by most of
their worshippers not for their heroism, but because they were
miracle-workers. Even the tales of martyrdom usually included instances of supernatural protection, although—paradoxically—
divine providence did not intervene to prevent the ultimate sacrifice. The *Peristephanon Liber* of Prudentius contains many examples. Thus, St. Romanus was saved from being burned alive by
a storm of rain, and was then enabled to continue preaching sermons after his tongue had been torn out, though God did not stop
his persecutors from finally killing him by breaking his neck; St.
Agnes was saved from rape when a man who cast lustful eyes
upon her was blinded by a thunderbolt, though she was soon after-

wards beheaded; St. Quirinus continued floating and preaching to
his disciples for some time after being thrown into a river with a
stone around his neck and was finally drowned only in answer to
his own prayers; the corpse of St. Vincent was first guarded
against hungry animals by a raven and afterwards, having been
dropped into the sea, was miraculously floated ashore in order that
it might receive Christian burial. These evidences of magical power
made the martyrs suitable objects of popular devotion, and it
quickly became the custom for their adherents to pray to them and
invoke their protection as though they were actually minor deities
and to cherish their bones and other relics in the belief that these
were still charged with a numinous force that could be used for the
curing of diseases. The trade in such objects was already so well
established by the later fourth century as to require legislative regulation. This was a prolongation of the old chthonian cult of dead
heroes which had inspired Sophocles' final celebration of the burial
of Oedipus in the soil of Attica. The popular belief in the magical
power of relics—a power exerted in total disregard of all ethical
considerations—was a survival of even more primitive layers of
human thought.[6]

Meanwhile, the main preoccupation of the leaders of the post-
Constantinean Church was not the promotion of Christian ethics
but the definition of Christian dogma. Previously, all converts at
baptism had been required to subscribe to a general profession of
the faith, but different branches of the Church had adopted
slightly different formulas, and there had been no generally accepted creed. But with the elevation of Christianity into the official
religion, it seemed important to secure agreement on the essential

---

[6] A letter of Pope Gregory the
Great, written at the end of the sixth
century, strikingly illustrates the survival of the old chthonian belief that
the corpses of great men retained a
numinous power which could be destructive as well as beneficent. Such
relics were "sacred" in the full primitive meaning of the word, so that it
was dangerous to touch them. According to Gregory, "the bodies of the
apostles Saint Peter and Saint Paul
glitter with so great miracles and ter-
rors in their churches that one cannot
even go to pray there without great
fear." When the corpse of Saint Lawrence was accidentally exposed during
building operations, those "who saw
the body of the same martyr, which
they did not presume to touch, all
died within ten days, so that none
might survive who had seen the holy
body of that righteous man." An attempt to remove the bodies of the
apostles from Rome produced a ter-
rific thunderstorm, after which the attempt was abandoned. See *Epistles* of
Gregory the Great, translated by
James Barmby, IV, 30.

elements of its theology. Unfortunately, it soon became apparent that Christians held sharply different opinions about the nature of the godhead, especially in the Greek Church with its metaphysical inclinations. Released from the perils of martyrdom and elevated to membership in the imperial ruling class, the bishops of the eastern provinces quickly became involved in speculative battles about the Trinity, launching anathemas against each other with reckless profusion and sometimes even inciting mobs to riot on behalf of their views. No sooner had one speculative problem been satisfactorily settled than a new one began to cause dissension, and the comprehensive formulation of Christian doctrine was not completed for centuries. During the reign of Constantine's son Constantius, according to the sardonic comment of the pagan historian Ammianus Marcellinus, bishops spent so much time hurrying to and fro to ecclesiastical synods that the imperial transportation service almost broke down. This dreary series of debates provided many lurid examples of the degeneration of Christianity through its fusion with Platonism. The religion that had triumphed, at least in the eastern provinces, owed more to Alexandria than to Jerusalem and emphasized the *gnosis* of the philosophical schools more than the *agape* of the gospel.

For several generations theologians were arguing about Christ's divinity. The phrase "Son of God" by which he had always been described seemed to imply that he was somehow distinct from God the Father and should not be regarded simply as a manifestation of the divine in human form, and his identification with the *Logos* of the philosophers meant that this distinction had existed eternally and had not originated with the Incarnation. Was Christ equal to the Father, or subordinate? The Pandora's box of Christological argument was opened by the Emperor Constantine when he summoned the first General Council of the Church to meet at Nicaea in 325, its primary function being to draft a statement of its beliefs. Owing largely to pressure from the Emperor, who himself took a leading part in the deliberations, the council succeeded in its objective. Asserting Jesus' full equality with God the Father, it described him as "God from God, light from light, true God from true God, begotten not made, of one substance with the Father." This formula, however, did not win universal approval, and dissenting churchmen soon began to rally their forces and resort to political maneuvering and intriguing in order to secure its revision. The Nicene Creed was disputed, in particular, by the followers of the Alexandrian theologian Arius, who declared that Jesus was subordinate to God the Father, *homoiousios* (of similar substance) instead of *homoousios* (of the same substance). For a period the homoiousians won the support of the imperial government and gained control of the Greek Church, but the homoousian position was valiantly championed by another Alexandrian, Athanasius, and by most of the Latin Church, and finally triumphed at the Council of Constantinople in 391. Thenceforth all Christians accepted the doctrinal position of the Nicene Creed.

The Council of Constantinople also affirmed the full divinity of the Holy Spirit, thus adopting a conception of the godhead as mysteriously divided into three persons. Formulas reconciling belief in the divine unity with belief in the divine trinity were sponsored by three theologians from Asia Minor, Basil of Caesarea, Gregory of Nazianzus, and Gregory of Nyssa. Some kind of trinitarian doctrine had been implicit in the teaching of the early Church: apostolic Christianity had spoken of the Holy Spirit as though it were a distinct manifestation of divine power, and converts had always been baptized in the name of the Father, the Son, and the Holy Spirit, and had been immersed three times. But the activity of the Spirit had never been clearly distinguished from that of Jesus, and had apparently been manifested only in the inspiration of Christian converts, not in the government of the cosmos. The strong appeal of Trinitarian doctrine to theologians owed more to Neo-Platonism than to the gospels. Plotinus had postulated two emanations from the godhead: the divine reason which became identified with Christ and the divine will which became identified with the Holy Spirit. It was chiefly the Greek Church that insisted on the distinction of the three persons within the godhead—a doctrine which, according to Gregory of Nyssa, represented a middle ground between Jewish monotheism and Hellenic polytheism. Latin Christianity always laid more emphasis on divine unity. The only Christological heresy that originated in the west was that of the Monarchians (also known as Sabellians, Modalists, and Patripassians), who erred in too closely identifying Jesus with God the Father.

After 381 the problem of Christ's divinity gave place to the problem of his humanity, which occupied the Greek Church through most of the fifth, sixth, and seventh centuries. As against the orthodox contention that he was in some mysterious fashion a union of God and man, the Monophysites and, at a later date, the more moderate Monothelites denied his full humanity, while the Nestorians maintained that he had two separate natures. The orthodox position was affirmed at the Council of Chalcedon of 451, but was not fully established until the third Council of Constantinople in 680.

Beneath all the hairsplitting and the political intriguing and wirepulling of this series of councils it is possible to discern some issues with real meaning. What was ultimately at stake in the Christological controversy involved the essential significance of the new view of life, and in spite of the loss of much of the original gospel affirmation, there can be no doubt that the orthodox formulation was truer to its spirit than any of the heresies. The Nicene Creed, asserting the unity in Jesus of full godhood and full manhood, implied the potential regeneration of the whole of human nature. As Irenaeus had declared, "How shall man be changed into God unless God has been changed into man?" [7] Athanasius insisted that what he was defending against the Arians was man's potential deification. Such a doctrine was humanistic, expressing in a new form the affirmation of human values that had been the essence of the early Greek tradition and had always distinguished Hellenic culture from that of the Orient. The denial of humanism was the underlying intention of the Christological heresies, all of which reflected a sense of the total separation of divinity and humanity.

Arianism represented the tendency of the Platonists to suppose that man could approach God only by shedding everything that made him fleshly and material and hence to regard Jesus as an intermediary between earth and heaven. A more fundamental divergence from Hellenic ways of thinking appeared in the Monophysite and Nestorian movements. These were theoretically in opposition to each other, as the Monophysites declared that Christ had only a divine nature while the Nestorians regarded him as both human and divine, but they were alike in their inability to ac-

---

[7] Quoted by McGiffert: op. cit., I, 145.

cept the fusion of manhood and godhead in one personality. These movements won their chief support among Oriental peoples who had never accepted the values of Hellenism, and became vehicles for the expression of the Oriental opposition to Helleno-Roman imperialism. The Monophysite position was defended by the native "Coptic" population of Egypt, which had been antagonistic to the dominant Greek minority since the time of the Ptolemies, and by most of the inhabitants of Syria. It had, in fact, been anticipated by third-century Syrian theologians, especially by Paul of Samosata, who had been both a Christian bishop and an official of the independent frontier kingdom of Palmyra. Nestorianism spread into territories farther east, beyond the boundaries of the Roman Empire, and became the dominant form of Christianity in Persia and in central Asia. In this manner the opposition between Hellenic humanism and the Oriental belief in divine transcendence, which had been a main factor in the cultural history of the Near East ever since Alexander had built his empire, reappeared in Christian theology. The Monophysites of Syria and Egypt became, in fact, so fanatically hostile to the orthodox Christology that they eventually welcomed the Mohammedan conquest of the seventh century. Mohammed was not a Christian, but he was at least an enemy of Hellenism and a spokesman for the Oriental concept of divinity.

Thus, the belief that manhood and godhood were so nearly akin that they could be united in the person of Jesus was enshrined at the heart of the orthodox Christian mythology, in opposition to the Oriental denial of humanistic values. According to Judaism, man had been made in the likeness of God; for pre-Platonic Hellenism he had become godlike when he most fully exercised his natural powers. Despite a revolutionary transformation in the concept of the human personality, Christian theology continued to affirm that the highest religious values were in accord with the nature of man and that their realization was a process of self-fulfillment rather than of self-suppression.

Probably, however, the ethical purposes of Christianity would have been better served if the Church had remained content with the simple affirmation that Jesus was a revelation of divinity in human form, instead of attempting to define this mystery in philosophical terms. All the verbal and dialectical ingenuity displayed by generations of theologians could not make the Christian conception of the nature of Jesus intelligible to the human mind. Even more incomprehensible, and more remote from ethical considerations, were the doctrines of the Trinity and of the separate identity of the Holy Spirit. Unlike the affirmation of Christ's twofold nature, these myths satisfied no emotional needs and symbolized no moral values. Incapable of imaginative representation, they survived in Christian theology only as monuments of misplaced speculative subtlety.

And although the creeds of Nicaea and Chalcedon represented a victory of humanism over Orientalism, this victory was perhaps more verbal than real, especially in the Greek Church. Christian thought had been so deeply influenced by the pessimistic mysticism of the Hellenic decadence that it could never afterwards be wholly disentangled from it. When Basil of Caesarea spoke of Christians as "not concerning themselves with the body, nor deigning to waste a thought upon it, but as if passing their lives in alien flesh" and declared that the mind enlightened by grace "is at last initiated into the great speculations, and observes the great mysteries," and when Gregory of Nyssa declared that the human spirit "must transfer all its powers of affection from material objects to the intellectual contemplation of immaterial beauty," they were echoing the Platonic tradition, not the teaching of Jesus.[8] The impulse to repudiate the material world had become a part of the Christian attitude in spite of its inconsistency with Christian theology. The clearest demonstration of this Platonization of Christianity was to be found in the art of the early Christian empire, which was the logical sequel of the art of late paganism, with no sharp break in the continuity of spirit and technique. It was significant that the Church found it possible to adopt the Hellenistic cosmology, as first expounded in the *Timaeus* and afterwards improved by the astronomers of Alexandria. Down to the Renaissance, Christians continued to regard the universe as a series of concentric circles in which the uncertainties of sublunar life were contrasted with the unfailing regularity of the stars and a vast extent of space separated human corruption from divine perfection. The soul could rise to heaven only by shedding everything that made it earthly.

[8] *Letters* of St. Basil, translated by R. J. Deferrari, CCXXIII, CCXXXIII. Gregory of Nyssa: *On Virginity*, translated by W. Moore and H. A. Wilson, V.

The meaning of this attitude became manifest in the monastic movement. This represented a diversion into new channels of the emotional currents originally responsible for Christianity's growth and triumph. With the absorption of the Christian Church into the Roman state, the revulsion against Helleno-Roman civilization and the hope of a new way of salvation could no longer find fulfillment simply in the profession of a new religion. During the fourth century a growing number of individuals sought personal salvation by withdrawing from society, giving away all their possessions, and devoting themselves, either singly or in groups, to the practice of asceticism. Exhibiting in a most extreme form the Christian conviction that the values of the gospel were totally opposed to those of worldly society and that the existing political and economic order was inherently sinful and unjust, monasticism reflected the failure of early Christian thought to establish a relationship between the temporal and the spiritual order. As long as this dichotomy continued, Christianity could not give new strength to the Roman Empire, but tended, on the contrary, to weaken it. The monastic withdrawal must have been an important contributing factor to the fifth-century collapse of Roman power in western Europe.

Affirming human brotherhood and equality, the monk put himself on a level with the poorest of his fellow creatures by surrendering all his property and living on the minimum necessary for survival. Regarding all fleshly desires as evil, he prepared himself for the millennium by trying to become a wholly spiritual being. The more extreme ascetics retired into total solitude, lived exclusively on bread and water, and cultivated every kind of physical discomfort in the hope that this would lead them to the knowledge of God.[9] Some men were broken by the struggle with the flesh, succumbing finally to sensual temptation or mental collapse. Contemporary records make it plain that others were victorious. Many ascetics retained a remarkable degree of physical and mental

---

[9] The aspect of the ascetic life toward which modern man is least sympathetic is the association of sanctity with dirt. Many of the early monks made a practice of never even touching water except for drinking purposes. Their belief that washing was sinful may have had deeper reasons than the mere desire to be as uncomfortable as possible. The public baths in the Roman cities were often centers of debauchery. Contempt for cleanliness was not restricted to Christianity. The Emperor Julian boasted of the lice that ran about in his beard (see his *Misopogon,* 338C).

health into extreme old age. Improbable as it may seem to the modern reader, there can be no doubt that long years of successful self-discipline gave them strength of character, serenity of spirit, psychological insight, and even some degree of worldly wisdom.

The movement began in the deserts of Egypt, where Apollonius of Tyana had encountered hermits long before the spread of the new religion, and owed much of its impetus to the impression made by one extraordinary individual. About the year 270 a young man named Anthony, the son of a prosperous farmer in a village of Upper Egypt, gave away his inheritance and fled into the wilderness.[1] It is significant that what impelled him to renounce all his worldly goods was the story of how Christ urged the rich young man to sell all his possessions and give the money to the poor. The protest against economic injustice was an important element in monasticism, though its remedy was to withdraw from society rather than to reform it. But while Anthony tried to practice the gospel ethic, he was also deeply influenced by superstitions inherited from the old Egyptian religion. Egyptian Christians still believed in a multitude of supernatural beings with magical powers, though the gospel had transformed them from gods into agents of the devil. Settling first in an empty tomb and then for twenty years in an abandoned fort near the top of a mountain, and living on bread and water left for him by his friends, Anthony had to fight a long series of battles against the demons who regarded the desert as their peculiar domain. They tempted him by showing him a desirable young woman and a handsome boy, tried to frighten him by assembling herds of lions, wolves, and snakes, and even physically assaulted him. The friends who brought him bread used to hear "the sound of tumult and of outcry, and to see flashing spears, and at night they would see the whole mountain filled with fiery phantoms."[2] Eventually they insisted on breaking in upon his solitude, chiefly because they were convinced that his long austerity must have given him miraculous powers for the cure

---

[1] St. Jerome, always jealous of other men's fame, insisted that the founder of monasticism was not Anthony, but a certain Paul, who had retired into the desert twenty years earlier. But his biography of Paul is too replete with miracles to have any historical validity. Athanasius' biography made it plain, however, that Anthony was not the first of the Christian hermits, though he was much the most influential.

[2] Palladius: *The Paradise of the Holy Fathers,* translated by E. A. Wallis Budge, I, 43.

of diseases. Anthony responded to their appeals, and demonstrated such impressive numinous powers that his fame quickly spread through all Egypt.

Down to his death close to his hundredth year Anthony continued to spend most of his time in the desert, settling finally in a little oasis close to the Red Sea where he could grow his own food; but in his later years he made occasional visits to Egyptian cities in order to cast out devils and perform other cures and to confirm the faith of his fellow Christians. In spite of his firm belief in the physical reality of the phantasms that assaulted him in his desert solitudes, he was plainly a man of magnetic personal force. Although he had the intellectual equipment of an Egyptian peasant, speaking no Greek and apparently not even learning to read, he became one of the most widely known men of his time, even receiving letters requesting advice from the Emperor Constantius.

Anthony gave such prestige to the ascetic life that thousands of other Egyptians were soon following his example, some of them assembling in communities, others preferring solitude. Throughout the fourth century the most flourishing monastic colonies were at Nitria, thirty-seven miles across the desert from Alexandria, and at Scete, across an additional forty miles of trackless sand. Here each candidate for sanctity lived in a stone hut roofed with branches and furnished with a sheepskin, a lamp, a jar of oil, and occasionally a few books, while his larder consisted of a few dried peas and lentils and a little bread and honey. The monks supported themselves by plaiting palm leaves into baskets and mats, which they carried into Alexandria to sell at infrequent intervals. Their austerities sometimes became competitive, each of them trying to support life on as little food as possible and to outdo his neighbor in the practice of prayer and fasting. In these colonies there was little collective discipline, and individuals made their own rules. Some ascetics, however, preferred a more rigidly organized type of community which would provide spiritual guidance and make possible a division of labor. In about 320 an ex-soldier named Pachomius founded an institution with a military type of discipline, which soon had over a thousand inmates. This was the first Christian monastery.

In the course of generations the flight to the desert evoked a considerable body of biographical literature, beginning with the life of Anthony written by Athanasius. Nothing illustrates more sharply the revolution of values that was transforming classical civilization. The hermits found peace and happiness by repudiating all civic obligations and ambitions and reducing existence to its barest essentials. They preferred the bleak expanses of the desert to the city life that had been regarded for a thousand years as necessary for truly human development. No doubt many ascetics were chiefly motivated by the fear of hell and the hope of earning eternal salvation; as they could no longer prove themselves worthy of heaven by risking martyrdom, they tried to demonstrate it by voluntary self-punishment. Yet one should not overemphasize the more morbid aspects of early Christian asceticism. The hermits wrestled with carnal desires which they had come to regard as sinful, but in the literature of the desert a pathological obsession with the corruption of the flesh appears as the exception rather than the rule. The strongest impression to be derived from many of the recorded sayings of the early desert fathers is that they found an immediate and positive contentment in their way of life. In spite of its austerity, the desert meant serenity and freedom. As one of the early recluses declared in his old age, after Scete had become overcrowded: "the sparseness of those who at that time dwelt in the desert was gracious to us as a caress; it lavished liberty upon us, in the far-flung vastness of that solitude." [3] The hermit was released from economic burdens and civic responsibilities and from the whole oppressive atmosphere of the Helleno-Roman decadence. There was a poetic quality in the lives of the desert fathers, though it was a poetry not of pagan daylight but of the starlit darkness. [4]

The monks did not forget the Christian ethic of charity, and

---

[3] Quoted by Helen Waddell: *The Desert Fathers*, p. 20.

[4] There was, in fact, a pastoral element about the whole movement; it represented the same idealization of the primitive, in contrast with urban sophistication, that had inspired the poetry of Theocritus. A wealthy Roman lady of the late fourth century who went into retirement at Bethlehem in Palestine made the parallelism explicit, though she emphasized the differences between Christian and pagan pastoralism. "In this little villa of Christ, everything is rustic, and apart from the singing of Psalms, there is silence. The ploughman driving his share sings an alleluia. The sweating reaper diverts himself with Psalms, and the vine dresser clipping the shoots with his curved pruning knife, hums some snatch from David. These are the songs of our district. These are the popular love-lays. This is what shepherds whistle; this is what heartens the tillers of the soil." Quoted by E. K. Rand: *Founders of the Middle Ages*, p. 119.

much of the literature emphasizes their courtesy and generosity. "A dry and even diet joined together with loving-kindness" was one man's formula for sanctity. The monk should hate "relaxation of the body and vainglory"; he was close to salvation if he had "humility and poverty and judgeth not another." Many of the anecdotes display a most scrupulous anxiety not to give offense to anyone. But the fundamental conviction that caused these men to go out into the desert was that God could be found only in private meditation, not in social activity, all civilization being necessarily corrupting. In the words of the Abbot Alois, "except a man shall say in his heart, I alone and God are in this world, he shall not find peace." [5] The whole movement was deeply influenced by the doctrines of Origen, as was demonstrated in the writings of its most influential theoretical exponent, the fourth-century theologian Evagrius. Following Origen, the monk sought salvation through a mystical *gnosis,* to be achieved by the suppression of all distracting emotions. Evagrius felt that he was close to salvation when, at the end of his life, he could say that for three years he had not felt fleshly desire.[6]

During the fourth century the Egyptian monks became generally known elsewhere, and in other parts of the empire men began to respond to the same impulse to repudiate civilization. Ascetics sought seclusion in forest huts and mountain caves and on uninhabited islands, though climatic conditions were nowhere else so favorable as in Egypt. The movement spread into Syria, where it was marked by the most extreme austerities, and into Asia Minor and the Balkans and the islands of the Mediterranean. It was carried into western Europe by Martin, a native of the Balkans who settled as a hermit near Tours, in Gaul, about the year 356, and who displayed some of the childlike simplicity and the love for nature and wild animals which afterward distinguished Francis of Assisi. Pagan writers, along with some more rationalistic Christians, violently denounced the monks for deserting their civic responsibilities and voiced their horror of the anti-civilized values and view of life inherent in the movement, but it reflected too much of the sensibility of the age to be checked by any reasonable argument.

---

[5] Waddell, op. cit., pp. 87, 88, 147.

[6] For Evagrius, see Owen Chadwick: *John Cassian.*

Some of the early monks came from upper-class backgrounds, but the large majority seem to have been men of humble parentage and little or no education. The whole movement had, in fact, a markedly democratic flavor, by contrast with the aristocratic and authoritarian tendencies represented by the bishops of the post-Constantinean Church. Asceticism not only offered a way of escape from civic obligations; it was a means of achieving power and prestige, becoming, in fact, the poor man's pathway to greatness. There was a deep significance in the words with which the theologian John Cassian spoke of one of the Egyptian monks, a certain Abbot John: "He sprang from obscure parents, but, owing to the name of Jesus, has become so well known to almost all mankind that the very lords of the temporal world who hold the reins of empire and are a terror to all powers and kings, venerate him as their lord, and from distant countries seek his advice." [7]

For theologians austerity led to the knowledge of God, but the popular mind was more interested in its concrete and utilitarian effects. There was a deeply rooted conviction, inherited from prehistoric times, that extreme asceticism and the mastery of all fleshly desires automatically resulted in a numinous power which would manifest itself in miracles of healing and in worldly wisdom. The saint was the successor of the primitive shaman and medicine man. For this reason the hermit's cell was not likely to remain secluded. The peasants of the neighborhood would seek his help and bring him offerings of food, as formerly they had come to the priests of local deities. When he died, his bones and other relics continued to be charged with power, and the possession of his corpse sometimes led to battles between rival communities.

The most widely read of the lives of the monks were those which especially emphasized their supernatural gifts, implying that anyone who devoted himself to praying and fasting, never bathed, and endured the most complete physical discomfort could always cure diseases, tame wild animals, and give advice on practical problems. The collection made by Palladius near the beginning of the fifth century, *The Paradise of the Holy Fathers*, was particularly replete with marvels. Some of the tales related by Palladius were pure folklore, such as his account of how a woman was changed into a

---

[7] Quoted by E. M. Pickman: *The Mind of Latin Christendom*, p. 333.

mare by a sorcerer with whom she had refused to commit adultery and how she was changed back into her proper form by the ministrations of a Christian hermit. Other marvels attributed to the desert fathers had a more specifically Christian flavor. Palladius told a story of a monk who, wishing to cross a river, was embarrassed by the necessity of undressing and thereby seeing his own naked body, but who was rescued from his dilemma by acquiring the power to walk across the top of the water. This may be described as Christian hagiology at its worst.[8]

Throughout the fourth century the more sober leaders of the Church resisted the degradation of the saint into the magician, admitting that miracles were sometimes possible but refusing to accept them without strong evidence and insisting that the only true purpose of the ascetic life was the knowledge of God. The conflict between sophisticated and vulgar Christianity was especially bitter in Gaul, where the bishops, most of whom belonged to the Gallic aristocracy, tried to check the fame that Martin of Tours was winning both as a miracle-worker and as a representative of democratic attitudes. But in the course of generations the belief in the magical power of sanctity grew more widespread and even the ruling classes came to believe in the virtues of asceticism. In 395 one of the richest and most cultivated of the Gallic landowners, Paulinus, gave up his wealth, abandoned the writing of secular poetry, and retired into religious seclusion with his wife and a few friends at Nola in Italy.[9] This sensational event, which was regarded by other Gallic aristocrats as a kind of betrayal, illustrated the trend of the times. One of Paulinus' friends, Severus, subsequently wrote a widely read life of Martin of Tours, laying great emphasis on his supernatural powers and arguing that he surpassed all the Egyptian hermits as a worker of miracles.

The most extraordinary examples of asceticism were the Eastern pillar saints. Toward the end of the fourth century an illiterate Syrian shepherd of the name of Symeon resolved to achieve sanctity by standing perpetually in the same spot, without moving or

---

[8] Palladius: op. cit., I, 50, 115.

[9] Accustomed to luxury, Paulinus and his wife found it difficult to live as austerely as was expected of them. A disciple of Martin of Tours who visited them at Nola was shocked by their continued use of wheaten bread and—to Paulinus' great dismay—insisted on cooking them meals according to the recipe given in Ezekiel, iv, 9–12.

sitting down. Not far from the city of Antioch his admirers built him a pillar over a hundred feet high, with a railing around its summit to protect him from falling, and here, through all weathers and vicissitudes, he continued to stand for thirty years. A ladder enabled disciples to bring him food and seek his guidance on spiritual and practical problems. When he died, troops prevented his corpse from being stolen by marauding Arabs, and transported it into Antioch, where it became one of the most prized treasures of the city. Even more remarkable was the career of Daniel, another Syrian of humble origin, who took his stand on a pillar in a suburb of Constantinople in the year 460, when he was fifty-one years of age. This manifestation of austerity earned such universal admiration that he became one of the most powerful figures in the empire, being frequently consulted on delicate political problems by the emperor himself. On one occasion when civil war was imminent, Daniel left his pillar and (the soles of his feet being completely worn away) was carried into the center of the city in order that he might use his influence as a peacemaker. He then returned to his pillar and continued to stand on it until his death at the age of eighty-four.

Eventually the ascetic impulse was brought under control and diverted into more constructive channels through the development of more organized forms of monasticism, with rules of behavior that struck a reasonable balance between laxity and austerity. After Pachomius the most influential figure in the early development of institutionalized asceticism was Basil of Caesarea. About the middle of the fourth century he founded a monastery in Asia Minor with a system of discipline which became a model for other communities. Institutional monasticism was soon afterwards introduced into Italy, chiefly by Jerome, but the most successful of the early western communities was that of Lerins, established in about 400 on an island close to the modern city of Cannes. The greatest leader of the movement in the west was John Cassian, a theologian of Balkan origin who spent some years in Egypt and Palestine and founded the monastery of St. Victor near Marseilles about 410. Distrusting miracles, emphasizing hard work as well as austerity, and providing much excellent moral advice, especially with reference to the sin of *accidia* to which monks were espe-

cially liable,[1] Cassian's *Institutes* and *Conferences* set the standards for the whole future of western monasticism.

By perpetuating in a new form the communal spirit that had
characterized the first-century Church, keeping the ascetic impulse
within reasonable limits, and promoting economic and intellectual
progress, monasticism performed most useful social services, especially during the Dark Ages of western Europe. Lerins, located
in an area that the modern world has dedicated to pleasure, was
for a long time an important center of learning and culture, and
its example was followed by other western institutions. Yet the
social value of monasticism was largely a by-product, unintended
by the founders of the movement. Monks were expected to devote
themselves to work, partly in order that they might be self-sup-
porting and partly because of its therapeutic value in guarding
them against carnal temptations. But their purpose was always
personal salvation, not the promotion of social welfare.

This whole impulse of escape from social life shows how deeply
Christianity had been influenced by the pessimism of its environment. During the fourth century the Church became so deeply
permeated with this attitude that it could never regain the original optimism of the gospel. Officially, it condemned the Gnostic
and Manichaean heresies and continued to affirm the goodness of
nature and the coming resurrection of the body; yet in practice
Christian ethics now displayed a growing revulsion against the
flesh as inherently sinful and unclean. In its fear of carnal desire
Christianity even began to find spiritual merits in physical disa-
bility. The fourth-century poet Prudentius described how the martyr Laurentius, ordered by pagan magistrates to produce the gold
and silver that the Church was supposed to have hidden, assembled a group of Christian invalids and cripples and declared that
these were its only true treasures. "These are the disciples of light
whom a feeble body contracts lest through the good health of the

---

[1] There is no precise English equivalent for *accidia*. Usually translated as
"sloth," it refers primarily to the emotional condition of which inactivity is
the result. Cassian defined it as "weariness or anxiety of heart" and observed that it was most prevalent in
the early afternoon. The French
word *ennui* has much the same connotations. It is perhaps a sign of spiritual
degeneracy that in modern civilization
ennui is no longer regarded as morally
reprehensible.

flesh the mind should swell to insolence. When sickness destroys the limbs the soul thrives more vigorously." [2]

The sense of sin attached itself particularly to the strongest of man's natural impulses. The Church never forgot that Jesus had taken part in the wedding feast at Cana, nor did it repudiate Paul's common-sense advice to his converts that it was better to marry than to be inflamed with sexual desire; yet by the fourth century it had come to believe that celibacy was a preferable condition, no matter what emotional conflicts it might entail. The fact that man's sexual organs responded only to carnal desire, not to conscious control by the will, came to be regarded as proof that the sexual act was essentially sinful. That children could not be propagated without lust was the curse inflicted on Adam and Eve in punishment for eating the forbidden apple. Christians who produced children in marriage were exempted from guilt, yet, according to St. Ambrose, it was through the inherent shamefulness of the sexual act that Adam's sin was transmitted to all his descendants. All men were worthy of hell because all men were conceived in lust. Such an attitude, which scarcely appeared in Christian writings before the fourth century, was closer to Manichaean dualism than to the teaching of the Gospel. It produced an obsessive craving for physical purity which had a lasting effect on Christian attitudes.

The psychological results were luridly illustrated in the letters of St. Jerome. Born in Illyria in 340 and educated largely in Rome, he became the greatest scholar of the early Latin Church, being mainly responsible for the standard translation of the Bible, the Vulgate. In temperament he was a typical man of letters, who seemed more akin to an Erasmus or a Voltaire than to the desert fathers. Because he loved the classics, he found it difficult to accept as the word of God Hebrew writings that seemed to him "harsh and barbarous," and believed that he had been rebuked in a vision for preferring Cicero to Christ. Cantankerous and egotistical, he was indeed not a likely candidate for sanctity, and his letters pungently reveal his low opinion of most of his contemporaries. Yet Jerome deemed it necessary to adopt a life of celibacy and do battle with his own fleshly impulses, chiefly, it would ap-

---

[2] Quoted by Pickman: op. cit., p. 318.

pear, from fear of hell. As a young man he spent three years as a hermit in the Syrian desert, punishing his body and dreaming constantly of Roman dancing girls. "My face was pallid with fasting," he declared afterwards, "but my heart was hot with desires in my cold body." After living in Antioch and Constantinople he returned to Rome in 382 at the request of the Pope in order to introduce monastic institutions into Italy, and then retired to a monastery at Bethlehem, where he spent the last thirty years of his life. His letters, most of which were written to aristocratic Roman women, consisted largely of exhortations to perpetual chastity. Lest they should be tempted to marry and bear children, he reminded them in crude detail of the physiological needs of infants. Virgins should be perpetually on guard against their own carnal desires; they should abjure wine and hot food and live solely on cold herbs, and they should never bathe lest they be corrupted by the sight of their own nakedness. The Behemoth that had been so admiringly described in the fortieth chapter of the Book of Job as the most remarkable of God's creations seemed to Jerome to symbolize the devil. Behemoth's "strength," according to Job, "is in his loins, and his force is in the navel of his belly." By loins and navel, Jerome declared, the Bible meant the male and female sexual organs.[3]

One of the most extraordinary documents of early Christianity is Jerome's dissertation *De Custodia Virginitatis,* which was written as a letter to a girl of fourteen. To this young protégée Jerome described his own early struggles with sensual desire. He went on to assure her that by devoting her life to Christ she could enjoy a heavenly lover who would more than compensate for the lack of an earthly husband. "Let the seclusion of your own chamber ever guard you; ever let the Bridegroom sport with you within. If you pray, you are speaking to your Spouse; if you read, he is speaking to you. When sleep falls on you, He will come behind the wall and will put his hand through the hole in the door and will touch your flesh. And you will awake and rise up and cry: 'I am sick with love.' "[4]

---

[3] Jerome: *Letters,* translated by F. A. Wright, XXII, 30, 7, 11; LIV, 4, 10; CVII, 11.

[4] Jerome: op. cit., XXII, 25. The original does not say 'flesh'; it says 'belly' (*ventrem*). This was apparently too strong for Jerome's English translator.

If all believers had lived in accord with Jerome's principles, Christianity would quickly have become extinct. The Church gradually worked out a double standard of morality, requiring strict asceticism from the clergy, but permitting laymen to earn salvation by following more humanistic rules of behavior. This dualism reflected a radical disharmony in Christian doctrine between the original teaching of Jesus and Paul and the otherworldly pessimism acquired during later generations. The impulse of ascetic escape was never again so strong as during the fourth century, and in later ages, under the influence of Augustine, Christian doctrine no longer made such a sharp separation between the Church and the world and laid increasing emphasis on the permeation of social life by Christian ethics. Yet a long series of Christian ascetics continued to affirm the transcendent value of total chastity and to project their sexual wishes, with little or no disguise, upon the heavenly bridegroom.

4

The Dawn of Western Civilization

There can be no doubt that Christianity brought new life to Helleno-Roman society. The vigor and experimentation displayed after the adoption of the new religion were in marked contrast to the dreary uniformity characteristic of the first and second centuries. But as long as the Church believed in a sharp separation between the natural and the spiritual order, it could give no new strength to the imperial government. A civilization cannot preserve its vitality unless its institutions are seen as embodiments of ultimate values and ideals. According to the teaching of fourth-century Christianity, ultimate values could be realized only in the coming kingdom of heaven, and all existing institutions were too deeply tainted with sin to be worth defending. Christian writings of this period make it plain that there was no longer any sufficient willingness to maintain the fabric of civilized society. Many of the most vigorous and idealistic citizens of the empire no longer cared to participate in social activities, but preferred to leave its preservation to divine providence. In spite of the fact that the rule of the emperors was declared to be in accord with the will of God, thus acquiring a new basis of legitimacy, devout citizens believed that the pursuit of individual salvation was more important than their duty to the state.

This attitude was justified by means of an irrational confidence in God's government of the world. Retaining the primitive belief

457

that religious observances were a guarantee of earthly good fortune and combining it with the otherworldliness of Christianity, the Church declared that God could be trusted to protect his worshippers and that the only way to secure peace and prosperity was to be worthy of them by pious living. During the barbarian invasions of the fifth century, Christian leaders repeatedly insisted that the people of the empire had brought their misfortunes upon themselves by their own wickedness. "By our sins the barbarians are strong," declared Jerome; "by our vices is the Roman army defeated." [1] But Jerome was not referring to the failure of the Roman people to perform their patriotic duties; he meant that the invasions were instigated by God as punishments for sin. According to the predictions of Paul and other New Testament writers, the empire was expected to last until the final time of troubles heralding the end of the world. When human wickedness had been sufficiently rebuked, God would restore the imperial peace and order. The ascetic who devoted his life to prayer did more to secure divine aid, and hence contributed more to the welfare of society, than the soldier or the statesman. Most Christian writers set out to minimize the catastrophes they were witnessing, in the belief that the adoption of the true religion must necessarily be a guarantee of God's protection.

The result of such an attitude was a gradual breakdown of central authority in the western provinces of the empire. Its immediate cause was the advent of barbarian invaders, but it should be emphasized that this was made possible only by the reluctance of citizens to perform their civic duties. The invaders were relatively few in number, and Roman-trained armies were usually capable of defeating them. But the will to defend the empire was lacking. Many Roman citizens, oppressed by high taxes and bureaucratic regimentation, actually preferred barbarian rule.[2] Especially sig-

[1] *Letters,* LX, 17.
[2] According to Orosius, writing in 417: "Certain Romans are to be found among them who prefer an impoverished freedom among the barbarians to the nightmare of taxation among the Romans." Salvian declared in 445: "Many of them, including persons well born and educated, are fleeing to the enemy lest they die under the afflictions of the State's persecution. . . . However much they differ from those to whom they have fled, both in customs and languages, and however much they are tried by the odor of the bodies and clothes of the barbarians, they nevertheless prefer to endure an unfamiliar life among the barbarians

nificant was the general reluctance to serve in the army, in consequence of which the imperial government had adopted the fatal policy of recruiting its forces largely from barbarian mercenaries. The legions supposed to defend the empire against German raiders were now composed largely of German troops and were even led by German-born generals.

In the late fourth century a new movement of peoples in the Germanic North was initiated by the arrival of the Huns from Asia. Flying from these formidable invaders, Germanic tribes began to press southward and westward and to seek refuge within the borders of the empire. Rome had admitted and absorbed similar groups in earlier centuries, and no particular difficulties were anticipated, especially as most of the Germans had already accepted Christianity, although in its Arian form. The influx of barbarians, however, was too large for successful assimilation; nor could the soldiers of the Roman army be trusted to defend the government against their kinsfolk. In consequence, the imperial authorities were unable to regain control of the situation.

In 378 the Visigoths, who had been admitted into the Balkans but afterwards mistreated by Roman officials, defeated and killed the Emperor Valens in the Battle of Adrianople. For the next generation they gave little further trouble, but early in the fifth century they began to move into Italy. The empire had recently been divided into eastern and western sections under different emperors, one of whom ruled at Constantinople and the other at Ravenna, which had replaced Rome as the imperial headquarters in the west.[3] The government at Ravenna promptly summoned most of the legions from the Rhine frontier to meet the threat, but they failed to prevent the Visigoths from seizing and plundering the City of Rome in 410. These were the first foreign invaders to capture the city for more than eight hundred years. Meanwhile, the withdrawal of the legions left the northern provinces inadequately

to an unjust harshness among the Romans." Quoted by E. M. Pickman: *The Mind of Latin Christendom*, pp. 273, 274.

[3] The experiment of setting up different administrations for the eastern and western provinces had first been tried by Diocletian, but the empire had been reunited by Constantine. In 395, on the death of the Emperor Theodosius, it was divided between his two sons. But in spite of this administrative separation, the empire was regarded as still a unity, the two emperors being considered as partners.

defended against other groups of barbarians. During the next generation, the Burgundians moved into eastern Gaul, the Angles and Saxons occupied eastern Britain, the Vandals swept across Spain into northern Africa, and the Visigoths, evacuating Italy, settled in southwestern Gaul and in Spain. Ravenna, guarded by its marshes from attack by land, remained at first the official capital of the western empire, but its emperors had little authority outside the city and were wholly dependent on the army. In 476 the last of these puppet rulers was removed by a German-born general. Shortly afterwards, the Ostrogoths invaded Italy, and yet another Germanic tribe, the Franks, took possession of northern Gaul. Thus the traditional order came to an end in all the Latin provinces of the empire.

For contemporaries, it should be emphasized, this was by no means the end of the Roman Empire. The traditional authority was still represented by the emperor at Constantinople, and after the deposition of the last of the puppet rulers at Ravenna he was re-garded as the rightful sovereign of the whole empire. Even the barbarian chieftains recognized his supremacy, at least in theory. Their rule was at first restricted to their own tribesmen, and it was only gradually that they began to organize new kingdoms. Nor did the advent of the Germans mean any immediate revolutionary change in social organization. They were now settled within the imperial domain, living side-by-side with the previous inhabitants, but most of the land remained in the possession of the same oc-cupants, and many of the wealthy families continued to control their estates and their tenants and to cultivate the arts and letters with a sublime unawareness that they were living through a major historical catastrophe. Contemporaries saw only a temporary break-down of the central authority and a consequent increase in disorder. Society began to be atomized into small units, and new responsibili-ties for the protection of life and property were assumed by the large landowners and more especially by the bishops of the Church, most of whom belonged to the aristocracy and were hence accustomed to rule. Thus the movement toward feudalism which had been initiated during the disturbances of the third century was carried farther. It was generally assumed, however, that the old order must eventually be re-established. This assumption continued, in fact, to dominate political thinking in western Europe through the whole of the Dark and early Middle Ages, as was shown by the establishment of the Holy Roman Empire.[4]

This lack of understanding was due in part to the teaching of the Church. God, it was supposed, would not permanently withdraw his protection from the empire that had so recently learned to honor and worship him. Christian writers like Augustine were much concerned to minimize the shock of such events as the sack of Rome, arguing that many comparable catastrophes had occurred in pagan times and that the practices of war had become more humane since the adoption of the new religion.[5] Persons who took refuge in churches, Augustine pointed out, had been spared from massacre; and even if a number of Christian virgins had been raped, this was probably permitted by God in order that they might not become sinfully proud of their chastity. An even more extraordinary incomprehension of events was exhibited by the writers of fifth-century Gaul, such as Sidonius Apollinarius. A wealthy aristocrat, man of letters, and Christian bishop, Sidonius was born in 430 and died in 488, thus witnessing the final collapse of Roman power in the west; yet, to judge from his writings, the Gallic upper-class families continued through all the disorders to live in much the same fashion as their ancestors of the previous century. Sidonius seems to have found the Germans disturbing chiefly because of their lack of social graces. He complained that they greased their hair with rancid butter, wore clothes of skins, tattooed their cheeks green, fed too heavily on unsavory messes, and spoke harshly and loudly. His letters show him performing his duties as landowner and bishop and taking measures to protect and feed the people of his diocese. Before assuming these administrative responsibilities he had continued to write poems in the traditional

---

[4] The most curious example of the persistence of this illusion is Dante's *De Monarchia*, written early in the fourteenth century. Dante affirmed that the Roman Empire was established by God in order to give peace to the world and prepare the way for Christianity, and regarded the current emperor (a German prince called Henry of Luxembourg) as the direct legal successor of Augustus. The continuity of the Roman and Holy Roman empires was assumed as a self-evident truth not requiring demonstration.

[5] The work of Orosius, *Adversum Paganos,* which remained the main source of historical information throughout the Middle Ages, was written in 417–18 at the suggestion of Augustine in order to demonstrate that the adoption of Christianity had brought about greater worldly prosperity. Orosius ransacked the whole record of pre-Christian society for evidences of continuous misery and misfortune.

rhetorical style. These have been described as marking "probably the utmost extreme of indurated conventionality that literary art has ever reached." [6]

Thus, the end of the Roman Empire in the western provinces was followed not by an abrupt break in the tradition of civilization, but by a slow and gradual decline. For centuries trade and industry continued to decrease, cities decayed, localities became economically and culturally dependent on their own resources, facilities for education disappeared, and disorder and insecurity were almost universal. Only the monasteries preserved vestiges of civilized life, thereby serving a practical purpose by no means envisaged by their founders. The decline continued until the Carolingian Renaissance of the eighth century. Then, after a brief revival, another fall was precipitated by the raids of the Northmen. Not until after 1000 was there a definite upward turn.

In the east, on the other hand, there was no dark age. The New Rome founded by Constantine on the Bosporus became the guardian of the ancient heritage, and its emperors retained control of the Hellenic provinces. During the period when the west was being overrun by the barbarians, the eastern empire, relatively free from attack, was able to reorganize its institutions and find new sources of strength. It remained rich and vigorous for another six hundred years, and was not finally extinguished until the Turkish capture of Constantinople in 1453. Though Byzantine civilization displayed little creativity in literature, philosophy, or the sciences, its vitality was proved by its capacity for survival and by its aesthetic expressions. The sixth century saw the greatest achievements in the visual arts since the Athenian golden age almost a thousand years earlier. The artistic genius of the Greeks continued to manifest itself down to the Turkish conquest, and even into the sixteenth century.

The Byzantine Empire was a continuation of that of Rome, with no break in institutional development; but it was able to reverse the trends toward social disintegration which had been so manifest in the western provinces. Civilization was more deeply rooted in the Hellenic provinces, where it had had a much longer

[6] Dill: op. cit., p. 334. See also   in Early Christian Gaul.
N. K. Chadwick: Poetry and Letters

and more inspiring history. In spite of elaborate bureaucratic regulations, trade and industry continued to flourish, and the concentration of landownership was checked, much of the land being held by small freeholders. Even more significantly, the government ceased to rely solely on barbarian mercenaries for the defense of the empire, and was able to find new reserves of citizen soldiers among the peasants of Asia Minor. The emperors retained the broad powers and the elaborate Oriental ceremonial inherited from Diocletian and Constantine, but they were expected to govern in accord with law, and could not otherwise claim obedience. Frequent rebellions against rulers who were felt to have abused their powers showed that the citizens of the empire were by no means the submissive victims of a military despotism. The spirit of Byzantine politics was, in fact, thoroughly Greek, and the volatile individualism, the passion for argument and intrigue, and the lack of mutual trust which had cursed Greek society during the era of the city-states continued to be conspicuous qualities of the citizens of Constantinople. Out of a total of one hundred and seven Byzantine emperors, no less than sixty-five were either forced to abdicate or removed by poison, strangulation, stabbing, or some other violent means. Yet, in spite of their stormy and often sordid history, the Byzantines, unlike their Greek ancestors, had acquired enough sense of unity to hold an empire together.

What made the Byzantine achievement possible was the transformation of Greek Christianity into an instrument of social stability. But this transformation meant the sacrifice of much of the ethical dynamism of the original gospel. The Christianity of Byzantium was the mystical and metaphysical faith of the Alexandrians, and was closer to Plotinus than to Jesus in its underlying spirit. It still meant giving to the poor—Constantinople was filled with institutions of public charity—but its main emphasis was on the hope of a mystical union with God rather than on the transformation of earthly life.[7] As the protector of the true religion, the

---

[7] The chief sources of Christian Neo-Platonism were the mystical writings attributed to the convert of Paul, Dionysius the Areopagite. These were probably written somewhere in the eastern provinces early in the sixth century. By a further confusion Dionysius was subsequently identified with the Christian martyr who became the patron saint of France under the name of St. Denis. In consequence, the writings bearing his name acquired almost canonical authority in western Europe during the Middle Ages.

Byzantine state claimed the loyal support of all Christians, but the emperors recognized little obligation to give practical effect to the teachings of the gospel. No other society in history has been so deeply permeated with Christian piety, but the piety of the Greek Church was compatible with an unblushing freedom from all moral scruples in the pursuit of worldly glory. The state had, in fact, absorbed the Church, making use of the Christian faith for its own temporal purposes. The emperor claimed broad ecclesiastical powers, and the official head of the Church, the Patriarch of Constantinople, was usually his subordinate. Even though some patriarchs were strong enough to claim independence and even to rebuke erring emperors, the religion they represented was mystical rather than ethical, with little practical efficacy.[8] The more devout Greek Christians continued to seek salvation by retiring into monasteries. Byzantine monasticism, unlike that of the Latin Church, performed few social services and, by withdrawing able citizens from the service of the state, remained an element of weakness in the social structure.

During part of the sixth century the empire was strong enough to undertake the reconquest of the western provinces, and the expected restoration of Roman authority seemed actually in process of realization. During the reign of Justinian, Byzantine armies regained control of northern Africa, Italy, and part of Spain, at the same time defending the eastern border provinces against the Persian kingdom of the Sassanids. But this ambitious program was ended by a new threat from the East. The early seventh century saw the sudden emergence from the deserts of Arabia of the religion of Mohammed. Mohammedanism preached a wholly transcendental deity congenial to the Near Eastern mind, and had a

---

[8] The famous patriarch of the early fifth century, John Chrysostom, declared: "When there is need of any good thing from above, the Emperor is wont to resort to the priest, but not the priest to the Emperor." (Quoted by Chester G. Starr: *Civilization and the Caesars*, p. 371.) But Chrysostom paid for his independence by being banished from Constantinople and dying in exile. In the course of the next thousand years a few later churchmen made similar claims, but more typical was the statement of a sixth-century patriarch: "Nothing must be done in the Church that is contrary to the will and commands of the Emperor." (Quoted by Charles Diehl: *Byzantium: Greatness and Decline*, translated by Naomi Walford, p. 166.)

strong appeal to those peoples in the border provinces, dominated by Greek ruling minorities since the conquests of Alexander the Great, who had never accepted the humanistic values and theology of Hellenism. Monophysite Christians, unable to believe in the union of God and man in the person of Christ, preferred the rule of the Arabs to that of the Greeks. Thus there began a new phase in the age-old conflict between East and West. Arabic armies conquered Syria and Egypt, occupied Persia, and moved across northern Africa into Spain. Meanwhile, much of northern Italy was seized by a new group of German invaders, the Lombards. The Byzantines were compelled to adopt a defensive policy and concentrate on holding Asia Minor and the Balkans, although they did not finally abandon their last foothold in Italy until the eleventh century.

The seventh century was marked by disorder and retreat, but through the eighth, ninth, and tenth centuries, under strong rulers, Byzantium was able to hold her own against the Mohammedans and at the same time to conquer and assimilate a series of barbarian invaders from the North who had settled in the Balkan peninsula. Protected from land assault by the immense line of ramparts built in the fifth century, and controlling the trade routes between Europe and the Orient, Constantinople, "the city guarded by God," remained a stronghold of Hellenic civilization. With its immense population, its architectural splendors, its institutions of learning, and its traditions of fine craftsmanship, it maintained a wealth and sophistication that were not equaled anywhere in the Western world until the time of the Renaissance.

In literature and thought, the prestige of the Hellenic heritage was an incubus that stifled creativity, but the Byzantine spirit flowered in its religious art. Technically, this represented an organic continuation of the art of late paganism, with no break in the line of development; but after the advent of Christianity, art acquired a new power and a new radiance and exuberance. How much it owed to its Hellenic and Roman background and how much it borrowed from Near Eastern countries like Syria, Armenia, and Iran are unsettled questions. Its most important sources appear to have been Roman, although it was certainly influenced by the decorative traditions of the East. But whatever was acquired from non-Christian cultures was molded into new forms appropriate to the sensitivity of Byzantine Christianity.[9]

Christian art had begun in the catacombs long before the time of Constantine. But the symbols used by the first Christian artists—anchors and doves and fishes and representations of the Good Shepherd in the form of a beardless Hellenic demigod—conveyed little of the Christian spirit and did not differ appreciably from the third-rate popular art of paganism. Not until after the official adoption of Christianity and the consequent diversion of the main current of Helleno-Roman art into Christian channels did a genuinely Christian art begin to develop. The main characteristics of late Roman painting and sculpture were then carried over into the art of the Church, at first with little change. Sarcophagi of the fourth and fifth centuries differ from those of earlier periods only in portraying scenes from the Bible rather than from pagan mythology. In the course of generations, however, art gradually became infused with a new spirit. During the fifth and sixth centuries distinctive styles and iconographic traditions became associated with Christian worship wherever the survival of civilization made artistic creation still possible. Although the most productive centers of Christian art were in the Hellenic and Asiatic provinces, some of its finest and most characteristic achievements occurred in Italy, so that it is somewhat misleading to speak of the work of this period as "Byzantine."

Sculpture was not the most appropriate medium for conveying a view of life which sought to negate corporeality and affirm a transcendent reality, and the characteristic art form of the post-Constantinean Church was mosaic, which had already had a long history as a mode of decoration and now became expressive. Most of the mosaics of the eastern provinces were obliterated after the Arabic and Turkish conquests. Early examples have survived in churches in Rome and Salonika,[1] but the finest extant achieve-

---

[9] The standard representation of Christ as bearded originated in Syria, and was not generally accepted elsewhere until the sixth century. This is one clear indication of Near Eastern influence on the development of Christian art.

[1] The church of Hagios Georgios at Salonika is a particularly interesting monument of the transition from paganism to Christianity. Originally built as a pagan temple similar to the Pantheon in its design, it became a church in the fifth century. Its brilliantly colored mosaics represent Christian saints standing in front of

ments are at Ravenna, especially the row of imperial dignitaries in San Vitale and the lines of saints and martyrs in San Apollinare, which date from the reign of Justinian. The immobile figures confronting the spectator, the lack of depth, the non-realistic enlargement of the more important figures, the unsmiling and somber intensity of the facial expressions—all this in the mosaics linked them with the bas-reliefs of late Roman paganism, while the rhythmic repetition of similar gestures and decorative patterns suggested the influence of Iran. But the figures in the bas-reliefs, however distorted, had remained corporeal, and Iranian art had conveyed no transcendental meaning. In the mosaics the figures appeared to float in air, the feet barely touching the ground; portrayed against gold or blue backgrounds, they seemed bathed in a celestial envelope of light. With their radiance of color and masterful unity of design, they affirmed an exuberant assurance of salvation which could not be paralleled in their pagan antecedents. This was the art of a society with an unquestioning trust in mystical realities.

The greatest expression of the Greek Christian spirit was the Hagia Sophia in Constantinople, completed in 537 during the reign of Justinian. This also was the product of a long evolution of aesthetic tendencies originating in Roman paganism. Although the designers of the building, Anthemius of Tralles and Isidore of Miletus, were Greeks from Asia Minor, they found their chief models in earlier buildings in the City of Rome.

Some early churches were round or octagonal, but the most frequent type had a structure derived from the Roman basilica, a rectangular building used as a law court or for other public purposes. With its broad central nave and flanking side-aisles with rows of columns, the basilica was easily adapted to the needs of Christian worship, which, unlike the worship of pagan deities, took place indoors. Could this form be fused with the domed style developed in late Roman baths and temples, thus fulfilling in a single structure both the practical needs of the new religion and its mystical sense? The engineering problem involved—that of placing a round dome over a square structure—was not easily solved, and Roman architects had begun to wrestle with it even before the

imaginary buildings and other decorative objects reminiscent of those portrayed in wall paintings at Pompeii.

adoption of Christianity, most notably in the mausoleum of Diocletian at Split. It was fully mastered for the first time in the Hagia Sophia, in which the dome was supported on pendentives, or curved triangles, placed at the four corners. Technically, therefore, this building represented the completion of trends inherent for centuries in Roman architectural development. The aesthetic result was that, while reproducing the feeling of a transcendental unity and totality that had been expressed in later Roman building, it conveyed also a new ethereal sense of lightness and airiness which made it an appropriate place of worship for the new religion.

Like the Roman domed buildings, the Hagia Sophia was designed as an organization of inner space, its external appearance being relatively unimpressive, but its unity was both more comprehensive and more complete than in any earlier structure. Studied in detail, its pillars and arches, balconies and side-aisles seemed to have an infinite complexity, while the brilliantly colored marbles and the vast expanses of gold mosaic gave an impression of overpowering richness. But the eye of the spectator never lost the immense central shell, and always came to rest finally on the slowly curving dome suspended over the building like the vault of the sky. By an extraordinary feat of technological genius, this appeared weightless and ethereal, floating in air like the figures in the mosaics. In the words of the contemporary historian Procopius, it seemed to be hanging by a golden chain from heaven rather than supported on solid masonry. The Hagia Sophia had none of the sense of restless stress and striving so powerfully conveyed by Gothic cathedrals. It was an affirmation of peace and mystical consummation.[2]

Was the Hagia Sophia Christian or Platonic? Christianity had given Byzantine civilization its trust in divine providence, but, as interpreted in terms of Hellenic philosophy, it had lost its originally dynamic and progressive quality. The kingdom of heaven was to be achieved not by human effort and suffering in the

---

[2] Unlike the Parthenon, the Hagia Sophia is still structurally intact and not a ruin, but it has probably lost even more by the passage of time. Its marbles are faded and its pavements broken, and relatively little of its mosaics (which once covered a space measuring four acres) have been uncovered. Deprived of its original brilliant coloring, what survives is merely a hollow shell. It is still disfigured, moreover, by quotations from the Koran.

temporal world, but immediately and eternally, by mystical union with God. The sense of peace and fulfillment of the Hagia Sophia recalled Plotinus' absorption into the One-All rather than the pity and charity of the gospel. The same loss of human sympathy was conveyed in the figure of the Pantocrator, which, in later phases of Byzantine art history, became the standard representation of Christ. This solemn embodiment of divine omnipotence had little in common with the loving and suffering Jesus of history, but was the appropriate expression of a religious faith that identified the worship of God with the service of the emperor.

The early eighth century saw a break in the continuity of the Byzantine cultural tradition. An imperial dynasty of Syrian origin, the first of whom was Leo the Isaurian, prohibited the use of religious pictures on the ground that spiritual realities could not be represented in material forms. This "iconoclastic" movement was an expression of the Asiatic denial of Hellenic humanism which had previously manifested itself in the Monophysite heresy, and was accompanied by an attack on the whole Hellenic heritage in culture and education. But after more than a century of controversy the Hellenists regained control of the Byzantine state and church, bringing about a renaissance both of religious art and of classical studies.[3] There was never much new development in Byzantine art, but both in architecture and in frescoes and mosaics the tradition retained its vitality through most of the Middle Ages. Through the medium of illuminated manuscripts, especially illustrated copies of sections of the Bible, the knowledge of Byzantine iconography was carried to western countries.

Western civilization owed an immense debt to Byzantium. Constantinople was the chief center from which, after the Dark Ages, culture was again diffused throughout western Europe. Yet, despite its borrowings from the eastern Mediterranean, Western civilization remained Roman rather than Greek in its essential spirit. It acquired its basic beliefs from the Latin rather than the Greek fathers, and Latin Christianity, in spite of its legalistic emphasis, had retained more of the original gospel spirit.[4] In the

---

[3] See R. R. Bolgar: *The Classical Heritage,* Chapter 2.

[4] The Byzantine spirit was transmitted directly to modern Greece and, through the medium of the Greek Church, to other Balkan countries and to Russia. In all these countries religion remained mystical rather than

western provinces the sense of duty and obligation that had
permeated Roman paganism were transmitted to the new religion.
Its spokesmen never forgot that Christianity was primarily ethical,
although their interpretation of its teaching often seemed closer to
Stoicism than to the Gospel. Even before the breakdown of Roman
rule, Latin religious leaders were beginning to overcome the dichotomy between the spiritual and the natural order and to affirm
that Christianity meant the permeation of all temporal institutions
by the spirit of the gospel. In the West, the Church was not
swallowed up by the state, but remained an independent organization capable of judging and rebuking the conduct of secular rulers.
The power acquired by the clergy of the Latin Church, and especially by their leader, the Bishop of Rome, could easily be abused,
but it was based on a recognition that Christianity should be a
guide to practice and not merely an assurance of otherworldly
salvation.

The first great champion of clerical authority in the Latin
Church was Ambrose, Bishop of Milan from 374 until 397. A
member of the Roman ruling class who had been a civil adminis-
trator before becoming a bishop, Ambrose was deeply influenced
by Stoicism, as was shown in his writings on ethics, and retained
some of its original republican spirit. When the Emperor Theodosius was guilty of ordering the massacre of several thousand
inhabitants of Salonika as a punishment for disobedience, Ambrose refused him admission to the church at Milan until he had
done penance and made restitution. "The bishops are wont to
judge Christian emperors," he declared, "not emperors the bishops." [5] This successful insistence that the emperor must conform
to Christian ethics had no precedents, and was rarely paralleled in
the history of the Greek Church.

During the period when the barbarian invaders were overrun-
ning the western provinces, the beliefs of the Latin Church were
comprehensively restated by Ambrose's convert and pupil Augustine, the greatest intellectual figure of the later empire and the most

ethical and practical, and served as
a support for secular political institutions and ambitions. Some of the
misunderstandings that have always
marked Russo-Western relations can
be traced back to the original differences between Greek and Latin Christianity.

[5] Quoted by Starr: op. cit., p. 371.

important Christian theologian since Paul.[6] Although his thinking was full of inconsistencies, and much of it reflected the superstition and the moral dualism and asceticism of his age, he reaffirmed the essential doctrines that differentiated Christianity from all pagan philosophies. More clearly than any other theologian, he found in Christianity a new beginning not only for personal morality, but also for sociology and metaphysics. Above all, by declaring that Christian love was the fulfillment of man's secular quest for social order, peace, and justice, he showed that it was possible to bridge the gulf between earthly kingdoms and the kingdom of heaven. He was the first Christian theologian to think politically as well as ethically. This was indicated in the title of his greatest book, in which the kingdom of heaven was described as a *civitas,* or community of citizens.[7] If the Hagia Sophia reflected the Byzantine conservation of the Helleno-Roman tradition, Augustine's *De Civitate Dei* looked forward to the new society that emerged after the collapse of Roman power. Although Augustine was in many ways the child of his time, his theology was at bottom the expression of a new sensitivity, leading to radically new views of reality and marking the dividing-line between classical and modern culture.

Born in North Africa in 354, the son of a pagan father and a Christian mother, and probably of Berber descent, Augustine was trained to be a teacher of rhetoric, and until his conversion at the age of thirty-two was concerned chiefly with professional success. While living the normal life of a young Latin intellectual, he sought explanations for the human situation first in Manichaeanism and afterwards in Neo-Platonism. Both these systems he seems to have accepted as intellectual formulations rather than as ethical guides, his resistance to his mother's Christianity being largely caused by fear of its moral rigor, especially in sex. His conversion occurred while he was a teacher at Milan, where he had come under the influence of Bishop Ambrose. Like that of Paul, it was an emotional convulsion, not an act of conscious choice; hearing a child in a

---

[6] C. N. Cochrane: *Christianity and Classical Culture* contains a stimulating appraisal of the work of Augustine, though it exaggerates the extent to which he freed himself from Platonic influences.

[7] The usual translation as the *City of God* does not convey the full significance of the word *civitas.*

neighboring house crying the words *"tolle, lege,"* "take up and
read," he interpreted this as a divine command, and on opening
his Bible found a passage in Paul's letters which condemned
"chambering and wantonness." Responding to what he believed
to be the will of God, he abandoned his professional career and
retired to North Africa to live a monastic life. Yet, although he
attributed his final conviction to divine grace, it is evident that he
had already been moving toward Christianity because of a growing realization that it explained human life more adequately than
any dualist philosophy and also because it promised personal
consolation through the direct communion of God and the individual soul. Man found God within himself, not as in Neo-
Platonism by becoming absorbed into the whole, but as a living
presence radiating love. "These pages present not the image of
this piety," he declared of the writings of Plotinus and his disciples, "the tears of confession, Thy sacrifice, a troubled spirit, a
broken and a contrite heart, the salvation of the people, the Bridal
City, the earnest of the Holy Ghost, the Cup of our Redemption.
No man sings there, Shall not my Soul be submitted unto God?
for of him cometh my salvation. For He is my God and my salvation, my guardian, I shall no more be moved. No one there hears
Him call, Come unto Me, all ye that labor. They scorn to learn of
Him, because He is meek and lowly in heart; for these things hast
Thou hid from the wise and prudent, and hast revealed them unto
babes." [8]

For Augustine, as for Paul, philosophy was rooted in personal
experience, deriving its postulates from the direct awareness of
spiritual realities. While expounding Christian metaphysics, he
therefore explored the processes by which he had found God. His
Confessions display a candid self-observation and a psychological
subtlety unknown in the literature of paganism. Marcus Aurelius
had written his meditations as a specimen of Stoicism, but Augustine did not set out to present a specimen of Christianity; he was
concerned with emotional truth, deducing his religious beliefs from
experience instead of twisting experience to make it conform with
theory. Interpreting the self with the aid of new categories, he was
like an explorer entering unknown territory; and his *Confessions*

---

[8] *Confessions,* translated by Edward Pusey, VII.

are filled with a sense of wonder at the complexities of the human psyche, and seem often to foreshadow the modern novel. His self-portrait is not wholly likable. Posterity has not easily condoned the callousness with which he dismissed his mistress in order to facilitate the good marriage that his mother planned for him, or the speed with which he formed a second liaison when his marriage was postponed. His concern with personal salvation leaves an impression of an egoistic self-concentration and almost feminine dependency. He can easily be analyzed as the victim of the domineering mother who—in spite of her concern for the salvation of his soul—was equally intent on his professional success. But Augustine's autobiography remains one of the supreme examples of the Christian acceptance of man as he was, not as he ought to be.

For Augustine, philosophy began with the consciousness of individuality; even if man's self-awareness was mistaken, it was still an awareness of something. This led to a recognition of the objective reality of truth and other values, and for Augustine, this meant a recognition of the existence of God. From his inner knowledge of God man derived the fundamental postulates by which he could proceed to knowledge of the external world. Christian faith was thus the essential prerequisite for the understanding of nature and history. The leap from the apprehension of values to belief in the Christian God was, of course, an intuitive affirmation and not a logical deduction, the knowledge of God being an inner certainty (at least for those who had received the gift of grace) which did not need to be demonstrated by external evidence. Augustine never tired of repeating the words attributed to Isaiah (by a mistranslation of the Hebrew) in the Latin version of the Bible: "unless you believe you will not understand." "Believe in order that you may understand" remained the guiding principle of all philosophical speculation for the next thousand years; and as long as belief meant a total acceptance of the whole structure of Catholic doctrine and practice, intellectual progress was inhibited. But any system of thought must be based on postulates that are prior to intellectual analysis, and are therefore matters of faith rather than of reason. In every age the current sensibility and climate of opinion cause certain assumptions to appear as self-evident, and the only test of their validity is operational. Implicit in the Christian view of God were assumptions about the nature of reality which would enable Western civilization to move beyond the levels achieved by Greece and Rome.

The chief postulate of Platonism had been the reality of the realm of ideas. Augustine retained much of the Platonic way of thinking that he had acquired before his conversion, particularly its epistemology and its mathematical mysticism; and the consequent inconsistencies in his philosophy led to long controversies among the medieval scholastics. But the God whom he learned to know at Milan was very different from the divine mind of Hellenic philosophy. He was the God who had revealed himself in the Jewish Scriptures and in the personality of Jesus, and was therefore dynamic as well as static, a source of love instead of an impersonal One-All. Interpreting reality by the postulates derived from knowledge of the Christian God, Augustine restated the three fundamental affirmations that had been absent from Platonism and were basic to the new Christian view: that the whole world, and not merely the forms and ideas, was the creation of God and therefore rational; that man was an individual soul endowed with personality, instead of being merely a spark of divinity imprisoned in matter; and that history was a meaningful process directed by the divine will.

Much in Augustine's thinking reflected the superstitions of the fourth century and had no permanent validity. Accepting the conventional notion of divine justice, he wasted much futile intellectual effort in trying to demonstrate that the righteous were rewarded and the wicked punished in this life. If a good man suffered misfortune, it was either a rebuke for an act of sin, a warning against wrongdoing, or a trial of his virtue. He believed in the power of relics to cure diseases, and recounted twenty-one miracles of healing which he had personally witnessed or could vouch for. But the main drift of his thinking was more enlightened and more realistic. As everything that happened was the work of God, and God was orderly, there was no distinction between what was normal and what was miraculous, or between knowledge and revelation. "Nature is all order and all miracle, but the miracle is the order, and greater than any miracle performed by man is man himself." [9] This meant that everything in nature, including those accidents

---

[9] Quoted by Cochrane: op. cit., p. 443.

and imperfections that Hellenic philosophy had attributed to the irrational influences of matter, was capable of rational explanation. In the distant future, with a different climate of opinion, this Christian world-view would make scientific advances possible. Like all the Church fathers, Augustine himself had no interest in science, regarding the knowledge of God as the only knowledge worth pursuing and interpreting all natural phenomena as merely symbols of divine truths. But implicit in his philosophy was a new concept of the natural order. Repudiating the Hellenic categories of idea and copy, form and matter, thought was moving beyond the impasse in which it had been trapped by Plato and Aristotle.

Augustine showed a similar fourth-century bias in his view of man. More vehemently than any earlier Christian writer, he insisted on man's bondage to original sin. Inheriting corruption from Adam, man was incapable of any good thing unless he was enlightened by grace, and grace came only from God and could not be earned by human effort. This doctrine of total depravity and divine election led Augustine into a number of controversies, especially with the British theologian Pelagius, who declared that man was free to choose or reject salvation. The Catholic Church did not wholly follow Augustine, but preferred the more moderate "Massilian" doctrine of John Cassian and other Gallic theologians. For Augustine, moreover, as for his master Ambrose, the especial sign and source of sin was sexual concupiscence. "Lust has to be waited for to set those members in motion, as if it had legal rights over them, and sometimes it refuses to act when the mind wills, while often it acts against its will. . . . From this concupiscence whatever comes into being by natural birth is bound by original sin." [1]

Yet in spite of Augustine's emphasis on original sin, he wholly repudiated the Manichaean dualism that he had accepted as a young man. Nature, being the creation of God, was good, and evil was not a positive force, but a negation. "No nature at all is evil, and this is a name for nothing but the want of good. . . . If sin be natural, it is not sin at all." Every desire was for something good, and the essence of sin was the choice of a partial rather than a universal good. "The soul, loving its own power, relapses from

---

[1] *On Marriage and Concupiscence;*   C. L. Cornish, III, 266, 275.
Works of St. Augustine, translated by

the desire for a common and universal good to one which is individual and private. . . . Not even Catiline himself loved his own villanies, but something else, for whose sake he did them." The universe, considered as a whole, was planned by God as a work of beauty in which sin and evil were necessary, the beauty being "achieved by the opposition of contraries, arranged, as it were, by an eloquence not of words, but of things"; and man, enlightened by grace, could learn to love and accept the divine order. "The right will is well-directed love, and the wrong will is ill-directed love." For the core of the human being was not a divine spark or a contemplative intelligence, but a loving and suffering person. Man was what he loved, and love was the source of all movement and all order. The ultimate purpose of human life was to be found not in knowledge but in love, not in freedom from disturbing emotions but in the attachment of man to the divine order and to his fellow men. "The citizens of the holy city of God, who live according to God in the pilgrimage of this life, both fear and desire, and grieve and rejoice. And because their love is rightly placed, all these affections of theirs are right." [2]

All Augustine's moral and philosophical works may be regarded as preparatory to the political and historical affirmations of the City of God. Begun as a defense of Christianity against pagan arguments that the new religion had failed to protect Rome from the Visigoths, it developed into a comprehensive interpretation of the new view of life. His mockery of the pagan gods, his insistence that the times were actually improving and catastrophes becoming less frequent, his descriptions of miraculous cures, and his attempts to prove the truth of every sentence in the Bible are of merely historical interest. But his general view of human life and human destiny has had a continuing influence on Western civilization.

The structure of the book, with its contrast between the earthly city built on human egoism and the heavenly city built on the love of God, reflected the fourth-century devaluation of all temporal institutions. Augustine did not believe in a terrestrial millennium, chiefly because it implied indulgence in carnal pleasures. Although

---

[2] City of God, translated by Marcus Dods, XI, 15, 18, 22; XIV, 9. Confessions, II. C. N. Cochrane: op. cit., p. 488. The Dods translation is not always accurate and should be used with caution.

the city of God was foreshadowed in the Church, it could become a reality only in the afterlife. This implied that progress was impossible and that history had no significance. But as he developed his theme Augustine did not maintain this sharp dichotomy between the two cities. Even though the earthly city could not achieve true justice, it nevertheless represented man's innate desire for peace and order, and hence should not be repudiated as evil. "The things which this city desires cannot justly be said to be evil. . . . They are good things and, without doubt, gifts of God." [3] The true importance of the *City of God* lies in its recognition, in contradiction to its initial premises, that all political order is good and therefore worthy of Christian support. In spite of Augustine's devaluation of earthly life, he regarded Christianity as not a negation but a fulfillment of man's earlier political and social development, providing him with the ideals and standards of justice that he had sought in vain as long as he was alienated from God.

The meaning of history was to be found in man's quest for a universal order and peace in which the unity of the whole would be in perfect harmony with the freedom of individuals. This ideal harmony was in accord with nature and with the will of God, though on account of man's sinfulness it could not be attained in this world. Looking back over the long history of the empire, Augustine insisted that the achievement of Rome, as of every earthly commonwealth, had been constantly corrupted by human pride and egoism. Alienated from God, the Romans had not known true justice; and "there is no republic where there is no justice. . . . Justice being taken away, then, what are kingdoms but great robberies?" [4] Yet at the same time Augustine also saw the empire in Virgilian terms as an expression of man's aspiration for peace. For Augustine, as for Paul, Roman power had been exerted to repress human wickedness, having been partially guided by the natural law that God had given to mankind. And although true justice could be realized only in the commonwealth of God, an earthly commonwealth could achieve an approximation of it by adopting Christian beliefs, so that progress within the temporal order was possible. Christianity, he declared, meant "security for the welfare and renown of a commonwealth; for no state is per-

---

[3] *City of God,* XV, 4.   [4] *City of God,* IV, 4; XIX, 21.

fectly established and preserved otherwise than on the foundations and by the bond of faith and of firm concord, when the highest and truest good, namely God, is loved by all, and men love each other in Him without dissimulation because they love one another for His sake." [5]

Thus, Augustine ended not by rejecting all earthly cities, but by seeing them with a double vision. In so far as they were guided by ideals of justice and order, they deserved loyal support; yet when judged by religious standards they were all corrupted by sin and should never be identified with absolute good. Law was necessary in order to control human egoism, yet obedience to law could never make men virtuous; it was "a means of intimidating the evil and enabling the good to live more quietly among them." [6] Rules of private property were necessary on account of human greed, though if men were guided by Christian love, all property would be held in common. All human government was good to the extent that it represented justice and natural law; but it was always imperfect, and could therefore claim only a limited allegiance from its citizens. The ultimate authority belonged to a higher law revealed to Christian believers. Combining the insights of Jewish prophets and Hellenic philosophers, and adding a new dimension to political theory by means of the gospel doctrine of the kingdom of heaven, this conception became the starting-point of Western thinking about the state. From it was derived the whole Western tradition of liberty under law.

After Augustine there were no important creative figures in the Western Christian tradition for six or seven hundred years. As the Western provinces sank into the Dark Ages, the Latin Church could preserve little of the classical heritage and displayed an increasing distrust of the mind and the senses. Struggling to maintain standards of order and morality in a barbaric society, it emphasized original sin and the hope of an otherworldly salvation and sought to control men's minds by a growing reliance on magic and miracle. Like the Greek Church, though in a very different environment, it preached an absolute religious unity and universalism, derived more from Plotinus than from the Gospel, in which the

---

[5] Quoted from Augustine's letters in C. Dawson (ed.): *A Monument to St. Augustine*, p. 64.

[6] Quoted by Cochrane: op. cit., p. 509.

diversity of the phenomenal world lost all meaning and value. Individuals could achieve salvation only by complying with the dictates of the Church; natural objects were significant only as symbols of transcendental realities. The sharp contrast between the unity affirmed by belief and the anarchy of actual social conditions was the most striking feature of Western culture during the Dark and early Middle Ages.

In the twelfth and thirteenth centuries, however, with the growth of political order and economic production, a new epoch of creativity began in western Europe. The affirmations of Christianity, chiefly in their Augustinian formulation, provided guidance and stimulation for aesthetic and intellectual exploration. These affirmations remained the basic postulates of Western thought, even for men who repudiated the moral and theological claims of the Church. Supported by the Christian faith in the unity and goodness of nature, in the value of the individual personality, and in the ultimate harmony of freedom and order, Western man began to create new political institutions establishing liberty under law, to produce literature and art that were increasingly infused with the enjoyment of natural phenomena, and, in the course of time, to apply the concept of natural law to the understanding and control of natural forces.

List of Books

A comprehensive bibliography, even one including only recent items, would, of course, be impossible. This list is restricted to books to which I have made direct reference and which are available in English, along with some others which I have found especially useful or suggestive.

TRANSLATIONS

THE King James Version of the Bible retains its literary pre-eminence. Since it is frequently misleading and sometimes incoherent, it should be used in conjunction with the recent Revised Standard Version (New York, 1952).

For those who have some knowledge of Latin and Greek, much the best way to read the classics is in the Loeb Classical Library (Cambridge, 1912–   ). This now includes almost all the writings of the leading Greek and Roman pagan authors, along with a few by Fathers of the early Church. Most of the translations are reliable, but a few fall markedly below the general level and must be used with caution.

The best translation of Homer into modern English prose is by E. V. Rieu (Penguin Classics). The translation by W. H. D. Rouse (New American Library) is excessively colloquial. Readers who like a style with an archaic flavor will prefer the Lang, Leaf, and Myers *Iliad* and the Butcher and Lang *Odyssey,* both of which are available in various editions.

W. J. Oates and Eugene O'Neill, Jr., have edited *The Complete Greek Drama,* 2 vols. (New York, 1938), with translations by various authors. L. R. Lind, ed.: *Ten Greek Plays in Contemporary Translations* (Riverside Editions) is a useful paperback collection. Among translations of separate plays, Dudley Fitts and Robert Fitzgerald: *The Oedipus Cycle of Sophocles* (Harvest Books) can be particularly recommended. But no translation of the Greek dramatists, especially of Aeschylus, can wholly convey the flavor of the original. Any English version that tries to retain the concision of the Greek necessarily sounds flat.

The Penguin Classics includes good versions of Herodotus by A. de Selincourt and of Thucydides by Rex Warner.

The Pre-Socratics are translated in Arthur Fairbanks: *The First Philosophers of Greece* (London, 1898) and in Milton C. Nahm: *Selections from Early Greek Philosophers*, rev. ed. (New York, 1947). The Jowett Plato, available in various editions, is complete and readable, but is frequently inaccurate. Some of the more important works have been well translated by W. H. D. Rouse in *Great Dialogues of Plato* (New American Library). There are excellent translations of the *Rebublic* by F. M. Cornford (Oxford, 1941) and by A. D. Lindsay (Everyman Paperbacks). Aristotle can be read in a twelve-volume edition edited by W. D. Ross (Oxford, 1908–52). Versions of the *Politics, Ethics,* and *Poetics* from this edition have been reprinted in various cheaper forms. The remains of the later philosophers are collected in W. J. Oates, ed.: *The Stoic and Epicurean Philosophers* (New York, 1940). Plotinus's *Enneads* has been excellently translated by Stephen Mackenna (rev. ed., London, 1957).

Modern translators have been less interested in the Latin writers, but there are excellent prose versions of the *Aeneid* by W. F. Jackson Knight (Penguin Classics) and of Lucretius by Ronald Latham (Penguin Classics). Cecil Day Lewis's verse *Aeneid* (Anchor Books) is inadequate. The verse translations of Ovid's *Metamorphoses* and *Ars Amoris* by Roffe Humphries (Indiana University Press, 1956–7) are quite free, but admirably convey the sophisticated flavor of the Latin. A large part of Tacitus has been well translated by Michael Grant in *On Imperial Rome* (Penguin Classics). Robert Graves's version of *The Golden Ass* of Apuleius (Pocket Books) is as lively and readable as the original.

The writings of all the important Church Fathers have been assembled in Alexander Roberts and James Donaldson, eds.: *The Ante-Nicene Fathers,* 10 vols. (Buffalo, 1885, and later editions), and Philip Schaff, ed.: *The Select Library of Nicene and Post-Nicene Fathers,* 28 vols. (Buffalo, 1886, and later editions). Ludwig Schapp, ed.: *The Fathers of the Church* (New York, 1948–   ) is a Catholic translation, of which thirty-three volumes have appeared so far. Augustine's *Confessions,* in the standard translation by Edward Pusey, has been reprinted in Pocket Books. Good modern versions of *The City of God* and other important early Christian writings are very much needed.

GENERAL CULTURAL HISTORY

Burke, Kenneth: *Attitudes toward History,* 2 vols. (New York, 1937).
   In spite of its frequent perversity, this study of social and cultural development by a literary critic contains many valuable insights.
Clark, Sir Kenneth: *The Nude: A Study in Ideal Form* (New York, 1956).
   An account of how artists through the ages have portrayed the human figure, which illuminates the whole history of culture.
Coon, Carleton S.: *The Story of Man* (New York, 1954).
   A lively survey of what is known about the origins and early development of the human race.

Hauser, Arnold: *The Social History of Art,* 2 vols. (New York, 1951).
     A provocative study of how the arts throughout history have reflected
     social conditions.
Herskovits, Melville J.: *Man and His Works* (New York, 1948).
     A comprehensive and authoritative account of the findings of modern
     anthropology.
Huntingdon, Ellsworth: *Civilization and Climate,* rev. ed. (New Haven,
     1924).
——: *Mainsprings of Civilization* (New York, 1945).
     In these and other books Huntingdon explores the influence of the
     environment on human society. They are pioneering expeditions into
     a field which deserves much fuller exploration.
Jaspers, Karl: *The Origin and Goal of History* (New Haven, 1953).
     An analysis of world history by a German philosopher, containing
     some useful generalizations, but very uneven in value.
Keith, Sir Arthur: *Evolution and Ethics* (New York, 1947).
     This short book is a most challenging application of Darwinism to
     human history.
Kroeber, A. L.: *Configurations of Culture Growth* (Berkeley, 1944).
     Illuminates (but does not satisfactorily solve) the problem of the
     intermittence of creativity.
Lethaby, W. R.: *Architecture,* revised by Basil Ward (New York, 1955).
     A sketchy but suggestive short account of its history.
Malraux, André: *Les Voix de silence* (Paris, 1951).
     In spite of the excellent translation by Stuart Gilbert (New York,
     1953), this study of the history of art should be read in French. It is
     a literary masterpiece, but on a second or third reading some of the
     intellectual content has a disconcerting tendency to evaporate.
Muller, Herbert J.: *The Uses of the Past* (New York, 1952).
     A most suggestive analysis of the achievements of different civiliza-
     tions, especially those of the eastern Mediterranean.
Sarton, George: *A History of Science* (Cambridge, 1952).
     Professor Sarton died before carrying the story beyond the age of
     Aristotle. Covers the history of science in the Near Eastern civiliza-
     tions and in Greece as far as the age of Aristotle. Comprehensive and
     reliable, but wholly lacking in interpretation.
Singer, Charles, and others: *A History of Technology,* 3 vols. (Oxford,
     1954–7).
     Comprehensive and authoritative.
Sorokin, Pitirim A.: *Social and Cultural Dynamics,* 4 vols. (New York,
     1937–41).
     Interprets the history of human culture as a series of oscillations be-
     tween religious and materialistic attitudes, with a strong bias in favor
     of religion.
Spengler, Oswald: *The Decline of the West,* 2 vols. (New York, 1926–8).
     Irving Babbitt's description of Spengler as a "charlatan of genius"
     remains true.
Toynbee, Arnold J.: *A Study of History,* 10 vols. (New York, 1945–54).
     Even for those who dissent in toto from Toynbee's view of history,
     his presentation of basic problems and the masses of recondite infor-
     mation with which he illustrates his theories make fascinating reading.

Turner, Ralph E.: *The Great Cultural Traditions*, 2 vols. (New York, 1941).
A useful textbook survey of the history of civilization.

EARLY CULTURES (INCLUDING JUDAISM)

Albright, W. F.: *From the Stone Age to Christianity* (Baltimore, 1940).
An admirable analysis of the evolution of religion in the ancient Near East.

Baron, S. W.: *Social and Religious History of the Jews,* vols. 1 and 2, rev. ed. (Philadelphia, 1952).
Authoritative, but much stronger on social than on religious development.

Breasted, J. H.: *Development of Religion and Thought in Ancient Egypt* (New York, 1912).
A standard work by a leading Oriental scholar of an earlier generation.

Ceram, C. W.: *The Secret of the Hittites* (New York, 1956).
A lively account of the rediscovery of a forgotten civilization.

Dawson, Christopher: *The Age of the Gods* (London, 1928).
The best short account of European and Near Eastern history prior to the first millennium B.C.

Finkelstein, Louis: *The Pharisees,* 2 vols. (New York, 1938).
A learned and sympathetic account of Pharisaic Judaism, which vastly exaggerates its influence in world history.

Frankfort, Henri: *Art and Architecture of the Ancient Orient* (Baltimore, 1954).
———: *Intellectual Adventure of Ancient Man* (Chicago, 1946).
———: *Kingship and the Gods* (Chicago, 1948).
These studies of cultural development in the ancient Near East contain much useful material, but are not easy reading.

Frazer, Sir J. G.: *The Golden Bough,* abridged edition (New York, 1922).
Though partially outmoded by later anthropological studies, this remains one of the great books of modern times.

Herzfeld, E. E.: *Zoroaster and His World,* 2 vols. (Princeton, 1947).
Authoritative, but badly in need of editorial rewriting and reorganization.

Hooke, S. H.: *Babylonian and Assyrian Religion* (London, 1948).
The best short survey.

Hughes, Pennethorne: *Witchcraft* (London, 1952).
Short and popular, but provocative, making a strong case for the existence of a witch-cult.

Meek, T. J.: *Hebrew Origins,* rev. ed. (New York, 1950).
Interesting and scholarly, though some of its theories are not wholly convincing.

Mekhitarian, A: *Egyptian Painting* (New York, 1954).
A volume in *The Great Centuries of Painting* series, published by Albert Skira. The text in these volumes is generally useful and reliable, but their outstanding features are the numerous and excellent colored illustrations.

Peters, J. P.: *Religion of the Hebrews* (New York, 1914).
An excellent general survey of the history of Judaism.

Pfeiffer, R. H.: *History of New Testament Times* (New York, 1949).
  Despite its misleading title, this book is largely a study of the Apocrypha.
——: *Introduction to the Old Testament* (New York, 1941).
  An invaluable compendium of useful information.
Rostovtzeff, M.: *History of the Ancient World* (Oxford, 1926).
  The best short account of the political and cultural development of the Near Eastern civilizations and of Greece and Rome.
Weber, Max: *Ancient Judaism* (Glencoe, 1952).
  Filled with Weber's characteristic intellectual vigor and perceptiveness.
Wilson, John A.: *The Burden of Egypt* (Chicago, 1951).
  The best one-volume analysis of Egyptian civilization.
Woolley, C. Leonard: *The Sumerians* (Oxford, 1928).
  A useful short survey.

GREECE

Burnet, John: *Early Greek Philosophy,* rev. ed. (London, 1930).
  The standard account of the pre-Socratics.
Chadwick, H. M.: *The Heroic Age* (Cambridge, England, 1912).
  A fascinating and illuminating comparison of two epic ages: that of the Homeric poems, and that of the Germanic invasions of the early Dark Age.
Clagett, Marshall: *Greek Science in Antiquity* (New York, 1955).
  A reliable general survey.
Cornford, F. M.: *From Religion to Philosophy* (London, 1912).
  This work by a leading English classical scholar of the early twentieth century is a most suggestive interpretation of the pre-Socratics.
Dodds, E. R.: *The Greeks and the Irrational* (Berkeley, 1951).
  A lively and scholarly study of the continuing influence of primitive superstitions in Greek culture.
Farrington, B.: *Greek Science,* 2 vols. (London, 1944–9).
  Based on the theory that science develops out of man's practical needs. Provocative but not always convincing.
Fite, Warner: *The Platonic Legend* (New York, 1934).
  A lively and well-argued attack on Plato and Platonism.
Guthrie, W. K. C.: *The Greeks and Their Gods* (London, 1950).
  The best general account of Greek religion.
——: *Orpheus and Greek Religion, rev. ed.* (London, 1952).
  An authoritative analysis of the Orphic movement.
Hadas, Moses: *History of Greek Literature* (New York, 1950).
  An excellent general survey, conservative in method and tone.
Harrison, Jane E.: *Prolegomena to the Study of Greek Religion* (Cambridge, England, 1922).
——: *Themis,* rev. ed. (Cambridge, England, 1937).
  Miss Harrison's studies of early Greek religious development emphasize the contrast between chthonian and Olympian beliefs. They are filled with anthropological learning, though their main thesis seems to some scholars to be overstated.
Jaeger, Werner: *Aristotle* (Oxford, 1934).
——: *Paideia,* 3 vols. (Oxford, 1939–44).

Jaeger, Werner: *Theology of Early Greek Philosophers* (Oxford, 1947).
  Jaegar is one of the leading authorities on Greek culture, and regards
  Plato as its culminating figure. *Paideia,* which is a comprehensive
  study of Greek thought down to Aristotle, is a work of profound
  learning, and easy to read, though scholars who do not share Jaeger's
  admiration for Plato disagree vigorously with his whole approach to
  Greek culture.
Kitto, H. D. F.: *Greek Tragedy,* rev. ed. (New York, 1954).
——: *The Greeks* (London, 1951).
  Admirable examples of how solid scholarship can be presented to the
  general reader.
Knox, Bernard M. W.: *Oedipus at Thebes* (New Haven, 1957).
  A brief but suggestive analysis of Sophocles's *Oedipus Rex.*
Levinson, R. B.: *In Defense of Plato* (Cambridge, 1953).
  A comprehensive reply to Fite, Popper, and other anti-Platonists.
Linforth, Ivan M.: *Solon the Athenian* (Berkeley, 1919).
  Assembles all the surviving information.
Little, Alan M. G.: *Myth and Society in Attic Drama* (New York, 1942).
  A well-argued restatement of the theories of George Thomson about
  the social forces reflected in the Greek drama.
Murray, Gilbert: *Five Stages of Greek Religion,* rev. ed. (Boston, 1952).
——: *Rise of the Greek Epic,* rev. ed. (London, 1934).
  Murray was a great humanist, though his scholarship was not always
  reliable. These are perhaps the best of his numerous books.
Nilsson, M. P.: *Greek Piety* (Oxford, 1948).
  A survey of Greek religious development by a great Swedish scholar.
Otto, Walter F.: *The Homeric Gods* (New York, 1954).
  The work of a German scholar of an earlier generation, this is a
  most penetrating introduction to the study of Greek culture.
Popper, K. R.: *The Open Society and Its Enemies,* 2 vols. (London, 1945).
  Popper regards Plato as the leading enemy of the open society, and
  presents a lively and well-documented argument.
Richter, Gisela M. A.: *Sculpture and Sculptors of the Greeks,* rev. ed. (New
  Haven, 1950).
  A standard work.
——: *Three Critical Periods in Greek Sculpture* (Oxford, 1951).
  Short but perceptive.
Robertson, D. S.: *Handbook of Greek and Roman Architecture* (Cam-
  bridge, England, 1929).
  Full of useful information, but not easy to read.
Robin, Leon: *Greek Thought* (New York, 1928).
  This is part of the multi-volume *History of Civilization.* Many of the
  volumes originally appeared in French under the general title of
  L'Evolution de l'humanité. Most of them represent an outstanding
  combination of solid scholarship and readability. A few items unac-
  countably and regrettably added by the English editor fall far below
  the general level.
Robinson, Charles A.: *Hellas* (New York, 1948).
  This brief popular survey of Greek history is a model of everything
  such a book should be.

Rohde, Erwin: *Psyche* (London, 1925).
  A study of the mystical element in Greek religion, perceptive but not always reliable, by a nineteenth-century German scholar.
Ross, W. D.: *Aristotle*, rev. ed. (London, 1956).
  A standard work.
Rostovtzeff, M.: *Social and Economic History of the Hellenistic World*, 3 vols., rev. ed. (Oxford, 1953).
  These volumes and the similar series on the Roman Empire are the outstanding works of one of the greatest of modern historians.
Tarn, W. W.: *Alexander the Great*, 2 vols. (Cambridge, England, 1948).
  Learned, well written, and eulogistic.
—— and Griffith, G. T.: *Hellenistic Civilization*, rev. ed. (London, 1952).
  An excellent textbook survey.
Taylor, A. E.: *Plato the Man and His Work*, rev. ed. (London, 1949).
  Taylor's scholarship is impeccable, but he is too inclined to interpret Plato as a sponsor of English middle-class morality.
Thomson, George D.: *Aeschylus and Athens* (London, 1941).
——: *Studies in Ancient Greek Society*, 2 vols. (London, 1949–55).
  Thomson demonstrates the value of a Marxist approach to early Greek culture, but spoils his case by too much vituperation of "bourgeois" scholarship.
Waerden, B. L. Van der: *Science Awakening* (Groningen, 1954).
  Despite its meaningless title, this book contains valuable material on the later development of Greek science, though much of it will be intelligible only to mathematicians.
Whitman, Cedric H.: *Sophocles* (Cambridge, 1951).
  A perceptive and well-written interpretation by a young American classicist.
Zimmern, A. E.: *The Greek Commonwealth*, rev. ed. (Oxford, 1931).
  A comprehensive description of the fifth-century polis, somwhat too idealized.

ROME

Altheim, Franz: *History of Roman Religion* (New York, 1938).
  An interesting interpretation, based on wide knowledge, but not always wholly convincing.
Bailey, Cyril, ed.: *The Legacy of Rome* (Oxford, 1923).
  A useful collection of essays.
Collingwood, R. G., and Myres, J. N. L.: *Roman Britain and the English Settlements* (Oxford, 1937).
  An authoritative work, somewhat pro-Celtic and anti-Roman.
Cruttwell, Robert W.: *Vergil's Mind at Work* (Oxford, 1946).
  A good analysis of Vergil's imagery.
Dill, Sir Samuel: *Roman Society from Nero to Marcus Aurelius* (London, 1905).
  Contains useful material on religion, philosophy, and literature under the Principate.
Duff, J. Wight: *Literary History of Rome from the Origins to the Close of the Golden Age* (London, 1920).

Duff, J. Wright: *Literary History of Rome in the Silver Age* (New York, 1931).
 Useful surveys, somewhat old-fashioned in tone.
Fowler, W. Warde: *Religious Experience of the Roman People* (London, 1911).
 The most reliable survey of the subject, very pleasant to read.
Frank, Tenney: *Roman Imperialism* (New York, 1914).
 A perceptive analysis of the building of the Roman Empire.
Grant, Michael: *Roman Literature* (Cambridge, England, 1954).
 The best short account.
Knight, W .F. Jackson: *Roman Vergil* (London, 1944).
 The best modern study.
Maiuri, A.: *Roman Painting* (Geneva, 1953).
Pallottino, M.: *Etruscan Painting* (Geneva, 1952).
 Two volumes in the Skira series *The Great Centuries of Painting*. See, under EARLY CULTURES: Mekhitarian.
Rostovtzeff, M.: *Social and Economic History of the Roman Empire*, 2 vols., rev. ed. (Oxford, 1957).
 A great work.
Starr, Chester G.: *Civilization and the Caesars* (Ithaca, 1954).
 Analyzes the transformation of Roman culture and civilization under the later empire.
Strong, E.: *Art in Ancient Rome*, 2 vols. (New York, 1928).
———: *Roman Sculpture from Augustus to Constantine* (London, 1907).
 Filled with useful information, though the presentation is not very critical.
Syme, Ronald: *The Roman Revolution* (Oxford, 1939).
 An admirable account of the building of the Principate.
Toutain, Jules: *Economic Life of the Ancient World* (New York, 1930).
 A volume in the *History of Civilization* series. See, under GREECE: Robin.

CHRISTIANITY AND THE END OF THE ANCIENT WORLD

Bolgar, R. R.: *The Classical Heritage* (Cambridge, England, 1954).
 An authoritative study of the preservation of classical literature in the Byzantine Empire and in medieval Europe.
Burleigh, J. H. S.: *The City of God* (London, 1949).
 A good short analysis of St. Augustine's main work.
Burrows, Millar: *The Dead Sea Scrolls* (New York, 1955).
 The most reliable and sensible of all the books on this subject.
Burckhardt, Jacob: *The Age of Constantine the Great* (London, 1949).
 A classic study of the transformation of the Roman Empire, by the great nineteenth-century historian.
Chadwick, Nora K.: *Poetry and Letters in Early Christian Gaul* (London, 1955).
 Reliable and interesting.
Chadwick, Owen: *John Cassian* (Cambridge, England, 1950).
 Useful for the early history of Western monasticism.

Cochrane, C. N.: *Christianity and Classical Culture* (Oxford, 1940).
 A most stimulating analysis of the difference between the pagan and
 the Christian views of life.

Dawes, E., and Baynes, N. H.: *Three Byzantine Saints* (Oxford, 1948).
 Short early biographies of Daniel the Stylite, Theodore of Sykeon, and
 John the Almsgiver, translated with a useful introduction.

Dawson, Christopher: *The Making of Europe* (London, 1932).
 This book and the book by Moss listed below are admirable short
 accounts of the transition from Classical to Medieval civilization.

——, ed.: *A Monument to Saint Augustine* (New York, 1930).
 An excellent collection of essays by Catholic writers, covering all
 aspects of Augustine's thought.

Diehl, Charles: *Byzantium: Greatness and Decline* (New Brunswick, 1957).
 A great French authority summarizes the Byzantine achievement.

Dill, Sir Samuel: *Roman Society in the Last Century of the Western Empire*
 (London, 1898).
 A fascinating account of life and literature in Gaul and Italy.

Dupont-Sommer, A.: *The Dead Sea Scrolls* (Oxford, 1952).
 Contains some useful material, but exaggerates the importance of the
 Scrolls for the history of Christianity.

Glover, T. R.: *The Conflict of Religions in the Early Roman Empire* (London, 1927).
 A Christian interpretation for the general reader, well written and
 informative.

Goguel, Maurice: *The Birth of Christianity* (London, 1953).
 An excellent account of the development of the Church during the
 first century.

Grabar, André: *Byzantine Painting* (Geneva, 1953).
 A volume in the Skira series *The Great Centuries of Painting.* See,
 under EARLY CULTURES: Mekhitarian.

Guignebert, Charles: *Christianity, Past and Present* (New York, 1927).

——: *Jesus* (New York, 1935).

——: *The Jewish World in the Time of Jesus* (London, 1939).
 From a rationalistic viewpoint, Guignebert is the most satisfying of
 the historians of early Christianity. His life of Jesus, a volume in
 the *History of Civilization* series, is especially good.

Harnack, Adolf: *History of Dogma*, 5 vols. (London, 1894–9).
 This comprehensive work by a nineteenth-century German scholar is
 still useful.

Hinks, Roger: *Carolingian Art* (London, 1935).
 The early chapters give an admirable short analysis of the development
 of art under the later empire.

Klausner, J.: *From Jesus to Paul* (New York, 1943).

——: *Jesus of Nazareth* (New York, 1926).
 These books present a Jewish interpretation of the origins of Christianity. They are informative and suggestive, though Christians will
 vigorously disagree with much of Klausner's approach.

Labriolle, P. de: *History of the Literature of Christianity from Tertullian
 to Boethius* (London, 1924).
 A volume in the *History of Civilization* series. See, under GREECE:
 Robin.

Latourette, K. S.: *History of the Expansion of Christianity*, vol. 1 (New York, 1937).
  Useful on the geographical growth of the early Church, though it says little about its doctrines and organization.

Lot, F.: *The End of the Ancient World* (New York, 1931).
  A volume in the *History of Civilization* series, covering Western Europe from the third to the seventh centuries. See, under GREECE: Robin.

McGiffert, A. C.: *History of Christian Thought*, vols. 1 and 2 (New York, 1932–3).
  Reliable, sensible, and easy to read.

Moore, G. F.: *Judaism in the First Century of the Christian Era*, 2 vols. (Cambridge, 1927).
  This authoritative study sheds a good deal of light on early Christianity.

Morey, C. R.: *Early Christian Art* (Princeton, 1942).
  The best general account.

Moss, H. St. L. B.: *The Birth of the Middle Ages* (Oxford, 1935).
  See under Dawson, above.

Pickman, E. M.: *The Mind of Latin Christianity* (New York, 1937).
  Mainly concerned with the Latin theologians of the fourth and fifth centuries. Contains much useful material and is easy to read, though the author's judgments are not always sound.

Rand, E. K.: *Founders of the Middle Ages* (Cambridge, 1929).
  Useful biographical essays on leading figures of the later empire and early Dark Age.

Rice, D. Talbot: *Byzantine Art* (Oxford, 1935).
  A good interpretive essay by a leading authority.

Rowley, H. H.: *The Zadokite Fragments and the Dead Sea Scrolls* (Oxford, 1952).
  One of the more useful studies of the Scrolls.

Runciman, Steven: *Byzantine Civilization* (London, 1933).
  A standard work by the leading English authority.

Schweitzer, Albert: *The Mysticism of Paul the Apostle* (London, 1931).
  A provocative application of Schweitzer's modernist views to early Christian theology.

Scott, E. F.: *Literature of the New Testament* (New York, 1932).
  A useful guide to the New Testament.

Strzygowski, Josef: *Origins of Christian Church Art* (Oxford, 1923).
  In this and other books Strzygowski argues that Christian art came from the East.

Swift, Emerson H.: *Roman Sources of Christian Art* (New York, 1951).
  A reply to Strzygowski. Swift makes a strong case, but is inclined to overstate it.

Waddell, Helen: *The Desert Fathers* (New York, 1936).
  An anthology of their sayings and biographies.

Wolfson, H. A.: *Philosophy of the Church Fathers* (Cambridge, 1956).
  Dealing mainly with the fusion of Greek and Jewish thought in the third and fourth centuries, this is the first volume of what promises to be the major work on the development of Christian theology.

Index

i

A Note on the Author

HENRY BAMFORD PARKES was born in Sheffield, England, in 1904. After attending Oxford (B.A.), he came to the United States in 1927. He did his graduate work at the University of Michigan (Ph.D., 1929). Since 1930 he has been a member of the faculty of New York University, at which he is Professor of History. Mr. Parkes has contributed widely to periodicals. His published books include *Jonathan Edwards; A History of Mexico; Marxism: An Autopsy; Recent America; The Pragmatic Test; The World after War; The American Experience;* and *The United States of America.* Mr. Parkes is married, and has two daughters. In 1956–7 he was Fulbright Professor at the University of Athens.

A NOTE ON THE TYPE

The text of this book was set on the Linotype in a face called TIMES ROMAN, *designed by* STANLEY MORISON *for* The Times (*London*), *and first introduced by that newspaper in 1932.*

Among typographers and designers of the twentieth century, Stanley Morison has been a strong forming influence, as typographical adviser to the English Monotype Corporation, as a director of two distinguished English publishing houses, and as a writer of sensibility, erudition, and keen practical sense.

In 1930 Morison wrote: "Type design moves at the pace of the most conservative reader. The good type-designer therefore realises that, for a new fount to be successful, it has to be so good that only very few recognise its novelty. If readers do not notice the consummate reticence and rare discipline of a new type, it is probably a good letter." It is now generally recognized that in the creation of Times Roman *Morison successfully met the qualifications of this theoretical doctrine.*

Composed, printed, and bound by Kingsport Press, Inc., Kingsport, Tennessee. Paper manufactured by S. D. Warren Company, Boston. Designed by

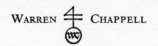

WARREN CHAPPELL